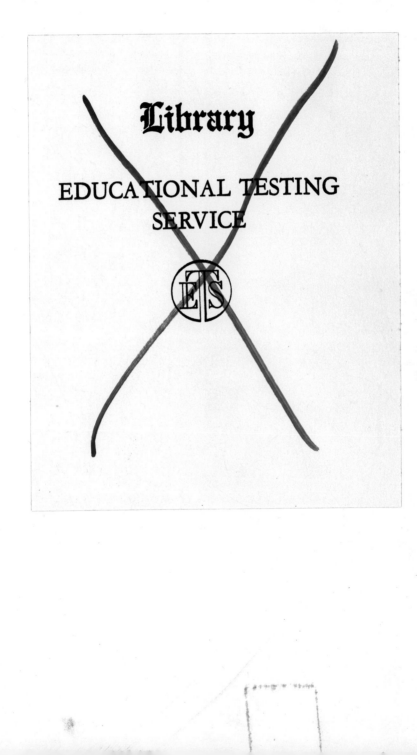

Item Response Theory
Application to Psychological Measurement

Item Response Theory
Application to Psychological Measurement

Charles L. Hulin

Fritz Drasgow

Charles K. Parsons

The Dorsey Professional Series

DOW JONES-IRWIN
Homewood, Illinois

ISBN 0-87094-284-0

Library of Congress Catalog Card No. 82–73929

Printed in the United States of America

1 2 3 4 5 6 7 8 9 0 K 0 9 8 7 6 5 4 3

To Tracy and Andrew,
Laura, and Sheila

Preface

Psychological measurement is the assignment of numerals, in accordance with rules, for quantitative representation of characteristics of individuals or objects. Measurement theories, then, consist of sets of rules by which one establishes unique correspondences between numerals and amounts or magnitudes of individuals' or objects' characteristics.

The measurement theories we consider in this book fall into a subarea of psychometrics. These theories are concerned with the specifications of rules for transforming individuals' responses to items on a psychological test or scale into estimates of the trait assumed to underlie the observable responses. Rules specified by some measurement theories can be very simple. For example, ability may be estimated by counting the number of questions answered correctly on a test. Other, more complex rules may weight responses to different items before the responses are combined into an estimate of ability. Such weights reflect the different degrees of difficulty and discriminatory power of the items and are chosen to maximize certain mathematical properties of the resulting estimates of individuals' characteristics.

In this book we discuss a particular class of measurement theories generally called *item response theory* or *latent trait theory*. The complexity of rules for converting item responses into estimates of an underlying trait range from very simple to complex. Indeed, the complexity of some of these theories may be one of the reasons for their lack of widespread adoption and use in applied measurement problems.

Unfortunately, in social science we have no well-articulated metatheory that specifies rules by which one can decide among competing theories on the basis of the propositions, assumptions, and conclusions of the theories. Of course, we do have some rules of thumb specifying that theories should be simple, general, and useful in practice. Some of the specific measurement theories we discuss in this book will very likely be judged deficient in the characteristic of simplicity. However, in the case of item response theories, it is sometimes necessary to sacrifice simplicity in order to gain general applicability and usefulness.

In this book, specifically in Chapters 2 and 3, we attempt to translate the mathematical formulations of item response theory into a language that can be readily grasped by individuals with a course in non-calculus statistics, a rudimentary knowledge of mathematical notation and concepts, and a basic knowledge of classical test theory. Although we occasionally use calculus when simpler methods prove inadequate, knowledge of calculus is not required. Thus, this book is different from currently available presentations of item response theories that require calculus-level probability and statistics courses, as well as graduate training in psychometric theory.

We expect that item response theory will become the standard approach to a broad class of practical measurement problems within this generation of applied social scientists. This class of problems generally involves questions of equivalence of measurement across subpopulations, individuals, and items. Therefore, we have intended the book to appeal to a very diverse audience. Applied researchers who were trained in classical measurement theory should be able to read and understand the materials contained in this book. Students enrolled in a variety of programs of study—educational psychology, industrial-organizational psychology, individual differences, personnel psychology, and psychometrics—as well as specialized branches of sociology, clinical psychology, personality theory, and organizational behavior should be able to follow our presentations and discussions with a minimum of confusion.

Finally, this book is designed in part for those individuals involved in programs of applied testing and measurement whose efforts occasionally bring them into contact with the law and public policy. The increased complexity and mathematical sophistication of some item response theories should not be taken as evidence that the theories are inappropriate for practical testing purposes. If increased complexity is accompanied by increased usefulness, the benefits may outweigh the costs.

Any book that is a collaborative effort must necessarily reflect the interests and training of the writers. This book indeed seems to reflect our collective training and research interests in the general areas of industrial-organizational psychology, psychometrics, and applied attitude research. We hope it also reflects the practical usefulness of item response theories in these diverse areas.

We, no less than most people, resist having our research and writing efforts neatly slotted into categories. But if anybody is going to do it, it might as well be us. Therefore, this book is probably best described as an introductory text and a practitioner's manual. It is a guide (but not an atlas) for the applications, advantages, and disadvantages of item response theories for many areas concerned with the measurement of psychological characteristics. However, the book can be adapted for use in an advanced undergraduate course or a beginning graduate course in measurement by excluding sections that contain more advanced material; these sections are indicated by an asterisk(*). Sections so marked contain information of a specialized nature and should be useful to testing practitioners.

Throughout we have attempted to maintain our orientation toward the *application* of measurement theories to diverse areas. Chapters 2 and 3 are intended to provide sufficient depth of coverage of these theories so that the applications follow with little additional explication. Applications were selected to include areas whose needs are ill-served by traditional methods. Thus, Chapter 4 presents appropriateness measurement as a means of determining the relevance of a test score as a measure of a specific individual's trait. Chapter 5 is devoted to a presentation of procedures for assessing measurement bias against specified subpopulations found within a larger, heterogeneous population. In Chapter 6 we present a straightforward generalization of these techniques that permits theory-based evaluations of the quality of translations of psychological scales and tests into foreign languages. We discuss in Chapter 7 the advantages and disadvantages of selecting items for presentation to individuals on the basis of each person's responses to items already presented. We discuss problems caused by one of the assumptions of item response theories in Chapter 8. This assumption, that the items are all measuring a single underlying trait, is surely violated in any set of real item responses. Finally, in Chapter 9 we discuss problems of public policy related to the use of tests for decision making in education and employment. No measurement theory can address, much less solve, all public policy aspects of testing. However, item response theories address some important and pressing issues that are beyond the limitations of traditional methods.

In our first chapter and in Chapter 9, we attempt to place the use of testing and psychological measurement into a broader perspective than one normally finds in books on measurement theory. Separation of scientists from the applications of their work is defensible from a number of perspectives. In the case of psychological testing, such separation seems shortsighted and, ultimately, self-defeating.

We have included Chapters 1 and 9 because we are convinced that social scientists should be sensitive to the impact of their work on individuals and society. This sensitivity to social issues seems especially important in the psychological measurement area, where theory and research are translated into practice with important, long-term implications for many individuals. In addition, we think that psychometricians can use item response theory (IRT) to address directly important social policy questions. Specifically, IRT can be used to study rigorously questions about measurement bias and questions related to the relevance of a test score as an estimate of an underlying trait for a specific individual. Thus, in Chapters 1 and 9 we attempt to relate measurement theory and practice to social policy issues and to delineate those issues that are matters of data and science and therefore should be addressed with the most rigorous means available. We recognize that the distinctions can sometimes be fuzzy between political awareness and the Lysenkoist trap of reporting and interpreting data and theories in accordance with the dictates of current political forces. We hope we have maintained the distinctions clearly.

The final draft of this book incorporates suggestions that have resulted from many hours of effort on the part of several of our colleagues and friends. Individuals who have contributed greatly to this effort are Jeanne Brett, Joseph Casagrande, James Drasgow, Daniel Eignor, Lloyd Humphreys, Dan Ilgen, Barbara Lerner, Mark Reckase, and David Weiss. May they be assigned to an interesting cell in that great item response data matrix in the sky as their ultimate reward. Numerous students read different drafts of several chapters for different courses we have taught during the past two years. We want to double out Anita Benjamin and Mary Roznowski for their efforts that went beyond those normally expected or encountered. In addition, we thank Robin Lissak for his contributions to Chapters 3 and 8 that included many analyses of empirical and Monte Carlo simulation data. We also wish to extend our appreciation to the College Board for providing the Scholastic Aptitude Test data that we used in a number of illustrative analyses.

Mary Welborn simultaneously solved the mysteries of the Vulcan editing system, our interlinear ciphers, theta, and human factors. Without her efforts, the two years in which we have been preparing this manuscript could easily have stretched interminably.

Charles L. Hulin
Fritz Drasgow
Charles K. Parsons

Contents

1

The Role of Measurement in Society

1.1 TESTS IN AMERICAN SOCIETY

Personnel decisions have historically been based on selection devices of varying degrees of sophistication and validity. Gideon, for example (Judg. 7:4–7), followed the Lord's advice and used a one-item performance test involving drinking from a nearby stream to reduce his army to an acceptable size. More recently, assessment centers were conducted by the Office of Strategic Services (OSS). The centers used structured and unstructured tests administered individually and in groups over the course of several days to select spies in World War II. Today, American Telephone & Telegraph selects supervisors by using assessment centers modeled after the early versions developed by the OSS.

As long as societies and groups have divisions of labor, there will be a need to classify or place individuals into different functional groups on some rational basis. Personnel decisions with long-term economic and social consequences are, for the most part, based on some form of systematic information about the individuals involved. To a substantial degree, psychological tests and measurement scales provide this information.

The widespread reliance on psychological tests for selection decisions in education[1] and employment in the United States is easily

---

[1] It needs emphasis that although tests are frequently required as part of a college application, they are rarely the sole determinant of rejection or selection. For example, based on a survey of college admission offices, Hargadon (1981) reported that about 60 to 65 percent of four-year colleges require test scores but only 2 percent use them as the single most important factor in admission decisions. Instead, high school performance (grade-point average or class rank) was much more frequently the single most important factor (cited by 31 percent). However, reliance on test scores as a component of the decision by nearly two thirds of the four-year colleges underscores the basis for the assumption that testing is a critical factor in college admission.

1

documented. Criticism of the use of psychological tests is also widespread. Designed to replace more subjective and arbitrary information upon which decisions were based, tests have not in fact resulted in a generally shared perception of fairness among all affected groups.

As we shall discuss in Chapter 9, controversies about test usage have resulted in part because psychometricians have rarely concerned themselves with issues of ethics and public policies. Indeed, scientists in general have traditionally avoided the political implications of their work. This posture has frequently been defended by arguing that knowledge is neutral and the role of scientists in any society is to extend human knowledge. Applications and implications of work by scholars were left to policymakers, administrators, courts, and politicians. Nonetheless, nuclear scientists have recently become involved in the development of atomic energy policies just as psychometricians are now beginning to consider the sociolegal consequences of selection decisions based on psychological tests. For example, Petersen and Novick (1976) provide an excellent analysis of several models of "culture fair" and "culture blind" selection. Most psychometricians, however, have concentrated on technical measurement issues and ignored the social implications of their work. The assumption underlying their decision apparently has been that if the technical problems associated with testing were solved, then objections to the use of such devices would wither away. This has not yet occurred, nor, we expect, will it occur in the immediate future.

The extent of the current controversies concerning testing is noteworthy, as is the active involvement of groups lobbying to influence governmental testing policy. In the period from September 1, 1980, to September 1, 1981, 17 individual states considered so-called truth-in-testing bills, although only New York and California enacted such legislation. The U.S. House of Representatives Subcommittee on Labor and Education held hearings on a series of federal truth-in-testing bills that would place politically determined restrictions on the practice of testing for education and employment opportunities in the United States. The federal legislation has not advanced to the point of a congressional vote. Nonetheless, psychologists who are involved with testing watch these legislative developments with concern.

Many of the issues covered by such truth-in-testing bills are matters of scientific concern that we believe should not be placed under governmental regulations. Others, such as disclosure of items on certain kinds of tests, are matters of public and social policy and should be addressed. However, it often appears that legislators and policymakers do not clearly separate political and social issues from technical and empirical issues when considering truth-in-testing regulations. Establishing the goals of racially and ethnically balanced work forces and college enrollments is a political decision. It is beyond the scope of psychometric theory. Neither of these political goals should be implemented under the guise of psychometric purity.

The increasingly close relation between psychometrics and sociolegal concerns can be illustrated by noting the watershed decision by the Supreme Court of the United States in *Griggs* v. *Duke Power* (1971) concerning fairness and discrimination in selection and the adoption and publication of the "Uniform Guidelines on Employee Selection" by four agencies of the U.S. government in 1978 (Equal Employment Opportunity Commission et al., 1978). During this past decade, the close relations between psychometrics and social policy have become manifest in all three branches of our government. Test users must now consider the long-term impact of tests on different groups as carefully as they consider technical psychometric issues.

Alternatives to testing exist, and the effects of such alternative procedures are worth considering. Pitting testing against alternatives as well as against antithetical counterproposals needs to be done explicitly by applied measurement psychologists. This inquiry might begin by considering the widespread use of merit as a basis of educational admissions and employment selection decisions. It should be noted, more seriously than in passing, that the decision for a society to rely on merit, however assessed, in choosing one individual instead of another is a political and not a scientific decision. Other criteria for decisions about individuals are available. Seniority, for example, is a criterion frequently used and actively promoted by unions. The results of an inquiry about alternatives to tests as measures of merit, or even reliance on merit as a basis for decisions, might result in substantially modified decision processes whose impact on different groups would, in turn, have to be assessed. Various combinations of merit, need, seniority, caste, and class could conceivably be recommended as bases for allocating opportunities.

In this book we shall assume that ability and achievement as measured by psychological and educational tests will continue to be used as an important basis for educational and employment decisions. We do so because we do not anticipate a decision by the various constituencies of American society to ban testing. A second reason is that if a substitute for merit is proposed and adopted, it may be a construct as complex and difficult to observe and quantify as merit; the basic measurement problems addressed in this book will remain. Finally, there are a number of applied measurement areas that are likely to remain important for the foreseeable future regardless of the outcomes of various testing controversies. Such problems as developing criteria for complex jobs with no countable output; measuring the economic worth of fundamentally dissimilar jobs; developing composite, multi-

ple-act, behavioral measures; and even assessing interests and apti-
tudes for guidance and counseling are likely to remain. In short, measurement and testing problems will probably continue, independent
of the current sociolegal controversies.

To the extent that item response theory can provide answers to
important scientific questions, some confusions between scientific
complexities and value differences can be eliminated. This should
clarify the current problems by making salient those problems that are
essentially psychometric in nature and those that are philosophical or
ethical in nature. A separation of the *issues* that must be considered
into those that are basically philosophical and those that are scientific
does not imply that scientists need not concern themselves with the
applications and results of their work. It does imply that we should
address matters of science with scientific procedures and matters of
public policy or ethics with philosophical methods of inquiry.

It is naive to believe that the measurement procedures and theories
discussed in this book will be sufficient to overcome all the problems
associated with testing as a basis for decision making. Many of the
problems of test-based decisions arise from issues of values and ethics; they are not addressable by scientific methods. However, the recent developments in measurement theory described in this book do
provide solutions to some problems that previously have been beyond
the scope of classical measurement theory. It is not always clear that
the answers provided by these new approaches will prove palatable to
the critics of testing. It *is* clear that these developments in measurement theory provide answers to a series of continuing problems and,
by these answers, demonstrate a sensitivity and awareness of the magnitude and scope of the problems.

1.2 ATTITUDE MEASUREMENT

Although we discuss problems and controversies about the use of
tests, the focus of this book is not on the "testing problem" or racial
differences in ability or the debate concerning the relative importance
of environmental and genetic influences in determining individual
ability. Measurement theory and ability testing will indeed be discussed. The applications of measurement theory, however, go far beyond these controversial areas and include many questions of interest
to educational psychologists, cross-cultural psychologists, attitude researchers, and organizational psychologists. One area of particular interest to a wide range of researchers is attitude assessments. The reason for the general interest in attitude assessments is quite simple:
Attitudinal differences are related to differences in most voluntary

actions and decisions of individuals, and most social scientists have interests in such individual behaviors.

The concept of attitudes was used over 100 years ago by Spencer (1862), but the history of attitude research reveals only occasional concerns with assessment of attitudes. Some individuals closely identified with measurement theories in general—Thurstone, Guttman, Lazarsfeld—made early contributions to the attitude assessment literature. Thurstone and Guttman, along with Likert, developed measurement models or scales that still bear their names and are very frequently used as attitude assessment techniques. However, with the exception of Anderson's (1976) work on functional measurement, the recent literature reveals little concern with measurement models of attitudes. Today's most prominent attitude theorists—Fishbein and Ajzen (1975), Ajzen and Fishbein (1980), Triandis (1979), and Abelson (1968)—pay little attention to measurement, appearing content to use the evaluative component from the semantic differential scales (Osgood, Suci, & Tannenbaum, 1957) to assess affect and to use probability scales to assess beliefs and behavioral intentions. Green (1954) provides discussions of some measurement issues in this area.

It is instructive to consider Fishbein and Ajzen's (1974) work on attitude-behavior consistencies. Their discussion was almost exclusively devoted to a consideration of the construction of multiple-act, behavioral composites to serve as criteria for attitude-behavior predictions. Assessments of attitudes were assumed as given. In their development of multiple-act criteria, however, Fishbein and Ajzen identified three different models specifying *item characteristic curves* that relate probabilities of endorsement of a specific attitude item to an underlying attitude. Two of these models are shown graphically in Figures 2.2.1 and 2.2.3 in Chapter 2. The Guttman model (Figure 2.2.1) specifies a step function that relates endorsement of an item to an underlying attitude. This model has been found to be unrealistic in practice because few behaviors or items meet the criterion of a sharp "step" in probability of endorsement.[2] The Likert model, which is functionally equivalent to the Lazarsfeld model shown in Figure 2.2.3, also has limitations because the probabilities of endorsement of behaviors can assume theoretically impossible values (less than 0.0, greater than $+1.0$) with extreme attitude positions. These limitations are discussed in more detail in Chapter 2.

The Thurstone model is a third attitude assessment model discussed by Fishbein and Ajzen. The Thurstone model can be used to

___

[2] A Guttman scale results when all items responses are functions of a single latent trait; knowledge of an individual's standing on this trait is sufficient to determine the individual's responses to all items.

describe a relation between probability of endorsement and underlying attitude strength that is nonmonotonic: At first the probability of item endorsement increases as the underlying attitude strength increases, but beyond a certain point the probability of endorsement *decreases* with further increases in attitude strength. The item characteristic curve for this model, shown graphically in Figure 1.2.1, im-

Figure 1.2.1
Nonmonotonic Relation between Probability of Endorsement of
Attitude Statement and Attitude Strength

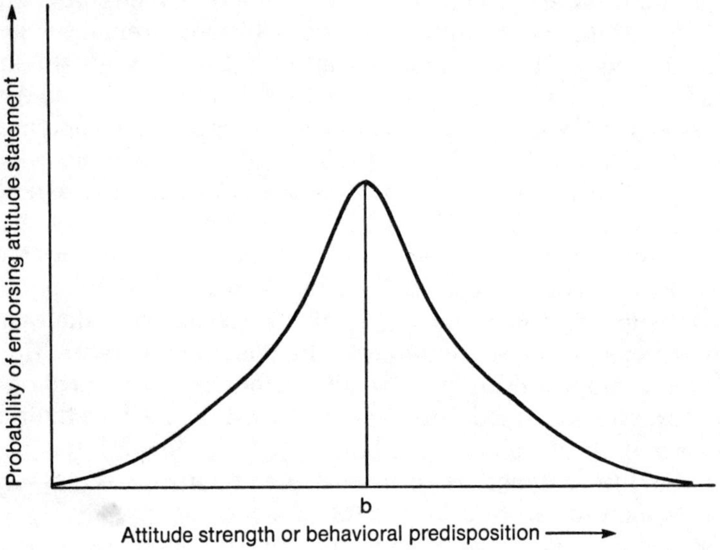

plies that when an individual's attitude closely matches the item's location (point *b* in Figure 1.2.1) on the underlying dimension, the probability of endorsement is high. As an individual's attitude toward the object or act departs in either direction from the item's value, the probability of endorsement decreases.

Guttman's step function, Lazarsfeld's linear model, and Thurstone's nonmonotonic model are mutually incompatible. If one of them correctly describes the relation between the probability of endorsing an attitude statement and an underlying attitude, then the other two cannot.

There has been relatively little basic psychometric work devoted to determining the specific relation between attitude strength and endorsement of attitude statements. Attitude scales would be expected to have more desirable properties if they were developed according to a model that allows convenient statistical analyses while accurately describing item responses. For example, we would expect to see stronger relations between attitude assessments and behavioral intentions or even subsequent behaviors. Although we shall not present extensive empirical research attempting to resolve this question in its most general form, we will demonstrate some of the advantages of applying item response theory methods that specify a particular nonlinear relation between probability of endorsement and underlying attitude.

1.3 SCOPE

The remaining chapters of this book present theory and applications of item response theory. Two chapters on theories and methods are followed by four chapters describing applications of item response theory to measurement problems. Each of these chapters is briefly described in this section.

Theory and method.   Chapter 2 contains the bulk of the theoretical developments of item response theory discussed and used in this book. The emphasis of this chapter is on presentation and discussion of the assumptions of item response theories and the related concepts necessary for an understanding of the theories. Derivations are avoided where possible, although at times a simple derivation is necessary to illustrate the basis for a development or an equation.

Chapter 3 has been written to parallel Chapter 2. In it, item response theories are applied to empirical data sets representing ability and attitude measurements. This chapter is intended to apply the concepts discussed in Chapter 2 and illustrate appropriate methods of analysis and frequently encountered problems.

Appropriateness measurement.   Even though a particular test contains no items that are biased against any identifiable subpopulation and provides excellent measurement for all samples of examinees, a score on this test may be seriously deficient as an estimate of ability for a small number of atypical examinees. Unusually creative examinees may read more into a question than was intended and, consequently, select an incorrect option based on this deeper analysis. Careless examinees and examinees unfamiliar with machine-scored answer sheets may record the answer to the $(i + 1)$th question in the ith space on the answer sheet for a block of items. Cheaters can copy responses to specific blocks of items (but probably not the entire test) from a high-ability neighbor. Some individuals may prepare for certain entrance examinations by memorizing questions and answers obtained by surreptitious means. In all these examples, it is clear that total test score is an unrepresentative measure of ability.

There are a variety of heuristic procedures designed to detect such aberrant response patterns; but these procedures are not well based in theory, and they generally function less than adequately. Appropriateness measurement methods based on item response theory (Levine & Rubin, 1979; Levine & Drasgow, 1982) provide powerful procedures for detection of aberrant response patterns. This topic is discussed and developed in Chapter 4.

Detection of test and item bias. The average scores on measures of ability of many minority groups in the United States are below the average performance of white, middle-class Americans. Similarly, females frequently have average scores on some (e.g., spatial) ability measures that are lower than their male counterparts. Japanese Americans have average scores on measures of quantitative ability that are greater than average scores of comparable Americans of non-Japanese ancestry. The magnitude of the differences among race, ethnic, or sex groupings depends on the tests involved. It is common to express the differences in terms of standard deviation units so that, say, male-female differences can be compared across different tests. For example, the magnitudes of differences between black and white means on standardized tests of cognitive ability frequently range between .5 and 1.3 standard deviation units. A cutting score on a selection or admission test that was set at the mean of the white population would eliminate 70 to 90 percent of the black applicants. Selection decisions based on such test scores severely limit opportunities for black applicants and raise serious questions about discrimination.

Questions have been and will continue to be raised by both critics and supporters of testing about the meanings of differences in mean test scores across different subpopulations. Do they reflect differences in "true" ability among subpopulations? Do they reflect differences in narrow, easily acquired skills and knowledge? Do they reflect measurement bias against minority group members because the tests assess little more than knowledge of white cultural values and content? At the heart of these questions is the issue of whether test items measure knowledge not equally available to all subpopulations.

A number of problems and misunderstandings in the area of measurement bias seem to be caused in part by differences between common usage of some terms and their technical definitions. For example, the differences in true, or real, ability referred to in the above paragraph have a very specific meaning in psychometrics. They refer to differences that are not bias or error, are important, and are difficult to change. Estimates of the underlying trait are useful for predicting future performance on related tasks across many different groups and tasks. But the latent trait estimated in item response theory is not real in the sense that most people would use the word; it is a mathematical abstraction used by researchers to summarize and integrate large amounts of observable data. Moreover, the latent trait does not refer to innate ability, but rather learned skills and knowledge.

A study of possible test bias based on item response theory examines the measurement equivalence of test items across subpopulations. An item provides equivalent measurement across subpopulations if the relation between probability of a correct response and ability is virtually identical in all subpopulations. If test items do not have this property, there is no reason to believe that the test scores provide comparable measurement across subpopulations. Thus test scores of individuals from one subpopulation, such as females, would *not* be directly comparable to test scores of individuals from a second subpopulation, such as males.

Evaluating translations of psychological scales. Classical measurement theory does not provide generally acceptable means for assessing the fidelity of an instrument's translation from the original to a target language. Most proposed solutions, for example, depend on the availability of large samples of bilingual subjects. Unfortunately, such individuals may have cognitive and affective structures that differ from the comparable structures of monolinguals of either language. These differences may invalidate evaluations of translations based on bilinguals. Hulin, Drasgow, and Komocar (1982) provide a procedure for investigating the comparability of an instrument across languages that does not rely on samples of bilingual subjects. This procedure is similar to methods designed to detect item bias across various subpopulations sharing a common language. The item response theory used in Hulin et al.'s method is developed in Chapters 2 and 3, and the method itself is discussed in detail in Chapter 6.

Adaptive testing. Many items on standardized tests are either too easy or too hard for any given examinee. As a result these items provide little information about the examinee's ability. By tailoring the items presented to an examinee so that they are of appropriate difficulty, it is possible to reduce substantially the number of items required to assess an ability or attitude. An efficient adaptive testing procedure, for example, will select items with difficulties that are near the current estimate of an examinee's ability. Thus, the $(i + 1)$th question presented to an examinee depends on the examinee's ability estimated on the basis of the first i items. Very easy items are not presented to high-ability examinees, and hard items are not presented to low-ability examinees.

Classical test theory does not provide a convenient method for placing into a common scale the test scores of examinees who take different sets of items, nor does it provide a good theory-based method for selecting items likely to yield the most information about an examinee's ability level. Adaptive testing methods based on item response theory yield test scores in a common metric. Early findings suggest they will prove to be economically feasible in the very near future. These methods are discussed in Chapter 7.

Dimensionality of a test or scale. One of the important assumptions of item response theory discussed in Chapter 2 is unidimensionality. This means that all the items on a test or ability scale are measuring a single latent trait of the individual. In Chapter 2 it will be made evident that unidimensionality is essential for all item response theories that are currently being applied. Because the theoretical developments leading to applications depend upon the assumption of unidimensionality, it is important to examine the extent to which any actual data set satisfies this property. The extent to which violations of this assumption lead to seriously misleading results is examined in Chapter 3.

Unfortunately, there is neither a straightforward nor simple process for determining or estimating the dimensionality of responses to a collection of items composing either an ability or an attitude scale. In Chapter 8 we describe the standard approaches and then present a procedure that appears to offer a partial solution to the problem of determining dimensionality. Although it is an heuristic procedure that depends on assumptions and invocations of faith, it does appear to yield reasonable answers when applied to Monte Carlo data sets whose dimensionality is known.

Public policy implications of testing. If it ever were possible to ignore the public policy implications of scientific practices in psychology and education, those days have passed. So long as objective assessments of merit or any other basis for selection decisions are used, measurement models will have implications for allocating opportunities in our society. They will, at times, be at odds with enunciated policies or even with constitutionally guaranteed rights. In Chapter 9, the role that measurement theory can play in the context of social and public policy is discussed.

1.4 SUMMARY

The range of applications discussed in Chapters 4, 5, 6, and 7 does not exhaust the possibilities of item response theory. Mastery and minimal-competency assessments, scale equating, estimating distributions of ability, and even graded response categories that could be used in attitude assessments have not been covered. We have focused on what we perceived to be the applications of greatest importance to a wide range of practitioners as well as those applications related to problems of public and social policy. The material contained in Chapters 2 and 3 should be sufficient to guide an interested researcher to the relevant primary sources and to develop applications to problems in a variety of areas. The materials and applications we have presented will be generally helpful to participants and spectators alike in the arena of applied psychological measurement.

REFERENCES

References for chapters that cite legal cases as well as articles and books will be separated into two sections to avoid confusion between the two different formats for citing reference material.

Articles and Books

Abelson, R. P., Aronson, E., McGuire, W. J., Newcomb, T. M., & Rosenberg, M. J. (Eds.). *Theories of cognitive consistency: A sourcebook.* Skokie, Ill.: Rand McNally, 1968.

Ajzen, I., & Fishbein, M. *Understanding attitudes and predicting social behavior.* Englewood Cliffs, N.J.: Prentice-Hall, 1980.

Anderson, N. H. How functional measurement can yield validated interval scales of mental quantities. *Journal of Applied Psychology,* 1976, *61,* 677–692.

Equal Employment Opportunity Commission, Civil Service Commission, Department of Labor, & Department of Justice. Adoption by four agencies of Uniform Guidelines on Employee Selection Procedures. *Federal Register,* 1978, *43,* 38290–38315.

Fishbein, M., & Ajzen, I. Attitudes toward objects as predictors of single and multiple behavioral criteria. *Psychological Review,* 1974, *81,* 59–74.

Fishbein, M., & Ajzen, I. *Belief, attitude, intention, and behavior: An introduction to theory and research.* Reading, Mass.: Addison-Wesley Publishing, 1975.

Green, B. F. Attitude measurement. In G. Lindzey (Ed.), *Handbook of social psychology* (Vol. 1). Reading, Mass.: Addison-Wesley Publishing, 1954.

Hargadon, F. Tests and college admissions. *American Psychologist,* 1981, *36,* 1112–1119.

Hulin, C. L., Drasgow, F., & Komocar, J. Applications of item response theory to analysis of attitude scale translations. *Journal of Applied Psychology,* 1982, *67,* 818–825.

Levine, M. V., & Drasgow, F. Appropriateness measurement: Validating studies and variable ability models. In D. J. Weiss (Ed.), *New horizons in testing: Latent-trait test theory and computerized adaptive testing.* New York: Academic Press, 1983. Reprinted from *British Journal of Mathematical and Statistical Psychology,* 1982, *35,* 42–56.

Levine, M. V. & Rubin, D. F. Measuring the appropriateness of multiple-choice test scores. *Journal of Educational Statistics,* 1979, *4,* 269–290.

Osgood, C. E., Suci, G. J., & Tannenbaum, P. H. *The measurement of meaning*. Urbana: University of Illinois Press, 1957.

Petersen, N., & Novick, M. An evaluation of some models for culture-fair selection. *Journal of Educational Measurement*, 1976, *13*, 3–31.

Spencer, H. *First principles*. New York: Burt, 1862. (Reprinted from 5th London edition.)

Triandis, H. C. Values, attitudes, and interpersonal behavior. In M. M. Page (Ed.), *Nebraska symposium on motivation*. Lincoln: University of Nebraska Press, 1979.

Legal Cases

Griggs, v. *Duke Power Co.*, 401 U.S. 424 (1971).

2

Introduction to Item Response Theory

2.0 OVERVIEW

In this chapter we present the concepts and theory that must be understood in order to use item response theory (IRT) properly. We focus on the development of various IRT models, assumptions, key results, and limitations on results. Our intent is to provide a broad overview of the essential ideas and assumptions of IRT. We therefore usually omit derivations in favor of providing relevant references.[1] The IRT results presented in this chapter are used in important ways in a variety of substantive applications in the chapters that follow.

In Section 2.1, we describe and define expressions that are used throughout this book and in the IRT literature. Some important early item response models are presented in Section 2.2, and their limitations are described. Two data sets are presented in Section 2.3. One data set consists of responses to multiple-choice ability test items and the other consists of responses to an instrument designed to measure attitudes. These data are used to motivate the IRT models presented in Section 2.4. Some additional assumptions that underlie the models as well as several very important implications are given in Section 2.5. Section 2.6 describes procedures for estimating parameters of IRT models and Section 2.7 defines and illustrates the concept of "information." Test models that allow responses to be classified into an arbitrary number of categories are described in Section 2.8. In Section 2.9, relations between IRT and classical test theory (CTT) are discussed. Finally, Section 2.10 contains a description of mathematical notation and methods that may be unfamiliar to some readers. Readers

---

[1] We do not mean to imply that studying derivations is without value; we strongly encourage consultation of original papers when they bear upon the reader's particular interest.

who wish to review this material may be well advised to read Sections 2.1 through 2.3, skip to Section 2.10, and then return to Section 2.4.

2.1 SOME IMPORTANT ITEM RESPONSE THEORY CONCEPTS

An item response theory includes a set of propositions concerned with individuals' responses to items used for psychological measurement. An essential part of each IRT presented in this book is a mathematical function that relates the probability of some type of response to an item by an individual to certain characteristics of the individual and the item. At the most abstract level, an IRT provides a probabilistic way of linking individuals' responses—the observable data—to theoretical constructs contained in psychological theories.

The different item response theories discussed in this book have been developed to deal with specific measurement problems encountered in psychology, education, and other social sciences. Of course, whether a particular IRT provides a satisfactory solution to some measurement problems is an empirical question. As the domain of IRT expands beyond the analytic and Monte Carlo studies by psychometricians and comes into wide use by practitioners, it becomes increasingly important that the form of one's IRT be critically examined for its applicability to a particular set of questions or problems.

Many different characteristics of individuals have been considered in IRT. In early work, Tucker (1946) and Lord (1952) developed an IRT for the situation in which the individual's characteristic was the ability, such as verbal or quantitative, measured by a mental test. Lazarsfeld (1950, 1959) developed several IRT models that were designed primarily for the investigation of attitudes. More recent applications of IRT include Wright and Mead's (1977) analysis of military police pistol marksmanship, Parsons's (1979) investigation of a frequently used instrument for measuring job satisfaction, and Hulin, Drasgow, and Komocar's (1982) procedure for investigating the quality of a translation of a psychological scale from one language to another.

All these investigations share a common perspective. They assume that the probability of an observable response or behavior is related to the individual's standing on an underlying latent characteristic. Thus, the probability of a correct response to a multiple-choice item on the Scholastic Aptitude Test–Verbal section (SAT-V) is stated as a function of an hypothesized latent characteristic, *verbal ability*; the probability of a military policeman shooting a bull's-eye is a function of an assumed pistol *marksmanship*; and the probability of workers agreeing that their work is "fascinating" is a function of their hypothesized *job satisfaction*.

In each case described above, the latent characteristic is *not directly observable*. An IRT provides a link between the responses and the latent variable. The point of IRT is to use observed behaviors—usually responses to many items—to estimate an individual's standing on the latent characteristic. The individual's standing on the characteristic can then be used to predict other behaviors—verbal ability may be used to predict freshman grade-point average—or make decisions of some type—one subunit of an organization might have many very dissatisfied workers and require an organizational intervention.

In our discussion we use the term *item* to describe the individual unit of observation, *test* or *scale* to describe the collection of items, and *trait* or *ability* to describe the latent characteristic of the individual, which is usually estimated from the individual's responses to test items. We will use the Greek letter theta (θ) to refer to a generalized value along the latent trait continuum.

Throughout most of this chapter we will consider measurement models for dichotomously scored items. In these models, the score of 1 is usually assigned to a positive or correct response to an item, and the score of 0 is usually assigned to a negative or incorrect response. Obviously, to be able to score responses requires knowledge of the correct answer. This is usually straightforward for most ability test items. However, scoring items that do not have options that are correct or incorrect (for example, attitude scale items) is more complicated. A method of scoring responses to this type of item is described in Section 2.3.

The latent trait θ is usually considered to be distributed continuously. However, the particular form of this distribution is usually *not* specified. We do *not* need to assume that ability is normally distributed. Lord (1974) has found that normality is only a moderately accurate approximation of the true distribution in some populations.

We should stress that we are discussing a general class of measurement theories that specify how to transform item responses, represented as 0s and 1s, into estimates of the trait assumed to underlie the item responses. Measurement theories must be differentiated from substantive or content theories that specify or define the meanings of the underlying traits in terms of their relations with other variables and behaviors. Thus, IRT can be used to estimate an individual's standing on the latent trait θ but does not provide guidance for construct validation of the trait.

2.2 SOME EARLY IRT MODELS

In this section, three IRT models developed in the 1950s are described. The models present interesting quantifications of the relation between response probability and the latent characteristic. However, these seminal models are little used in present-day research because more sophisticated models with wider applicability have been developed. Nevertheless, their place in the development of modern IRT is important and merits serious discussion.

The first model we consider is the Guttman "perfect scale" (Guttman, 1950). Figure 2.2.1 presents a perfect "monotone" (Guttman

Figure 2.2.1
Guttman Perfect Scale Item

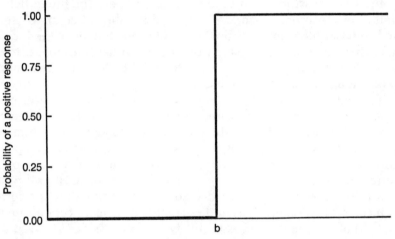

item (Torgerson, 1958). The "curve" in Figure 2.2.1—actually a step function—states the probability of a response to an item as a function of the trait under consideration.

The interpretation of Figure 2.2.1 is straightforward. An individual with less than b units of the latent trait will not make a correct response—the probability of a correct response is 0.0 for all individuals with $\theta < b$. Individuals with more than b units of the trait will always respond correctly; here the probability of a correct response is 1.0.

The curve in Figure 2.2.1 is called an item characteristic curve (ICC). Lazarsfeld (1950), Torgerson (1958), and others have called this type of curve the "item trace line" because it traces "the probability for an item as a 'respondent' moves along the latent continuum" (Lazarsfeld, 1959, p. 493). We follow the terminology established by Tucker (cited by Lord, 1952, p. 5) and Lord (1952), calling these curves ICCs because this term has been widely adopted in the recently published literature.

Although the IRT model presented in Figure 2.2.1 is very interesting from a theoretical standpoint, it is rare that actual data of interest to social scientists will meet its very stringent requirements. For this reason, deterministic models such as the Guttman perfect scale are rarely employed by practitioners.[2] Stochastic (i.e., probabilistic) models that allow probabilities of positive responses greater than zero but less than one are more appropriate for the types of data commonly seen. Consequently, we shall only consider stochastic models in the remainder of this book.

A stochastic IRT model that retains the step-function ICC is the *latent-distance model*. Figure 2.2.2 presents an ICC that satisfies the

Figure 2.2.2
Latent Distance Model

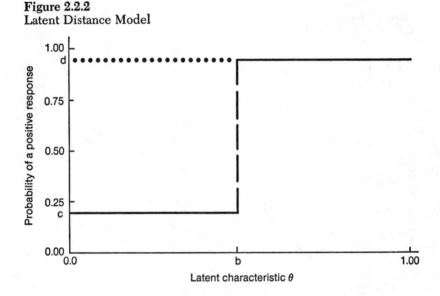

latent-distance model described by Lazarsfeld (1950), Green (1954), and Torgerson (1958). Individuals whose standings on the trait are less than b have probability c $(0 \leq c < d)$ of making the desired response. Individuals with θ greater than b have probability d $(c < d \leq 1.0)$ of making a positive response.

Again, it appears unlikely that social science data sets will be reasonably represented by ICCs of the form presented in Figure 2.2.2. Although the latent-distance model is a stochastic model, both the discontinuity at the *breaking point* (b) of the latent trait and the flatness of the ICC before and after b seem implausible because people almost never behave with such consistency. We refer researchers who

---

[2] See Cliff (1979, 1981) for some recent theoretical developments that are quite interesting.

suspect that their data sets are adequately described by the latent-distance model to Lazarsfeld (1950) and Torgerson (1958, chap. 13).

Lazarsfeld (1959) developed an IRT model that avoids the step-function discontinuity by assuming that the probability of a correct response to an item is proportional to an individual's standing on the underlying latent trait. The ICCs are linear functions of θ:

(2.2.1) $P(\theta) = \text{Prob(Positive Response}|\theta) = c + a\theta,$

where a is the slope of the ICC relating $P(\theta)$ to θ and c is the intercept of the function.[3] Figure 2.2.3 illustrates this model, which Torgerson

Figure 2.2.3
Two Linear Model ICCs

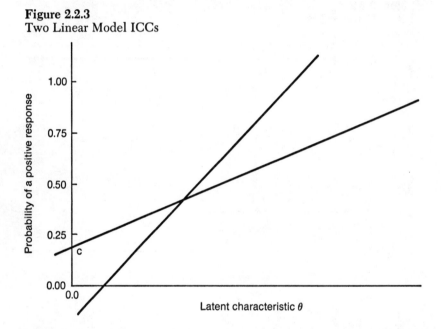

(1958) termed the *linear model*. Here an individual with θ equal to zero has probability c of making a positive response. Individuals with higher standings along the latent continuum have correspondingly higher probabilities of positive responses.

The most obvious limitation of the linear model is that, unless a is zero, individuals with sufficiently low standings on the latent trait will have negative probabilities of a positive response, and individuals with sufficiently high standings will have probabilities greater than unity. In other words, only if the item responses are unrelated to θ,

---

[3] Prob(positive response$|\theta$) is the conditional probability of a positive response to a particular item given a level of θ on the latent trait continuum.

which implies a is zero, will the linear model yield probabilities of responses that are always between 0 and 1.0. But if the item responses are unrelated to θ, the item provides no information about θ. Thus only items with $a > 0$ would be included in a measurement scale, and probabilities less than zero or greater than one would occur. Clearly, negative probabilities and probabilities greater than unity create theoretical problems for any IRT model. Lazarsfeld (1959, p. 509) recognized this difficulty and dealt with it by requiring that "there is 'nobody at home' " when an ICC is less than zero or greater than unity. That is, the distribution of θ is such that there is no individual for whom $P(\theta)$ is less than zero or $P(\theta)$ is greater than one.

Lazarsfeld's linear model can be interpreted as a linear approximation to a general class of ICCs in which $P(\theta)$ is monotonically increasing but not necessarily linearly related to θ. There are many examples ranging from applied psychology to physics where a linear approximation of a nonlinear function is quite good. For Lazarsfeld's linear model, the adequacy of the approximation will depend on the range of item difficulties, the discriminating power of the items (i.e., steepness of the ICCs) and the range of θ for the population of individuals under consideration. Torgerson (1958, p. 368) notes that the problems caused by negative probabilities and probabilities greater than unity put "a real limitation on the model." Further information about the linear model can be found in Torgerson (1958, chap. 13) and Lazarsfeld (1959).

2.3 EMPIRICAL ITEM CHARACTERISTIC CURVES

At this point it is useful to examine data from two psychological scales. The first, the SAT-V, has been studied extensively by Lord (1968, 1980). The second instrument is the Job Descriptive Index (JDI), which was developed by Smith, Kendall, and Hulin (1969) to assess five facets of job satisfaction (Satisfactions with Work Itself, Coworkers, Supervision, Pay, and Promotion Opportunities). Recent empirical results (Parsons & Hulin, 1980; Hulin et al., 1982) suggest that treating the JDI as a unidimensional scale as we do here does little violence to the structure of JDI data under certain circumstances.

In this section we shall present several *empirical ICCs* which we will use to motivate the mathematical form of the ICCs presented in Section 2.4. To obtain an empirical ICC, we use various characteristics of the items (described and defined more fully in Sections 2.4 and 2.6) to estimate θs for a large sample of examinees. Then the examinees are sorted into a number of mutually exclusive and exhaustive categories on the basis of their estimated abilities ($\hat{\theta}$s). Finally, the proportions of examinees with positive responses to the item in each $\hat\theta$ interval are determined. The empirical ICC for an item is a plot of these proportions against the median $\hat\theta$ of each interval.

Empirical ICCs simply display the proportions of individuals who responded correctly or positively to an item at various levels of θ. The general shape of an empirical ICC should be a good approximation to the mathematical form of the ICC that is specified by an IRT model. A close approximation of an empirical ICC to the theoretical ICC illustrates the applicability of the model. A large discrepancy between the empirical ICC and the theoretical ICC for some item indicates that the IRT model may be inappropriate for the item.

SAT-V. Figure 2.3.1 presents the empirical ICC for an SAT-V item based on the responses of 49,470 examinees. The $\hat\theta$ continuum

Figure 2.3.1
Empirical ICC for an SAT-V Item, Based on the Responses of 49,470 Examinees

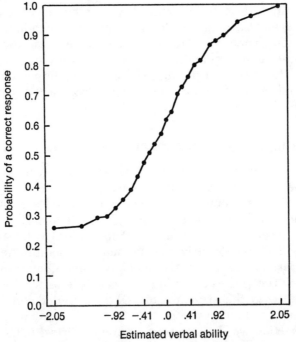

was divided into 25 intervals by using the 2d, 6th, 10th, . . . , percentile points from the standard normal distribution. (Ability estimates are usually scaled to have a mean of zero and a standard deviation of one.) This yielded approximately 2,000 examinees in each $\hat\theta$ interval.

Thus, each point plotted in Figure 2.3.1 is based on a large number of examinees and should be stable.

There are several features of Figure 2.3.1 that merit attention. First, note that even very low–ability examinees answer this item correctly with probability .25. This is not surprising because SAT-V items have five multiple-choice options. An examinee guessing randomly would have a .20 probability of a correct response. As ability increases, the empirical ICC in Figure 2.3.1 rises slowly at first, and then more sharply. Finally, at very high ability levels, examinees are almost certain to answer this item correctly. In addition, the empirical ICC has again become almost horizontal. Note that equal changes in $\hat{\theta}$ at different points along the continuum are not translated into equal increases in the probability of a correct response.

If the reader were to select a smooth curve to fit to the points in Figure 2.3.1, the S-shaped cumulative normal ogive might well suggest itself. Indeed, the early IRT models developed by Lawley (1943; 1944), Lord (1952), and Tucker (1946) used normal ogive ICCs. The fit of the normal ogive at the lower asymptote is not usually very good for multiple-choice items. An S-shaped curve, like the normal ogive, with a nonzero lower asymptote would provide a very good description of the empirical ICC presented in Figure 2.3.1.

Figure 2.3.2 presents empirical ICCs for several other SAT-V items obtained from the responses of the 49,470 examinees described previously. For each item, it is possible to envision part of an S-shaped curve with a nonzero lower asymptote that accurately describes the probabilities of a correct response. In panel A, for example, only the upper part of the curve is needed because this is a very easy item. Panel B presents a very difficult item. Here roughly half the examinees answered the item correctly with the probability described by the lower asymptote. The item discriminates quite sharply among high-ability examinees: The curve rises dramatically at high values of $\hat{\theta}$. A less sharply rising empirical ICC is presented in panel C. Again, this is a difficult item. Panel D depicts an ICC from an extremely difficult item: Examinees in the bottom three-quarters of the ability distribution have less than 1 chance in 10 of answering correctly. Consequently, for this item it is clear that the low- to moderate-ability examinees are *not* answering randomly. If they were, their probabilities of responding correctly would be close to .2. The items presented in panels C, E, and F are reminiscent of Lazarsfeld's (1959) linear model. From the perspective of modeling with S-shaped curves, we interpret these empirical proportions as drawn from the center of the curve. The linear relations result because there are not enough examinees of sufficiently low or high ability for the lower or upper asymptotes to appear. Finally, panel F shows an item that appears to have a lower

Figure 2.3.2
Empirical ICCs for SAT-V Items

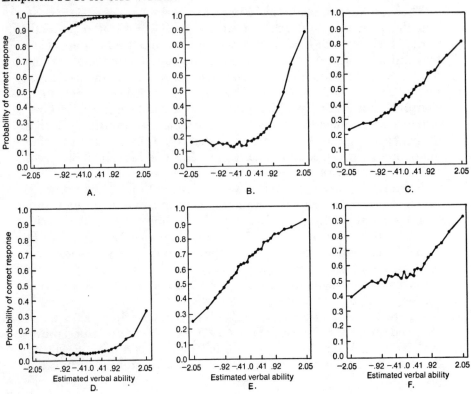

asymptote that is relatively high. Apparently, one or more of the incorrect options is not attractive to low-ability examinees.

The empirical ICCs presented in Figures 2.3.1 and 2.3.2 result from the responses to multiple-choice items where examinees are encouraged to guess if they can eliminate one or more options. The empirical ICCs support the obvious intuition that even very low-ability examinees will have nonzero chances of answering correctly. We have introduced the concept of an S-shaped curve with a nonzero lower asymptote in order to provide a theoretical model for this type of item.

JDI. We shall now present empirical ICCs for the JDI (Smith et al., 1969). For these items, the worker responds either no, yes, or ? to each of 72 adjectives, depending on whether or not the adjective describes the individual's job. The JDI is scored using a somewhat more complicated scoring procedure than for the SAT-V. The scoring procedure developed by Smith et al. assigns a score of +3 to a yes response to a positive item (e.g., fascinating) or a no response to a negative item (e.g., underpaid). Yes responses to negatively worded items and no responses to positively worded items are assigned a score of 0. All ? responses were assigned a score of $+1$. Throughout this book we will score the JDI items with a 0 for a negative response (no to a positively worded item, or yes to a negatively worded item), a $+1$ for a positive response (yes to a positively worded item, or no to a negatively worded item) and a 0 for a ? response.

Figure 2.3.3 presents the empirical ICC for the item "pleasant" based on the responses of 3,812 workers. The sample consists of per-

Figure 2.3.3
Empirical ICC for the Item "Pleasant" from the JDI
Satisfaction with the Work Itself Scale

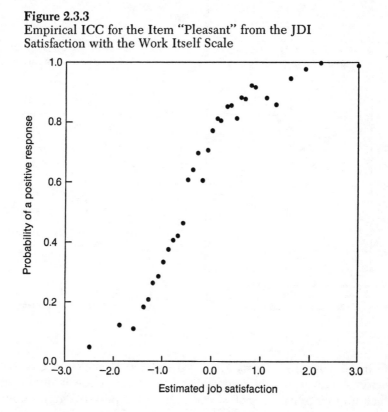

sonnel in a wide range of nonmanagerial jobs in a retail firm and two military organizations. The empirical ICC in Figure 2.3.3 was obtained by the same methods used to obtain empirical ICCs for SAT-V items. Estimates of θ (overall job satisfaction) were based on responses to 60 JDI items. (The nine-item Pay scale was excluded because this scale was not appropriate for the military sample, and three items from the Coworkers scale were excluded due to incomplete

24

Figure 2.3.4
Empirical ICCs for JDI Items

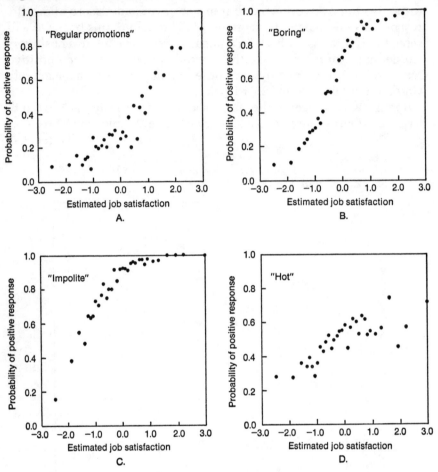

data in all samples.) Thirty-three satisfaction strata were created to provide a wide range of satisfaction categories while maintaining a sufficiently large number of workers in each stratum. The number of workers per stratum ranged from 58 to 179. The strata medians are $-2.5, -1.9, -1.6, -1.4, -1.3, -1.2, \ldots, .8, .9, 1.1, 1.3, 1.6, 2.2, 3.0.$ These strata were selected as a compromise between forming a large number of strata and including a large number of workers in each stratum.

Note that the empirical ICC in Figure 2.3.3 appears to have a lower asymptote that is very close to zero. This should not be too surprising; a thoroughly disgruntled worker is unlikely to guess the positive response to this item. Thus, an S-shaped curve, with a lower asymptote of zero and an upper asymptote of one, seems to be an appropriate model for this item. Additional research and discussion concerning the lower asymptotes of JDI items is presented in Chapter 3.

Figure 2.3.4 presents the empirical ICCs for a number of JDI items. Panel A shows the empirical ICC for the item "regular promotions." This is a somewhat extreme item; only very satisfied workers endorse this item with high probability. The empirical ICC for the item that asks whether the work itself is "boring" is shown in panel B. This item is more popular (less extreme) than the item in panel A. An even less extreme item is shown in panel C; here moderately dissatisfied workers state with high probability that their supervisor is not "impolite." Finally, panel D presents a relatively nondiscriminating item. This item, which asks whether the work itself is "hot," does not have a sharply rising empirical ICC. The empirical ICCs in panels B and C provide a sharp contrast to panel D. Because its empirical ICC is relatively flat, the item "hot" does little to discriminate among various levels of satisfaction and, consequently, does little to aid in the measurement of job satisfaction.

2.4 S-SHAPED ITEM CHARACTERISTIC CURVE MODELS

The normal ogive model.   The empirical ICCs presented in Section 2.3 demonstrate the need for IRT models with S-shaped ICCs. In this section, we describe the normal ogive and logistic IRT models that have S-shaped ICCs.

We begin with the normal ogive model, which preceded the logistic model in development. Early work on this model was done by Lawley (1943; 1944), Tucker (1946), and Lord (1952). Bock and Lieberman (1970) and Kolakowski and Bock (1970) have presented more recent work.

The ICC used in the normal ogive model is the cumulative normal ogive. It may be written:

$$(2.4.1) \qquad P_i(\theta) = \frac{1}{\sqrt{2\pi}} \int_{-\infty}^{a_i(\theta - b_i)} e^{-y^2/2} \, dy,$$

which expresses the area under the standardized normal curve from a z-score of $-\infty$ to a z-score of $a_i(\theta - b_i)$. The normal ogive is used as an ICC because its height at θ, which is given by Equation 2.4.1, can be interpreted as the probability of a correct response for examinees with ability θ. The interpretation of $P_i(\theta)$ as a probability is possible because the lower asymptote of the normal ogive is zero and its upper asymptote is one. Thus, in contrast to the linear model, negative probabilities and probabilities greater than one cannot occur for the normal ogive model at any value of θ.

For some data sets, values of a_i and b_i can be selected so that the normal ogive given by Equation 2.4.1 for each item is close to the points forming the item's empirical ICC. Then b_i can be interpreted as an index of the item's difficulty and a_i can be interpreted as the discriminating power of the item. Unfortunately, the integration in Equation 2.4.1 is not easily performed; this is a major reason for use of the logistic models.

Values of θ in a given population (as well as $\hat\theta$s) are usually scaled to have a mean of zero and a standard deviation of one. It is possible to rescale θ to have a different mean and variance. For example, if it were convenient to rescale the abilities to have a mean of 500 and a standard deviation of 100, we could perform the following transformations:

$$\theta^* = 100\theta + 500$$

$$a_i^* = a_i/100$$

$$b_i^* = 100b_i + 500.$$

Thus the mean and standard deviation of θ^* would be 500 and 100, respectively. However,

$$a_i^*(\theta^* - b_i^*) = \frac{a_i}{100}\left[(100\theta + 500) - (100b_i + 500)\right]$$

$$= a_i(\theta - b_i),$$

and so using θ^*, a_i^*, and b_i^* in Equation 2.4.1 produces the same $P_i(\theta)$ as θ, a_i, and b_i. This shows that linear transformations of the θ-metric are permissible. By convention, the θ-metric is usually scaled to have a mean of zero and a standard deviation of one.

We shall not deal with the problem of estimating θ, b_i and a_i for the normal ogive model. Interested readers should consult Lord (1952), Bock and Lieberman (1970), and Kolakowski and Bock (1970) for maximum likelihood estimates. Figure 2.4.1 presents a normal ogive using $b_i = -.50$ and $a_i = .91$ in Equation 2.4.1. These values of a_i and b_i were selected by inspection to fit the points in the empirical ICC presented in Figure 2.3.3. Note that the empirical proportions of correct responses are all quite close to the theoretical curve. Thus, we can summarize the set of 33 points that form the empirical ICC by a curve with only two item parameters: a_i and b_i. In addition, the normal ogive allows us to interpolate between pairs of empirical ICC points, as well as extrapolate beyond the range of empirical ICC points.

Figure 2.4.1
Normal Ogive Fitted to the Empirical ICC for the Item
"Pleasant" from the JDI Satisfaction with the Work Itself Scale

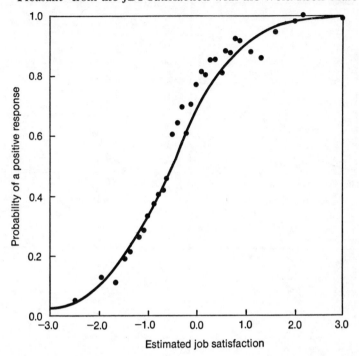

Figure 2.4.2 presents four more normal ogives fitted to the empirical ICCs presented previously in Figure 2.3.4. Again, the normal ogives are generally quite close to the empirical proportions of correct responses. Note that the ogive in panel D is essentially flat. This tells us that this item has little value for estimating job satisfaction, at least within the sample of workers considered here.

The normal ogive model is important for a number of theoretical reasons. These reasons are discussed in Chapter 8. Due to the integration in Equation 2.4.1, however, logistic models are used in most practical applications of IRT.

Logistic function. One class of S-shaped curves that is relatively convenient to use is the logistic ogive (or, more precisely, the logistic cumulative distribution function). The form of this curve is

$$(2.4.2) \qquad \text{Height of logistic ogive at } x = \frac{1}{1 + e^{-x}},$$

where e is a mathematical constant approximately equal to 2.71828.

Figure 2.4.2
Normal Ogives Fitted to Empirical ICCs for JDI Items

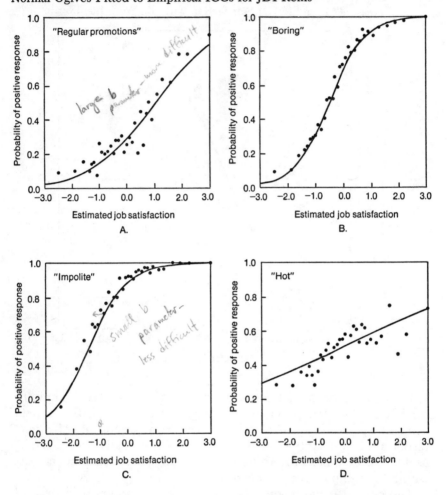

A.

B.

C.

D.

Note that there is no integral in this equation; the height of the ogive can be evaluated directly and easily. The logistic ogive in Equation 2.4.2 is particularly attractive because it is virtually identical to the normal ogive in Equation 2.4.1 (Birnbaum, 1968, p. 399; Haley, 1952):

$$(2.4.3) \qquad \left| \frac{1}{\sqrt{2\pi}} \int_{-\infty}^{x} e^{-v^2/2} \, dy - \frac{1}{1 + e^{-1.7x}} \right| < 0.01.$$

Thus the logistic ogive can be used as an approximation of the normal ogive and conversely, the normal ogive can be used as an approximation of the logistic ogive. This property is useful because it is sometimes easier to derive a relationship using one ogive instead of the other. Due to Equation 2.4.3, a relationship or property that can be derived for one ogive should be approximately true for the other ogive.

The three-parameter logistic model. The three-parameter logistic model (Birnbaum, 1968) is the most general of the three logistic models that we shall discuss. This model has received a substantial amount of study (Lord, 1968, 1970, 1974, 1975, 1980; Hambleton & Traub, 1971; Marco, 1977) as well as criticism (Wright, 1977). An S-shaped curve with a nonzero lower asymptote, the three-parameter logistic ICC is designed to model data of the nature presented in Figures 2.3.1 and 2.3.2. The model is particularly appropriate when individuals with low standings on the latent trait can occasionally respond correctly to difficult items. Ability tests using multiple-choice formats and attitude instruments where substantial acquiescent response sets occur are examples of situations where the three-parameter model might be especially useful.

The form of the three-parameter logistic model[4] is

$$(2.4.4) \qquad P_i(\theta) = c_i + (1 - c_i) \frac{1}{[1 + \exp\{-Da_i(\theta - b_i)\}]}.$$

In this equation, a_i reflects the steepness of the ICC at its inflection point (panels B and C of Figure 2.4.2 show ICCs that are steep at their inflection points and, hence, these items have large a parameters; panels A and D show relatively flat ICCs, and these items have small a parameters), b_i is an index of item difficulty and corresponds to the value of θ at the inflection point of the ICC (panel A of Figure 2.4.2 shows an item that is endorsed infrequently and therefore has a large b parameter while the item in panel C is endorsed more frequently and therefore has a smaller b parameter), and c_i is the lower asymptote of the ICC and corresponds to the probability of a correct response among respondents with very low levels of θ. D is a scaling constant usually set equal to 1.7 or 1.702. Using this value of D in Equation 2.4.4 scales the logistic ICC to take advantage of the relation between logistic and normal ogives shown in Equation 2.4.3. The interpretations of the item parameters a_i, b_i, and c_i become apparent from studying Equation 2.4.4. In the following paragraphs, we vary a_i, b_i, and c_i to illustrate the effects of these item parameters on the ICC.

First, consider the empirical ICC originally presented in Figure 2.3.1 and reproduced in Figure 2.4.3. Assume for the moment that we

---

[4] When the constant e is raised to some power x, the notation $\exp(x) = e^x$ is occasionally used. One reason for using this notation is that sometimes an exponent of e includes subscripts or superscripts (see Equation 2.4.4). Using the exp notation, one may avoid writing a subscript or superscript on a superscript.

Figure 2.4.3
Empirical ICC Based on the Responses of 49,470 SAT-V
Examinees, and Probabilities Computed from Equation 2.4.5

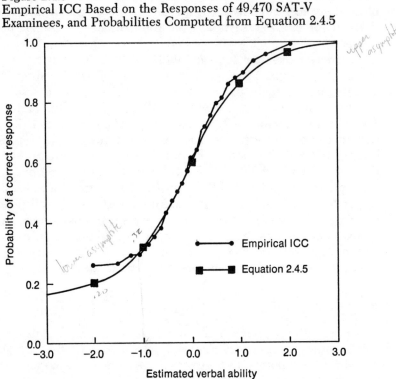

have estimated the item parameters for this item to be $\hat{a}_i = .90$, $\hat{b}_i = -.08$, and $\hat{c}_i = .155$. (Methods for estimating item parameters are discussed in Section 2.6.) Substituting the parameter estimates for the parameters in Equation 2.4.4, we see

$$\hat{P}_i(\theta) = .155 + .845 \frac{1}{[1 + \exp\{-(1.702)(.90)[\theta - (-.08)]\}]}$$

(2.4.5)

$$= .155 + .845 \frac{1}{[1 + \exp\{-1.53(\theta + .08)\}]}.$$

According to this model, examinees with ability $\theta = -1$ have probability

$$\hat{P}(-1) = .155 + .845 \frac{1}{[1 + \exp\{-1.53(-1 + .08)\}]}$$

$$= .155 + .845 \frac{1}{1 + 4.09}$$

$$= .32$$

of a correct response. This probability is indicated in Figure 2.4.3 by the "■" plotted above −1 on the $\hat{\theta}$ axis. Note that the estimated probability is very close to the observed probabilities.

The probability of a correct response among examinees with $\theta = -2$ is

$$\hat{P}(-2) = .155 + .845 \frac{1}{[1 + \exp\{-1.53(-2 + .08)\}]}$$

$$= .20,$$

which is also plotted in Figure 2.4.3. Note that here the model's probability is slightly smaller than the observed value. Similar computations at values of 0, +1, and +2 yield probabilities of .60, .86, and .97, respectively. The model's probabilities are smaller than the empirical probabilities for θ values of 1 and 2, and quite close at θ values of −1 and 0.

Now consider a hypothetical item with the same a_i and b_i parameters, but a different c_i parameter. If $c_i = .50$, then Equation 2.4.5 becomes:

$$(2.4.6) \qquad P_i(\theta) = .50 + .50 \frac{1}{[1 + \exp\{-1.53(\theta + .08)\}]}.$$

The probabilities of a correct response for this item at θ values of −2, −1, 0, 1, and 2 are .52, .60, .76, .92, and .98, respectively. These compare to corresponding values of .20, .32, .60, .86, and .97 from Equation 2.4.5. The upper asymptote of the ICC has not changed. In contrast, the lower asymptote has been substantially affected. The ICCs defined by Equation 2.4.5 and Equation 2.4.6 are plotted in Figure 2.4.4.

Note that for very small (i.e., negative values that are large in magnitude) values of θ, the term

$$\frac{1}{[1 + \exp\{-Da_i(\theta - b_i)\}]}$$

becomes approximately zero, leaving

$$P_i(\theta) = c_i.$$

Consequently, c_i is the lower asymptote of the ICC. It is interpreted as the probability of a correct response among examinees of very low ability. The parameter c_i is sometimes called the "guessing" parameter. It is important to note that although c_i is certainly affected by guessing, these guesses are frequently *nonrandom*. Returning to Figure 2.3.2, panel D, the lower asymptote of this ICC is obviously not .2, which is the probability of obtaining a correct answer by guessing

Figure 2.4.4
ICCs for Equations 2.4.5 and 2.4.6

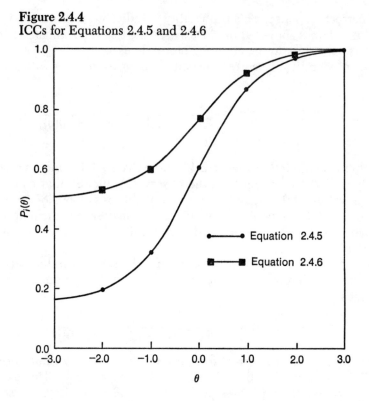

randomly. Lord (1974) notes that estimates of c are frequently less than the probability of randomly guessing the correct response, and attributes this phenomenon to item writers making one or more incorrect options very attractive to low-ability examinees.

Note also that items with nonzero c parameters have ICCs that are compressed between c and 1.00. This effectively reduces the total discriminatory power of the item. In Equation 2.4.6 the lower asymptote is .5 and the difference between $P_i(\theta)$ for individuals with a θ of -2 and those with a θ of $+2$ is $.98 - .52 = .46$. In Equation 2.4.5, the difference is $.77 (=.97 - .20)$ because the c parameter is .155. Thus an item with a large c parameter distinguishes less clearly among those examinees with high and low abilities than an item with a lower c parameter (provided the two items have the same a and b parameters). We shall return to this point in our discussion of item information.

The effects of varying the b_i parameter are straightforward. Let us compare the ICC for a hypothetical item with parameters $a_i = .90$, $b_i = -1.08$, and $c_i = .155$ to the ICC defined in Equation 2.4.5. The new ICC is

$$(2.4.7) \quad P_i(\theta) = .155 + .845 \frac{1}{[1 + \exp\{-1.53(\theta + 1.08)\}]},$$

which differs from Equation 2.4.5 only in the b_i term ($b_i = -.08$ in Equation 2.4.5). The probabilities of a correct response at θ values of $-2, -1, 0, 1$, and 2 are .32, .60, .86, .97, and .99, respectively. The ICCs for Equation 2.4.7 and Equation 2.4.5 are plotted in Figure 2.4.5. It

Figure 2.4.5
ICCs for Equations 2.4.5 and 2.4.7

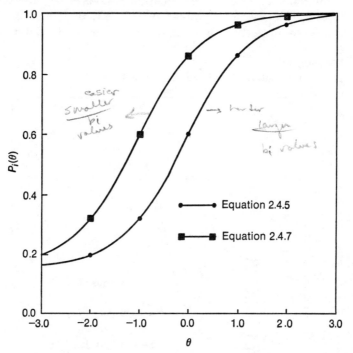

should be clear that the change in b_i from $-.08$ to -1.08 has merely displaced the original ICC to the left by one θ unit; in all other respects, the two curves are identical.

The implication of moving an ICC to the left is that the new item is *easier* than the item described by Equation 2.4.5. In a discussion of attitude measurement, the item would be said to be more popular or less extreme. The parameter b_i is referred to as the "item difficulty" parameter. Other things being equal, smaller values of b_i correspond to easier or more popular items, and larger values of b_i indicate harder or less popular items.

The final item parameter of the three-parameter logistic model is a_i. Again, we can understand its role in Equation 2.4.4 by varying a_i while holding the other parameters constant. Let us select $a_i = 1.90$, and compare the ICC

$$P_i(\theta) = .155 + .845 \frac{1}{[1 + \exp\{-D(1.90)(\theta + .08)\}]}$$

(2.4.8)

$$= .155 + .845 \frac{1}{[1 + \exp\{-3.23(\theta + .08)\}]}$$

to Equation 2.4.5. The values of Equation 2.4.8 are .16, .20, .63, .98, and 1.00, respectively, for θ values of -2, -1, 0, 1, and 2. These probabilities are plotted in Figure 2.4.6. Note that the ICC defined by

Figure 2.4.6
ICCs for Equations 2.4.5, 2.4.8, and 2.4.9

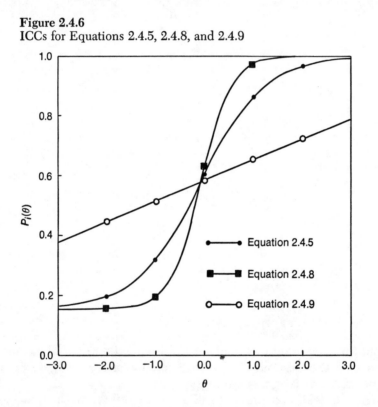

Equation 2.4.8 is more angular than the ICC for Equation 2.4.5. In fact, if a_i is sufficiently large, a three-parameter logistic ICC will look like the step-function ICC (with an upper asymptote of unity) shown in Figure 2.2.2 for the latent-distance model.

It is clear that the a_i parameter controls the steepness of the ICC in the region near b. For this reason, a_i is called the "discriminating power" of the item. Note that when a_i is large (as in Equation 2.4.8), the ICC is very steep near b_i, and flat elsewhere. In contrast, when a_i is small, say .2, the ICC rises smoothly for a wide interval, centered at b_i. An item with the ICC

$$(2.4.9) \qquad P_i(\theta) = .155 + .845 \; \frac{1}{[1 + \exp\{-D(.2)(\theta + .08)\}]}$$

is also plotted in Figure 2.4.6. The ICC for this item rises gradually but consistently throughout the range of θ values plotted.

Figure 2.4.6 illustrates the sense in which a_i indexes the "discriminating power" of an item. Consider two examinees, examinee 1 with $\theta_1 = -1.0$, and examinee 2 with $\theta_2 = 1.0$. The item described in Equation 2.4.8 will very likely discriminate between the two examinees in that examinee 1 will respond incorrectly (with probability $1 - P_i(-1) = 1 - .2 = .8$), and examinee 2 will answer correctly (with probability $P_i(1) = .98$). In contrast, the item described by Equation 2.4.9 is much less able to discriminate between the two examinees: $P_i(-1) = .51$ and $P_i(1) = .65$. Thus, in the area near b_i, an item with a larger a_i value rises more rapidly and can be used by a test maker to discriminate more sharply among examinees with abilities near b_i.

It is interesting to note that, although items with large a_i values rise rapidly near b_i, elsewhere their ICCs are relatively flat. For example, the ICC for Equation 2.4.8 has value .155 at $\theta = -3$, and rises to .156 at $\theta = -2$. Consequently, this item has essentially no ability to discriminate among examinees at these low ability levels. The item described by Equation 2.4.9, on the other hand, rises from .38 at $\theta = -3$ to .44 at $\theta = -2$, which indicates some discriminating power. In sum, items with smaller a_i values have less discriminating power than items with larger values of a near their b_i values, but more discriminating power for θ values relatively far from b_i. Thus, they provide some information about ability over a wide range of θ. In contrast, items with large a_i values provide a great deal of information about θ values near their corresponding b_i values but provide little information about θ elsewhere. Items with low to moderate a_i values can be valuable to test and scale makers when little is known about the distribution of θ prior to administration of the instrument, because they provide some information for a wide range of θ values.

We conclude our presentation of the three-parameter logistic model by discussing the theoretical limits on item parameters and noting typical ranges for item parameter estimates. First, note that the a_i parameter must be a positive, real number for the ICC to be monotonically increasing. (See Section 2.10 for a discussion of *monotonic* functions.) For dichotomously scored (correct/incorrect) items, it is generally assumed that ICCs are monotonically increasing, and therefore we shall make this assumption throughout this book. Estimated a_i

values usually range from about .30 to about 2.0. The b_i parameter can be any real number, but is normally estimated to be between -3.0 and 3.0. Finally, the lower asymptote is restricted to the interval $0.0 \leq c_i \leq 1.0$. Estimates of c_i are frequently close to $1/m$ for multiple-choice ability test items with m options. In attitude measurement, nonzero values of c_i may be infrequent and, except for general response tendencies, their meaning is not obvious. Estimating c_i is usually difficult because there are very few individuals with extremely low values of θ whose item responses can be used to help determine c_i.

The two-parameter logistic model. This model is the special case of the three-parameter logistic model where all c_i values are zero. Consequently, the lower asymptotes of two-parameter logistic ICC curves are zero, which means that, according to the model, very low-ability individuals have almost no chance of making a positive or correct response to difficult items. ICCs of this form seem appropriate for modeling responses to open-ended questions such as:

Find $\int 2x dx$,
Define homunculus,

and

Complete the following analogy:
oxymoronic : onomatopoeia :: tintinabulation :_____.

It appears unlikely that an examinee could "guess" the answers to these items. In addition, the two-parameter logistic model seems appropriate for attitude measurement items that intermix positive and negative stems to minimize or eliminate acquiescent response sets.

The equation for the two-parameter logistic model is

(2.4.10)
$$P_i(\theta) = \frac{1}{1 + \exp[-Da_i(\theta - b_i)]},$$

which results from setting c_i equal to zero in Equation 2.4.4. To illustrate two-parameter logistic ICCs, consider the following hypothetical items:

Item	a_i	b_i
1	1.0	0.0
2	1.0	1.0
3	1.0	-1.0
4	.5	0.0
5	1.5	0.0

ICCs for these items are presented in Figure 2.4.7.

Figure 2.4.7
ICCs for Two-Parameter Logistic Items

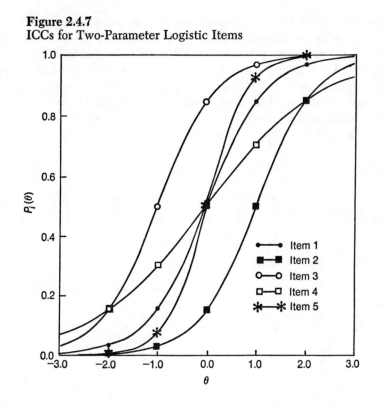

Note that the ICCs for items 1, 2, and 3 are identical up to a translation along the abscissa. It is clear that the lower asymptote is zero for these curves, and that the upper asymptote is one. For all the ICCs in Figure 2.4.7, $P_i(\theta) = .5$ at $\theta = b_i$; this leads to the interpretation of b_i in the two-parameter model not only as the item difficulty parameter, but also as the point along the θ continuum at which examinees have a 50 percent chance of responding correctly. This latter interpretation of b_i does not hold for the three-parameter logistic model.

By comparing ICCs for items 1, 4, and 5, it is clear that a_i controls the steepness of the ICC in the neighborhood of b_i. In particular, the slope of the ICC can be obtained by differentiating Equation 2.4.10 with respect to θ. At $\theta = b_i$, it can be shown that the slope of the ICC is 42.55 percent of a_i if D is set equal to 1.702. This simple relation is not true for the three-parameter logistic model. Instead, the slope of the three-parameter logistic ICC is $(1 - c_i)(D/4)a_i$ when evaluated at $\theta = b_i$ and, consequently, the slope depends upon both a_i and c_i. Note again that a larger c parameter acts to decrease the steepness of the ICC.

The one-parameter logistic model. The special case of the three-parameter logistic model that results from setting $c_i = 0$ and $a_i = 1$ for all items is called the one-parameter logistic or *Rasch* model. This model is perhaps most useful when a researcher has carefully pre-tested a set of items that were written in a format that minimizes guessing. Then it may be possible to select a subset of these items with approximately equal discriminating powers. Under these conditions the simplicity of the one-parameter model makes it very attractive to practitioners. The model was originally developed by the Danish mathematician Rasch (1960), and has the form

(2.4.11) $$P_i(\theta) = \frac{1}{1 + \exp[-D(\theta - b_i)]},$$

Figure 2.4.8 presents ICCs for three one-parameter logistic items. Note that all one-parameter logistic curves are identical up to a trans-

Figure 2.4.8
Three One-Parameter Logistic ICCs

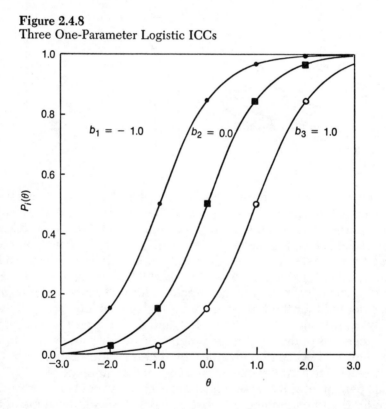

lation along the abscissa, which reflects the particular value of b_i for each ICC. Consequently, one-parameter logistic ICCs can never cross, as do the two-parameter logistic ICCs for items 1 and 4 in Figure 2.4.7 and the three-parameter logistic ICCs in Figure 2.4.6.

The one-parameter logistic model has many desirable features. It is the simplest of the logistic models, has many statistically elegant properties and is the least expensive to use in practice. Practitioners whose data are adequately modeled by the one-parameter logistic model are strongly encouraged to use it. The simple form of this model, however, can be its chief weakness when applied to empirical data. Empirical ICCs do not necessarily all have the same slope, nor do they necessarily have lower asymptotes of zero. The choice of an IRT should reflect the nature of one's data. We suspect that the one-parameter logistic model will be appropriate only for carefully pretested and selected sets of items.

2.5 ADDITIONAL IRT CONCEPTS AND ASSUMPTIONS

Interpretation of $P_i(\theta)$. It is convenient to note here that $P_i(\theta)$ does not necessarily refer to the probability of a positive response from a particular individual at the specified θ level. It is apparent that for a given individual, the probability of a positive response may be as low as zero—the examinee might surely select a particular incorrect option—or as high as one—the examinee might know the answer. Further, the probability of a positive response can be any value between zero and one for a given individual. Consider Lazarsfeld's (1959, p. 493) "brainwashing" experiment (also see Lord & Novick, 1968, pp. 29–30):

> Suppose we ask an individual, Mr. Brown, repeatedly whether he is in favor of the United Nations; suppose further that after each question we "wash his brains" and ask him the same question again. Because Mr. Brown is not certain as to how he feels about the United Nations, he will sometimes give a favorable and sometimes an unfavorable answer. Having gone through this procedure many times, we then compute the proportion of times Mr. Brown was in favor of the United Nations. This we could call the probability of Mr. Brown's being in favor of the United Nations.

$P_i(\theta)$ is usually interpreted as the probability of a positive response among individuals with ability θ. Note that here the height of the ICC is interpreted as the relative frequency of positive responses in the subpopulation of individuals with that particular value of θ. This is a weaker assumption than the assumption that $P_i(\theta)$ is the probability of a correct response for *a given individual* with ability θ. In many practical applications, the weaker assumption is appropriate, useful, and quite realistic. We note, however, in some theoretical work it is convenient to assume (or possible to deduce) that $P_i(\theta)$ is the probability of a positive response for a given individual with ability θ.

Unidimensional latent trait space. Throughout this book we treat the probability of an item response as a function of a single characteristic of the individual: θ. Since we *assume* that response probabilities are a function of a single latent characteristic of the individual, it is important to examine this assumption for real data sets. How can one test statistically the null hypothesis that an instrument is unidimensional? Unfortunately, no general significance test yet exists. In the following paragraphs, we discuss some general considerations concerning the dimensionality of a set of items. In Chapter 3 we examine the robustness of IRT to multidimensionality, and in Chapter 8 we discuss several methods for examining dimensionality.

It is important to realize that no actual psychological measurement instrument is likely to be exactly unidimensional. Instead, it is overwhelmingly likely that myriad minor dimensions will affect item responses. *Whether or not an instrument is sufficiently unidimensional to allow application of IRT is the central question.*

We agree with Lord and Novick (p. 383) that the practical usefulness of a psychological model provides one crucial criterion for evaluating a model and its assumptions. The JDI provides an interesting example of how conclusions about the effective dimensionality of a psychological instrument can differ. First, we note that many analyses clearly demonstrate that the JDI measures at least five separate dimensions (Drasgow & Miller, 1982). A number of studies have shown that these separate dimensions are important and scientifically meaningful, when JDI scales are used as *dependent variables* (Adams, Laker, & Hulin, 1977; Herman, Dunham, & Hulin, 1975). In this context, it is misleading and inappropriate to treat the JDI as a unidimensional instrument. However, a general affect dimension of the JDI seems to account for much of the variance in JDI scale scores, and the JDI may be treated as a unidimensional instrument for some purposes (Hulin et al., 1982; Parsons & Hulin, 1980).

How can investigators, without the extensive preliminary study that exists for the JDI, determine whether their instruments are reasonably unidimensional? Lord and Novick suggest that a one-dimensional model may be appropriate

> for tests that appear as though they ought to be homogeneous: for example, certain tests of vocabulary, reading, spelling, and some kinds of spatial ability. On the other hand, we should expect a mathematics test made up half of arithmetic reasoning items and half of plane geometry items to show at least $k = 2$ latent dimensions. (p. 381)

In other words, careful application of common sense and knowledge of the trait or traits being measured may provide valuable insights.

In general, the latent dimensionality of an instrument may not be evident from inspection of the items. Because the unidimensional assumption is essential in the theoretical developments of all IRTs currently available, we believe the dimensionality of any instrument must be examined prior to the routine application of an IRT. Factor analysis, a method commonly used to study the dimensionality of psychological measuring instruments, can be used under certain restrictive conditions. In Chapter 8 we discuss methods for factoring item correlation matrices and illustrate some of the problems that are likely to be encountered in practice.

Local independence. In this subsection, one consequence of a unidimensional latent trait space is considered. As shown in Section 2.6 this consequence, termed *local independence,* is essential for estimation of IRT parameters.

Returning to the example of Mr. Brown, let us assume that we have conducted the brainwashing experiment many times and found that the probability is .50 that Mr. Brown will respond positively to the question, "Are you in favor of the United Nations?" Also assume that we have found that Mr. Brown will respond positively to the question, "Should the United States contribute millions of dollars to the United Nations every year?" with probability .167. Finally, assume that a single latent dimension, attitude toward the United Nations, underlies the probabilities of responses to these questions. If Mr. Brown's standing on this latent attitude variable is denoted by θ_B, we can write

$$P_1(\theta_B) = \text{Prob}(u_1 = 1|\theta_B) = .50$$

and

$$P_2(\theta_B) = \text{Prob}(u_2 = 1|\theta_B) = .167$$

to indicate the probabilities of positive responses to the two questions.

Suppose that we identify 1,000 individuals with precisely the same attitude, θ_B, toward the United Nations as Mr. Brown and pose the same two questions. Imagine that the following data are obtained:

		Item 2		
		$u_2 = 1$	$u_2 = 0$	
Item 1	$u_1 = 1$	86	420	506
	$u_1 = 0$	83	411	494
		169	831	1,000

Except for sampling fluctuations, it is clear that $\text{Prob}(u_1 = 1|\theta_B)$ is .50 and $\text{Prob}(u_2 = 1|\theta_B)$ is .167. Now, let us consider the proportion of favorable responses to the second question among examinees who responded *positively* to the first question:

$$\text{Sample Prob}(u_2 = 1|\theta_B, u_1 = 1) = \frac{86}{506} = .170,$$

which is equal to $\text{Prob}(u_2 = 1|\theta_B)$, except for sampling error. Similarly:

$$\text{Sample Prob}(u_1 = 1|\theta_B, u_2 = 1) = \frac{86}{169} = .508,$$

which is equal to $\text{Prob}(u_1 = 1|\theta_B)$, except for sampling error.

The point of this example is to illustrate the idea that at a particular value of θ, say θ_B, item responses are independent. This property is called "local independence." More generally,

(2.5.1) $\quad \text{Prob}(u_n = 1|\theta, u_1 = 1, u_2 = 1, \ldots, u_{n-1} = 1)$
$$= \text{Prob}(u_n = 1|\theta).$$

This states that all the information that we can know about the probability of a positive (or negative) response is contained in θ. Moreover, if we know θ, then observing responses to $n - 1$ items provides *no additional information* about the response to the nth item.

What would it mean if

$$\text{Prob}(u_2 = 1|\theta, u_1 = 1) \neq \text{Prob}(u_2 = 1|\theta, u_1 = 0)?$$

Clearly, response propensities in the subpopulation of examinees with attitude θ who answered item 1 positively are different from the subpopulation of examinees with the same attitude but who answered item 1 negatively. Thus, responses in the two subpopulations must be affected by some *second latent dimension,* which implies the latent trait space *cannot* be unidimensional.

Returning to the hypothetical data presented above, note that

Sample $\text{Prob}(u_1 = 1 \text{ and } u_2 = 1|\theta_B)$
$$= 86/1000 = .0860$$
$$\doteq \text{Sample Prob}(u_1 = 1|\theta_B) \cdot \text{Sample Prob}(u_2 = 1|\theta_B)$$
$$= \frac{169}{1000} \cdot \frac{506}{1000} = .0855.$$

In general, local independence implies that

$$\text{Prob}(u_1 = 1, u_2 = 1, \ldots, u_n = 1|\theta)$$
(2.5.2)
$$= \prod_{i=1}^{n} \text{Prob}(u_i = 1|\theta).$$

Equations 2.5.1 and 2.5.2 are equivalent: Equation 2.5.1 can be used to define local independence and Equation 2.5.2 can then be derived;

or Equation 2.5.2 can be taken as the definition of local independence, with Equation 2.5.1 resulting.

In a similar fashion, local independence of item responses when conditioning on a single θ, as in Equation 2.5.2, implies that the item pool is unidimensional (i.e., there is not a second ability, unrelated to θ, that affects responses to items), and unidimensionality of an item pool implies local independence as stated in Equation 2.5.2. Readers are referred to Lord and Novick (1968, pp. 360–361) for a more mathematically rigorous discussion of local independence.

For the purposes of applied researchers, it may be more convenient first to examine the dimensionality of an item pool. If a unidimensional latent trait space is found to provide a reasonable approximation of the latent structure of the item pool, then local independence can be taken as a consequence and the estimation procedures of Section 2.6 can be used.

It is important to note that local independence does not mean that the responses to any two items are uncorrelated *in general*. Local independence implies responses to any two items are uncorrelated *in a homogeneous subpopulation* with a particular level of attitude or ability θ. In a heterogeneous population *where θ varies*, item scores should be correlated.

Item parameter invariance. The sense in which IRT item parameters are invariant across subpopulations is discussed in this subsection. To understand the invariance property, it is useful to interpret ICCs as nonlinear regression lines. In particular, the item response u_i is taken as the "dependent" variable, and θ is taken as the independent variable. Then the regression of u_i onto θ consists of the points $[\theta, E(u_i|\theta)]$ where $E(u_i|\theta)$ is the expected value (i.e., average) of u_i among individuals with ability or attitude θ. At a given value of θ, this expectation is simply

$$(2.5.3) \qquad E(u_i|\theta) = 1 \cdot \text{Prob}(u_i = 1|\theta) + 0 \cdot \text{Prob}(u_i = 0|\theta) = P_i(\theta).$$

Thus, an ICC can be interpreted as the regression of u_i on θ.

Figure 2.5.1 illustrates a hypothetical situation where:

1. θ is normally distributed in the overall population with a mean of 0 and a standard deviation of 1.
2. A job applicant was hired if his or her ability estimate, $\hat{\theta}$, was greater than .60.
3. $d = \theta - \hat{\theta}$ is the error of estimate, which is normally distributed with mean zero. In order to examine the effects of selection on $\hat{\theta}$ (instead of θ), we shall arbitrarily assume that d has a standard deviation of .10 in the neighborhood of $\theta = .60$.

The distributions of θ that result from these assumptions are shown at the bottom of Figure 2.5.1.

Note that the two subpopulations in Figure 2.5.1 share a common ICC. In fact, subpopulations can be formed in any manner whatsoever

Figure 2.5.1
ICC and Two Subpopulations

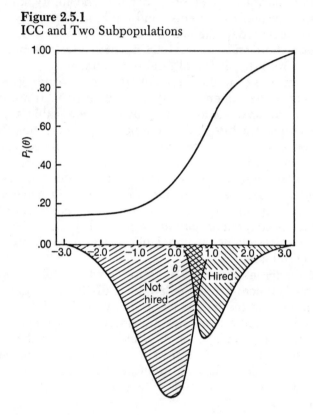

without affecting the subsequent regression of u_i on θ, provided that the probability of a positive response is a function of the single ability or attitude θ and that individuals' responses to item i are not used when forming subpopulations. Thus, if the ICC has the form of a three-parameter logistic ogive with parameters a_i, b_i, and c_i for some population, it will have the same form and parameters in any subpopulation. This is the sense in which IRT item parameters are invariant across subpopulations.

It is important to note that IRT item parameter *estimates* will not be identical when calculated in different samples. Obviously, sampling fluctuations will occur. In addition, the θ-metric can vary from sample to sample. For example, the distributions of θ for the two subpopulations in Figure 2.5.1 could *both* be separately standardized to have mean zero and unit variance. Then the item difficulties in the "hired" subpopulation would be linearly related to item difficulties in the "not hired" subpopulation. Methods for *equating θ-metrics* and transforming separately estimated b_is to the same scale are discussed in Chapter 5.

Another advantage of this invariance property of IRT becomes apparent when the IRT item difficulty parameter b_i is compared with the traditional item difficulty index p_i. The parameter p_i is defined as

(2.5.4) $$p_i = E(u_i),$$

that is, p_i is the proportion of correct responses to item i. It is important to note that p_i is subpopulation dependent. For example, p_i will be larger in "smarter" subpopulations and smaller in less able subpopulations. In contrast, b_i does *not* vary across subpopulations if $θ$-metrics have been equated.

Lord (1977, 1980) presents an interesting example where p_is for two items have different rank orders in different subpopulations. Figure 2.5.2 portrays a second ICC for the two subpopulations described

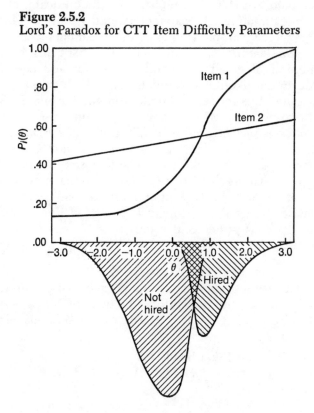

Figure 2.5.2
Lord's Paradox for CTT Item Difficulty Parameters

above. Note that item 2 is an easier item among hypothetical job applicants not hired ($p_2 > p_1$), but is more difficult for job applicants who were hired ($p_2 < p_1$). For this reason, Lord does not believe that p_i provides a measure of item difficulty, but is instead a measure of item difficulty *vis-a-vis some subpopulation*. In contrast, b_i describes item difficulty *irrespective of subpopulation*. Note that items with one-parameter logistic ICs do not suffer from "Lord's Paradox" because the paradox depends on items having ICCs that cross.

2.6 ESTIMATION

After an IRT model has been selected for a particular data set, it is necessary to estimate person and item parameters. In all the models considered here, a single ability parameter θ is estimated for each individual. In contrast, the parameters that must be estimated for each item depend upon the IRT model selected: b_i for the one-parameter logistic, a_i and b_i for the two-parameter normal ogive and logistic models, and a_i, b_i, and c_i for the three-parameter logistic model. In this section we describe some general principles of estimation, one class of estimators of IRT parameters, some theoretical problems encountered in estimating IRT parameters, and widely available computer programs that can be used to estimate parameters.

General considerations. Mathematical statisticians have developed a number of general methods for estimating parameters of models. Maximum likelihood estimation (MLE) is perhaps the most widely used and theoretically important method available. The central idea that underlies MLE is remarkably simple: *Parameter estimates are chosen by selecting the values that make an observed data set appear most likely in light of a particular model.*

To illustrate the method of MLE, consider a simple example that is related to IRT. Imagine that we are given a coin that may be biased in the sense that the probability, P, of obtaining a head is not necessarily .5. The data to be used to estimate P consist of the dichotomously scored coin tosses (1 = heads, 0 = tails):

1, 1, 1, 1, 0, 1, 1, 1, 1, 1, 0, 0, 1, 0, 1, 0, 0, 1, 0, 1, 1, 1, 1, 1, 0.

Thus, on 25 tosses, 17 heads are observed.

One model for these data states that (1) successive coin tosses are independent; and (2) the probability of a head on a toss is P and the probability of a tail is $Q = 1 - P$. Then the *likelihood* of the data presented above is

(2.6.1)
$$L = \text{Likelihood}(\text{Data}|P)$$
$$= P\,P\,P\,P\,Q \cdots P\,Q = P^{17}Q^8.$$

The maximum likelihood estimate, $\hat{P}$, of P is the value of P in Equation 2.6.1 that maximizes L.

Figure 2.6.1 illustrates the likelihood function. This is simply a plot of L for various values of P. The values of L were computed from

Figure 2.6.1
Likelihood Function for Equation 2.6.1

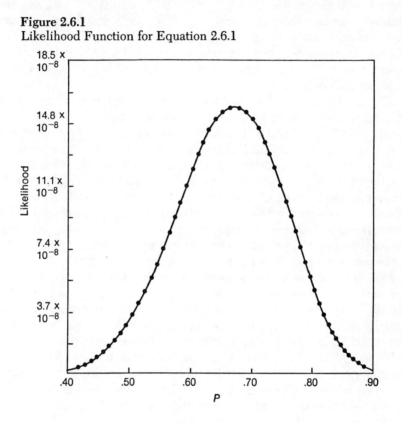

Equation 2.6.1 using $P = .40$, $P = .41$, . . . , $P = .90$. The maximum of the function is at $P = .68$; consequently, .68 is the maximum likelihood estimate of P.

For more complicated data sets and more complicated models, maximizing the likelihood function is much more difficult. However, the essential notion of picking parameter estimates such that they maximize the likelihood function, and hence, maximize the likelihood of the data, remains unchanged. A detailed description of maximum likelihood methods and properties of maximum likelihood estimators can be found in Kendall and Stuart (1979). In the remainder of this subsection we shall provide elementary descriptions of three important properties of maximum likelihood estimators that hold under certain regularity conditions.[5]

The first property of maximum likelihood estimators is *consistency*. An estimator m of a parameter μ is consistent if there is a sample size N for which the probability that $|m - \mu| > \varepsilon$ (ε is a small, positive number) can be made arbitrarily small. Loosely speaking, this says that if sample size is large enough then m will almost surely be very close to μ. Note that consistency is a statistical formulation of the commonsense idea that larger sample sizes should yield "better" estimates of parameters.

Maximum likelihood estimators are also asymptotically normal and efficient under certain regularity conditions. *Asymptotic normality* means that the sampling distributions of maximum likelihood estimates become normally distributed as sample size increases. *Asymptotic efficiency* means that in large samples the sampling variance of maximum likelihood estimates reaches a theoretical lower bound: No other consistent estimator can have a smaller sampling variance. Thus, the consistency and asymptotic efficiency properties of maximum likelihood estimators imply that this type of estimator converges (in probability) to the parameter as sample size increases, and no other estimator converges faster (i.e., has smaller sampling variance).

Estimating θ when item parameters are known. Let us begin our discussion of estimating parameters of IRT models by assuming that the item parameters are known. This unrealistic assumption, which greatly simplifies the problems encountered in estimation, will be examined further in the last paragraph of this subsection.

To use MLE to estimate θ, it is necessary to write the likelihood function. Let $Q_i(\theta) = 1 - P_i(\theta)$ equal the probability of an incorrect response to item i given ability θ, $u_i = 1$ indicate a correct response to item i, and $u_i = 0$ indicate an incorrect response. Note that

$$[P_i(\theta)]^{u_i}[Q_i(\theta)]^{1-u_i} = \begin{cases} P_i(\theta) & \text{if } u_i = 1 \\ Q_i(\theta) & \text{if } u_i = 0. \end{cases}$$

Using this convenient relation, the likelihood function can be written as

(2.6.2) $$L = \prod_{i=1}^{n}[P_i(\theta)]^{u_i}\,[Q_i(\theta)]^{1-u_i}$$

for an individual with responses u_i. Since the ICCs are known (by the assumption that item parameters are known), the maximum likelihood estimate, $\hat{\theta}$, of ability is the value of θ that maximizes Equation 2.6.2.

---

[5] The regularity conditions involve assumptions concerning continuity of functions and existence of derivatives.

To illustrate methods for maximizing Equation 2.6.2, suppose that an examinee is administered a three-item test and suppose further that the items have the three-parameter logistic ICCs shown in Figure 2.6.2. The item parameters for these ICCs are:

Item	a_i	b_i	c_i
1	0.75	−2.00	0.10
2	1.25	0.00	0.18
3	1.00	1.75	0.16

Figure 2.6.2
Three-Parameter Logistic ICCs for Three Hypothetical Items

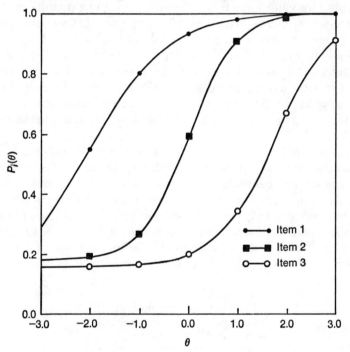

Finally, suppose that the examinee responds correctly to items 1 and 2 and responds incorrectly to item 3. Thus, $u_1 = 1$, $u_2 = 1$, and $u_3 = 0$.
The likelihood function from Equation 2.6.2 for this examinee is

$$(2.6.3) \quad \begin{aligned} L &= [P_1(\theta)^1 Q_1(\theta)^0][P_2(\theta)^1 Q_2(\theta)^0][P_3(\theta)^0 Q_3(\theta)^1] \\ &= P_1(\theta)P_2(\theta)Q_3(\theta), \end{aligned}$$

because any number raised to the zero-th power is 1, i.e., $k^0 = 1$, and raising any number to the first power leaves the number unchanged, i.e., $k^1 = k$. The maximum likelihood estimate $\hat{\theta}$ of θ is the value along the θ continuum that maximizes Equation 2.6.3.

Unfortunately, it is not simple to find $\hat{\theta}$. This is because the expression for $P_i(\theta)$ given in Equation 2.4.4 is complicated. One straightforward, albeit tedious, procedure for determining $\hat{\theta}$ is to substitute many different values of θ into Equation 2.6.3 and then plot L as a function of θ. This is analogous to Figure 2.6.1, where L is plotted as a function of P. For Figure 2.6.2, we could compute L at, say, θ values of -3.0, $-2.9, \ldots, 3.0$. If we inspected the resulting 61 values of L, and took $\hat{\theta}$ to be the θ value associated with the largest value of L, our $\hat{\theta}$ would be within 0.1 of the θ value that maximizes L. We can only say that our $\hat{\theta}$ is within 0.1 of the θ value that truly maximizes L because L was computed for values of θ that differed by 0.1. For example, the θ value that truly maximizes Equation 2.6.3 might be 1.0527, but our "grid search" method would compute L only at θ values of 1.0 and 1.1, and yield an error of .0527 or .0473, depending upon whether the former or latter θ value was selected as $\hat{\theta}$. If errors of up to 0.1 are considered to be too large, a second grid search with smaller differences between θ values could be performed. This grid search would only compute L for θ values up to 0.1 away from the θ that maximized L in the first grid search.

A procedure that reduces the number of times that L must be computed might proceed as follows. First, an interval for θ is selected that depends on the examinee's number of correct responses. For the items in Figure 2.6.2 and the examinee described previously with $u_1 = u_2 = 1$ and $u_3 = 0$, it seems reasonable that $\hat{\theta}$ should lie between -1 and $+2$. Table 2.6.1 contains values of $P_1(\theta)$, $P_2(\theta)$, $Q_3(\theta)$, and L for several values of θ in this interval. The probability of correct and incorrect responses can be computed using the ICC parameters and

Table 2.6.1
ICC Values and Likelihood
Function Values at Several Points
along the θ Continuum

θ	$P_1(\theta)$	$P_2(\theta)$	$Q_3(\theta)$	L
-1.00	.80	.27	.83	.179
0.00	.94	.59	.80	.444
1.00	.98	.91	.66	.589
2.00	1.00	.99	.33	.327
0.50	.96	.79	.75	.569
1.50	.99	.97	.51	.490
0.75	.97	.86	.71	.592
1.25	.99	.95	.59	.555

Equation 2.4.4, or read from Figure 2.6.1. The values of L for the first four θ values (-1.0, 0.0, 1.0, and 2.0) in Table 2.6.1 show that $0.0 < \hat{\theta} < 2.0$. This interval can be reduced by computing L at $\theta = 0.5$ and $\theta = 1.5$. The values of L that result from these calculations indicate that $0.5 < \hat{\theta} < 1.5$. Now L can be determined at $\theta = .75$ and 1.25. Results here indicate that $0.5 < \hat{\theta} < 1.0$. This process can be continued until the interval for $\hat{\theta}$ is as narrow as desired.

Although the procedure just described requires fewer calculations than the grid search method, it is clear that many calculations would be required to reduce the interval for $\hat{\theta}$ to less than, say, .0001. Consequently, more efficient methods are required.

Directly maximizing Equation 2.6.2 is quite difficult because it is written as a *product* of many terms. It can be shown, however, that the natural logarithm of L, $l = \ln L$, obtains its maximum at the same value of θ as does L (because l is a strictly increasing monotonic function of L). Thus, rather than maximize Equation 2.6.2, we can take its logarithm and maximize

$$(2.6.4) \qquad l = \sum_{i=1}^{n} [u_i \ln P_i(\theta) + (1 - u_i) \ln Q_i(\theta)],$$

which now requires maximization of a *sum* of terms. It is much easier to maximize Equation 2.6.4 than Equation 2.6.2 because it is easier to differentiate sums than it is to differentiate products. To maximize Equation 2.6.4, note that the *slope* of l is zero at the maximizing value of θ.[6] Thus to maximize Equation 2.6.4, we take the *derivative* of l with respect to θ (because the derivative of a function equals the slope of the function), set the derivative equal to zero (because the derivative is zero at the function's maximum), and solve for $\hat{\theta}$. The *likelihood equation* is the derivative of l set equal to zero:

$$(2.6.5) \qquad \frac{\partial l}{\partial \theta} = \sum_{i=1}^{n} \left[u_i \frac{P_i(\theta)'}{P_i(\theta)} - (1 - u_i) \frac{P_i(\theta)'}{Q_i(\theta)} \right] = 0,$$

where $P_i(\theta)'$ is the derivative of $P_i(\theta)$ with respect to θ. Simplifying Equation 2.6.5 yields

$$(2.6.6) \qquad \sum_{i=1}^{n} \left\{ [u_i - P_i(\hat{\theta})] \frac{P_i(\hat{\theta})'}{P_i(\hat{\theta}) \, Q_i(\hat{\theta})} \right\} = 0$$

as the equation that must be solved to obtain $\hat{\theta}$. The value of $\hat{\theta}$ that satisfies Equation 2.6.6 is not easily obtained by hand. A numerical algorithm programmed on a computer can obtain $\hat{\theta}$ quite quickly for most IRT models.

---

[6] Figure 2.6.1 shows that the slope of a function is zero at the function's maximum value.

Estimates of θ obtained in this fashion have the optimal properties described previously (consistency, asymptotic efficiency, and asymptotic normality). Note that the items on the test, not the individuals, compose the "sample" for estimating θ when item parameters are known. Thus as the number of items increases for each examinee, $\hat{\theta}$ converges to θ with the smallest possible standard error of estimate of any estimator of θ.

In practice we, of course, never know the item parameters. At best, previous research may provide item parameter *estimates*. Consequently, the theorems that prove $\hat{\theta}$ is consistent and asymptotically efficient are not exactly appropriate for practical applications. However, research presented in Chapter 3 illustrates that estimated ICCs are close to the true ICCs under wide circumstances. Consequently, it appears that maximum likelihood estimates of $\hat{\theta}$ based on previously estimated ICCs should have approximately the optimal properties noted above, although a rigorous proof of this statement is not yet available.

Estimating ability and item parameters. Normally researchers and practitioners will have data obtained from N individuals responding to n items where neither ability nor item parameters are known. Typically, we wish to estimate both ability, θ, and item parameters a_i, b_i, and c_i simultaneously from this one data set.

Lord (1968, 1980) and Birnbaum (1968) describe an iterative procedure for estimating both ability and item parameters. The procedure operates in the following general fashion. First, ad hoc methods are used to obtain initial, "starting" values for ability and item parameter estimates. Then, the likelihood equations for item parameters are solved, holding constant the initial ad hoc estimates of the ability parameter. Then these item parameter estimates are used to estimate ability parameters. With the newly obtained $\hat{\theta}$s, item parameters are reestimated; and with the reestimated item parameters, ability parameters are reestimated; and so on. This iterative procedure is continued until both item and ability parameters converge.[7] Further technical details of this procedure can be found in Lord (1980).

We shall denote the maximum likelihood estimates of a_i, b_i, and c_i by $\hat{a}_i$, $\hat{b}_i$, and $\hat{c}_i$, respectively.

Unfortunately, the properties of maximum likelihood estimates obtained in this fashion are unknown. The optimal properties of maximum likelihood estimators are derived under the assumption that parameters are estimated in only one direction of a two-way (examinees by items) data table. In IRT, this assumption corresponds to estimat-

---

[7] Convergence simply means that the estimates of θ or item parameters changed by an arbitrarily small value from the ith to the (i + 1)th iteration.

ing ability parameters or item parameters, *but not both sets of parameters simultaneously*. Wright (1977), for example, believes that irresolvable problems arise for some IRT models when both item and ability parameters must be estimated simultaneously. However, simultaneous estimation of subject *and* item parameters using an iterative procedure such as the one described above appears to be sufficiently accurate for many applications of IRT (see Section 3.3). By increasing sample size and test length, errors of estimation apparently can be made small enough for IRT to be useful in solving many practical testing problems. We encourage readers to study carefully the Monte Carlo results presented in Chapter 3 to determine whether ability and/or item parameter estimates are likely to be adequate for their purposes.

Computer programs. In this subsection we briefly describe computer programs that are available to estimate item and ability parameters for the logistic and normal ogive models.

BICAL (Wright & Mead, 1977) is a highly portable FORTRAN program for the one-parameter logistic model. This program is quite inexpensive to run. We strongly encourage researchers and practitioners with data sets that are adequately described by the one-parameter logistic model to use this model and a suitable one-parameter logistic estimation program.

LOGIST (Wood & Lord, 1976; Wood, Wingersky, & Lord, 1976) is a FORTRAN program that can be used to estimate parameters of the one-, two-, and three-parameter logistic models.[8] This program contains several assembly language subroutines and is therefore not easily adapted to non-IBM computers, although a CDC Cyber version is now available. More information about LOGIST can be obtained from Marilyn S. Wingersky, Educational Testing Service, Princeton, N.J. 08541. LOGIST is roughly 5 to 10 times as expensive to run as BICAL.

NORMOG (Kolakowski & Bock, 1970) is a FORTRAN program designed to estimate parameters of the normal ogive model. The program is written for an IBM 360 or IBM 370 computer. The program can be obtained from the International Educational Services, 1525 East 53rd Street, Chicago, Ill. 60615.

2.7 ITEM AND TEST INFORMATION

Introduction. Information can be defined in terms of the uncertainty of some event. The less the uncertainty that, for example, an

---

[8] LOGIST was designed for the three-parameter logistic model, but can be used for the two-parameter logistic model by restricting all c_i values to equal zero. Similarly, settings all c_i to zeros and all a_i to ones causes LOGIST to estimate parameters of the one-parameter logistic model.

event will occur or an observation will fall within a specified interval along some continuum, the more information one has. As an introduction to the use of this general concept in IRT, consider the process of statistical inference. Typically, we gather data from a sample and compute the sample value of a particular statistic, say, the sample mean $\bar{X}$. The value of the sample statistic is then used to make inferences about the value of the population parameter, μ. Prior to gathering any data or computing any statistics, we have no information about the population parameter. Our uncertainty about its value is theoretically infinite—it could be any where between $-\infty$ and $+\infty$. After gathering N observations and computing $\bar{X}$, our uncertainty about the value of μ is reduced. We have some information, and because of that information our uncertainty has been reduced. But how much have we reduced our uncertainty and how much information do we have?

Our uncertainty about population or theoretical parameters could be expressed in terms of the sampling variance of sample estimates around the parameter or the length of the confidence interval for the parameter. If we are estimating a population mean, the squared standard error of the mean is $\sigma_{\bar{x}}^2 = \sigma_x^2/N$. The smaller this squared standard error, the greater our information. Thus, it is natural to define information about a parameter as the reciprocal of the squared standard error:

$$I_{\bar{x}} = 1/\sigma_{\bar{x}}^2.$$

Information is important in IRT because tests and scales developed using IRT procedures can be evaluated in terms of the accuracy of estimates of θ that they provide. The squared standard error of θ, or information, which is the reciprocal of the squared standard error, is normally used as the measure of estimation accuracy. Information is not necessarily constant throughout the range of θ. The information at a particular value of θ depends on the number and attributes of the items used to estimate θ. For example, little information about ability is provided at high levels of θ by very easy items that nearly all high-ability examinees answer correctly. These same items may provide a substantial amount of information about ability at low levels of θ.

Item and test information functions. We have no information about the ability of an individual prior to obtaining item responses and converting these responses into estimate of θ. After estimating θ from the item responses, we can assess how much information we now have about the location of θ: What is our uncertainty about θ? Just as information about the population mean was given by $1/\sigma_{\bar{x}}^2$, the information about θ is given by $I(\theta) = 1/\sigma_{\hat{\theta}|\theta}^2$, or the reciprocal of the squared standard error of $\hat{\theta}$ given θ. The standard error of $\hat{\theta}$ given θ is interpreted as the standard deviation of the distribution of $\hat{\theta}$s for all

individuals with a common θ. Using the relation between informa-
tion and squared standard error, it is easy to show that $\sigma_{\hat\theta|\theta}$ is equal to
$1/\sqrt{I(\theta)}$.

Birnbaum (1968) and Lord (1980) approach the problem of obtaining a formula for test information by defining the test information
function $I(\theta)$ as the reciprocal of the *asymptotic sampling variance of
maximum likelihood ability estimates $\hat\theta$ for individuals with a common ability* θ. This means that as the number of items becomes large,
$1/\sqrt{I(\theta)}$ is the standard error of $\hat\theta$ when the method of maximum
likelihood is used to estimate θ. Lord (1980, Chapter 5) proves that

(2.7.1)
$$I(\theta) = \sum_{i=1}^{n} \frac{[P_i(\theta)']^2}{P_i(\theta)Q_i(\theta)},$$

where $P_i(\theta)'$ is the derivative (i.e., slope) of the ICC for item i at θ.
(The derivatives for the one-, two-, and three-parameter models are
listed in the last subsection of Section 2.7 for the reader's convenience.)

A very important feature of Equation 2.7.1 is that item information
functions $I(\theta, u_i)$ add up to the test information function. Define the
information function for item i as

(2.7.2)
$$I(\theta, u_i) = \frac{[P_i(\theta)']^2}{P_i(\theta)Q_i(\theta)}.$$

Then

(2.7.3)
$$I(\theta) = \sum_{i=1}^{n} I(\theta, u_i).$$

From Equation 2.7.3, which shows that $I(\theta)$ is the sum of $I(\theta, u_i)$, it is
apparent that the extent to which a given item provides information
about θ is independent of all other items on the test when the method
of maximum likelihood is used to estimate ability. This is a convenient property because it means that an item's contribution to accuracy
in ability estimation can be easily examined. A plot of $I(\theta, u_i)$, computed by Equation 2.7.2, against θ shows exactly how much the test
information curve would increase at each point along the θ continuum
if the item would be added to the test.

Example. The item information functions for the first nine JDI
work scale items are plotted in Figure 2.7.1. The item parameter estimates used to generate Figure 2.7.1 are shown in Table 2.7.1. Note
that each item information function reaches its maximum value when
θ equals the item's difficulty, b_i. At its maximum, the value of the
information curve is $\frac{1}{4}D^2 a_i^2 = .721 a_i^2$. These relations are always true
for the two-parameter logistic model. In contrast, for three-parameter

Figure 2.7.1
Item Information Functions for Items from the JDI Satisfaction with the
Work Itself Scale

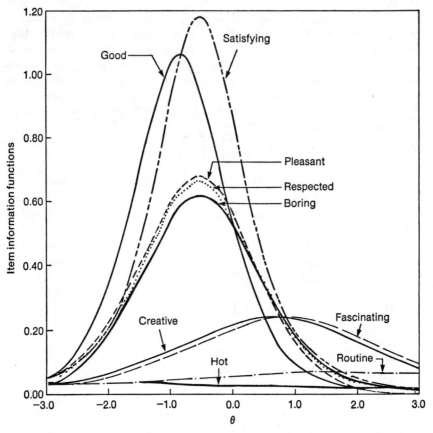

Table 2.7.1
Item Parameter Estimates
for Nine JDI Work Scale
Items

Item	a_i	b_i
Fascinating	0.57	0.88
Routine	0.31	2.19
Satisfying	1.28	−0.54
Boring	0.92	−0.51
Good	1.21	−0.86
Creative	0.57	0.66
Respected	0.96	−0.57
Hot	0.18	−0.15
Pleasant	0.96	−0.53

logistic items, the item information curve reaches its maximum at a θ value slightly larger than b_i. See Birnbaum (pp. 460–464) for proofs.

Further details about the relation between item parameters and $I(\theta, u_i)$ as well as the specific item information functions can be learned from examining Figure 2.7.1. It is not surprising that the item "satisfying" has the largest value of $I(\theta, u_i)$. There is an obvious relation between the content of this item and the meaning of the latent trait. In contrast, responses to "hot" and "routine" provide little information about job satisfaction at any θ value. "Fascinating" and "creative" have a parameters of modest size and provide a moderate amount of information about job satisfaction for θ values roughly between -1.0 and 2.5.

Figure 2.7.2 presents the *test* information function for the nine JDI items. Note that the function reaches its maximum near $\theta = -0.6$ and falls off sharply in both directions. This type of instrument would be primarily useful for separating workers into two categories: moderate to high work satisfaction and low work satisfaction. Note that such an instrument provides very little information about the work satisfaction of workers with θ greater than 1.0. For the purposes of research in

Figure 2.7.2
Test Information Functions for Various Methods of Scoring the Nine Items from Table 2.7.1

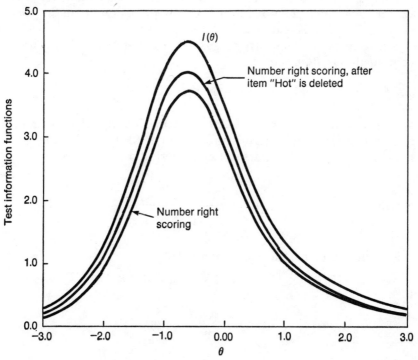

 58

which correlations between variables are studied, this level of information is probably adequate because correlations are relatively insensitive to small to moderate amounts of measurement error. However, if satisfaction scores are used to make decisions about individuals along the entire continuum of θ, then more accurate measurement is needed at high and low levels of θ.

Other methods of scoring a test. In the preceding subsection, we considered only maximum likelihood estimates of ability. Note that $\hat{\theta}$ can be thought of as a "test score" since $\hat{\theta}$ is a function of item responses. There are many other ways to score a test; perhaps the most common is the number right score, Σu_i.

Since maximum likelihood estimates are asymptotically efficient, no test scoring procedure can (asymptotically) provide more information about θ than the maximum likelihood estimate $\hat{\theta}$. Thus when n is large, the 95 percent confidence interval for θ,

$$(2.7.4) \qquad (\hat{\theta} - 1.96/\sqrt{I(\theta)}, \ \hat{\theta} + 1.96/\sqrt{I(\theta)}),$$

based on the maximum likelihood estimate $\hat{\theta}$, is the smallest possible 95 percent confidence interval. Lord (1980, Chapter 5) describes a method of constructing confidence intervals for $\hat{\theta}$ that can be used for any scoring procedure. If a nonoptimal procedure is used to score a test, perhaps for the sake of convenience, how much information about θ is lost? In particular, how much larger is the confidence interval for θ, based on the nonoptimal scoring procedure, than the confidence interval in Equation 2.7.4?

These questions are easy to answer if a test score X is a linear combination of item scores

$$(2.7.5) \qquad X = \sum_{i=1}^{n} w_i u_i,$$

where w_i is the weight given to the ith item. Note that if $w_i = 1$ for all i, then X is the number right score. Lord (1980) shows that the information function for the class of linear scoring procedures is

$$(2.7.6) \qquad I_x(\theta) = \frac{\left[\sum_{i=1}^{n} w_i P_i(\theta)'\right]^2}{\sum_{i=1}^{n} w_i^2 P_i(\theta) Q_i(\theta)}.$$

If X is the number right score, then

$$(2.7.7) \qquad I_x(\theta) = \frac{\left[\sum_{i=1}^{n} P_i(\theta)'\right]^2}{\sum_{i=1}^{n} P_i(\theta) Q_i(\theta)}.$$

There are several important points concerning Equation 2.7.6 and Equation 2.7.7. First, $1/\sqrt{I_x(\theta)}$ is the asymptotic standard error of estimate of θ if test score X is used to estimate θ by Lord's method. In principle, this standard error could be used to construct a confidence interval for θ as in Equation 2.7.4. Perhaps more importantly, $I_x(\theta)$ can be compared to $I(\theta)$ to assess the benefits of using the computationally complex but asymptotically efficient maximum likelihood method instead of a more convenient scoring method.

It is also important to note that the contribution of an individual item to $I_x(\theta)$ *cannot* be determined without considering the remaining $(n - 1)$ items. This is because the numerator of Equation 2.7.7 contains the square of a sum of terms; the cross-products of each $P_i(\theta)'$ with the other $(n - 1)$ terms in the sum affect $I_x(\theta)$. Thus it is *not* possible to write an equation analogous to Equation 2.7.3, which shows that the contribution of each item to $I(\theta)$ is unaffected by the other $n - 1$ items. The complexities of Equations 2.7.6 and 2.7.7 are made salient by "Birnbaum's Paradox." Birnbaum (1968, p. 474) showed that adding items to a test can actually *reduce* information about ability when a nonoptimal scoring procedure is used: $I_x(\theta)$ can be made smaller and the standard error of $\hat{\theta}$ larger by lengthening the test.

Figure 2.7.2 presents the information function $I_x(\theta)$ for number right scoring of the nine JDI work scale items in Table 2.7.1. Note that $I_x(\theta)$ is roughly 75 to 80 percent as large as $I(\theta)$ for most values of θ. Figure 2.7.2 also illustrates Birnbaum's Paradox: Deleting the item "hot" increases $I_x(\theta)$. Note that this increase in measurement accuracy can be effected without using the computationally complex maximum likelihood estimates. Items like "hot" and "on your feet" would likely not have been retained in the final version of the JDI if the scale developers (Smith et al., 1969) had employed test information curves in their developmental studies.

Optimal methods of scoring a test.* If the weights

$$(2.7.8) \qquad w_i(\theta) = \frac{P_i(\theta)'}{P_i(\theta)Q_i(\theta)}$$

are used in Equation 2.7.6, then

$$(2.7.9) \qquad I_x(\theta) = \frac{\left[\displaystyle\sum_{i=1}^{n} \frac{[P_i(\theta)']^2}{P_i(\theta)Q_i(\theta)}\right]^2}{\displaystyle\sum_{i=1}^{n} \frac{[P_i(\theta)']^2}{P_i(\theta)Q_i(\theta)}}$$

$$= \sum_{i=1}^{n} \frac{[P_i(\theta)']^2}{P_i(\theta)Q_i(\theta)} = I(\theta).$$

Thus the information about θ provided by these scoring weights equals the maximum possible information. For this reason, the weights in Equation 2.7.8 are called "optimal scoring weights" by Lord (1980) and "locally best weights" by Birnbaum (1968).

Equation 2.7.8 reduces to

$$(2.7.10) \qquad w_i(\theta) = \frac{Da_i}{1 + c_i \exp[-Da_i(\theta - b_i)]}$$

for the three-parameter logistic model (Lord, 1980) and to

$$(2.7.11) \qquad w_i = Da_i$$

for the two-parameter logistic model (Birnbaum, 1968). Interestingly, $w_i = 1.0$ for all items is the optimal weight for the one-parameter logistic model. Thus the convenient number right scoring method provides optimal information about ability if the one-parameter logistic model is correct. This is another statistically desirable property of the one-parameter logistic model.

The optimal scoring weights for the three logistic models are quite natural; they correspond to the assumptions of each model in compelling ways. For example, the one-parameter model assumes that all items are equally discriminating; consequently differential weighting of these items seems inappropriate. The optimal scoring procedure for the one-parameter model is congruent with this intuition. In contrast, two-parameter logistic items are assumed to vary in their discriminating powers. The optimal scoring procedure weights each item score by the item's discriminating power. In effect, this discounts responses to items with low discriminating power and emphasizes responses to items with high discriminating power. Finally, optimal weights for the three-parameter logistic items shown in Figure 2.6.2 are plotted in Figure 2.7.3. Note that $w_i(\theta)$ approaches zero as an individual's chance of responding correctly approaches the lower asymptote of the ICC. Furthermore, $w_i(\theta)$ approaches Da_i as an individual's probability of a correct response approaches one. Thus, these weights discount responses that are likely to be guesses, and emphasize responses to discriminating items when guessing is unlikely.

It bears reiterating that $w_i(\theta)$ is not always a constant applied to the ith item for all respondents; $w_i(\theta)$ varies as a function of θ in the three-parameter logistic model. The same response to a given item will receive different credit for individuals with different θs. These differences in weighted scores are intended to reflect the likelihood of correctly guessing an answer on an ability measure. In the two-parameter model where there is no guessing, such corrections are not necessary.

Figure 2.7.3
Optimal Scoring Weights Plotted as a Function of θ for Three
Three-Parameter Logistic Items

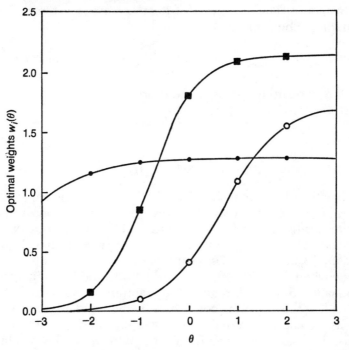

Accuracy of item parameter estimates.* The test information function $I(\theta)$ presented in Equation 2.7.1 can be used to determine standard errors of maximum likelihood ability estimates $\hat{\theta}$. The accuracy of maximum likelihood estimates of *item* parameters can be determined by defining analogous information functions. These information functions can be used to compute standard errors of item parameter estimates and, consequently, are helpful in interpreting these estimates. Moreover, item information functions are needed to compute some of the *item bias* indices discussed in Chapter 5.

Lord (1980, p. 191) presents formulae for information functions of maximum likelihood estimates of three-parameter logistic item parameters that are analogous to $I(\theta)$. For the b parameter of item i,

$$(2.7.12) \qquad I_{b_i} = \frac{D^2 a_i^2}{(1 - c_i)^2} \sum_{j=1}^{N} \left[(P_i(\theta_j) - c_i)^2 \frac{Q_i(\theta_j)}{P_i(\theta_j)} \right],$$

and for the a parameter,

$$(2.7.13) \qquad I_{a_i} = \frac{D^2}{(1 - c_i)^2} \sum_{j=1}^{N} \left[(\theta_j - b_i)^2 (P_i(\theta_j) - c_i)^2 \frac{Q_i(\theta_j)}{P_i(\theta_j)} \right].$$

Here θ_j is the ability of the jth individual in a sample of size N. Notice that the summation in Equations 2.7.12 and 2.7.13 is over individuals, not items as in Equation 2.7.1.

To compute standard errors of item parameter estimates, a third quantity must be computed:

$$(2.7.14) \qquad I_{a_i b_i} = -\frac{D^2 a_i}{(1-c_i)^2} \sum_{j=1}^{N} \left[(\theta_j - b_i)(P_i(\theta_j) - c_i)^2 \frac{Q_i(\theta_j)}{P_i(\theta_j)} \right].$$

Then the standard errors of $\hat{b}_i$ and $\hat{a}_i$ are

$$(2.7.15) \qquad \text{SE of } \hat{b}_i = \sqrt{I_{a_i}/(I_{a_i} I_{b_i} - I_{a_i b_i}^2)}$$

and

$$(2.7.16) \qquad \text{SE of } \hat{a}_i = \sqrt{I_{b_i}/(I_{a_i} I_{b_i} - I_{a_i b_i}^2)}.$$

In practice, Equations 2.7.15 and 2.7.16 cannot be computed because a_i, b_i, c_i, and the θ_j are unknown parameters. Approximate expressions for I_b, I_a, and I_{ab} can be obtained by substituting maximum likelihood estimates of item and person parameters into Equations 2.7.12, 2.7.13, and 2.7.14. These approximations should be reasonably accurate when the numbers of individuals (N) and items (n) are large.

In Chapter 5 we shall require the "sampling covariance" of $\hat{a}_i$ and $\hat{b}_i$.[9] Dividing this sampling covariance by the standard errors of $\hat{a}_i$ and $\hat{b}_i$ yields the correlation of $\hat{a}_i$ and $\hat{b}_i$ over repeated samples of N individuals. The sampling covariance of $\hat{a}_i$ and $\hat{b}_i$ can be obtained by computing

$$(2.7.17) \qquad \text{Cov}(\hat{a}_i, \hat{b}_i) = -I_{a_i b_i}/(I_{a_i} I_{b_i} - I_{a_i b_i}^2).$$

Again, an approximate value of $\text{Cov}(\hat{a}_i, \hat{b}_i)$ can be obtained by substituting estimates of item and person parameters into Equations 2.7.12, 2.7.13, and 2.7.14.

Lord (1980) also presents functions involving the lower asymptote parameter c_i: I_{c_i}, $I_{a_i c_i}$, and $I_{b_i c_i}$. We shall not list these formulae because

---

[9] Sampling covariances are also important in multiple regression. For example, consider the situation where high school average (HSA) and SAT total score (SAT-V + SAT-M) are used to predict freshman grade point average (GPA). In most populations, HSA and SAT total scores have a positive correlation. Assuming this to be the case, imagine that samples of size N are drawn repeatedly and sample regression weights (b_{HSA} and b_{SAT}) for HSA and SAT total score are computed in each sample. Across samples, b_{HSA} and b_{SAT} will have a negative correlation: If b_{HSA} is large in a given sample, b_{SAT} will probably be small; conversely, if b_{SAT} is large then b_{HSA} is likely to be small. Because HSA and SAT total scores have a positive correlation, tradeoffs between a large regression weight for one variable and a small weight for the other variable can occur, especially in small samples. The correlation of b_{SAT} and b_{HSA} over repeated samples is a "sampling correlation;" and the product of the sampling correlation, the standard error of b_{HSA} and the standard error of b_{SAT}, is the "sampling covariance" of b_{HSA} and b_{SAT}.

attempts to estimate c_i by the method of maximum likelihood are not usually successful (Lord, 1968, p. 1014). Instead, values of c_i are usually selected by ad hoc methods, and only a_i and b_i are estimated by the method of maximum likelihood.

Equations 2.7.1, 2.7.15, 2.7.16, and 2.7.17 can be used with the two-parameter logistic model by setting $c_i = 0$. Similarly, Equations 2.7.1 and 2.7.15 can be used with the one-parameter logistic model by setting $a_i = 1$ and $c_i = 0$.

Limitations. It is important to note two limitations on Equations 2.7.1, 2.7.15, 2.7.16, and 2.7.17. First, these equations provide asymptotic expressions for standard errors. Thus the formulae are valid in "large" samples. Minimum values of N and n that are required for the formulae to be reasonably accurate are unknown at present.

A second limitation is that Equation 2.7.1 is derived using the assumption that θ is estimated using item parameters—not item parameter *estimates*. Equations 2.7.15 through 2.7.17 are based on the assumption that the θ_j are known—not estimated—when item parameters are estimated. Thus, strictly speaking, these formulae are not appropriate when item and person parameters are estimated simultaneously. The formulae in this section *underestimate* the true standard errors of estimate when item and person parameters are estimated simultaneously (Lord, 1980, p. 181). The magnitudes of the discrepancies between the true standard errors and the approximate standard errors are unknown, but it appears that the discrepancies are likely to be small when N and n are reasonably large.

Derivatives and information functions for logistic models.* The derivatives of $P_i(\theta)$ with respect to θ and item information functions for the three-, two-, and one-parameter logistic models are given in Table 2.7.2 on the following page.

The equations presented in this subsection can be rearranged in various ways. We have selected forms that are relatively simple to program and are conducive to efficient calculations.

2.8 POLYCHOTOMOUS TEST MODELS*

It has long been believed that there is information about examinees' ability in their selection of incorrect responses. However, all of the test models previously considered in this chapter have scored items dichotomously as either correct or incorrect. A *polychotomous* test model for multiple-choice items allows each option to be considered separately; the various incorrect options are *not* grouped together into a single incorrect category. If there are degrees of incorrectness of the various options or if examinees of different ability

Table 2.7.2
Derivatives and Information Functions of the Three Logistic Models

	Derivative of $P_i(\theta)$ with respect to θ: $P_i(\theta)'$	Item Information Function: $I(\theta, u_i)$
Three-parameter model	$\dfrac{(1-c_i)Da_i \exp\{-Da_i(\theta-b_i)\}}{[1+\exp\{-Da_i(\theta-b_i)\}]^2}$	$\dfrac{(1-c_i)\, D^2 a_i^2 \exp\{-Da_i(\theta-b_i)\}}{[1+c_i\exp\{-Da_i(\theta-b_i)\}][1+\exp\{-Da_i(\theta-b_i)\}]^2}$
Two-parameter model	$\dfrac{Da_i \exp\{-Da_i(\theta-b_i)\}}{[1+\exp\{-Da_i(\theta-b_i)\}]^2}$	$\dfrac{D^2 a_i^2 \exp\{-Da_i(\theta-b_i)\}}{[1+\exp\{-Da_i(\theta-b_i)\}]^2}$
One-parameter model	$\dfrac{D \exp\{-D(\theta-b_i)\}}{[1+\exp\{-D(\theta-b_i)\}]^2}$	$\dfrac{D^2 \exp\{-D(\theta-b_i)\}}{[1+\exp\{-D(\theta-b_i)\}]^2}$

levels show different patterns of incorrect option selection, a poly-chotomous test model should be useful in estimating θ.

In this section we shall present empirical option characteristic curves (OCCs) for several SAT-V items. We shall also examine the pattern of option selection among examinees who respond incorrectly. A crude polychotomous test model that has been successfully used by Drasgow, Levine, and Williams (1982) is briefly described.

Empirical OCCs. An empirical OCC is obtained by the procedure described in Section 2.3 for empirical ICCs with the additional fea-ture that *the frequencies of selection of each incorrect option are tabulated.* Using the SAT-V data described in Section 2.3, Levine and Drasgow (1983) formed 10 ability strata on the basis of ability esti-mated using the three-parameter logistic model. Ability estimates were scaled to have a mean of zero and a standard deviation of one. The 10th, 20th, . . . , percentile points from the standardized normal distribution were used to divide the $\hat{\theta}$ continuum into 10 ability strata. The empirical OCCs for two items are presented in Figure 2.8.1.

Figure 2.8.1
Empirical OCCs for SAT-V Items*

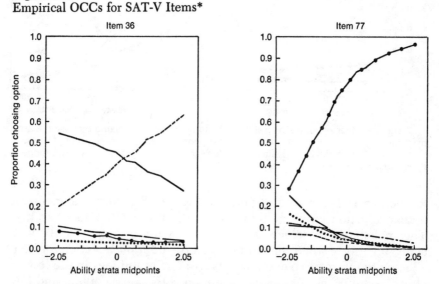

* Option A is indicated by long dashes, B by dots, C by connected dots, D by short dashes, E by the solid line, and omits by short and long dashes.
Source: Copyright 1983, Educational & Psychological Measurement. Reproduced by permission.

Conditional OCCs. The extent to which incorrect option choice is useful in estimating ability may perhaps be seen more clearly by examining the frequencies of option selection among examinees who responded incorrectly to an item. A conditional OCC is obtained by

determining the proportions of examinees in each ability stratum selecting each option, after removing all examinees who answered the
item correctly (Levine & Drasgow, 1983). This double conditioning
(first on incorrect responses, then on $\hat{\theta}$ for those who responded incorrectly) allows us to examine the information contained in wrong responses as it relates to θ. Figure 2.8.2 presents the conditional OCCs

Figure 2.8.2
Proportions of Examinees Choosing Incorrect SAT-V Options among
Examinees Who Responded Incorrectly*

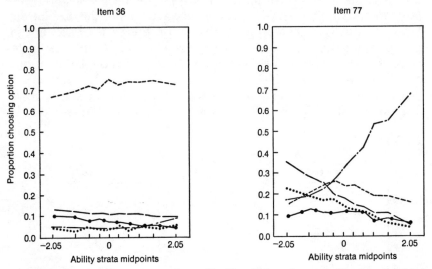

* The first incorrect option is indicated by long dashes, the second by dots, the third
by connected dots, the fourth by short dashes, and omits by short and long dashes.
Sources: Copyright 1983, Educational & Psychological Measurement. Reproduced
by permission.

for the two SAT-V items presented in Figure 2.8.1. Note that incorrect
option selection for item 36 provides little information about ability:
The probability of selecting the fourth incorrect option is about .7
across all ability strata. In contrast, incorrect option selection for item
77 is quite informative about ability. Among examinees in the lowest
ability stratum, the first incorrect option is the most popular and few
examinees omit the item. As ability increases, the first incorrect option
is less likely to be chosen, and this option is selected by only 5 percent
of the examinees in the highest ability stratum who responded incorrectly. The decision to omit the item is made more frequently as
ability increases, with the conditional percent of examinees omitting
the item reaching 68 percent in the highest ability stratum.

Models. Empirical OCCs can be used to construct a very simple
polychotomous test model: Probabilities of option selection are ob-

tained from empirical OCCs by linearly interpolating between strata midpoints. There are many problems with this crude model—very large samples are required, it is impossible to extrapolate below the lowest stratum midpoint and above the highest stratum midpoint, the number of strata is chosen arbitrarily, etc. Nonetheless, this model has been used successfully by Drasgow et al. (1982). Their application is described in Chapter 4.

Little use of more sophisticated polychotomous test models, such as the ones developed by Bock (1972) and Samejima (1969, 1972) has been made to date. However, the research of Drasgow et al. (1982) indicates that polychotomous test models can provide advantages over dichotomous test models. It seems likely that more extensive use of polychotomous test models will be made by practitioners in the future.

2.9 RELATION BETWEEN IRT AND CLASSICAL TEST THEORY

Although it may be tempting to view IRT and classical test theory (CTT) as rival theoretical frameworks, it is perhaps more appropriate to view the theories as partially overlapping. IRT models make stronger assumptions (e.g., local independence, logistic ICCs) than are made in CTT, and obtain stronger results. In this section we shall describe some relations between IRT concepts and corresponding CTT concepts and point out some advantages of IRT concepts.

True scores and θ. In CTT, an individual's true score, τ, is defined as the expected observed score X of that individual. If the number right scoring method is used, and if the assumptions of IRT are correct, then

$$\tau = E(X) = E \sum_{i=1}^{n} u_i = \sum_{i=1}^{n} E(u_i)$$

$$(2.9.1) \qquad = \sum_{i=1}^{n} [1 \cdot \text{Prob}(u_i = 1|\theta) + 0 \cdot \text{Prob}(u_i = 0|\theta)]$$

$$= \sum_{i=1}^{n} P_i(\theta).$$

Since each $P_i(\theta)$ is a monotonically increasing curve, it is clear that τ is a monotonically increasing function of θ. For any set of items, it is possible to plot the function $\tau = \Sigma P(\theta)$ against θ. Two of these plots are presented in Section 3.2. It is important to note that the relation between θ and τ is one-to-one; when the assumptions of IRT are true, *θ and τ are the same ability expressed in different metrics.*

There is an essential difference between θ and τ, however. Once the mean and variance of the θ-metric have been established, an individual's θ does not depend upon the particular measuring instrument (although the accuracy of $\hat{\theta}$ as an estimate of θ does depend on the number and quality of items). Thus an individual's ability measured in the θ-metric can be compared across different sets of test items. This property is used in essential ways in adaptive testing where items may be selected by a computer to have the appropriate difficulty for an examinee on the basis of the examinee's previous responses. At the end of an adaptive testing session, examinees may have taken partially overlapping but distinct sets of items. Nonetheless, their estimated θs will be directly comparable. However, τs cannot be used similarly. Examinees who answer easier items will receive an advantage, as will examinees who answer more items. Since τ is defined in terms of the particular items answered, τs from two sets of items that measure the same construct are not comparable unless the sets of items are "parallel" in the sense of CTT. If the sets of items are strictly parallel, one may compare observed scores. Note, however, adaptive tests are unlikely to be parallel because they are tailored to the ability of individual examinees by selecting appropriately difficult or easy items.

Item parameters. In Section 2.5 the item parameter invariance property of IRT item parameters was described. Strictly speaking, *item* parameters are not defined in CTT. However, practitioners who develop measuring instruments using CTT typically use the item difficulty parameter, p_i, from Equation 2.5.4 to index item difficulty, and the item–test biserial correlation, r_b, as a measure of item discriminating power. Lord's Paradox, described in Section 2.5, illustrates the subpopulation-dependent nature of p_i. It is easy to show that r_b is also subpopulation-dependent. In IRT the item parameters do *not* depend upon the examinee subpopulation, and the ability parameter does *not* depend upon the item pool. Analogous statements cannot be made for CTT.

Precision of measurement. In IRT, the accuracy of ability estimates is characterized by $I(\theta)$ in Equation 2.7.3 for maximum likelihood estimates of θ and by $I_x(\theta)$ in Equation 2.7.6 for a weighted sum of item scores. Since the standard error of $\hat{\theta}$ is $1/\sqrt{I(\theta)}$, the test information function provides a clear indication of the accuracy of estimation. Furthermore, $I(\theta)$ and $I_x(\theta)$ can be used during the construction of a measuring instrument to select items: select items, compute $I(\theta)$ or $I_x(\theta)$, and determine whether $\hat{\theta}$ has a sufficiently small standard error across the range of θ values of interest to the researcher. Note that $I(\theta)$ may be adequate for some θ intervals (e.g., between roughly -1 and 0 in Figure 2.7.2), but perhaps not adequate in other θ intervals (e.g., between roughly 1 and 2 in Figure 2.7.2). Thus, $I(\theta)$ can be used to determine what type of items should be added to increase measurement accuracy and what type of items might be deleted without seriously degrading estimation accuracy.

The two principal indices of measurement accuracy in CTT are the test reliability $\rho_{xx'}$, and the variance of error scores σ_e^2, which is also called the squared standard error of measurement. True score variance, σ_τ^2, and σ_e^2 are defined as the variances of true scores and error scores, respectively, in a population of individuals. Consequently, test reliability

$$\rho_{xx'} = \frac{\sigma_\tau^2}{\sigma_\tau^2 + \sigma_e^2} = \frac{\sigma_\tau^2}{\sigma_x^2}$$

is also defined with respect to a population. This leads Samejima (1977) to state, "Reliability is a dead concept in test theory since it differs from one group of subjects to another, and its generalizability is narrowly limited" (p. 243). It is also important to note that $\rho_{xx'}$ and σ_e^2 are indices of measurement accuracy that are typically aggregated over individuals and refer to the scale as a whole. They may *not* be especially useful in characterizing measurement accuracy for specific intervals or for particular individuals.

IRT can be used to calculate the standard error of measurement of number right score X at a specific τ value (Lord, 1980). Denote this conditional standard error $\sigma_{e|\tau}$. To determine $\sigma_{e|\tau}$, first note that since τ and θ stand in a one-to-one relation, specifying τ indirectly specifies θ. Thus, the conditional variance of number right score $\sigma_{x|\tau}^2$ equals $\sigma_{x|\theta}^2$ for corresponding τ and θ values. Using the local independence assumption of IRT and the formula for the variance of a binomial distribution, we see that

(2.9.2) $$\sigma_{x|\tau}^2 = \sum_{i=1}^{n} P_i(\theta)Q_i(\theta).$$

Finally, for a fixed value of τ, all the variance in observed scores is error variance. Consequently, Equation 2.9.2 can be used to compute the squared standard error of measurement of number right score for individuals with true score τ.

Equation 2.9.2 notwithstanding, indices such as split-half reliability, test-retest reliability, coefficient α, and σ_e reflect average measurement accuracy in a population. Furthermore, the various measures of reliability can vary across different populations even though $\sigma_{e|\tau}$ is exactly the same in all populations for all values of τ. Thus, test reliability is meaningful only in describing average measurement accuracy vis-à-vis some particular population. In contrast, $I(\theta)$ and $I_x(\theta)$ do not depend upon the examinee population; instead they depend only upon the items that form the measuring instrument.

Limitations. The invariance properties of IRT parameters and test information functions are derived using the assumptions of local independence and a particular model for ICCs. It is an empirical question whether any given set of items can approximately satisfy the IRT assumptions. Further, the extent to which various IRT models are robust to violations of assumptions has not yet been fully determined.

2.10 REVIEW OF SOME NOTATION AND MATHEMATICS

In this section, we briefly review some terms and methods that may be unfamiliar to readers.

Monotonic functions. A function f for which $f(a) > f(b)$ if $a > b$ is a *strictly increasing monotonic function.* Function A in Figure 2.10.1

Figure 2.10.1
Various Functions

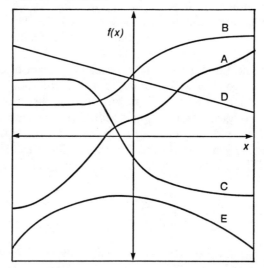

is a strictly increasing monotonic function because the function always increases as x increases. Curve B is a *monotonically increasing function* but is not strictly increasing because the curve is horizontal in some places. Function C is a *monotonically decreasing function,* and D is a *strictly decreasing monotonic function.* Finally, curve E is a *nonmonotonic* function because it first increases and then decreases. Periodic functions, such as sine and cosine curves, are also nonmonotonic if considered over a sufficiently large range of x values.

The constant e. The number e, which equals 2.7183 . . . , is an irrational number like $\pi = 3.14159$ . . . . It is also one of the most important numbers in mathematics and statistics. For example, the height of the bell-shaped standard normal curve is

(2.10.1) $$f(x) = \frac{1}{\sqrt{2\pi}} e^{-x^2/2}.$$

The logistic and normal ogive IRT models described in Section 2.4 all involve raising e to some power. For notational convenience, it is common to define the term exp as

(2.10.2) $$\exp(x) = e^x.$$

Then raising e to some power, say e^2, can be expressed as

$$\exp(2) = e^2 \doteq (2.7183)^2 \doteq 7.3892.$$

Integration and differentiation. In this subsection, we shall describe integration and differentiation in terms of the applications of these methods that are made in Chapter 2. It should be noted that our descriptions are neither rigorous nor general. Further information concerning these methods can be obtained in an introductory calculus book such as Thomas (1969).

We shall denote the derivative of a function $y = f(x)$ as $f(x)'$. If a function contains several variables (e.g., $y = x^2 + z^2$), we denote the derivative of y with respect to x as $\partial y / \partial x$. In Chapter 2, we use the important fact that the derivative of a function yields the *slope* of the function. For example, if $f(x) = x^2$, then $f(x)' = 2x$. The slope of the curve $f(x) = x^2$ at $x = 3$ is then 6.

Integration is a method that can be used to find the area under a curve. For example, if we wished to know the area under the normal curve in Equation 2.10.1 from $-\infty$ to, perhaps, $x = 1$, we would calculate the integral

$$\begin{matrix} \text{Area under normal} \\ \text{curve from } -\infty \text{ to } 1 \end{matrix} = \int_{-\infty}^{1} \frac{1}{\sqrt{2\pi}} \exp\{-x^2/2\}dx.$$

The symbol $\int$ means "integrate the following expression;" the numbers below and above the integral sign indicate the range of values for which the integration should occur; and dx indicates that the integration should be performed with respect to x.

REFERENCES

Adams, E. F., Laker, D. R., & Hulin, C. L. An investigation of the influence of job level and functional speciality on job attitudes and perceptions. *Journal of Applied Psychology*, 1977, 62, 335–343.

Birnbaum, A. Some latent trait models and their use in inferring an examinee's ability. In F. M. Lord & M. R. Novick, *Statistical theories of mental test scores*. Reading, Mass.: Addison-Wesley Publishing, 1968.

Bock, R. D. Estimating item parameters and latent ability when responses are scored in two or more nominal categories. *Psychometrika*, 1972, *37*, 29–51.

Bock, R. D., & Lieberman, M. Fitting a response model for *n* dichotomously scored items. *Psychometrika*, 1970, *35*, 179–197.

Cliff, N. Test theory without true scores? *Psychometrika*, 1979, *44*, 373–393.

Cliff, N. Evaluating Guttman scales, 1941–1981: Old and new thoughts. Paper presented at the meeting of the American Psychological Association, Los Angeles, Calif., August, 1981.

Drasgow, F., Levine, M. V., & Williams, E. Advances in appropriateness measurement. Manuscript under review, 1982.

Drasgow, F., & Miller, H. E. Psychometric and substantive issues in scale construction and validation. *Journal of Applied Psychology*, 1982, *67*, 268–279.

Green, B. F. Attitude measurement. In G. Lindzey (Ed.), *Handbook of social psychology*, Reading, Mass.: Addison-Wesley Publishing, 1954.

Guttman, L. Chap. 2, 3, 6, 8, and 9. In S. A. Stouffer et al. (Eds.), *Measurement and prediction*. Princeton, N.J.: Princeton University Press, 1950.

Haley, D. C. *Estimation of the dosage mortality relationship when the dose is subject to error* (Technical Report No. 15). Stanford, Calif.: Stanford University, Applied Mathematics and Statistics Laboratory, 1952.

Hambleton, R. K., & Traub, R. E. Information curves and efficiency of three logistic test models. *British Journal of Mathematical and Statistical Psychology*, 1971, *24*, 273–281.

Herman, J. B., Dunham, R. B., & Hulin, C. L. Organizational structure, demographic characteristics, and employee responses. *Organizational Behavior and Human Performance*, 1975, *13*, 206–232.

Hulin, C. L., Drasgow, F., & Komocar, J. Application of item response theory to analysis of attitude scale translations. *Journal of Applied Psychology*, 1982, *67*, 818–825.

Kendall, M., & Stuart, A. *The advanced theory of statistics* (Vol. 2, 4th ed.). New York: Macmillan, 1979.

Kolakowski, D., & Bock, R. D. *A Fortran IV program for maximum-likelihood item analysis and test scoring: Normal ogive model* (Research Memorandum No. 12). Chicago: University of Chicago, Department of Education, 1970.

Lawley, D. N. On problems connected with item selection and test construction. *Proceedings of the Royal Society of Edinburgh*, 1943, *61*, 273–287.

Lawley, D. N. The factorial analysis of multiple-item tests. *Proceedings of the Royal Society of Edinburgh*, 1944, *62*, 74–82.

Lazarsfeld, P. F. Chap. 10 and 11. In S. A. Stouffer et al. (Eds.), *Measurement and prediction*. Princeton, N.J.: Princeton University Press, 1950.

Lazarsfeld, P. F Latent structure analysis. In S. Koch (Ed.), *Psychology: A study of a science* (Vol. 3). New York: McGraw-Hill, 1959, 476–542.

Levine, M. V., & Drasgow, F. The relation between incorrect option choice and estimated ability. *Educational and Psychological Measurement,* 1983, in press.

Lord, F. M. A theory of test scores. *Psychometric Monograph,* No. 7, 1952.

Lord, F. M. An analysis of the Verbal Scholastic Aptitude Test using Birnbaum's three-parameter logistic model. *Educational and Psychological Measurement,* 1968, *28,* 989–1020.

Lord, F. M. Item characteristic curves estimated without knowledge of their mathematical form—A confrontation of Birnbaum's logistic model. *Psychometrika,* 1970, *35,* 43–50.

Lord, F. M. Estimation of latent ability and item parameters when there are omitted responses. *Psychometrika,* 1974, *39,* 247–264.

Lord, F. M. The "ability" scale in item characteristic curve theory. *Psychometrika,* 1975, *40,* 205–217.

Lord, F. M. A study of item bias, using item characteristic curve theory. In Y. H. Poortinga (Ed.), *Basic problems in cross-cultural psychology.* Amsterdam: Swets & Zeitlinger, 1977, 19–29.

Lord, F. M. *Applications of item response theory to practical testing problems.* Hillsdale, N.J.: Erlbaum, 1980.

Lord, F. M., & Novick, M. R. *Statistical theories of mental test scores.* Reading, Mass.: Addison-Wesley Publishing, 1968.

Marco, G. L. Item characteristic curve solutions to three intractable testing problems. *Journal of Educational Measurement,* 1977, *14,* 139–160.

Parsons, C. K. Measuring appropriateness in the assessment of job satisfaction. Unpublished doctoral dissertation, University of Illinois, 1979.

Parsons, C. K., & Hulin, C. L. *An empirical comparison of latent trait theory and hierarchical factor analysis in applications to the measurement of job satisfaction* (Technical Report 80-2). Urbana: University of Illinois, Department of Psychology, 1980.

Rasch, G. *Probablistic models for some intelligence and attainment tests.* Copenhagen: Danish Institute for Educational Research, 1960.

Samejima, F. Estimation of latent ability using a response pattern of graded scores. *Psychometric Monograph,* No. 17, 1969.

Samejima, F. A general model for free-response data. *Psychometric Monograph,* No. 18, 1972.

Samejima, F. A use of the information function in tailored testing. *Applied Psychological Measurement,* 1977, *1,* 233–247.

Smith, P. C., Kendall, L. M., & Hulin, C. L. *The measurement of satisfaction in work and retirement.* Skokie, Ill.: Rand McNally, 1969.

Thomas, G. B., Jr. *Calculus and analytic geometry* (4th ed.). Reading, Mass.: Addison-Wesley Publishing, 1969.

Torgerson, W. S. *Theory and methods of scaling.* New York: John Wiley & Sons, 1958.

Tucker, L. R. Maximum validity of a test with equivalent items. *Psychometrika,* 1946, *11,* 1–13.

Wood, R. L., & Lord, F. M. *A user's guide to LOGIST* (Research Memorandum 76–4). Princeton, N.J.: Educational Testing Service, 1976.

Wood, R. L., Wingersky, M. S., & Lord, F. M. *LOGIST—A computer program for estimating examinee ability and item characteristic curve parameters* (Research Memorandum 76–6). Princeton, N.J.: Educational Testing Service, 1976.

Wright, B. D. Solving measurement problems with the Rasch model. *Journal of Educational Measurement,* 1977, *14,* 97–116.

Wright, B. D., & Mead, R. J. *BICAL: Calibrating items and scales with the Rasch model* (Research Memorandum No. 23). Chicago: University of Chicago, Department of Education, 1977.

3
Methods

3.0 OVERVIEW

In this chapter we show how to use the theory that was described in Chapter 2. Emphasis is placed on presenting examples of IRT analyses and showing the relations between results of these analyses and results from traditional methods.The assumptions, methods, and goals of the two approaches are also compared.

In Section 3.1 we apply concepts and methods discussed in Chapter 2 to analyze sets of items designed to measure psychological traits. IRT analyses are preceded by corresponding traditional analyses in order to highlight important similarities and differences between the procedures. Also, we shall illustrate the construction of a scale assessing job satisfaction using the two-parameter logistic model, and illustrate the development of a scale assessing verbal ability using the three-parameter logistic model.

Section 3.2 further illustrates relations between IRT and traditional approaches by graphically displaying statistics computed in Section 3.1. In Section 3.3 we review research investigating the effects of sample size, number of items, IRT model, and multidimensionality on IRT person and item parameter estimation.

Finally, we have simplified some points in order to retain clarity. It should be understood from the outset that some problems and issues are more complex than presented in this chapter. Several of these problems are addressed later in this book (e.g., the use of factor analysis to assess dimensionality), but others are altogether avoided (e.g., the use of multitrait-multimethod matrices to study construct validity).

3.1 DEVELOPMENT OF ATTITUDE AND ABILITY SCALES

In this section illustrative analyses of two data sets are presented. One analysis is conducted using responses to the items that form the

Job Descriptive Index (JDI), which was originally developed by Smith, Kendall, and Hulin (1969). The two-parameter logistic model is used in this analysis. Otis-Lennon Intelligence Test data are used in the second analysis. Here the three-parameter logistic model is applied because the multiple-choice response format of this latter test allows guessing and it is reasonable to assume that examinees are motivated to achieve the maximum possible score. Two analyses are presented for each data set. Traditional item analysis techniques are used in one analysis, and the other is conducted using IRT procedures.

Traditional Test Development

We assume in this section that the goal of test construction is to measure a single trait or characteristic of an individual rather than to predict an external criterion. Therefore, all test and item statistics reflect *internal* comparisons and criteria.

Traditional test development usually involves the use of two statistics: item difficulty and item validity (Guilford, 1954). A wide range of item difficulty indices exist, but the simplest is the proportion of examinees passing an item or "p."[1] Item validity is sometimes based on the relation between item score and an external criterion of interest (college GPA, job performance, etc.), but in the present analysis we use the biserial correlation between dichotomously scored item responses and total test scores, which is an internal criterion.[2]

A simplified version of traditional test development might proceed through the following stages:

Stage I: Writing items and computing item statistics. In all cases we assume that the researcher begins with a theory in which one or more constructs are defined and are measurable. The theory guides item writing and item selection. Sometimes an investigator may have available a pool of items that have been written previously and shown empirically to measure a particular construct. In other cases, the investigator must write new items. If an item pool is being used for the first time, Nunnally (1978) suggested that the initial item pool should contain at least twice as many items as desired in the final instrument.

---

[1] Actually p, or proportion passing an item, is an easiness rather than a difficulty index.

[2] The biserial correlation in effect corrects the Pearson product moment correlation between item score and total test score for the dichotomous $(0 - 1)$ scoring of the item. Chapter 8 contains a discussion of different types of correlations. The assumptions used in the derivation of the biserial correlations are frequently violated. However, the effects of these violations appear to be less serious than the distortions in the Pearson product moment correlation between item score and total test score caused by differences in item difficulty.

With either new or previously used items, item statistics should be based on a sample large enough to provide stable item difficulty and validity statistics.

Item difficulty and validity statistics alone do not demonstrate conclusively that a set of items measures the construct defined by the researcher's theory. Additional evidence, perhaps obtained from factor analysis and the multitrait-multimethod matrix (Campbell & Fiske, 1959), is required. Chapter 8 provides some information about factor analysis and how it applies to test development. The reader may also consult Nunnally (1978) or Kim and Mueller (1978a, 1978b) for discussions of factor analysis. Cronbach and Meehl (1955), Campbell and Fiske, and Messick (1981) provide important discussions of construct validity.

Stage II: Initial item selection. Nunnally (1978) argued that the most important statistic for test construction is the item–total test score correlation. Items with the highest biserial correlations should be included in the test because, when combined, they form a scale with high internal consistency.[3] High internal consistency gives some evidence that a set of items is measuring one rather than several traits. It is important to note, however, that internal consistency can be high for sets of items that are multidimensional. Thus, internal consistency and dimensionality of item pools must be assessed separately.

One common index of internal consistency is Cronbach's (1951) coefficient α. It is computed as

$$(3.1.1) \qquad \text{coefficient } \alpha = \frac{n}{n-1}\left(1 - \frac{\Sigma\sigma_i^2}{\sigma_x^2}\right),$$

where n is the number of items in the scale, $\Sigma\sigma_i^2$ is the sum of the item variances, and σ_x^2 is the variance of the total test scores. For a given number of items, higher correlations among items lead to higher internal consistency. When item-item correlations are sufficiently high, more items lead to higher internal consistency. Although it may not be apparent from Equation 3.1.1, choosing items with high item–total correlations yields a scale with a relatively large value of coefficient α. Birnbaum's Paradox (see Section 2.7) results when an instrument includes items with low item–total test score correlations. Coefficient α can also decrease when items with low item–total test score correlations are added to a test (see Drasgow & Miller, 1982, for an example).

Stage III: Obtaining the desired score distribution. After acceptable internal consistency is obtained, the next concern might be the

---

[3] We hold the position that high internal consistency, rather than the weaker condition of high reliability, is essential in the measurement of a theory-based construct. Low internal consistency is evidence of items with poor measurement characteristics or of items measuring several *separate* constructs.

test score distribution. The distribution of test scores in the original sample can be computed for the items tentatively selected for the test. If the obtained distribution does not match the distribution desired by the test developer (perhaps a normal distribution), then some item switching must occur. Figure 3.1.1 shows two hypothetical distribu-

Figure 3.1.1
Hypothetical Obtained and Target Total Test Score Distributions

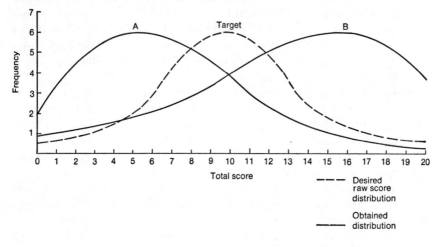

tions, A and B, of raw scores and the desired, or target, distribution. If an investigator had proceeded through Stage III and obtained a distribution similar to A, then the item difficulty statistics can be used to substitute items; appropriate replacement of items will reduce the positive skew and create a more nearly symmetric distribution. In order to change distribution A to the desired distribution, some difficult items (low p values) should be replaced by easy items (high p values). The opposite is true if the obtained distribution resembles B.

IRT Test Development

As in the preceding discussion of the traditional approach, we again assume that the objective of test development is to measure a psychological trait. Scale development is again based on internal rather than external criteria. IRT analysis involves the use of ICCs computed from one, two, or three estimated item parameters and estimates of the person parameter. The item discrimination parameter a_i is analogous to item validity from the traditional approach, and the item difficulty parameter b_i is analogous to p. The c_i parameter does not have a direct analogue in the traditional approach. Comparisons among IRT and traditional item parameters are further described in Section 3.2.

A general approach for using IRT to develop a test is described next.

Stage I: Item writing and the assumption of unidimensionality. We assume in the traditional approach that items are written to measure a single construct motivated by a substantive theory. *Unidimensionality,* an assumption of all IRT models described in this book, is the technical term used in IRT to formalize the idea that all items measure a single latent trait. Chapter 8 contains a discussion of methods for investigating the unidimensionality assumption. For now, let us simply say that items should be written to measure a single psychological trait.

Stage II: Computing ICCs. Investigators must first decide which IRT model is most appropriate for their data. If examinees have the opportunity and motivation to guess when they do not know the correct answer (multiple-choice aptitude or achievement test items), then three-parameter logistic ICCs are likely to be appropriate. If guessing is not likely to occur, then two-parameter ICC logistic models may be appropriate. The one-parameter logistic model may be appropriate if (1) items have been selected to have approximately equal values of a_i and (2) item content or item format precludes guessing.

After choosing the appropriate model, item parameters are estimated with a program such as LOGIST (Wood, Wingersky, & Lord, 1976). Item parameter estimates are then used to construct a test with the desired features.

Stage III: Item selection. IRT-based item selection proceeds in a more direct fashion than item selection by traditional methods. Rather than choosing items on the basis of item–total test score correlations and item difficulties, we can specify the desired *test information curve* (TIC) and choose items so that ability estimates have the desired accuracy at each θ level. (Recall that test information is inversely related to the squared standard error of estimate for θ.) There is no direct way to ensure that some prespecified level of measurement accuracy is achieved in traditional approaches to item selection.

Equation 2.7.3 states the IRT property that is essential for item selection. This equation states that item information functions can be summed to obtain the TIC, provided that maximum likelihood ability estimates (or the optimal scoring weights in Equation 2.7.8) are used. For example, imagine that a "peaked test" with maximum information at some value θ_o is desired. Item information would be computed at θ_o for all available items by the methods described in Section 2.7. The items could then be ranked from most informative to least informative, and the n most informative items would be selected for the test. By concentrating on item and test information functions, a test can be tailored to have the desired measurement accuracy.

Development of an Attitude Scale: Traditional Approach

The first analysis described here concerns the development of a measure of general job satisfaction. We shall use JDI items, which were developed using traditional methods. We expect that only a few items will be unacceptable in terms of IRT parameter estimates obtained for a new sample of workers. However, note that JDI items were writtten and selected on the basis of their relation to five specific facets of job satisfaction (the Work Itself, Supervisor, etc.). Selecting items to assess a general satisfaction dimension is different than the original developmental strategy, and a different type of instrument will result from the present analysis.

The data for this exercise were obtained from a sample of 1,349 workers who completed the JDI in 1977–1978. Their item responses were scored dichotomously by the process described in Section 2.3. Table 3.1.1 shows 60 JDI items rank-ordered by their item-total biser-

Table 3.1.1
IRT Item Parameter Estimates and Traditional Statistics for Job Descriptive Index Items

	Traditional Item Statistics			IRT Item Parameter Estimates		Estimated Information at $\theta = .25$
Item	$\hat{r}_b$	$\hat{r}_{pb}$	$\hat{p}$	$\hat{a}$	$\hat{b}$	
41	.707	.407	.890	1.209	−1.587	.093
38	.677	.448	.809*	1.073	−1.192	.209
34	.664	.492	.760*	1.087	−.958	.299†
42	.662	.462	.817*	1.127	−1.207	.200
29	.645	.450	.778*	.943	−1.110	.234†
53	.639	.453	.766*	.817	−1.138	.214
3	.635	.458	.756*	.850	−1.064	.237†
18	.614	.446	.760*	.843	−1.088	.229†
5	.611	.397	.853	.854	−1.616	.123
45	.607	.318	.910	.885	−2.033	.068
30	.603	.377	.855	.888	−1.590	.126
27	.598	.469	.375*	1.109	.421	.866†
9	.596	.435	.764*	.796	−1.147	.209
47	.593	.378	.846	.724	−1.731	.112
7	.585	.439	.712*	.768	−.910	.252†
33	.582	.460	.583*	.832	.325	.499†
40	.580	.415	.772*	.878	−1.123	.225
23	.579	.445	.324*	1.071	.624	.740†
19	.575	.437	.306*	1.053	.698	.685†
22	.575	.459	.498*	.903	.003	.568†

Table 3.1.1 (*concluded*)

Item	Traditional Item Statistics			IRT Item Parameter Estimates		Estimated Information at $\theta = .25$
	$\hat{r}_b$	$\hat{r}_{pb}$	$\hat{p}$	$\hat{a}$	$\hat{b}$	
58	.572	.412	.755	.690	−1.202	.179
24	.570	.454	.544	.844	−.172	.470†
31	.568	.428	.685	.787	−.771	.290†
21	.565	.446	.423	.907	.287	.594†
50	.563	.316	.898	.677	−2.287	.064
51	.563	.394	.800	.682	−1.478	.141
55	.561	.421	.681	.659	−.839	.221
4	.560	.403	.754	.677	−1.208	.176
32	.550	.426	.649	.743	−.631	.297†
26	.537	.380	.214*	.873	1.243	.334†
44	.535	.400	.708	.712	−.930	.229
13	.529	.392	.727	.651	−1.088	.185
57	.519	.267	.906	.580	−2.649	.050
59	.517	.396	.628	.559	−.645	.189‡
39	.514	.377	.744	.689	−1.137	.189
60	.500	.388	.652	.559	−.777	.180
35	.490	.374	.665	.616	−.792	.206‡
11	.477	.380	.476	.503	.144	.182‡
56	.475	.346	.784	.539	−1.623	.108
20	.471	.338	.226*	.724	1.319	.253†
25	.471	.355	.314*	.657	.893	.275†
46	.470	.372	.546	.512	−.235	.181‡
1	.462	.360	.391*	.517	.612	.188‡
49	.460	.366	.515	.498	−.068	.176‡
10	.455	.281	.894	.602	−2.434	.059
36	.446	.324	.761	.559	−1.423	.127
48	.433	.329	.694	.438	−1.214	.104
28	.427	.341	.605	.532	−.542	.180‡
37	.426	.341	.515	.515	−.327	.180‡
52	.426	.339	.520	.540	−.090	.206‡
6	.403	.314	.389*	.432	.712	.131‡
54	.378	.290	.672	.385	−1.179	.087
2	.356	.269	.311	.342	1.520	.074
15	.323	.258	.389	.321	.920	.068
17	.272	.208	.331	.244	1.809	.039
12	.271	.206	.305	.280	1.864	.049
8	.201	.157	.616	.179	−1.550	.021
16	.185	.145	.617	.171	−1.643	.020
43	.043	.030	.798	.020	−39.790	.000
14	.039	.029	.272	.032	18.417	.001

* Item included in final version of the general job satisfaction scale developed by traditional methods.

† Item information is among top 17.

‡ Additional items included in final version of scale developed by IRT analysis.

ial correlations ($\hat{r}_b$) and also includes point biserial correlations[4] ($\hat{r}_{pb}$) and proportion right ($\hat{p}$). The 20 items with the highest $\hat{r}_b$ were included in the first version of the scale, which produced a coefficient α of .85.

The distribution of total scale scores for this 20-item scale is presented in Figure 3.1.2A. The distribution is clearly asymmetric with a

Figure 3.1.2A
Relative Frequency of Scores on the First Version of the General Job Satisfaction Scale (developed by traditional methods)

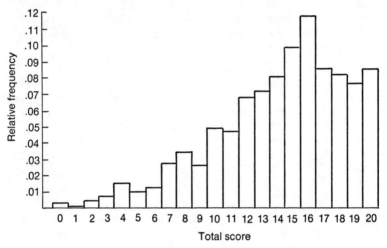

pronounced negative skew (tail to the left). In fact, the skew is −.736. Assume that we desire a distribution that is closer to the normal distribution in shape. In order to eliminate the skew, 5 of the easier items were replaced with 5 more difficult items from the remaining 40 items. The items deleted, items 5, 30, 41, 45, and 47 had high $\hat{p}$ values; the new items, items 1, 6, 20, 25, and 26, had lower $\hat{p}$ values and reasonably high item-total correlations. The revised raw-score distribution appears in Figure 3.1.2B. Here the skew is −.075, which confirms the visual impression of a symmetrical distribution. Because the item statistics are based on a large sample, we can expect that the scale would yield a similar distribution of scores in another random sample of individuals from the same population. Reshaping the score distribution did not appreciably affect the scale internal consistency

---

[4] A point biserial correlation is the usual Pearson product moment correlation between a dichotomous variable (here, item score) and a continuous variable (total test score).

Figure 3.1.2B
Relative Frequency of General Job Satisfaction Scores after Substituting
Five Items with Low $\hat{p}$ Values for Five Items with High $\hat{p}$ Values

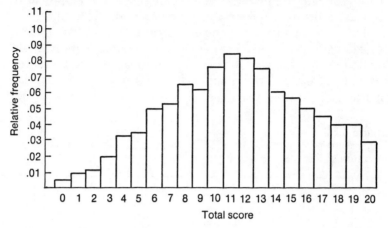

(coefficient α = .85). The final 20 items selected are marked with an *
in Table 3.1.1.

Development of an Attitude Scale: IRT Approach

The first step in applying IRT is to examine the assumption of
unidimensionality. As mentioned earlier, carefully written, theory-
based items might be sufficiently unidimensional for IRT. From other
analyses (not presented here), we believe that a strong general attitude, general job satisfaction, underlies responses to the JDI and that
the items are sufficiently unidimensional to apply IRT.

The choice of a model is the next step in the IRT analysis. The
model selected here is the two-parameter logistic model with a_i and b_i
free to vary across items, but with c_i fixed at 0.0. The two-parameter
logistic model was chosen because, in attitude measurement, individuals with very low satisfaction should have no reason to guess the
correct response to an item. There may well be exceptions. For example, it might be hypothesized that even a thoroughly disgruntled employee would not respond negatively to every item because of a generalized "Panglossian" tendency to find something good about even
the worst situation. If there is a tendency by low-θ individuals occasionally to respond positively, and these responses are made randomly throughout the JDI, then ICCs would not have lower asymptotes of zero; small positive values of c would result. Acquiescent
response sets, socially desirable responses, and various other influ-

ences may affect the lower asymptote of the ICC. For these reasons, it is important to check the form of the ICC.

To investigate the lower asymptote of JDI ICCs, empirical item–total scale score regressions can be computed.[5] This plot is determined in the same manner as the empirical ICCs in Chapter 2, except that total scale score is used to partition the sample of individuals and is plotted on the horizontal axis. An empirical item–total regression for item 6, "creative" work, appears in Figure 3.1.3. Notice that the proportion of positive responses is only .036 and .015 for the two

Figure 3.1.3
Proportions of Positive Responses for Item 6, "Creative" Work, as a Function of Total Score on 60 JDI Items

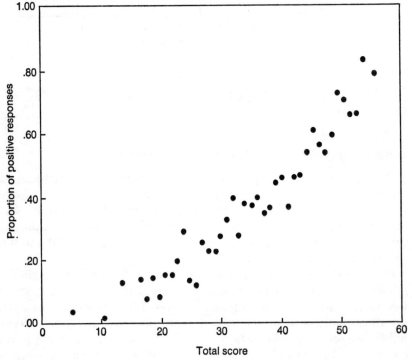

---

[5] Note that total scale score is based on the responses to all items including the item under consideration. This creates an artifactual relation between the item and total test score. The artifactual relation can be eliminated by plotting proportion correct on item i against the "reduced" total test score, Y_i, where

$$Y_i = \sum_{j=1}^{n} u_j - u_i.$$

lowest satisfaction strata. The lower asymptote for this item is effectively zero.

Lower asymptotes of many JDI items were not as well defined as the near-zero lower asymptote of "creative." For example, items with high p values are not likely to have well-determined lower asymptotes. Among more difficult JDI items—items with $\hat{p} < .50$ in Table 3.1.1—the mean proportion of positive responses was .093 in the lowest satisfaction stratum.

After an IRT model is selected, item parameter for all items must be estimated. The dichotomously scored item responses from the 1,349 workers described earlier were input to LOGIST, allowing a_i and b_i to vary but holding c_i fixed at 0. The resulting parameter estimates appear in Table 3.1.1. Two items, items 14 and 43, have very low values of $\hat{a}_i$ and extreme values of $\hat{b}_i$. These item parameters are not well-estimated and should be removed from further consideration. Items 8, 12, 16, and 17 are also unlikely to be useful.

In order to describe the use of information curves to develop tests, consider the following hypothetical situation. Assume that an organization wants to use the results of a job satisfaction survey to select individuals for an intervention that is designed to improve job satisfaction. Because interventions are costly, individuals should only be selected who are below a point on the satisfaction continuum that would be described verbally as "neutral." Assume that it is known from past experience that satisfaction scores below $-.50$ are low enough to cause concern. Suppose further that we would like to be about 98 percent sure that an individual with a true attitude of $\theta = .25$ will have an observed $\hat{\theta}$ greater than $-.50$ (so that individuals with θs of .25 or greater—well above the neutral point—are not included in the intervention). Thus we want .25 to be two standard errors above $-.50$.[6] One standard error of $\hat{\theta}$ must then be .375. We can specify the information needed to achieve this value because the $\sigma_{\hat{\theta}|\theta} = 1/\sqrt{I(\theta)}$. Therefore, the TIC must equal or exceed 7.11 at $\theta = .25$ because $1/\sqrt{7.11} = .375$. In this way, a practical need for measurement accuracy can be translated into the target TIC that appears in Figure 3.1.4. The remainder of the target TIC in Figure 3.1.4 was selected on the basis of subjective judgments. In the context of an actual organization, additional points on the TIC would probably be selected so that the job satisfaction scale met other organizational needs.

---

[6] This results because the maximum likelihood estimate $\hat{\theta}$ is normally distributed with a mean of .25 when the true value of θ is .25 and the number of test items is large (i.e., maximum likelihood estimates are consistent and asymptotically normal). Because 98 percent of the area under a standardized normal curve is to the right of a z-score of -2, we want $[(-.50) - .25]/(\sigma_{\hat{\theta}|\theta}) = -2$.

Figure 3.1.4
Target and Actual Test Information Curves for Scales Measuring General
Job Satisfaction

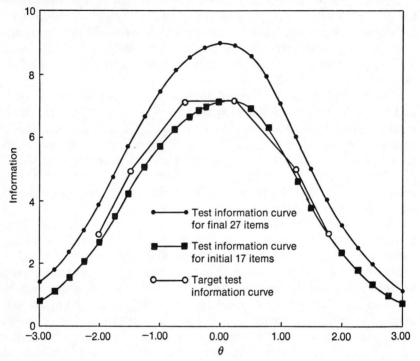

Item selection is designed to produce a set of items whose information curves sum to produce a TIC that matches or exceeds the target
TIC. In order to use the IRT property that the test information function is the sum of item information functions, the method of maximum
likelihood must be used to estimate θ. As noted in Chapter 2, using
nonoptimal test scores (such as raw scores) results in the loss of information about θ. Therefore the maximum likelihood estimate $\hat{\theta}$ is used
throughout this chapter.

For this example, the first step involves rank ordering the items in
terms of their information $\theta = .25$. By using the formula for the item
information function presented in Chapter 2, the *estimated* information (because we have only *estimated* item parameters) can be computed for each item at $\theta = .25$. These values appear in Table 3.1.1. The
top 17 items are indicated by "†", and the sum of their information at
$\theta = .25$ is 7.12. The TIC for these 17 items appears in Figure 3.1.4.
The obtained test information curve is deficient at $\theta < 0.0$. Therefore,
10 items with substantial information were added. These items are
indicated by "‡" in Table 3.1.1.

It is interesting to compare the scale developed by IRT analysis to the scale developed by traditional methods. There are 12 items appearing in the scale developed by IRT methods that did not appear on the scale developed by traditional methods. The biserial correlations of these items tend to be lower than the biserial correlations of items selected for the traditional scale. They were included in the IRT scale due to their contribution to information at $\theta = .25$. If we had desired to maximize information at some other point, all or none of these items may have been included. After selecting items with the highest biserial correlations in the traditional analysis, items were added or deleted only to obtain a different raw-score distribution, which says little about the accuracy with which a trait is estimated in different θ intervals. However, in most cases some overlap between scales developed through IRT and traditional methods is expected because of the association between IRT parameters and traditional item statistics.

Development of a Test of Verbal Ability: Traditional Approach

The next test, the Otis-Lennon School Abilities Test, was developed in English and then translated into Canadian French for francophone Canadian school children. It contains 100 multiple-choice items with five response options. Used here are item responses from 1,373 children in grades 7, 8, and 9, to 60 verbal reasoning items.

For illustrative purposes, assume that we wish to shorten the test drastically to 20 items, yet retain an internal consistency value of about .85. We begin by computing item-total biserial correlations, $\hat{r}_b$, and difficulty indices, $\hat{p}$. The item statistics, rank-ordered by $\hat{r}_b$, appear in Table 3.1.2. The 20 items with the highest $\hat{r}_b$ yield a scale with a coefficient α of .85. The frequency distribution of total scores for these 20 items, $X = \Sigma_{i=1}^{20} u_i$, appears in Figure 3.1.5A.

Table 3.1.2
IRT Item Parameter Estimates and Traditional
Statistics for Otis-Lennon Items

Item	Traditional Item Statistics			IRT Item Parameter Estimates		
	$\hat{r}_b$	$\hat{r}_{pb}$	$\hat{p}$	$\hat{a}_i$	$\hat{b}_i$	$\hat{c}_i$
35	.761	.578	.687*	1.539	−.288	.160
2	.753	.356	.951	.824	−2.652	.160
4	.750	.359	.943	.744	−2.795	.160
36	.725	.476	.838	.911	−1.151	.160
20	.706	.516	.760*	1.350	−.556	.160

88

Table 3.1.2 (*continued*)

Item	$\hat{r}_b$	$\hat{r}_{pb}$	$\hat{p}$	$\hat{a}_i$	$\hat{b}_i$	$\hat{c}_i$
	Traditional Item Statistics			IRT Item Parameter Estimates		
47	.705	.510	.753*	1.007	− .683	.160
42	.701	.530	.682*	1.224	− .275	.160
55	.700	.528	.735*	1.329	− .459	.160
14	.694	.334	.944	.783	−2.443	.160
41	.690	.537	.663*	1.303	− .212	.120
10	.681	.292	.958	.702	−2.968	.160
37	.661	.520	.623*	1.406	.045	.199
19	.656	.390	.894	.741	−1.949	.160
18	.650	.385	.893	.766	−1.788	.160
15	.636	.344	.916	.782	−2.017	.160
11	.628	.466	.746*	.876	− .721	.160
43	.617	.485	.628*	1.242	− .036	.160
23	.616	.489	.586*	1.035	.055	.160
59	.603	.480	.489*	1.324	.411	.120
26	.591	.361	.886	.712	−1.902	.160
8	.590	.438	.746	.905	− .625	.160
27	.590	.404	.815	.801	−1.131	.160
25	.589	.463	.565*	1.071	.125	.160
46	.580	.451	.633	.899	− .151	.160
45	.578	.461	.500*	1.893	.449	.160
5	.572	.455	.548*	1.046	.214	.160
48	.565	.450	.537*	1.149	.323	.160
56	.563	.447	.554	.919	.208	.160
32	.551	.438	.552	1.314	.350	.210
30	.545	.469	.693	.875	− .453	.160
16	.542	.406	.701	.807	− .457	.160
22	.519	.390	.755	.671	− .907	.160
40	.519	.347	.825	.595	−1.373	.160
53	.513	.408	.566	1.060	.337	.190
1	.504	.209	.874	.570	−3.911	.160
60	.503	.401	.436*	.967	.566	.120
50	.499	.393	.592	.888	.083	.160
57	.494	.380	.328*	1.425	.950	.120
29	.490	.355	.792	.622	−1.085	.160
13	.489	.359	.763	.581	−1.081	.160
21	.457	.317	.795	.520	−1.376	.160
49	.452	.349	.358*	2.000	.849	.160
7	.431	.286	.842	.476	−1.893	.160
12	.418	.330	.599	.620	.021	.160
58	.418	.321	.685	.525	− .474	.160
52	.390	.161	.962	.436	−4.192	.160
9	.379	.261	.190*	1.070	1.586	.074
34	.361	.269	.747	.431	−1.118	.160
39	.321	.238	.724	.383	−1.063	.160
44	.318	.246	.355*	.795	1.317	.160
6	.306	.161	.929	.253	−5.745	.160

Table 3.1.2 (*concluded*)

Item	Traditional Item Statistics			IRT Item Parameter Estimates		
	$\hat{r}_b$	$\hat{r}_{pb}$	$\hat{p}$	$\hat{a}_i$	$\hat{b}_i$	$\hat{c}_i$
54	.294	.227	.350	.660	1.441	.150
51	.292	.226	.679	.323	− .963	.160
33	.288	.223	.355	.622	1.519	.160
28	.282	.223	.372	.687	1.312	.160
31	.265	.188	.787	.275	−2.339	.160
24	.245	.196	.457	.332	1.263	.160
38	.226	.178	.500	.330	.841	.160
17	.204	.146	.208	.649	2.381	.120
3	.181	.096	.926	.202	−7.030	.160

* Item included in the final version of the verbal ability test developed by traditional methods.

Figure 3.1.5A
Relative Frequencies of Total Test Scores on the Initial Version of the 20-Item Verbal Ability Test

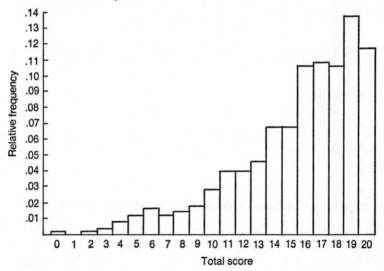

This distribution has a negative skew (skew = −1.043). If a more symmetrical distribution is desired, some item switching is necessary. To illustrate item switching, the remaining 40 items from the original pool were examined for $\hat{p}$ values less than or near .50, while still having a $\hat{r}_b \doteq .40$. Nine items (items 5, 9, 25, 44, 45, 48, 49, 57, and 60)

were substituted for items 2, 4, 10, 14, 15, 18, 19, 26, and 36 because these latter items had the highest $\hat{p}$ values of the initial 20 items. Coefficient α for the new set of items is .86, or an increase of .01 over the original 20 items. The items included in the final version of the scale are indicated by a "*" in Table 3.1.2.

Total scores were recomputed for the new 20-item test and are plotted in Figure 3.1.5B. This frequency distribution has less negative

Figure 3.1.5B
Relative Frequencies of Total Test Scores after Substituting Nine Items with Low $\hat{p}$ Values for Nine Items with High $\hat{p}$ Values

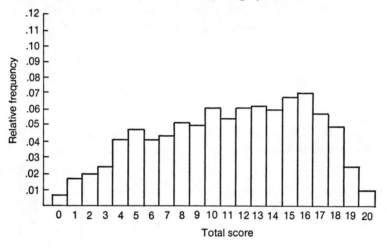

skew (skew = −.248) than the original 20-item scale. One further iteration might be desirable to obtain a more nearly symmetrical distribution.

Development of a Test of Verbal Ability: IRT Approach

Using the data set obtained from the sample of Canadian school children, parameters were estimated for the three-parameter logistic model. LOGIST was again used, this time allowing a_i, b_i, and c_i to vary. These parameter estimates appear in Table 3.1.2.

For this example, suppose that accurate estimates of θ across a broad range of θ values are required, rather than a peak at only one value as in the previous example. Suppose further that the standard error of estimate can be no larger than .5 across the range $-2 \leq \theta \leq +2$. These would be reasonable requirements if decisions about individuals must be made across a broad range of verbal ability. The standard error of $\hat{\theta}$ equals $1/\sqrt{I(\theta)}$; therefore, the information function must equal or exceed 4.0 across the θ range of interest. This target TIC appears in Figure 3.1.6.

Because information at the extremes of the θ interval (-2 and $+2$) will probably be most difficult to obtain, initial item selection should

Figure 3.1.6
Target and Actual Test Information Curves for Tests Measuring
Verbal Ability

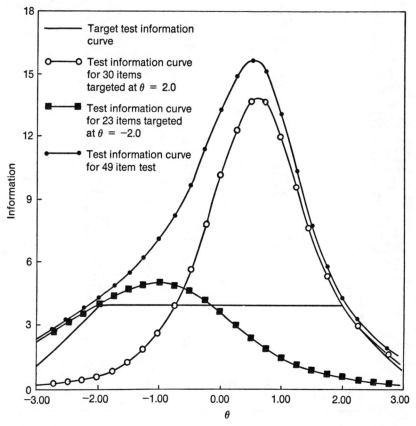

concentrate on obtaining sufficient information at these θ values. Estimated information was evaluated at $\theta = -2$ and $\theta = +2$ for each item using the item parameter estimates in Table 3.1.2. The items that provided maximum information at these θ values are presented in Table 3.1.3. Notice that only four items (items 16, 22, 34, and 58) appear on both lists; a total of 49 items is needed to meet the minimum information requirements.

Table 3.1.3
Estimated Information for Otis-Lennon Items at Two
Values of θ

Item	Estimated Information $\theta = -2$	Item	Estimated Information $\theta = 2$
2	.359	9	.563
15	.321	57	.346
14	.314	44	.294
18	.289	54	.225
19	.284	28	.228
26	.260	17	.217
4	.249	33	.201
36	.211	60	.191
10	.207	49	.186
27	.184	53	.118
40	.150	59	.118
29	.132	48	.112
22	.122	56	.110
13	.120	5	.102
21	.119	50	.095
7	.117	32	.094
11	.101	12	.090
1	.090	25	.085
47	.084	23	.079
8	.082	46	.068
34	.078	58	.059
58	.067	24	.058
16	.065	45	.058
		38	.055
		16	.051
		43	.049
		30	.046
		37	.042
		22	.037
		34	.037

	$\theta = -2$	$\theta = 2$
Total number of items	23	30
Sum of item information	4.005	4.014

The estimated TICs that result from treating the two sets of items that appear in Table 3.1.3 as separate tests are plotted in Figure 3.1.6. These curves show that a set of items can be useful for estimating ability in one range of θ but not another. The estimated TIC for all 49 items is also shown in Figure 3.1.6. Note that it is much easier to attain sufficient information for accurate ability estimates at intermediate values of θ than at $\theta = +2$ or -2.

There are interesting contrasts between the 49-item test developed using the IRT analysis and the 20-item test developed by traditional methods. Of course, substantial overlap exists in the two tests—there are 15 items in common—because the IRT test contains 49 items. However, the set of items selected on the basis of information at θ = -2 had only 2 items in common with the traditionally developed test, while the items selected due to their information at θ = $+2$ had 13 items in common. In fact, it can be seen in Tables 3.1.2 and 3.1.3 that the nine items providing the most information at θ = -2 were the same nine items that appeared in the initial item selection for the traditional scale but were discarded because they were too easy (high $\hat{p}$ values). It is apparent that desires for symmetrical score distribution can detract from accurate measurement at some θ values.

Summary

IRT and traditional approaches to scale development both require a pool of items that is larger than needed for the final version of the scale. Both methods require large samples of respondents for computing the item statistics that are used to select items and evaluate alternative forms of the final instrument.

There are important differences between IRT and traditional methods. The traditional approach is based on the relatively simple statistics of proportion right and item–total test score correlation; the cost associated with computing these statistics is low. The IRT approach is based on a more sophisticated theory and uses parameter estimation methods that require a high-speed computer. The traditional approach allows the test developer to construct a scale that has a specified internal consistency for the sample as a whole and a particular raw-score distribution. These properties of the scale or test can be expected to be obtained in future samples if development were based on large, representative samples of respondents and if future samples were randomly drawn from the same population. The IRT approach allows test developers to construct psychological scales with specified TICs. In particular, test information can be carefully controlled at points or intervals along the θ continuum corresponding to levels of θ where decisions—costly if wrong—must be made. The distribution of total test scores and internal consistency (i.e., coefficient α) are not explicitly considered. This is reasonable because an internal consistency estimate of test reliability refers to the average measurement accuracy of the scale throughout the entire score distribution. A scale can be developed with an acceptable level of internal consistency *for the scale as a whole,* yet fail to have sufficient information at important cutting scores or in important θ intervals. In this regard, it should be noted that the original JDI provides substantial information at $\theta = -.5$ but relatively little information at $\theta = 1.0$. This is appropriate for many purposes. Interventions are normally targeted toward dissatisfied employees rather than neutral or satisfied employees. For other innovative purposes, such as rewarding supervisors who have done a particularly good job on the human relations aspects of supervision, the information provided by the JDI may be deficient.

3.2 THE RELATION BETWEEN IRT ITEM PARAMETERS AND TRADITIONAL ITEM PARAMETERS

This section further illustrates relations that were discussed in Section 2.9. Under certain conditions, there are functional relations between IRT and traditional item parameters. The assumptions that must be made to derive precise relations between the two are difficult or impossible to realize in empirical data. Therefore, the results presented in this section are used to illustrate IRT concepts; they are not arguments for the interchangeability of indices or measurement theories.

Computation of $\hat{\theta}$

Estimation of the person parameter θ in IRT is frequently a source of confusion. One often-asked question is "How does $\hat{\theta}$ relate to total score?" Bivariate scatterplots presented in this section illustrate relations between the maximum likelihood estimate of θ, true score, and observed score.

For the two-parameter logistic model, the relation between total score and $\hat{\theta}$ can be seen in a plot of total scores and $\hat{\theta}$s for the 60 JDI items described in Section 3.1. Figure 3.2.1 shows the scatterplot of total score and $\hat{\theta}$ for 100 workers. The relation is decidedly nonlinear. At the tails of the scatterplot, there are wide ranges of $\hat{\theta}$ for the same or very similar total scores. Lord (1980) states that this "compression of a wide range of ability into one or two discrete values necessarily results in inaccurate measurement" (p. 49). The difference between total score and $\hat{\theta}$ results because total score depends only on the number of positive responses whereas $\hat{\theta}$ is a function of both the number of positive responses *and* characteristics of these items. For example, a positive response to an item with a low a_i is relatively discounted when computing $\hat{\theta}$, and a positive response to an item with a high a_i is given relatively more emphasis.

The solid line plotted in Figure 3.2.1 shows the (approximate) relation between true score and $\hat{\theta}$. In Section 2.9 it was shown that the true score associated with a given θ value is $\tau = \Sigma_{i=1}^{n} P_i(\theta)$. The esti-

Figure 3.2.1
JDI Total Score Plotted as a Function of $\hat{\theta}$

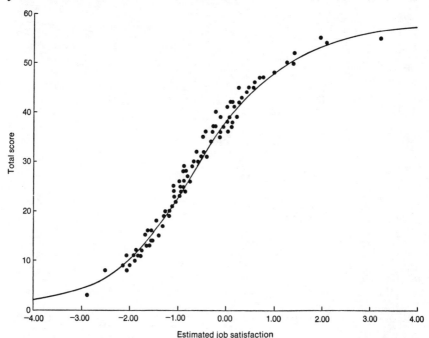

mated item parameters from Table 3.1.1 were used to compute the
true score corresponding to each $\hat{\theta}$ value. Note that the relation between true score and $\hat{\theta}$ is S-shaped.

A comparison between $\hat{\theta}$ and total score can also be made for the
three-parameter logistic model. The parameter estimates for 60 verbal
reasoning items shown in Table 3.1.3 were used to compute $\hat{\theta}$ for 100
francophone Canadian school children who were tested with the Canadian French version of the Otis-Lennon Intelligence Test. Figure
3.2.2 presents the scatterplot of total score and $\hat{\theta}$ for verbal reasoning.
Notice first that these points describe the same general relations obtained for the two-parameter logistic model. However, the scatter of
total score at a given $\hat{\theta}$ value is greater among low-ability examinees
than the scatter among moderate- to high-ability examinees. This
shows the effect of guessing, which is greatest at the lowest levels of
ability. In contrast, the scatter is relatively constant for all $\hat{\theta}$ values
shown in Figure 3.2.1. The relation between true score and $\hat{\theta}$ is
plotted as the solid line in Figure 3.2.2.

Item statistics.   The relations between IRT item parameters and
traditional item statistics are explored in this subsection. Some of

Figure 3.2.2
Otis-Lennon Total Score Plotted as a Function of $\hat{\theta}$

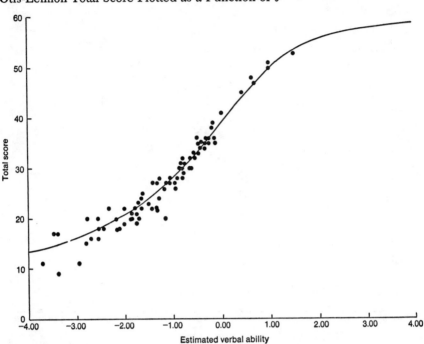

these relations can be illustrated by plotting parameter estimates from Table 3.1.1 and Table 3.1.2. As described in Section 3.1, $\hat{a}_i$ and $\hat{b}_i$ were obtained by LOGIST for 60 JDI items using a sample of 1,349 workers. The traditional statistics, $\hat{p}$, $\hat{r}_b$, and $\hat{r}_{pb}$, were also computed for this sample. Two items, 14 and 43, with bs that are very large in absolute value and have very large sampling errors are excluded in subsequent analyses.

The first comparison is between item difficulty indices. The plot of the points $(\hat{p}_i, \hat{b}_i)$ in Figure 3.2.3 shows a negative relation, which is expected because more difficult items have higher $\hat{b}$ values (and lower $\hat{p}$ values). There is also some scatter among $\hat{b}_i$ values for a given $\hat{p}$ value and nonlinearity at the extremes of the scale.

Turning to item discrimination, the points $(\hat{r}_b, \hat{a}_i)$ are plotted in Figure 3.2.4. Once again the scatter and nonlinearity are apparent. Note that there is more scatter in the $(\hat{r}_b, \hat{a}_i)$ plot than in the $(\hat{p}_i, \hat{b}_i)$ plot. This is expected because it is usually more difficult to estimate accurately a_i parameters than b_i parameters.

Plots of $(\hat{p}_i, \hat{b}_i)$ and $(\hat{r}_b, \hat{a}_i)$ for the Otis-Lennon data are not pre-

Figure 3.2.3
Estimated Item Difficulty ($\hat{b}_i$) Plotted as a Function of Proportion Correct
for 58 JDI Items

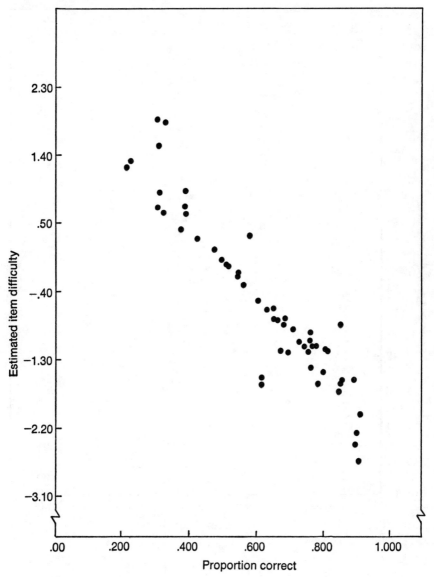

Figure 3.2.4
Estimated Item Discrimination ($\hat{a}_i$) Plotted as a Function of Biserial
Correlation for 58 JDI Items

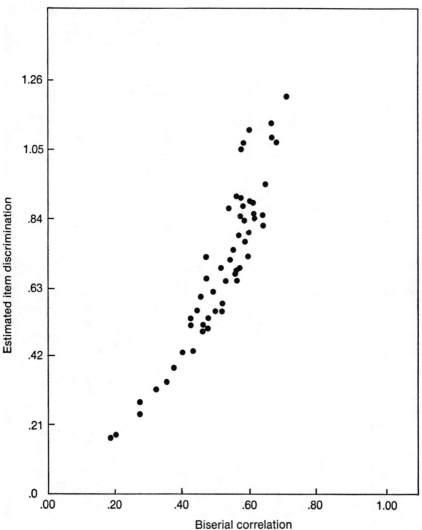

sented because they are similar to Figures 3.2.3 and 3.2.4. There is,
however, more scatter in the relation between $\hat{r}_b$ and $\hat{a}_i$ for the Otis-
Lennon data.

3.3 FACTORS THAT AFFECT PARAMETER ESTIMATION: EFFECTS OF SAMPLE SIZE, TEST LENGTH, IRT MODEL, AND MULTIDIMENSIONALITY

In applications of IRT, parameters can only be estimated; their true values are never observed. Consequently, it is important to understand what factors affect the accuracy of these estimates. In this section we begin by discussing the effects of sample size, test length, and the IRT model on parameter estimation.

Researchers usually must estimate item parameters and θs simultaneously. As noted in Section 2.6, there is not a mathematical proof that estimates of item and ability parameters obtained simultaneously become more accurate as test length (n) and sample size (N) increase. In this section, Monte Carlo research is described that shows estimates of a, b, and θ *do improve* as N and n increase, provided that there is a reasonable match between item difficulties and examinees' abilities.

Monte Carlo simulation studies used to investigate estimation accuracy usually begin by specifying a set of values for the a, b, and c parameters. Ideally, the (a, b, c) combinations realistically simulate actual items. Then, a distribution of ability is chosen. Responses by a simulated examinee are generated by sampling a θ from the ability distribution (this is actually done by a computer program that generates pseudorandom numbers in accordance with the previously selected ability distribution), and then generating a sequence of simulated item responses using θ and the item parameters. Finally, a program such as LOGIST uses the binary responses to estimate item and subject parameters. These estimated parameters are compared to the original "true" parameters. Results of several of these studies are described below.

The first of these two studies was conducted by Swaminathan and Gifford (1979). In this study, four test lengths (10, 15, 20, and 80) and three sample sizes (50, 200, and 1,000) were used to investigate accuracy of parameter estimation for the *three*-parameter logistic model. The measure of estimation accuracy used by Swaminathan and Gifford was the Pearson product moment correlation between true and estimated parameters.

Using a normal distribution of θ, Swaminathan and Gifford found that correlations between a_i and $\hat{a}_i$ ranged from $-.02$ for a 15-item test with 50 examinees to .88 for an 80-item test with 1,000 examinees. Correlations generally increased as sample size and test length increased, although there were some exceptions. In a skewed distribution of θ, the correlations between a_i and $\hat{a}_i$ ranged from near zero for all sample sizes with a test of 10 items to .82 for an 80-item test and

1,000 simulated examinees. The largest correlations for each test length occurred in the largest samples; smaller samples yielded generally poor results. In a uniform distribution of θ (on the interval -1.7 to 1.7), correlations for 10-, 15-, and 20-item tests were generally poor regardless of sample size. However, the $(a, \hat{a})$ correlation was .94 for an 80-item test with 1,000 examinees. The correlation was .73 for the 80-item test in a sample of 200 examinees.

The requirements for estimating b, in terms of sample size and number of items, are less severe. For a normal distribution of θ, a test with as few as 10 items and a sample of 50 examinees produced a correlation between b and $\hat{b}$ of .95. Longer tests and more examinees produced even larger correlations. Similar results were obtained for the skewed distribution of θ, although an extreme value of $\hat{b}$ occasionally occurred. For the uniform distribution of θ, a test with 10 items and a sample of 50 examinees resulted in a correlation between b and $\hat{b}$ greater than .80. Longer tests and larger samples generally produced $(b, \hat{b})$ correlations in excess of .95.

Swaminathan and Gifford did not compute correlations between c_i and $\hat{c}_i$ because a constant c_i (.25) was used throughout the study. In general, mean $\hat{c}$ values (across all test items) approached .25 as test length and sample size increased. In a similar study, Ree (1979) reported a correlation between c and $\hat{c}$ of .379 for a test of 80 items and a sample of 2,000 with normally distributed θs. The correlation was .233 with a skewed distribution of θs and .557 in a uniform distribution. Clearly, even long tests and large samples do not necessarily allow accurate estimation of c.

'The results of the preceding Monte Carlo studies show that accuracy of item parameter estimation in the three-parameter model will vary depending on which parameter is estimated. Swaminathan and Gifford's results are in general agreement with Lord's (1968) conjecture that as many as 50 items and 1,000 examinees may be required for accurate estimation of the a parameter of three-parameter logistic ICCs.

Although a close relation between parameters and parameter estimates surely indicates "good" estimation, this criterion may be overly stringent for some purposes. Linn, Levine, Hastings, and Wardrop (1981), for example, present two hypothetical items with vastly different a and b parameters that nonetheless have virtually identical ICCs in the θ interval $[-3.0, 3.0]$. Thus, ICCs may be relatively unaffected by large errors in the estimates of item parameters. This was the motivation for a study by Hulin, Lissak, and Drasgow (1982) that investigated the recovery of ICCs rather than the recovery of the a, b, and c parameters.

The difference between actual and estimated ICCs can be assessed by computing the squared distances between the curves at a number of points along the θ continuum. The squared distances are averaged, and then the square root is taken. This statistic, the root mean squared error (RMSE) of the recovered ICC is expressed as:

$$(3.3.1) \qquad \text{RMSE} = \sqrt{\frac{1}{m} \sum_{j=1}^{m} \left[\hat{P}_i(\theta_j) - P_i(\theta_j) \right]^2}$$

where $P_i(\theta)$ is the true ICC for item i; $\hat{P}_i(\theta)$ is the recovered ICC and is computed using the estimates $\hat{a}_i$, $\hat{b}_i$, and $\hat{c}_i$, and m is the number of θ points used in the sum. The RMSE can be interpreted as the approximate distance between true and recovered ICCs.

Hulin et al. investigated the effects of sample size, test length, and IRT model on the accuracy of recovered ICCs. They generated binary item response data for both the two- and three-parameter logistic models. Sixty sets of item parameters were selected by sampling bs from a uniform distribution on the interval $[-3.0, 3.0]$, and sampling cs (where applicable) from a uniform distribution on the interval $[.11, .33]$. The a_i parameters were generated by first sampling numbers x_i from a uniform distribution on the interval $[.3, 1.4]$ and then applying a power transformation: $a_i = x_i^{1.4}$. Two thousand θs were randomly sampled from a normal distribution with a mean of zero and a standard deviation of one.

Hulin et al. analyzed four tests of 15 items, two tests of 30 items, and one test of 60 items and four sample sizes (200, 500, 1,000, and 2,000) for each test length. The data sets for each model were input to LOGIST to estimate item parameters. The resulting parameter estimates were then used to compute the recovered ICCs for each data set. Each RMSE was computed by comparing a recovered ICC to its corresponding true ICC at 31 θ values chosen at equal intervals from -3.0 to $+3.0$. Finally, RMSEs were averaged over all 60 items in each test length–sample size combination.

Results for the *two*-parameter logistic model are displayed in Figure 3.3.1. With test lengths of 60 and 30 items and sample sizes of 500, 1,000, and 2,000, the average RMSEs are less than .05. In the 15-item tests with samples of 2,000 and 1,000, the RMSEs are slightly greater than .05. However, the 15-item tests with samples of 200 resulted in an average RMSE of nearly .09.

The results for the three-parameter model, displayed in Figure 3.3.2, are less impressive: The RMSEs are somewhat higher. For sample sizes of 2,000 and 1,000 and tests of 60 and 30 items, the average RMSEs are less than .06. The other combinations of sample sizes and

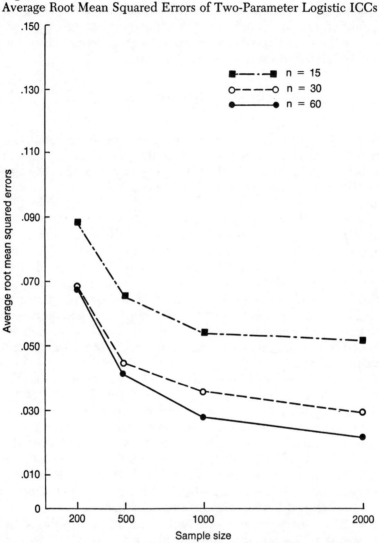

Figure 3.3.1
Average Root Mean Squared Errors of Two-Parameter Logistic ICCs

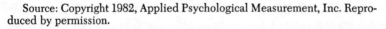

test lengths resulted in RMSEs that were marginally to substantially larger.

In another analysis, root mean squared errors of $\hat{\theta}$ and Pearson product moment correlations between true θ and $\hat{\theta}$ were computed. The correlations and RMSEs were computed using $\hat{\theta}$s that were less than 3.0 in absolute value. Only these $\hat{\theta}$s were used, because some $\hat{\theta}$s

Figure 3.3.2
Average Root Mean Squared Errors of Three-Parameter Logistic ICCs

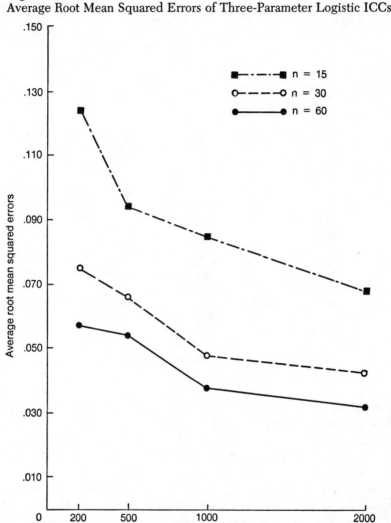

outside this interval were very large in magnitude and tended to distort correlations and RMSEs. The results for two- and three-parameter logistic item responses are presented in Table 3.3.1. For the two-parameter model, 30 items with any sample size down to 200 seem to be sufficient for accurate estimation of θ for most conditions ($r(\theta, \hat{\theta}) \geqslant$ .90). For the three-parameter model, the 60-item test with any sample

Table 3.3.1
Root Mean Squared Errors of $\hat{\theta}$, Correlations between θ and $\hat{\theta}$, and Proportions of $\hat{\theta}$ in -3 to $+3$ Interval

| | Number of Items | | | | | |
| | 60 | | 30 | | 15 | |
Sample Size	2-PL	3-PL	2-PL	3-PL	2-PL	3-PL
$N = 2{,}000$						
RMSE	.276	.377	.383	.529	.535	.744
$r_{\theta\hat{\theta}}$	.961	.928	.926	.860	.854	.739
Proportion	.985	.983	.995	.982	.990	.948
$N = 1{,}000$						
RMSE	.278	.377	.397	.534	.545	.771
$r_{\theta\hat{\theta}}$	.961	.927	.920	.860	.845	.718
Proportion	.994	.987	.999	.984	.987	.946
$N = 500$						
RMSE	.289	.373	.398	.570	.577	.806
$r_{\theta\hat{\theta}}$	.958	.929	.915	.834	.834	.696
Proportion	.990	.992	.994	.970	.987	.941
$N = 200$						
RMSE	.290	.351	.423	.548	.613	.849
$r_{\theta\hat{\theta}}$	.962	.936	.907	.845	.821	.654
Proportion	.990	.985	.990	.975	.978	.914

Source: Copyright 1982, Applied Psychological Measurement, Inc. Reproduced by permission.

size results in accurate estimation of θ. Tests of length $n = 30$ for the three-parameter logistic model and tests of length $n = 15$ for both the two- and three-parameter logistic models yield ability estimates with relatively large RMSEs and low $r(\theta, \hat{\theta})$. These ability estimates may not be sufficiently accurate for some purposes.

Before discussing the importance of these results, two limitations should be noted concerning the generalizability of these RMSEs. First, the assumption of a normally distributed θ may be reasonable in many situations, but it is unlikely that mean item difficulty would be exactly identical to the mean of the ability distributions. Hulin et al. found that when a θ distribution with a mean of $-.5$ was used, but with mean b still 0, the pattern of RMSEs remained about the same, but the RMSEs were slightly larger. The second limitation on the results of Hulin et al. occurs because the models they fit to their simulation data sets were perfectly appropriate. For example, they generated data by the two-parameter logistic model and then estimated parameters for this model. In practice, it is unlikely that there will be a perfect match between model and data: Actual ICCs are unlikely to be, say, two-parameter logistic ogives; the assumption of unidimensionality is unlikely to be perfectly satisfied; etc. Therefore, the RMSEs reported in Table 3.3.1 should be considered as lower limits to what one might find in practice, with larger RMSEs resulting to the extent that mean item difficulty is too high or too low for the examinee population and to the extent that there is misfit of the model to the data.

The results obtained by Hulin et al. indicate that the numbers of items and examinees required for estimation of parameters depends on the questions being asked. For questions that require the comparison of ICCs, such as item bias studies (the topic of Chapter 5) and the evaluation of scale translations into a foreign language (the topic of Chapter 6), the primary emphasis is on accurate estimation of ICCs. Apparently, large numbers of items are not needed for these kinds of studies. Not surprisingly, however, large numbers of subjects are necessary. Test lengths as short as 30 items, if combined with sample sizes of 500 examinees for two-parameter data or 1,000 for three-parameter data, appear sufficient for accurate estimation of ICCs. Larger samples yield more accurate estimates.

If an investigator is using IRT to answer a question that requires accuracy in θ estimation, then sample size and test length requirements are different. For instance, in adaptive testing, (described in Chapter 7) an estimate of θ is made following an individual's response to a block of items. New items are selected for presentation based on the most recent estimate of θ. The results of the study by Hulin et al. indicate that initial item calibration of long tests ($n = 60$) does *not* require large numbers of examinees: when $n = 60$ and $N = 200$, the correlation between θ and $\hat{\theta}$ was .96 and .94 for the two- and three-parameter logistic models, respectively. However, for the tests of length $n = 15$, test calibration samples of 500 and 200 examinees reduced the accuracy of $\hat{\theta}$.

The results also suggest there are tradeoffs between test length and sample size. Doubling test length and halving sample size, at least for tests of 30 and 60 items and sample sizes of 500, 1,000, and 2,000, resulted in comparable average RMSEs of estimated ICCs. Taken as a whole, the results suggest that hard and fast rules about minimum numbers of items and sample sizes are not appropriate, because requirements differ depending upon the questions being studied.

Effects of Multidimensionality

In the studies previously described in this section, the accuracies of parameter estimates obtained from LOGIST were examined for several test lengths and sample sizes using the two- and three-parameter logistic models. In the remainder of this section, some effects of violations of the assumption of a unidimensional latent trait space are described.

Actual data sets are unlikely to satisfy exactly the assumption of unidimensionality. One way in which this assumption can be violated is by clusters of items having higher within-cluster correlations than expected on the basis of a single latent trait. Clusters might result on a test of verbal ability from the use of various item types (paragraph comprehension, analogies, etc.) or on a scale measuring general job satisfaction, from the use of items that refer to various aspects of the job (co-workers, pay, supervision, etc.). Separate scales or subtests could be constructed from each cluster, but they would be moderately to highly correlated. This would occur because all test items are affected at least in part by a general latent trait. For example, responses to paragraph comprehension items, analogies, and sentence completion items are all influenced to some extent by the examinees' overall verbal ability.

It is useful to think of the influence of the general latent trait on the intercorrelations among the items as the prepotency of the general trait. At one extreme, the latent space is truly unidimensional. Here the intercorrelations among the items are solely due to the general latent trait. A verbal ability test that uses items stressing different kinds of content and formats (such as those mentioned above) could be thought of as corresponding to a situation where there is a small shift away from strict unidimensionality. In this case, each item might measure the general latent trait of verbal ability *and a specific ability* related to the content of the item (sentence completion, vocabulary, verbal analogies). Thus, both the general latent trait *and* the specific abilities would influence the intercorrelations of the items within the different content clusters. Only the general latent trait would influence the intercorrelations among the items selected from different content clusters. Thus, the items would correlate somewhat more highly within content clusters than they would between clusters.

The general trait assessed by a test of algebra achievement or by a collection of general job satisfaction items would likely be less prepotent than the general trait from a verbal ability test. The influence on the item intercorrelations by the specific traits measured by the different areas studied in algebra, or the different aspects of one's job, might be as strong or stronger than the general latent trait of algebra achievement or general job satisfaction.

Finally, it is possible to consider cases where there is no general trait: a general trait with zero prepotency. In these cases, the influence on the item intercorrelations would all come from the specific content areas. Thus we would expect sizable item intercorrelations within each content area but zero correlations between items from different content areas. These latter kinds of scales would lie at the opposite end of the prepotency continuum from the tests consisting of items all measuring the same general latent trait.

Drasgow and Parsons (1983) used five levels of prepotency of the general latent trait to simulate item response data with and without guessing. At one extreme were truly unidimensional data sets; at the other extreme were data sets with substantial multidimensionality. If subtests had been formed in the most highly multidimensional data sets by grouping clusters of items with high within-cluster correlations, the subtest intercorrelations would have ranged from .02 to .14, after correcting for the attenuation due to subtest unreliability.

All of Drasgow and Parsons's data sets had 50 simulated items, and responses to all items were influenced in part by a general latent trait. Drasgow and Parsons used *group factors* to cause clusters (or groups) of items to have within-cluster correlations higher than expected on the basis of the general latent trait. They used 5 group factors and 5 to 15 items per group factor. Thus clusters of from 5 to 15 items had higher than expected within-cluster correlations.

The extent to which violations of unidimensionality degrade IRT parameter estimates can be examined by inspecting the correlations between $\hat{\theta}$ and scores on the general latent trait. Drasgow and Parsons were able to compute these correlations, which cannot be computed for actual data sets, because scores on the general latent trait and group factors are known in a simulation study. They used LOGIST to (1) estimate parameters of the two-parameter logistic model for their data set without guessing, and (2) estimate parameters of the three-parameter logistic model for their data sets with guessing. Their results are shown in Table 3.3.2.

Data sets 1 and 6 were truly unidimensional. The correlations between $\hat{\theta}$ and the general latent trait would be 1.0 if there were no errors of estimation. The observed correlations, .96 and .94, indicate that the effects of errors of estimation are relatively small. The prepotency of the general trait in data sets 2 and 7 is quite high. Nonetheless, there is some multidimensionality in these data sets: if five subtests were formed from these item pools—one subtest for each group factor—the subtest intercorrelations would range from .68 to .90, after correcting for attenuations due to subtest unreliability. From Table 3.3.2, it is clear that LOGIST recovered the general latent trait because $\hat{\theta}$ was highly correlated with the general trait and virtually uncorrelated with the group factors.

The general latent trait has moderate prepotency in data sets 3 and 8. After correcting for subtest unreliability, subtest intercorrelations range from .46 to .60. The correlations between $\hat{\theta}$ and the general

Table 3.3.2
Correlations between Ability Estimates from
LOGIST and Scores on the General Latent Trait
and Group Factors

Data Set	General Latent Trait	Group Factor				
		1	2	3	4	5
Data sets with no guessing						
1	.96	—	—	—	—	—
2	.94	.04	.07	.17	.08	.05
3	.84	.32	.08	.15	.13	.15
4	.74	.46	.06	.14	.21	.22
5	.38	.77	.06	.04	.06	.08
Data sets with guessing						
6	.94	—	—	—	—	—
7	.91	.12	.03	.08	.10	.10
8	.83	.28	.04	.12	.14	.21
9	.72	.44	.13	.14	.08	.13
10	.35	.71	−.03	.02	.06	.15

Note: Correlations between group factors and ability estimates are zero for the truly unidimensional data sets 1 and 6. $N = 1,000$ for data sets without guessing, and $N = 1,500$ for data sets with guessing.
Source: Copyright 1982, Applied Psychological Measurement, Inc. Reproduced by permission.

latent trait are .84 and .83. These correlations are probably high enough for many practical purposes. Note, however, that the correlations of the first group factor with $\hat{\theta}$ are .32 and .28. The first group factor affects the largest number of items (15) of any of the group factors.

It is probably inappropriate to use IRT in data sets 4 and 9. About half the variance in $\hat{\theta}$ can be associated with the general latent trait, and about 20 percent can be associated with the first group factor. In these data sets, the correlations between subtests range from .25 to .39 after correcting for subtest unreliability. Finally, in data sets 5 and 10 it is clear that LOGIST has been drawn to the strongest group factor.

Summary. The importance of the study conducted by Drasgow and Parsons lies in its demonstration that LOGIST can tolerate a reasonable amount of heterogeneity. This suggests that applications of IRT are not limited to item pools assessing very narrow constructs. Instead, item pools for reasonably broad constructs can be developed and analyzed by IRT methods. In Section 8.5 we describe a method that can be used to determine whether a data set is too multidimensional for analysis by IRT.

REFERENCES

Campbell, D. T., & Fiske, D. Convergent and discriminant validation by the multitrait-multimethod matrix. *Psychological Bulletin*, 1959, 56, 81–105.

Cronbach, L. J. Coefficient alpha and the internal structure of tests. *Psychometrika*, 1951, 16, 297–334.

Cronbach, L. J., & Meehl, P. E. Construct validity in psychological tests. *Psychological Bulletin*, 1955, 52, 281–302.

Drasgow, F., & Parsons, C. K. Application of unidimensional item response theory models to multidimensional data. *Applied Psychological Measurement*, 1983, in press.

Drasgow, F., & Miller, H. Psychometric and substantive issues in scale construction and validation. *Journal of Applied Psychology*, 1982, 67, 268–279.

Guilford, J. P. *Psychometric methods*. New York: McGraw-Hill, 1954.

Hulin, C. L., Lissak, R. I., & Drasgow, F. Recovery of two- and three-parameter logistic item characteristic curves: A Monte Carlo study. *Applied Psychological Measurement*, 1982, 6, 249–260.

Kim, J.-O., & Mueller, C. W. *Introduction to factor analysis*. Beverly Hills, Calif.: Sage Publications, 1978. (a)

Kim, J.-O., & Mueller, C. W. *Factor analysis*. Beverly Hills, Calif.: Sage Publications, 1978. (b)

Linn, R. L., Levine, M. V., Hastings, C. N., & Wardrop, J. L. Item bias in a test of reading comprehension. *Applied Psychological Measurement*, 1981, 5, 159–173.

Lord, F. M. *Applications of item response theory to practical testing problems*. Hillsdale, N. J.: Erlbaum, 1980.

Messick, S. Constructs and their vicissitudes in educational and psychological measurements. *Psychological Bulletin*, 1981, 89, 575–588.

Nunnally, J. C. *Psychometric theory* (2d ed.). New York: McGraw-Hill, 1978.

Ree, J. M. Estimating item characteristic curves. *Applied Psychological Measurement*, 1979, 3, 371–385.

Smith, P. C., Kendall, L. M., & Hulin, C. L. *The measurement of satisfaction in work and retirement*. Skokie, Ill.: Rand McNally, 1969.

Swaminathan, H., & Gifford, J. A. *Estimation of parameters in the three-parameter latent-trait model*. Laboratory of Psychometric and Evaluation Research (Report No. 90). Amherst, Mass.: University of Massachusetts, School of Education, 1979.

Wood, R. L., Wingersky, M. S., & Lord, F. M. *LOGIST: A computer program for estimating examinee ability and item characteristic curve parameters* (Research Memorandum 76–6). Princeton, N.J.: Educational Testing Service, 1976.

4

Appropriateness Measurement

4.0 OVERVIEW

Test performance data can be summarized in an N row by n column matrix of zeros and ones indicating the incorrect and correct responses of N subjects or examinees to the n test items. As we have seen in Chapters 2 and 3, the response of any one subject to any specific item provides little evidence about the process underlying item responses and about the relevance of the item to the latent trait. A well-designed instrument administered to appropriate individuals does, however, have certain characteristics that can be examined through a careful consideration of the response matrix of 0's and 1's.

Two different perspectives can be taken when examining the response matrix: One can examine row vectors of responses to the n items individual by individual, or one can examine column vectors representing the N subjects' responses to items. The first method, examining an individual's responses to the n items, searches for patterns of responses that indicate deviance from expected patterns. Deviance is indicated, for example, when a high-ability individual misses many easy items, a low-ability examinee responds correctly to many difficult items, an examinee omits too many easy items, or an examinee appears to respond randomly throughout the test. Examining the *appropriateness* of a test score as a measure of ability for a given *individual* is the topic of this chapter.

The alternative view of the response matrix compares responses of identifiable *groups* of individuals to the same item. Here individuals of similar ability from different groups should have similar probabilities of responding correctly to a particular item. Items that do not have this property are said to be *biased;* methods for detecting biased items are the subject of Chapter 5.

Problems with test appropriateness occur because occasionally a test may fail to measure properly the characteristic of interest in a particular individual *even though the test provides excellent measurement for the group as a whole.* Standard methods for developing and assessing tests—for example, classical test theory and factor analysis—make little or no provision for the possibility that the latent trait of some individuals may only be poorly reflected in their test scores. We use the term *appropriateness measurement* (which was originally proposed by Levine and Rubin, 1979), to refer to any method of detecting individuals for whom test scores fail as measures of the latent characteristic of interest.

In Section 4.1 several types of inappropriate test scores are described. Three more or less heuristic procedures for appropriateness measurement are summarized in Section 4.2 and several IRT-based methods are presented in Section 4.3. Studies examining appropriateness measurement are reviewed in Section 4.4. Because appropriateness measurement is a recent development, emphasis is placed on thorough descriptions of all methods and empirical findings.

Appropriateness measurement provides a clear example of a problem that is difficult to address by traditional measurement procedures but is readily studied by IRT-based techniques. Item bias, discussed in Chapter 5, is another. Classical test theory and factor analysis are inherently group-based and do not provide measures of the fit of the model to a particular individual's responses. In contrast, an IRT explicitly states a formal model for the item responses of each individual. Consequently, the goodness of fit of the model to a particular individual's responses can be quantified and studied.

Many of the ideas presented in this chapter were originally proposed by Michael Levine. We have not provided citations for every idea of Levine's because many were communicated in personal conversations, seminars, and colloquia; an accurate reconstruction of these exchanges is impossible. Instead, we acknowledge his contributions to appropriateness measurement by noting that the use of IRT to study test-taking anomalies systematically was first proposed by Levine, and many subsequent developments in appropriateness measurement have been greatly influenced by his work.

4.1. EXAMPLES OF INAPPROPRIATE TEST SCORES

In this section several examples of inappropriate test scores are described. It is easy to think of more examples (which the reader is encouraged to do). The few presented here illustrate several important points. In each example, the test-taking anomaly produces an unusual pattern of responses: several correct responses to hard items and several incorrect responses to easy items. Currently available appropriateness measurement methods are limited to this type of testing problem. The reason for this limitation is made explicit in Section 4.3.

As a first example, consider the test performance of a hypothetical examinee with high ability but limited experience with machine scored tests. This individual's high ability is apparent in the first half of the test; correct responses are given to all easy and moderately difficult items as well as many of the most difficult items. After responding to all items on the first half of the test, the examinee decides to omit a particularly complex item. Upon solving the following item, the examinee forgets that the previous item was omitted. Thus, for the second half of the test, the examinee's response to the ith item is recorded as the $(i - 1)$th answer on the answer sheet, the $(i + 1)$th answer is recorded in the ith place, and so on. Due to time limits, the examinee does not reach the final items, and the mistake remains unnoticed.

It is apparent that the total score for this particular answer sheet substantially underestimates the examinee's ability. However, routine scoring of the answer sheet assigns a *spuriously low* score to the individual. Further, the inappropriate test score may be used in a college admissions or job selection decision.

Note that the pattern of responses made by the hypothetical examinee is atypical: There are many correct answers to difficult items on the first half of the test and many incorrect answers to easy items on the second half. Consequently, these item responses would not be very well fitted by an IRT model that assumes the probabilities of correct responses are functions of a single ability of the examinee.

In this example there is no bias inherent in the test, nor is this testing anomaly likely to occur systematically for a given individual or subpopulation. Because the anomaly is probably not stable and may not be related to group membership, it would go unnoticed by standard test scoring and item analysis procedures. Even the procedures to be discussed in Chapter 5 would not detect this problem.

Consider another example: An extemely creative examinee gives novel interpretations to some of the easier items on a test. Hoffman (1962) has criticized standardized intelligence tests as catering to those examinees who are not creative. Suppose the creative examinee provides correct answers to several difficult items. This indicates a higher than average ability. However, on first reading, the very easy items appear so trivial to this examinee (as the test developers intended) that the examinee reinterprets the items. Construed in this manner, the items may ask deep, challenging questions. Options that are usually scored as incorrect may now provide the best answer and, consequently, may be selected. Unfortunately, the test scorer will be unaware of the process generating the selection of the options and give the creative examinee a spuriously low score.

Again, total score is not a representative measure of the individual's ability. However, as in the earlier example, the examinee's answer sheet provides evidence that total test score is not a good measure of ability.

Spuriously high scores may result from cheating. *Newsweek* (Sewall, Drake, & Lee, 1980) reports that, in a recent survey on four college campuses, one out of three students admitted cheating at least once. With such widespread acceptance among the potential examinee population coupled with the importance of test scores for career opportunities, cheating may be a serious problem. Recently, the *American Journal of Nursing* (1979) reported that 12,000 Nursing Board examinees in New York were reexamined because Nursing Board officials had received numerous anonymous letters alleging that test booklets were available two weeks prior to the test date for prices ranging from $300 to $2,000. In such large-scale incidents, there is a tremendous cost associated with massive reexamination. It would be a great benefit to all parties if a means were available for identifying a subset of examinees who were more likely than others to have previewed the exam.

Again, there may be evidence of cheating in the examinee's pattern of responses. It is not likely that all cheaters, either those who occasionally glance at a neighbor's exam or those with a test preview, will achieve perfect scores on the test. The length of most aptitude tests probably prevents complete memorization of all items by an examinee. Careful vigilance by test proctors should preclude precise reproduction of a neighbor's answer sheet. It is more likely that an examinee may copy or memorize answers to blocks of items. The resulting answer sheet for a low-ability examinee may appear to have been generated by a bizarre process: Blocks of correct responses are intermixed with blocks of responses that are nearly all incorrect. This type of response pattern is quite different from that of the general exam-taking population and may be detectable by appropriateness measurement.

Incidents of *tampering* with answer sheets have also been reported. In his study of bias in mental testing, Jensen (1980) states that some school teachers admitted that they completed students' tests. The teacher would simply record the correct response on the answer sheet whenever the student had skipped or failed to reach the item. Such efforts add an unknown degree of error to measurement and also are likely to produce atypical patterns of responses.

The list of possible measurement anomalies could continue. Rather than further belabor the point, we assert that failures of tests to measure ability are not routinely sought, studied, or identified. An examinee who receives a spuriously high score may cause a more deserving candidate to be denied admission to an educational program or entry into an organization. Truly qualified examinees with spuriously low scores may also be denied admission. Costs to organizations include those associated with both selecting possibly unqualified applicants and rejecting qualified applicants.

4.2 HEURISTIC METHODS FOR APPROPRIATENESS MEASUREMENT

In this section we describe three procedures that can be used to identify individuals for whom test scores are inappropriate measures of a latent trait. As each of the three procedures is described, the reasoning that underlies the method should be both apparent and compelling. However, the lack of a theoretical foundation for each method should also be obvious. This is primarily a weakness of traditional measurement theory. In Section 4.3, model-based appropriateness measurement methods are described that have strong theoretical justifications.

Ghiselli's prediction of predictability. In many applied prediction problems, one or more predictor variables are used to predict one or more criterion variables. For example, analyses of SAT scores used to predict first-year grade point average (GPA) consistently show correlations in the range of .30 to .50. Similar correlations often result when occupational success is predicted from test scores (Ghiselli, 1966). Since prediction is less than perfect, errors in admission and selection decisions occur. Ghiselli (1960) sought to reduce these errors by identifying individuals for whom test scores failed to predict accurately criterion performance. Thus, Ghiselli's methods were not explicitly designed for the purposes of appropriateness measurement but may nonetheless be so used.

Consider the relation between one predictor and one criterion appearing in Figure 4.2.1. Let Y_j denote GPA and X_j denote SAT total score for the jth individual. The least squares regression line, $\hat{Y}_j = a + bX_j$, provides the standard means of predicting criterion scores from predictor scores. From the scatter of points around the line, it is obvious that some criterion scores lie quite close to the regression line (points A, E, G, and K, for example) and others are quite distant (points C, F, I, and M). The distance between actual and predicted criterion score for subject j is

$$(4.2.1) \qquad \delta_j = |Y_j - \hat{Y}_j|.$$

Figure 4.2.1
Hypothetical Plot of Grade Point Average and SAT Total Score

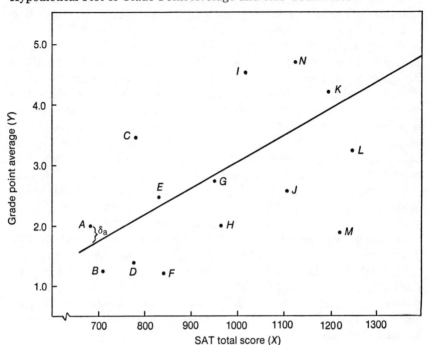

Ghiselli attempted to find another variable, Z, that was related to δ. Such a variable, called a "predictor of predictability," could be used to identify individuals who are likely to have large errors of prediction.

In three studies, Ghiselli (1963) used the 64-item forced choice, Self-Description Inventory (SDI) to develop a predictor variable, X. Supervisory ratings of job performance of factory workers, foremen, and executives served as criterion variables in the three studies. In each of the three studies, Ghiselli followed the same procedure. Initially, the total sample was divided into two subsamples, termed the *derivation* sample and the *cross-validation* sample. In the derivation sample, Ghiselli computed δ for each individual, and then used item analysis to identify a subset of the 64 SDI items that discriminated between predictable (low values of δ) and unpredictable (high values of δ) individuals. These items formed the predictor of predictability variable, Z. Ghiselli then used Z in the cross-validation sample to predict which individuals should be predictable. By excluding individuals predicted to be unpredictable, Ghiselli found that the validity of the predictor variable, X, was substantially increased in all three studies. This result confirmed previous research (Ghiselli, 1960) that had used students as subjects.

One difficulty with prediction of predictability is that the predictability variable appears to be very situation specific (Ghiselli, 1963; Brown & Scott, 1966; Wiggins, 1973). Consequently, a new predictor of predictability must be developed for each application of Ghiselli's method. This is both time-consuming and costly. A second problem with the method is that the predictability variable is developed by purely empirical methods; the only theory involved in the research lies in specifiying the original item pool. As a result, the substantive processes underlying the unpredictability of some individuals may not be revealed. Finally, developing a predictability variable is sometimes difficult. Brown and Scott, for example, reported three studies in which they were unable to develop predictability variables.

Jacobs's weighted average. Jacobs (1963) presented a statistic that can be construed as a quantitative estimate of response pattern atypicality (although this was not his original intent). We shall call such statistics *appropriateness indices.* Jacobs's index is obtained by first ordering test items from least difficult to most difficult and then separating the items into quintiles. Jacobs's appropriateness index score for an individual is

$$(4.2.2) \qquad \mathcal{J} = \frac{M_2 + 2M_3 + 3M_4 + 4M_5}{X}$$

where M_k is the number of correct responses to items in the kth quintile for that examinee and

$$(4.2.3) \qquad X = \sum_{k=1}^{5} M_k .$$

$\mathcal{J}$ can vary from zero to four. $\mathcal{J}$ is zero when all the correct responses made by an examinee are in the first quintile, so that the numerator of Equation 4.2.2 is zero and the denominator is greater than zero. If an examinee only responds correctly to items in the fifth quintile, then the numerator of Equation 4.2.2 is four times as large as the denominator. Relatively high scores on this index indicate that an examinee has correctly answered many difficult items while incorrectly answering many easy items. Thus, a high $\mathcal{J}$ score indicates response pattern atypicality.

The data presented in Table 4.2.1 can be used to illustrate Jacobs's appropriateness index. In this table, the items have been ordered by difficulty level so that items 1 and 2 form quintile 1, items 3 and 4 form quintile 2, items 5 and 6 form quintile 3, items 7 and 8 form quintile 4,

Table 4.2.1
Simulated Responses of Two Hypothetical Examinees to a
10-Item Test

Item	Proportion of Correct Answers in Norming Sample	ETS Δ	Examinee 1	Examinee 2
1	.80	9.64	1	0
2	.75	10.32	1	1
3	.65	11.44	1	1
4	.60	11.96	1	0
5	.50	13.00	1	1
6	.40	14.04	1	1
7	.35	14.56	0	1
8	.30	15.08	1	0
9	.25	15.68	0	1
10	.20	16.36	0	1

Note: Proportion correct was used to sort items into quintiles on the basis of their difficulty for the $\mathcal{F}$ index. The ETS Δ statistic is used when computing Donlon and Fischer's (1968) personal biserial correlation.

and items 9 and 10 form quintile 5. Examinee 1 has a response pattern that appears normal. Here 2, 2, 2, 1, and 0 items in difficulty levels 1, 2, 3, 4, and 5, respectively, have been answered correctly. Therefore, the numerator of Equation 4.2.2 is $0(2) + 1(2) + 2(2) + 3(1) + 4(0) = 9$, and X is simply the total number right, which is 7. Thus, for examinee 1, $\mathcal{F}$ = 1.29.

The responses for examinee 2 were generated by a two-stage experiment. In the first stage, a coin was flipped. The results of the first stage were used to select the response process simulated in stage two. If a head was obtained in stage one, a random response to a four-item multiple-choice item was generated in stage two (i.e., the probability of a simulated correct response was .25, and the probability of a simulated incorrect response was .75). If a tail was obtained in stage one, the item was scored as correct. The responses generated by this process can be interpreted as simulating a very low-ability examinee who has been given the answers to half of the items on a test or who copies half of the answers from a very high-ability neighbor.

For examinee 2, there are 1, 1, 2, 1, and 2 correct responses in the five quintiles. Consequently,

$$\mathcal{F} = \frac{1 + 2(2) + 3(1) + 4(2)}{1 + 1 + 2 + 1 + 2}$$

$$= 2.29,$$

which is substantially larger than the index value of the simulated normal examinee.

There are a number of problems with $\mathcal{J}$ as an appropriateness index. First, categorizing items into quintiles loses information about item difficulty; presumably a more powerful appropriateness index would result if the information regarding item difficulty were not discarded. Second, the weighting in Equation 4.2.2 is arbitrary: there is no evidence to indicate the particular weights (0, 1, 2, 3, and 4) used by Jacobs are optimal. A third problem is that, in effect, $\mathcal{J}$ is a measure of the average difficulty of items answered correctly by an examinee (where all items in the first quintile have difficulties of zero, all items in the second quintile have difficulties of one, etc.). Consequently, examinees who answer more items correctly should tend to have higher $\mathcal{J}$ values. Jacobs found correlations between $\mathcal{J}$ and total test score that ranged from .58 to .85 for several SAT-V and SAT-M tests. Thus, $\mathcal{J}$ should *not* be used as an appropriateness index to compare examinees with different total test scores. All three of these difficulties occur because $\mathcal{J}$ is only a heuristic measure.

Donlon and Fischer's personal biserial. Donlon and Fischer (1968) proposed a statistic that was explicitly designed to be an appropriateness index. Donlon and Fischer's index, the *personal biserial correlation,* reflects the similarity between item difficulties as experienced by a particular individual and the item difficulties in a norming sample.

To derive the personal biserial correlation, an examinee's right and wrong answers, scored 1 and 0 respectively, are taken as the *observed* measures of item difficulties *for that examinee.* Then it is assumed that there is a latent variable, Y, which underlies the examinee's observed item responses and is normally distributed across items.[1] This assumption, stated less formally, asserts that the difficulty the examinee experiences in solving items (not the pattern of 1s and 0s) is normally distributed across items. If the perceived item "easiness" is greater than some threshold value, the examinee responds correctly; otherwise an incorrect response is made. Finally, it is assumed that across items there is a linear regression of difficulties experienced by a norm group onto the difficulties experienced by a particular examinee. Given these assumptions, the personal biserial correlation can be computed as the biserial correlation (see Chapter 8) between the examinee's pattern of 0s and 1s and item difficulties in the norm group.[2]

The personal biserial correlation can also be derived from the assumption that Y and the observed group-based item difficulties follow

---

[1] Actually, Y is an item "easiness" variable.

[2] Both *personal* biserial correlations and *item-total* biserial correlations are computed as biserial correlations. A personal biserial is computed across items for one person whereas an item-total biserial is computed across people for one item.

a bivariate normal distribution. Although Donlon and Fischer (1968) did not discuss this point, they apparently found that the group-based *proportion correct* index of item difficulty was not normally distributed. Consequently, Donlon and Fischer transformed the proportion-correct measure of item difficulty to another measure that should follow a distribution that is more similar to the normal distribution. They used the "Education Testing Service delta" (ETS Δ) measure of item difficulty that is defined as

$$\Delta_i = 4\Phi^{-1}(1 - \hat{p}_i) + 13,$$

where $\hat{p}_i$ is the proportion correct on item i in the test norming sample, and Φ^{-1} is the inverse normal transformation that transforms a probability value into a normal deviate with unit variance. The delta for an item is then "that value on the baseline of a normal curve with mean 13.0 and standard deviation 4, above which the area under the curve is equal to the proportion passing the item among those who reach it" (Donlon & Angoff, 1971, p. 23). Note that if values of p_i are evenly spread throughout the interval from zero to one, then Δ_i will be normally distributed.

The equation Donlon and Fischer used to compute the personal biserial correlation is

(4.2.4) $$r_{\text{perbis}} = \frac{\bar{\Delta}_r - \bar{\Delta}_c}{s_\Delta} \frac{k}{h},$$

where $\bar{\Delta}_r$ is the mean Δ for items reached, $\bar{\Delta}_c$ is the mean Δ for items answered correctly, s_Δ is the standard deviation of Δ across all items reached, k is the number of correct answers given by the examinee divided by the number of items reached, and h is the height of the standard normal curve (i.e., ordinate of the $N(0, 1)$ density function) at the point dividing the area under the curve into sections with areas k and $(1 - k)$. Equation 4.2.4 can be obtained from formulas given by McNemar (1969, pp. 218–219).

The information contained in Table 4.2.1 can be used to illustrate the personal biserial correlation. For examinee 1,

$\bar{\Delta}_r = (9.64 + 10.32 + \ldots + 16.36)/10 = 13.21$

$\bar{\Delta}_c = (9.64 + 10.32 + 11.44 + 11.96 + 13.00 + 14.04 + 15.08)/7$
$\quad = 12.21$

$s_\Delta = \{[(9.64 - 13.21)^2 + (10.32 - 13.21)^2 + \ldots + (16.36 - 13.21)^2]/10\}^{1/2} = 2.18$

$k = 7/10 = .7$

$h = .348$, because a z-score of .52 separates the area under the normal curve into two sections with area .7 and $(1 - .7)$, and the height of the curve is .348 at this z-score.

Thus

$$r_{\text{perbis}} = \frac{13.21 - 12.21}{2.18} \frac{.7}{.348} = .92$$

for examinee 1. This very high correlation indicates that the pattern of item difficulties experienced by examinee 1 is quite similar to the pattern seen in the norming sample.

For the aberrant responses simulated for examinee 2, we see

$$\bar{\Delta}_c = 13.63$$
$$k = .7$$
$$h = .348$$

with $\bar{\Delta}_r$ and s_Δ unchanged. Then

$$r_{\text{perbis}} = \frac{13.21 - 13.63}{2.18} \frac{.7}{.348} = -.39.$$

This indicates that the pattern of item difficulties for examinee 2 is *inversely* related to the item difficulties in the norming group. Thus, the personal biserial succeeds in detecting the aberrant responses.

Fischer (1970) investigated the personal biserial for two samples of college freshmen using SAT data. In particular, Fischer hypothesized that the multiple correlation would be significantly increased by adding personal biserial correlations for the SAT-V and SAT-M as two additional predictor variables to a regression equation that predicted college GPA from high school average, SAT-M, and SAT-V. Despite large sample sizes ($N = 437$ and 532), Fischer found that treating the personal biserial coefficients as predictor variables failed to increase significantly the multiple correlation.

For two reasons we do not believe that Fischer's method for examining the personal biserial provided a valid evaluation of this index. First, Fischer considered whether the personal biserial *predicted* GPA. However, it is more appropriate to think of the personal biserial as *moderating* the relation between SAT scores and the criterion, rather than *predicting* the criterion (see Wiggins, 1973, chap. 2). That is, relations between test score and criterion should be stronger for those with high personal biserials. Consequently, Fischer has only performed the first step of Zedeck's (1971) procedure for testing moderator variables: showing that the moderator variable is not directly related to the criterion. The crucial test involves testing the *interaction* between the moderator and predictor variables. The interaction is tested by comparing the multiple correlation from the equation

(4.2.5) $\widehat{\text{GPA}} = a + b_1(\text{H.S. Ave.}) + b_2(\text{SAT-V}) + b_3(\text{SAT-M})$

to the multiple correlation from the equation

(4.2.6)
$$\widehat{GPA} = a + b_1(\text{H.S. Ave.}) + b_2(\text{SAT-V}) + b_3(\text{SAT-M})$$
$$+ b_4[(\text{SAT-V})(r_{\text{perbis}} \text{ for SAT-V})]$$
$$+ b_5[(\text{SAT-M})(r_{\text{perbis}} \text{ for SAT-M})].$$

Unfortunately, Fischer did not test Equation 4.2.6 against Equation 4.2.5.

From our thinking about appropriateness measurement, we are not convinced that testing the variance accounted for by Equation 4.2.6 against the variance accounted for by Equation 4.2.5 for statistical significance is a fair means for evaluating the personal biserial as a measure of inappropriateness. Nor, for reasons that will be discussed below in Section 5.1, should we expect different test score–criterion correlations for groups of individuals with high and low personal biserials: Correlations are extremely insensitive to departures from linearity, individual differences in appropriateness, and bias. In addition, we suspect that only a very small percentage (perhaps 3 to 5 percent) of SAT scores are truly inappropriate measures of ability. For the individuals affected, the consequences can be profound. However, we believe the vast majority of individuals' test scores are appropriate, and for these individuals Equation 4.2.6 should be no better than Equation 4.2.5. Methods more sensitive than differences in correlations must be used to examine the effectiveness of appropriateness indices. We shall discuss one such approach in Section 4.4.

Summary. The appropriateness indices discussed in this section are heuristic in the sense that they were not derived from some theory of psychological measurement. Instead, they reflect various *intuitions* concerning the properties of normal and aberrant response patterns. Without a theory of measurement, it is difficult or impossible to characterize precisely the properties of normal response patterns. Consequently, departures from normal response patterns are not always evident. In the next section, theory-based appropriateness indices are described.

4.3 IRT-BASED APPROPRIATENESS MEASUREMENT

In this section, three distinct classes of IRT-based appropriateness indices are presented. The first two classes, the ℓ_o and Gaussian model classes, were developed and studied by Levine and his associates (Levine & Rubin, 1979; Levine & Drasgow, 1982a; Drasgow, Levine, & Williams, 1982; Drasgow, 1982a; Parsons, in press). The squared standardized residual, the third class of indices, was developed by Wright (Wright, 1977; Wright & Stone, 1979). Empirical research examining the indices developed by Levine is summarized in Section 4.4.

The ℓ_o class of appropriateness indices. As Levine and his colleagues have studied this class of indices, they have made a series of revisions in the index that were designed to improve its properties. We shall describe each of these indices and the intuitions that motivated each revision.

The rationale for the ℓ_o indices is closely associated with one idea that motivates maximum likelihood estimation. As noted in Section 2.6, the purpose of maximum likelihood estimation is to select as parameter estimates those values that make a given data set appear most likely. The intuition that guided Levine and his associates is: Suppose there is no value of θ that makes the likelihood of a particular examinee's responses large. Then the IRT used in test norming and ability estimation is inappropriate for this individual, and it is unlikely that test score is a representative measure of ability. All the examples of inappropriate test scores described in Section 4.1 can produce response vectors for which no value of θ yields a relatively large value of the likelihood function. An ℓ_o index would detect such response vectors, and thus function as an appropriateness index in the desired fashion.

The first and simplest of the ℓ_o indices studied by Levine and Rubin and Levine and Drasgow (1982a) is

(4.3.1) $\ell_o = \log \max_{\theta} \mathrm{Prob}(\mathbf{U}|\theta) = \log \mathrm{Prob}(\mathbf{U}|\hat{\theta}),$

where $\mathbf{U}$ is a vector of item responses, $\mathrm{Prob}(\mathbf{U}|\theta)$ is the likelihood function discussed in Section 2.6 and $\hat{\theta}$ is the maximum likelihood estimate of θ. Note that ℓ_o is just the natural logarithm of the maximum of the likelihood function.

The artificial data in Table 4.3.1 can be used to illustrate ℓ_o. For simplicity, assume that both examinees in Table 4.3.1 have the same maximum likelihood estimate of ability (as they would if the IRT model under consideration were the one-parameter logistic model) and the probabilities of correct and incorrect responses are as given in the table. Then the maximum of the likelihood function for examinee 1 is

$$\mathrm{Prob}(\mathbf{U}|\hat{\theta}) = (.9)(.7)(.5)(.7)(.9)$$
$$= .198,$$

and

$$\ell_o = \log(.198) = -1.62.$$

Table 4.3.1
Response Vectors and Response Probabilities for
Two Hypothetical Examinees

			Examinee	
Item	$P_i(\hat{\theta})$	$1 - P_i(\hat{\theta})$	1	2
1	.9	.1	1	0
2	.7	.3	1	0
3	.5	.5	1	1
4	.3	.7	0	1
5	.1	.9	0	1

In contrast, the maximum of the likelihood function for examinee 2 is

$$\text{Prob}(\mathbf{U}|\hat{\theta}) = (.1)(.3)(.5)(.3)(.1)$$
$$= .00045,$$

and ℓ_o is -7.71.

It is clear that ℓ_o succeeds in detecting the aberrant response pattern of examinee 2. More generally, ℓ_o will be a negative number that is relatively large in magnitude for any response vector with many correct responses to hard items and incorrect responses to easy items. These values of ℓ_o result because the many correct responses to hard items indicate θ cannot be low and, simultaneously, the incorrect responses to easy items indicate that θ cannot be high.

As described in Section 4.4, ℓ_o detects aberrant response vectors surprisingly well. Note, however, that there is no explicit provision in ℓ_o for omitted responses. When omitted items were present, Levine and Drasgow (1982a) computed ℓ_o for answered items and ignored omits. For tests in which examinees omit varying numbers of items, however, comparing values of ℓ_o may be misleading. This is because an examinee who answers more items than another examinee will be likely to have a response vector with a smaller ℓ_o value and *appear* more aberrant. To see this, rewrite the logarithm of the likelihood equation as

(4.3.2)
$$\ell_o = \log \text{Prob}(\mathbf{U}|\theta)$$
$$= \sum_i \log \text{Prob}(u_i|\theta).$$

Because the logarithm of any number between zero and one is negative, $\log \text{Prob}(u_i|\theta)$ is negative for every item that is answered. Thus, smaller values of ℓ_o should result for examinees who answer more items.

To improve the ℓ_o index, Drasgow (1982a) computed ℓ_o for all items answered, and then calculated the geometric mean likelihood,

(4.3.3) $$\ell_g = \exp(\ell_o/n),$$

where n is the number of items attempted by the examinee. Equation 4.3.3 expresses the likelihood of a response vector as the geometric mean likelihood across answered items. Clearly, a small value of ℓ_g indicates an atypical response vector.

Some properties of the ℓ_o and ℓ_g indices can be observed from examining Table 4.3.2, which contains response vectors for three hy-

Table 4.3.2
Response Vectors and Response
Probabilities for Three Hypothetical
Examinees

Item	$P_i(\hat{\theta})$	$1 - P_i(\hat{\theta})$	Examinee 1	2	3
1	.90	.10	1	1	*
2	.70	.30	1	1	0
3	.50	.50	0	0	*
4	.30	.70	1	1	1
5	.10	.90	0	0	*
6	.61	.39	*	1	0
7	.39	.61	*	0	*
Items Answered			5	7	3

* Item was omitted.

pothetical examinees. Again, assume that all examinees have identical maximum likelihood estimates of θ. First, note that ℓ_o for examinee 1 is

$$\ell_o = \log[(.9)(.7)(.5)(.3)(.9)] = -2.46,$$

and for examinee 2,

$$\ell_o = \log[(.9)(.7)(.5)(.3)(.9)(.61)(.61)] = -3.45.$$

Thus, ℓ_o indicates that the response pattern of examinee 2 is more atypical than the response pattern of examinee 1. This result is misleading because the response patterns of examinees 1 and 2 are identical across the items answered by examinee 1, and examinee 2 made the most probable responses on items 6 and 7. For examinee 3,

$$\ell_o = \log[(.3)(.3)(.39)] = -3.34,$$

which indicates that the response vector of examinee 2 is *more atypical* than the response vector of examinee 3. Again this is misleading.

The geometric mean likelihood for examinee 1 is

$$\ell_g = \exp(-2.46/5) = .61.$$

For examinee 2, ℓ_g is also .61, and ℓ_g is .33 for examinee 3. The value of ℓ_g as an appropriateness index is apparent: Examinees 1 and 2 have comparable index scores, while examinee 3 has a substantially lower index score. The effect of the differential omitting rates has been eliminated by transforming ℓ_o to ℓ_g.

Both ℓ_o and ℓ_g can be misleading if examinees at different ability levels are compared. Drasgow, Levine, and Williams (1982) showed that the expected value of ℓ_o and ℓ_g varies as a function of θ. Let

$$\hat{P}_{ik} = \text{Prob}(u_i = k|\hat{\theta}), \qquad k = 0, 1,$$

denote the probabilities of incorrect ($k = 0$) and correct ($k = 1$) responses for an examinee with estimated ability $\hat{\theta}$. Then Drasgow et al. showed

(4.3.4) $$E(\ell_o) \doteq \sum_i [\hat{P}_{i1} \log \hat{P}_{i1} + \hat{P}_{i0} \log \hat{P}_{i0}].$$

Since the $\hat{P}_{ik}$ are functions of $\hat{\theta}$, it is clear that $E(\ell_o)$ depends upon ability level.

The dependence of ℓ_o on θ is illustrated in Figure 4.3.1. This figure is based on item parameters estimated by Drasgow (1979), who fit the one- and three-parameter logistic models to the GRE-V test. Item parameters were estimated by LOGIST and BICAL in a sample of 2,470 examinees. The expectation of ℓ_o was approximated by Equation 4.3.4.

The relation between $E(\ell_o)$ and θ is approximately symmetric for the one-parameter logistic model. In part, this is because ICCs for the one-parameter logistic model have lower asymptotes of zero and upper asymptotes of unity. The three-parameter logistic model, in contrast, has nonzero lower asymptotes. As a result, the relation between $E(\ell_o)$ and θ is asymmetric.

The importance of noting the relation between θ and $E(\ell_o)$ can be seen by considering an examinee with estimated ability $\hat{\theta} = 3.0$ and a three-parameter logistic model ℓ_o of -35.0. Compared to other examinees at this ability level, an ℓ_o of -35.0 is quite low and indicates response vector atypicality. Compared to examinees of moderate ability (θ near zero), however, an ℓ_o of -35.0 is quite high and seems to indicate a very good fit of the model to the response vector. Of course, the former interpretation should be adopted.

Figure 4.3.1
Expectation of ℓ_o as a Function of θ

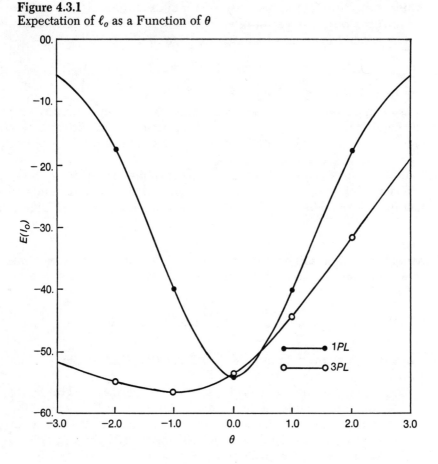

Drasgow et al. derived an approximation for the variance of ℓ_o for examinees of ability θ, which can be used in conjunction with Equation 4.3.4 to *standardize* ℓ_o. Their approximation is

$$(4.3.5) \qquad \mathrm{Var}(\ell_o) \doteq \sum_i \hat{P}_{i1} \hat{P}_{i0} [\log(\hat{P}_{i1}/\hat{P}_{i0})]^2.$$

Then, ℓ_o can be standardized by

$$(4.3.6) \qquad \ell_z = \frac{\ell_o - E(\ell_o)}{[\mathrm{Var}(\ell_o)]^{1/2}}.$$

Furthermore, Drasgow et al. found that the distribution of ℓ_o was approximately normal for the SAT-V, which consisted of 85 items.

Var(ℓ_o) can be computed for those items that are answered. Then use of ℓ_z allows comparisons among index scores for examinees answering different numbers of items. In addition, ℓ_z eliminates the

Table 4.3.3
Item Responses and Response Probabilities for a Hypothetical
Examinee

Item	$P_i(\hat{\theta})$ $= \hat{P}_{i1}$	$1 - P_i(\hat{\theta})$ $= \hat{P}_{i0}$	Item ℓ_o Expectation	Item ℓ_o Variance	Response
1	.9	.1	−.325	.434	1
2	.7	.3	−.611	.151	1
3	.5	.5	−.693	.000	0
4	.3	.7	−.611	.151	1
5	.1	.9	−.325	.434	0

dependence upon θ, so that index scores for examinees at different ability levels can be compared.

The data in Table 4.3.3 can be used to illustrate the ℓ_z index. For item 1, the expectation of ℓ_o is

$$E(\ell_o) \text{ for item } 1 \doteq \hat{P}_{11} \log \hat{P}_{11} + \hat{P}_{10} \log \hat{P}_{10}$$
$$= .9 \log(.9) + .1 \log(.1)$$
$$= -.325,$$

and the variance of ℓ_o is

$$\text{Var}(\ell_o) \text{ for item } 1 \doteq \hat{P}_{11}\hat{P}_{10}[\log(\hat{P}_{11}/\hat{P}_{10})]^2$$
$$= (.9)(.1)[\log(.9/.1)]^2$$
$$= .434.$$

Across the five-item test, the expectation of ℓ_o is

$$E(\ell_o) \doteq -.325 - .611 - .693 - .611 - .325$$
$$= -2.565,$$

and the variance of ℓ_o is approximately

$$\text{Var}(\ell_o) \doteq .434 + .151 + 0 + .151 + .434$$
$$= 1.170.$$

The value of ℓ_o for this examinee is −2.46, and

$$\ell_z = \frac{-2.46 - (-2.565)}{(1.170)^{1/2}} = .097.$$

Thus, the fit of the model used to estimate θ is quite near the expected fit.

Appropriateness indices based on the Gaussian model. As described in Chapter 2, the latent trait θ is usually assumed to be unidimensional. Levine and Rubin (1979) refer to IRT models employing a single latent-trait dimension as "standard models." Levine and Rubin developed an alternative model where a new ability level, θ_i, is sampled for each item, i. For example, in a 60-item test, Levine and Rubin's model allows 60 distinct values of θ. These θs are assumed to be independently sampled from a normal distribution with mean θ_0 and variance σ_g^2. Levine and Rubin called this model the *Gaussian model*.

To describe how the Gaussian model might aid in detecting unusual response patterns, consider again the low-ability examinee who manages to copy occasional answers from high-ability neighbors. The low-ability examinee's answer sheet contains some item responses that accurately reflect his or her ability and some that reflect the abilities of neighboring examinees. In this case, an item response model that allows varying levels of ability should fit the observed response pattern better than a standard model with a single ability level throughout the test.

Methods for estimating examinee parameters of the Gaussian model are presented by Levine and Dragow (1982b). In essence, they first estimate ICCs for a standard logistic model using LOGIST. Then they write the likelihood of a vector of item responses as a function of θ_0, σ_g^2, and the individual θ_i. The θ_i can be integrated out of the likelihood equation, leaving

$$l_n = \log \text{Prob}\,(\mathbf{U}|\theta_0,\,\sigma_g^2)\,.$$

Finally, θ_0 and σ_g^2 can be estimated using numerical methods.

Levine and Rubin (1979) suggested two appropriateness indices based on the Gaussian model. The first is the logarithm of the likelihood ratio comparing a Gaussian model to its corresponding standard model:

$$(4.3.7) \qquad\qquad LR = l_n - \ell_o.$$

For ICCs of a given form (e.g., three-parameter logistic), the Gaussian model will fit a response vector *at least as well as the standard model*. This is because the standard model is the limiting case of the Gaussian model where $\sigma_g^2 = 0$. To the extent that a varying-ability model provides a better fit than a constant-ability model, l_n will be greater than ℓ_o and a large value of LR will result. Values of l_n should be substantially larger than l_o for the types of aberrant test taking described in Section 4.1.

The second index obtained from the Gaussian model is the estimate, $\hat{\sigma}_g^2$, of the variance of the θ_i distribution. This index should be near zero when the major determinant of a vector of responses is a single ability. If other factors influence the examinee's responses (cheating, misunderstanding directions, etc.), then $\hat{\sigma}_g^2$ should be greater than zero.

Wright's squared standardized residual. Wright (1977) suggested that the fit between a model and an examinee's responses can be assessed by examining the differences between the model's probabilities of correct responses and the examinee's pattern of correct and incorrect responses. In particular, the *residual* on item i is

$$R_i = u_i - P_i(\theta),$$

where u_i is 1 or 0 and $P_i(\theta)$ is the probability of a correct response.

The residuals are aggregated across items to obtain a measure of test appropriateness for a particular individual. However, the R_i must first be standardized. Standardizing is useful because it makes the residual terms more comparable across items. Adding unstandardized residuals to obtain an appropriateness index is analogous to adding grade point average (on a four-point scale) and GRE total score to obtain a measure of academic competence. The variance of grade point average is much less than the variance of GRE total scores; consequently these two terms should be standardized before they are combined. Similarly, the residuals R_i should be standardized before they are added.

To standardize R_i, we must obtain its mean and variance. The expectation of R_i is approximately zero because

$$E(u_i) = P_i(\theta) \doteq P_i(\hat{\theta}).$$

The variance of u_i can be obtained from the well-known formula for the variance of a binomial:

$$\begin{aligned} \text{Var}(u_i) &= P_i(\theta)\,[1 - P_i(\theta)] \\ &\doteq P_i(\hat{\theta})\,[1 - P_i(\hat{\theta})]. \end{aligned}$$

Thus, the standardized residual for item i is

$$(4.3.8) \qquad SR_i = \frac{u_i - P_i(\hat{\theta})}{[\text{Var}(u_i)]^{1/2}}.$$

Wright's squared standardized residual is

$$(4.3.9) \qquad W = \sum_i SR_i^2.$$

Wright stated that W follows an appropriate chi-square distribution, with $(n - 1)(N - 1)/N$ degrees of freedom. Here N refers to the number of individuals in the test norming sample, and n refers to the number of items on the test. W assumes a particularly simple form for the one-parameter logistic model:

$$(4.3.10) \quad W = \sum_i \{u_i \exp[-D(\hat{\theta} - b_i)] + (1 - u_i) \exp[D(\hat{\theta} - b_i)]\}.$$

Table 4.3.4 illustrates Wright's squared standardized residual for the one-parameter logistic model. For examinee 1,

$$W = .03 + .18 + 1.00 + .18 + .03 = 1.42,$$

and the squared standardized residual for examinee 2 is

$$W = 30.08 + 5.48 + 1.00 + 5.48 + 30.08 = 72.12.$$

Table 4.3.4
Item Difficulties, Item Responses, and Squared Standardized Residuals for
Two Hypothetical Examinees with $\hat{\theta} = 1.0$

				Examinee	
Item	b_i	$exp[-D(\hat{\theta} - b_i)]$	$exp[D(\hat{\theta} - b_i)]$	1	2
1	−1.0	0.03	30.08	1	0
2	0.0	0.18	5.48	1	0
3	1.0	1.00	1.00	1	1
4	2.0	5.48	0.18	0	1
5	3.0	30.08	0.03	0	1

W is relatively small for the examinee who answered the three easiest items correctly and responded incorrectly to the two most difficult items. In contrast, the aberrant response pattern of examinee 2 yields a much larger value of W. Thus relatively large values of W are associated with unusual response vectors, and W can be used as an appropriateness index.

Summary. If item parameters have already been estimated, the appropriateness indices presented in this section can be computed at very little cost. For example, the most sophisticated index in the ℓ_o class, ℓ_z, costs perhaps a penny to compute. The Gaussian model indices are more expensive: both can be obtained for approximately 5 to 10 cents.

The ℓ_o class of indices provides a good example of how theory-based measurement allows careful evaluation of the properties of an appropriateness index. Equation 4.3.4 gives the mean of the ℓ_o index, Equation 4.3.5 gives the variance, and Drasgow et al. (1982) have shown that the index approximately follows a normal distribution. Using these results it is possible to compute ℓ_z, which approximately follows a standardized normal distribution. Similar analyses for heuristic appropriateness indices such as the personal biserial are difficult or impossible.

4.4 INVESTIGATION OF IRT-BASED APPROPRIATENESS INDICES

In this section, we review the research and results of Levine and his colleagues. Their studies have carefully assessed the strengths and weaknesses of a number of appropriateness indices. Taken as a whole, these studies have moved from examining appropriateness measurement via Monte Carlo simulation, to research using actual responses of examinees. None of the appropriateness indices studied by Levine and his colleagues has yet been implemented by a testing organization. Applications of appropriateness measurement methods by practitioners should occur in the near future for reasons noted in Chapter 1 and discussed in Chapter 9.

Design of Appropriateness Measurement Studies. The studies conducted by Levine and his colleagues have more or less followed one experimental design. For convenience, this design is presented here.

The studies begin with a test norming sample that consists of N examinees' responses (either real or simulated) to n items. Item parameters for a test model are estimated using the test norming sample. These item parameter estimates are used to estimate ability and compute appropriateness indices throughout the rest of the study.

A normal sample consists of response vectors that are considered to have been generated by the test model under consideration. Here each subject's responses to the n items are contained in a vector that consists of 0s and 1s indicating incorrect and correct responses. For simulated response vectors, the process used to generate the data is known and the normal sample can truly be "normal" (in the sense that the test model perfectly matches the data simulation process). In contrast, the processes underlying an actual examinee's responses are not known. Consequently, a normal sample of actual examinees consists of a set of response vectors *assumed* to be normal. Note that unidentified aberrant examinees in the normal sample will cause an appropriateness index to appear less effective than if the normal sample consisted entirely of normal response vectors.

There are two types of samples of aberrant response vectors: spuriously high and spuriously low samples. An examinee with a spuriously high test score is simulated by randomly selecting k percent of the examinee's original responses without replacement and rescoring these responses as correct. An examinee with a spuriously low score is simulated by first randomly selecting k percent of the examinee's responses without replacement and then replacing original responses with random responses. For five-option, multiple-choice items, there is a .2 probability that the random response will be correct and a .8 probability that it will be incorrect.

Appropriateness indices are then computed for the normal and aberrant response vectors. The effectiveness of an index is evaluated by examining the extent to which it can separate normal and aberrant response vectors *solely on the basis of appropriateness index scores.*

Receiver operating characteristic (ROC) curves are used to illustrate index effectiveness. Basically, an ROC curve displays the probabilities of correctly identifying aberrant response vectors at various false-alarm rates, where a false alarm is defined as the incorrect classification of a normal response vector as aberrant. An ROC curve is obtained by first specifying a value, t, of the appropriateness index. This value is sometimes called a cutting score. Then the proportions of examinees with index values less than t are determined in the normal and aberrant sample (assuming that small index values indicate aberrance). Let

$x(t)$ = proportion of normal response vectors with index scores $\leq t$

$y(t)$ = proportion of aberrant response vectors with index scores $\leq t$

Plotting the $< x(t), y(t) >$ pairs for several values of t produces an ROC curve. An ROC curve that indicates a good detection of aberrance is one that rises sharply from the origin to the upper left hand corner of the plot. Because the base rate for normal examinees will probably be much higher than the base rate for aberrant examinees, our interest in the ROC curve lies in the detection rates (i.e., values of y) at low false-alarm rates (i.e., low values of x).

As an example of drawing an ROC curve, imagine that the following values of ℓ_z were obtained for a normal sample of 10 response vectors and a spuriously low sample of 10 response vectors:

Normal		Spuriously Low	
2.25	1.00	−0.21	0.09
0.55	0.22	0.27	−0.89
−1.20	−0.31	−0.80	−1.33
−1.21	0.35	−1.83	0.56
0.79	0.64	−1.18	−1.98

It is convenient to sort each set of index scores into ascending order (i.e., from most aberrant to least aberrant). Here,

Normal	−1.21	−1.20	−0.31	0.22	0.35	0.55	.064
	0.79	1.00	2.25				

Spuriously Low:	−1.98	−1.83	−1.33	−1.18	−0.89	−0.80	−0.21
	0.09	0.27	0.56				

The choice of cutting scores is arbitrary to some extent. It is important to use enough cutting scores so that the ROC curve accurately represents the detectability of aberrant response vectors. For the present example, let us use cutting scores of $-2.00, -1.90, \ldots, 2.30$. A larger number of cutting scores would be used in an actual appropriateness measurement study.

When $t = -2.00$, the proportion of normal examinees with index scores less than or equal to t is 0. Thus $x(-2.00) = 0$. Similarly, $y(2.00) = 0$. Therefore, the first ROC curve point is (0,0). The next ROC curve point is (0, .10) because $x(-1.90) = 0$ (no normal response vector is misclassified as spuriously low) and $y(-1.90) = .10$ (1 of 10 spuriously low response vectors is classified as spuriously low). The ROC curve point obtained from $t = -1.80$ is (0, .20). When $t = -1.70$, we see $x(-1.70) = 0$ and $y(-1.70) = .20$. Because we have already obtained the ROC curve point (0, .20) for $t = -1.80$, it is not necessary to plot the same point again.

The ROC curve points obtained by this process are

(0, 0)	(.30, .70)
(0, .10)	(.30, .80)
(0, .20)	(.40, .90)
(0, .30)	(.50, .90)
(.20, .30)	(.60, 1.00)
(.20, .40)	(.70, 1.00)
(.20, .60)	(.80, 1.00)
(.30, .60)	(.90, 1.00)
	(1.00, 1,00)

The ROC curve corresponding to these ROC curve points is plotted in Figure 4.4.1. A diagonal line is also plotted to serve as a reference. An ROC curve lying along the diagonal indicates that detection of aberrance is no better than chance.

The ROC curve in Figure 4.4.1 is jagged due to the very small sample sizes (10 values of ℓ_z for both normal and aberrant groups). ROC curves for larger samples are usually much smoother.

Levine and Rubin (1979). The first large scale IRT appropriateness measurement study was conducted by Levine and Rubin. They investigated the ℓ_o, LR, and $\hat{\sigma}_g$ indices using artificial data generated according to the three-parameter logistic model for an 85-item test with five multiple-choice options per item. Levine and Rubin bypassed test norming and instead used the exact (simulation) parameters to compute appropriateness indices. Spuriously high and spuriously low examinees were simulated by the 4, 10, 20 and 40 percent spuriously high and spuriously low modifications.

Figure 4.4.1
Example of an ROC Curve

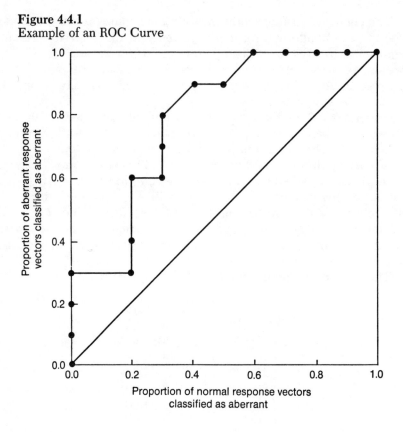

Figure 4.4.2 presents Levine and Rubin's results for the *LR* index computed in *spuriously low* samples. As expected, tampering with more items increases detectability. Note that the 4 and 10 percent modifications are not especially detectable. The results for the ℓ_o and $\hat{\sigma}_g$ indices were quite similar to results for the *LR* index and, consequently, are not shown here.

Levine and Rubin recomputed the *LR* ROC curve for the 20 percent spuriously low modification using only response vectors that had more than 10 percent of the item responses changed due to tampering (i.e., more than eight item responses were changed). This ROC curve is shown in Figure 4.4.3. Detection rates for this sample are very good.

The results of applying the $\hat{\sigma}_g$ index in the *spuriously high* sample are shown in Figure 4.4.4. Note that detection rates are excellent for the 40 percent modification and very good for the 20 percent treatment. Results similar to these were obtained for the other appropriateness indices.

Figure 4.4.2
ROC Curves for the *LR* Appropriateness Index for
the Spuriously Low Modification

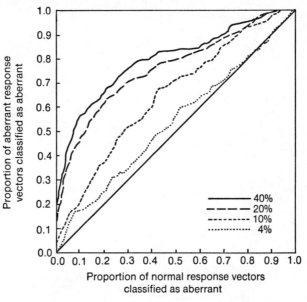

From "Measuring the Appropriateness of Multiple-Choice
Test Scores" by M. V. Levine and D. F. Rubin, *Journal of
Educational Statistics*, 1979, *4*, 279.

The importance of the Levine and Rubin study lies in its demonstration that IRT-based appropriateness indices can achieve very high
rates of detection of aberrant response vectors. These detection rates
were achieved under ideal conditions: Simulation parameters (and
not parameter estimates) were used to compute appropriateness indices, and the IRT model used to compute indices perfectly matched
the model by which the item responses were generated. The research
conducted by Levine and Drasgow (1982a) continued and extended
Levine and Rubin's work by determining whether currently available
IRT models and estimation techniques were adequate for applications
of appropriateness measurement to actual data sets.

Levine and Drasgow (1982a).   These researchers began by reana-
lyzing some of Levine and Rubin's simulated data. In particular, they
used LOGIST to estimate item parameters from Levine and Rubin's
normal sample of 2,800 simulated examinees. Then ℓ_o was computed
for the normal response vectors and for the 20 percent spuriously low,
large-score-change sample.[3] The ROC curve based on ℓ_o computed

---

[3] Note that here the normal and norming samples are identical.

Figure 4.4.3
ROC Curve for the *LR* Appropriateness Index for 102
Spuriously Low Response Vectors with Nine or More
Item Responses Changed in the 20 Percent
Spuriously Low Modification

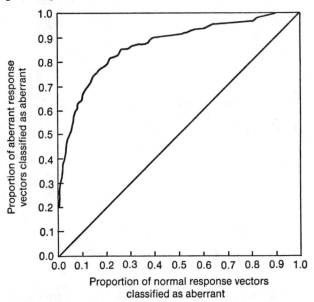

Proportion of normal response vectors
classified as aberrant

From "Measuring the Appropriateness of Multiple-Choice
Test Scores" by M. V. Levine and D. F. Rubin, *Journal of
Educational Statistics, 1979, 4,* 285.

from *estimated* item parameters was virtually identical to the ROC
curve in Figure 4.4.3. Thus, estimating item parameters in a large
sample of normal response vectors did not degrade appropriateness
measurement.

In their next study, Levine and Drasgow investigated the effects of
including unidentified aberrants in the test norming sample. Using
Levine and Rubin's simulation data, they combined 2,800 normal response vectors with 200 spuriously low response vectors (20 percent
modification) to form the test norming sample. Item parameters were
again estimated by LOGIST, and ℓ_o was computed for all response
vectors. The ROC curve for the large-score-change, spuriously low
sample was again nearly identical to Figure 4.4.3. Consequently, it is
apparent that unidentified aberrant response vectors in the test norming sample do not necessarily affect appropriateness measurement.

Because they had obtained uniformly positive results using simulation data, Levine and Drasgow next examined the ℓ_o and *LR* indices
using actual SAT-V data. The most important issue addressed here
lies in determining whether the three-parameter logistic model is suf-

Figure 4.4.4
ROC Curves for the $\hat{\sigma}_g$ Index for the Spuriously High
Modification

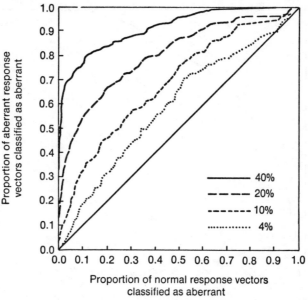

From "Measuring the Appropriateness of Multiple-Choice
Test Scores" by M. V. Levine and D. F. Rubin, *Journal of
Educational Statistics*, 1979, *4*, 284.

ficiently descriptive of actual examinees' responses to allow detection
of aberrant response vectors.

Levine and Drasgow selected 3,000 examinees who had responded
to at least 90 percent of the SAT-V items and used LOGIST to estimate item parameters. An aberrant sample was created by applying
the 20 percent spuriously low modification to 200 examinees from the
test norming sample. Then ℓ_o and *LR* were computed for the 2,800
normal examinees and the 200 spuriously low examinees. Again,
results for the ℓ_o and *LR* indices were very similar. Figure 4.4.5 indicates that aberrant response vectors are detectable, at least among
examinees with low omitting rates.

In summary, the Levine and Drasgow investigations are important
because they showed that appropriateness measurement can be implemented in samples of SAT-V examinees with low omitting rates,
using the three-parameter logistic model and LOGIST.

Drasgow (1982a). In this research a number of theoretical and
applied issues concerning appropriateness measurement were examined. They included:

1. Estimation of item parameters for the three-parameter logistic

Figure 4.4.5
ROC Curve for Levine and Drasgow's ℓ_o Index for the 20 Percent
Spuriously Low Modification

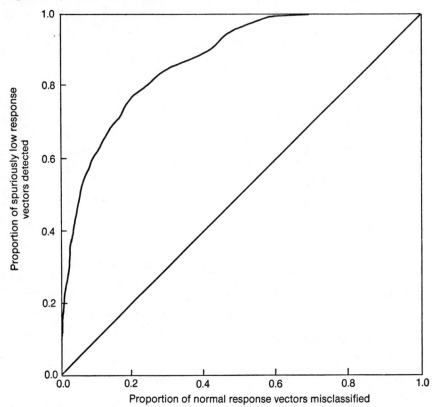

model. Wright (1977) has argued that, despite its psychometric virtues, parameter estimation for the three-parameter logistic model is impossible. The one-parameter model, in contrast, has optimal statistical properties but seems psychometrically inappropriate for multiple-choice items. Drasgow empirically investigated the adequacy of item parameter estimation by comparing the power of appropriateness indices based on the three-parameter logistic model to indices based on the one-parameter logistic model. In addition, Donlon and Fischer's (1968) personal biserial was compared to the IRT-based appropriateness indices.

2. *Explicit comparison of appropriateness indices.* In previous studies, detection rates among the various appropriateness indi-

ces were not directly compared. Drasgow evaluated the relative statistical powers of the indices.

3. *Sample size.* Lord (1968) indicated that samples of perhaps 1,000 examinees are necessary to estimate the three-parameter logistic model's item parameters. Drasgow compared the effectiveness of appropriateness indices based on item parameters estimated in samples of 500 and 3,000 examinees.

4. *Appropriateness measurement generality.* Levine and Rubin (1979) developed and evaluated appropriateness indices using simulated SAT-V data. Drasgow used GRE-V data to investigate the possibility of systematic differences between the SAT-V and GRE-V.

The experimental design used by Drasgow closely follows the design previously described. Item parameters were estimated in norming samples of 500 and 3,000 GRE-V examinees. The spuriously low sample included 200 examinees with GRE-V scores from 600 to 630 prior to tampering. Twenty items on the 95-item test were subjected to the spuriously low modification. The spuriously high sample was composed of 115 examinees with GRE-V scores from 420 to 460 prior to tampering. The spuriously high modification was also performed on 20 items.

Drasgow took several steps to ensure fair comparisons between the various indices. First, only examinees with low omitting rates were selected for the normal and aberrant samples. Second, the ℓ_g index was used to control further the effects of differential omitting rates. Finally, the ability distributions of the aberrant samples were examined after tampering. The two distributions were found to be quite similar; consequently, a single normal sample with a comparable ability distribution was selected. Control for the relation between ℓ_g and θ is accomplished by choosing a normal sample such that its ability distribution matches a corresponding aberrant sample.

Detection rates for the spuriously low sample and the test norming sample of 3,000 are presented in Table 4.4.1. Note that (1) detection rates for indices based on the three-parameter logistic model are consistently higher than detection rates for the corresponding one-parameter logistic indices; (2) all IRT-based indices have detection rates substantially higher than the personal biserial; and (3) it is very difficult to ascertain which of the three-parameter logistic indices is most effective.

Table 4.4.2 presents results for the spuriously low sample when appropriateness indices were computed using parameter estimates obtained from the test norming sample of 500. The detection rates in this table are remarkably similar to the rates presented in Table 4.4.1, which were obtained using the norming sample of 3,000. The finding

Table 4.4.1
Proportions of Spuriously Low Response Vectors
Detected

Model	Index	Proportion of Normal Response Vectors Misclassified as Aberrant				
		.02	.04	.06	.08	.10
1-PL	ℓ_g	.16	.35	.51	.55	.61
	$\hat{\sigma}_g$	.20	.42	.53	.58	.62
	LR	.19	.37	.50	.59	.63
3-PL	ℓ_g	.22	.43	.54	.65	.68
	$\hat{\sigma}_g$	.21	.49	.58	.67	.72
	LR	.22	.43	.53	.65	.72
	r_{perbis}	.13	.27	.38	.42	.59

Note: Appropriateness indices were computed using item parameters estimated in the norming sample of 3,000 examinees.

Table 4.4.2
Proportions of Spuriously Low Examinees Detected

Model	Index	Proportion of Normal Response Vectors Misclassified as Aberrant				
		.02	.04	.06	.08	.10
1-PL	ℓ_g	.15	.33	.51	.53	.60
	$\hat{\sigma}_g$	.19	.43	.54	.57	.62
	LR	.19	.36	.52	.59	.63
3-PL	ℓ_g	.20	.40	.53	.63	.65
	$\hat{\sigma}_g$	.22	.48	.56	.65	.70
	LR	.24	.41	.48	.61	.67

Note: Appropriateness indices were computed using item parameters estimated in the norming sample of 500 examinees.

that appropriateness measurement was not seriously degraded when item parameters were estimated in a norming sample of 500 examinees is surprising: much larger sample sizes are usually suggested. Investigations in still smaller samples are needed to determine the minimum sample size required for appropriateness measurement.

Results for the spuriously high sample using parameter estimates obtained from the test norming sample of 3,000 are presented in Table 4.4.3. These detection rates are poor, which indicates spuriously high examinees are *not* detectable for the GRE-V using the indices studied

Table 4.4.3
Proportions of Spuriously High Response Vectors
Detected

Model	Index	Proportion of Normal Response Vectors Misclassified as Aberrant		
		.033	.067	.100
1-PL	ℓ_g	.07	.22	.27
	$\hat{\sigma}_g$	.04	.19	.26
	LR	.04	.19	.30
3-PL	ℓ_g	.06	.19	.30
	$\hat{\sigma}_g$	.03	.22	.27
	LR	.07	.18	.27
	r_{perbis}	.09	.15	.31

Note: Appropriateness indices were computed using item parameters estimated in the norming sample of 3,000 examinees.

by Drasgow. This result is quite different from Levine and Rubin's excellent detection rates for simulated SAT-V item responses. An explanation lies in an important difference between the SAT-V and GRE-V exams: The SAT-V has many more difficult, discriminating items with *low* lower asymptotes (i.e., small c_i values) than does the GRE-V. Spuriously low examinees are detectable *if they miss items they should answer correctly with high probability,* and spuriously high examinees are detectable *only if they correctly answer several items they should miss with high probability.* Consequently, a low-ability examinee who answers several hard SAT-V items correctly is indicated to be aberrant. The GRE-V has very few difficult, discriminating items with low c_i values; thus, spuriously high examinees are difficult to detect. These results show that *the types of aberrance detectable depend upon the characteristics of the items that compose the test.*

Drasgow's results provide insights into the previously described issues concerning appropriateness measurement. For example, Tables 4.4.1 and 4.4.2 clearly indicate that problems of estimation for the three-parameter logistic model have been overstated, at least with respect to appropriateness measurement. However, the differences between indices based on the one- and three-parameter models are not so large that we unequivocally advocate the three-parameter model under all circumstances. For example, a researcher may wish to investigate the correlation between test score and some personality trait for theoretical purposes. If the researcher believes that it is important to delete examinees with inappropriate test scores, it is unlikely that the decision regarding the selection of the one- or three-parameter model would affect the correlation. Here simplicity and cost indicate that the one-parameter model should be selected. In applied work where test scores affect individuals' careers and educations, we believe that optimal methods for aberrance detection should be used. Drasgow's work indicates that the three-parameter logistic model provides superior aberrance detection for the GRE-V.

Tables 4.4.1 through 4.4.3 show that the differences among indices in aberrance detection are small. Because the indices based on the Gaussian model ($\hat{\sigma}_g$ and LR) are substantially more expensive to compute than an ℓ_o class index, practitioners may wish to use the latter type of index. A practical problem with the ℓ_o and ℓ_g indices is that they suffer from a statistical dependence upon θ; the ℓ_z index does *not* have this problem. Finally, Drasgow's results concerning detectability of spuriously low examinees is quite similar to the findings of Levine and Rubin (1979) and Levine and Drasgow (1982a).

Drasgow, Levine, and Williams (1982). This study had three broad, yet interrelated objectives. First, Drasgow et al. explicitly studied the properties of the ℓ_o index. As described in Section 4.3, they derived approximate expressions for the mean (Equation 4.3.4) and variance (Equation 4.3.5) of ℓ_o, and showed that ℓ_o approximately follows a normal distribution.

The problems caused by differential omitting rates were the second focus of the Drasgow et al. research. In particular, how should omitted and not-reached items be handled by an appropriateness index? In the studies described above, the problem caused by omitting was sidestepped by restricting the normal and aberrant samples to include only examinees with low omitting rates. However, in practical applications, it is clear that an appropriateness index score should be computed for each examinee.

The third objective of this research involved the use of a *polychotomous* test model for appropriateness measurement. Scoring omitted and not-reached items as a separate response category might solve the omits problem. In addition, a polychotomous test model may provide better aberrance detection by identifying individuals whose patterns of *incorrect* responses are very atypical. Note that the types of spuriously low aberrance discussed in Section 4.1 all yield atypical incorrect option selections as well as atypical patterns of correct and incorrect responses.

Drasgow et al. developed an index analogous to ℓ_z for polychotomous test models. Let p_o denote the logarithm of the maximum of the polychotomous model's likelihood function. In addition, let $\hat{P}_{ij}$ denote the estimated probability of selecting option j of the ith multiple-choice item for an examinee with estimated ability $\hat{\theta}$. Then Drasgow et al. showed that

$$(4.4.1) \qquad E(p_o) \doteq \sum_i \sum_j \hat{P}_{ij} \log \hat{P}_{ij},$$

and

$$(4.4.2) \qquad \mathrm{Var}(p_o) \doteq \sum_i \left[\sum_j \sum_k \hat{P}_{ij} \hat{P}_{ik} \log \hat{P}_{ij} \log(\hat{P}_{ij}/\hat{P}_{ik}) \right].$$

Thus, p_o can be standardized to yield p_z, which approximately follows a normal distribution.

Drasgow et al. used the polychotomous histogram model, which was described and illustrated in Section 2.8. Option characteristic curves (OCCs) were obtained by linearly interpolating proportions between median estimated abilities in adjacent categories. The lines connecting proportions for each option in Figure 2.8.1 illustrate linear interpolation. To determine the probability of selecting option j for an examinee with estimated ability $\hat{\theta}$, Drasgow et al. merely computed the height of the line above $\hat{\theta}$ that connected proportions for option j.

Drasgow et al. used SAT-V data in their study. Histograms for each of 85 items were constructed from the responses of 49,470 examinees, using 25 ability strata. The three-parameter logistic model was used as the dichotomous test model throughout this study.

In preliminary analyses it was found that examinees who omitted more than 35 percent of the test items, or who reached less than 77 percent of the test items, typically had very small p_z index values. For example, in one sample of 500 examinees, the 6 examinees who reached less than 77 percent of the test items had a mean p_z score of -3.08. Drasgow et al. concluded that these two categories of examinees actually constituted groups of examinees with aberrant response patterns, because these examinees did more than simply omit many items: They omitted *too many easy items*, or items with very effective distractors. If these examinees had attempted more items, in all likelihood their test scores would have increased substantially. Excluded from all subsequent analyses, therefore, were examinees who omitted more than 35 percent of the test or reached less than 77 percent of the test items.

Detection rates for the ℓ_z and p_z indices were then compared. As expected, it was found that p_z substantially increased detectability of spuriously low response vectors. For example, among examinees who had moderately high estimated ability ($0.24 < \hat{\theta} < 0.80$) prior to the 30 percent spuriously low modification, p_z detected 59 percent of the aberrant sample at the cost of a 3 percent false-alarm rate; ℓ_z detected 35 percent at this false-alarm rate.

Drasgow et al. found that spuriously high examinees who had low to moderate ability prior to tampering were very detectable by the ℓ_z index. (Again, note that the SAT-V has many hard, discriminating items with low c_i values.) In contrast, the p_z index was less effective. After careful investigation, Drasgow et al. concluded that p_z was less effective than ℓ_z because the spuriously high modification induced a "signal" of the same magnitude for both dichotomous and polychotomous models. However, there was more "noise" in the p_z index because most normal examinees choose a few improbable incorrect options. Because detectability depends on the magnitude of the signal in relation to background noise, detectability for the p_z index was reduced.

In sum, Drasgow et al. provided a powerful method for detecting spuriously low examinees in samples where there is unrestricted omitting, by developing a standardized appropriateness index based on a polychotomous test model. Unfortunately, there is an interaction between appropriateness index and type of aberrance, i.e., p_z is better for detecting spuriously low examinees whereas ℓ_z is better for detecting spuriously high examinees. This leaves the practitioner with a choice between ℓ_z and p_z, which seems to rest on the type of aberrance the practitioner would rather detect. Of course, both indices could be computed if cost is not a concern.

Parsons (in press). During the decade following the publication of Lord and Novick's (1968) *Statistical Theories of Mental Test Scores*, almost all theoretical studies and practical applications of IRT have focused on ability testing. Parsons, in his dissertation, undertook the task of revising and applying IRT methods in order to apply appropriateness measurement methods to the assessment of attitudes. One very difficult problem in generalizing existing IRT methods to attitude measurement lies in the short "tests" commonly used to assess attitudes. For example, the Job Descriptive Index (JDI; Smith, Kendall, & Hulin, 1969) uses either 9 or 18 items to assess satisfactions with various facets of work and the work environment. At the time Parsons was conducting his dissertation research, it was unknown whether the two- or three-parameter logistic model could be used with instruments that contained fewer than perhaps 40 items. The following paragraphs describe the procedures developed by Parsons to utilize IRT with small sets of items.

The need for appropriateness measurement in the area of attitude assessment can be seen by considering the following hypothetical questionnaire respondents:

1. A nearly illiterate laborer ordered by his or her supervisor to participate in an attitude survey. The worker feels compelled to provide responses to all items, even those that he or she cannot read.

Obviously, responses to items the worker cannot read are essentially random.

2. A highly educated professional amused by some seemingly trivial items. Rather than describing his or her true feeling on these items, capricious responses are made.
3. A worker who suspects that a supervisor or co-worker will see his or her responses. To protect personal relationships, the worker provides what he or she believes to be positive responses to some items. Note that without knowing the scoring key, the examinee may not be able to guess the "correct" answer.

In all three of these examples, some responses are unrelated to the latent traits of interest. Parsons's work centered around using appropriateness measurement to identify respondents for whom scale scores provide misleading measures of attitudes.

The JDI scales that Parsons studied were the 18-item Work scale, the 9-item Promotions scale, and the 18-item Supervisor scale. In addition, he included 15 items from the Co-workers scale. Parsons estimated item parameters from the responses of 1,906 individuals holding a variety of nonmanagerial jobs in a retail sales firm and two military organizations. For the purposes of item parameter estimation, Parsons treated the 60 JDI items as if they were unidimensional, and used LOGIST to estimate the a_i and b_i parameters of the two-parameter logistic model.[4] These item parameter estimates were used in all subsequent analyses.

The appropriateness index score for a response vector was calculated by the following procedure. First, a separate $\hat{\theta}$ was estimated for each of the 18-item scales and the 15-item scale. (Responses to the 9-item Promotions scale were ignored.) Then the geometric mean likelihood of the response vector was computed by the equation

$$(4.4.3) \qquad \ell_g = \left\{ \prod_{\substack{18 \\ \text{Work} \\ \text{items}}} P_i(u_i|\hat{\theta}_w) \cdot \prod_{\substack{18 \\ \text{Supervisor} \\ \text{items}}} P_j(u_j|\hat{\theta}_s) \cdot \prod_{\substack{15 \\ \text{Co-workers} \\ \text{items}}} P_k(u_k|\hat{\theta}_c) \right\}^{1/51}$$

where $\hat{\theta}_w$, $\hat{\theta}_s$, and $\hat{\theta}_c$ are the estimated attitudes for the Work, Supervisor, and Co-workers scales respectively. Note that this procedure allows satisfaction levels to vary across scales, while providing an overall measure of the appropriateness of the JDI as a measuring instrument.

As an initial study of the feasibility of the appropriateness index in Equation 4.4.3, Parsons simulated 100 response vectors using the item

---

[4] Drasgow and Parsons's (1983) research, which was summarized in Section 3.3, provides a partial justification for this procedure.

parameters already estimated for the 60 JDI items. Each response vector was generated using Equation 2.4.10 and the single value of $\theta = 2.0$. Then 20 items were randomly selected and replaced by random responses. Appropriateness index values were computed for this spuriously low sample by two procedures. In the first procedure, θ was estimated from all 60 item responses, and ℓ_g was computed by Equation 4.3.3. This process is entirely appropriate because it involves applying a unidimensional model (two-parameter logistic) to unidimensional (two-parameter logistic) item responses. In Parsons's second procedure, three separate attitudes (θ_w, θ_s, θ_c) were estimated from disjoint blocks of 18, 18, and 15 items, chosen to correspond to the three JDI scales. Then Equation 4.4.3 was used to compute an appropriateness index value. Note that this procedure purposely ignores the unidimensionality of the 60 items. Finally, a normal sample of 1,000 response vectors was generated. Values of θ in this sample were selected to match the distribution of $\hat{\theta}$ (estimated from 60 items) for the spuriously low group.

Figure 4.4.6 presents the results of this simulation. Estimating atti-

Figure 4.4.6
Appropriateness Index ℓ_g Based on Three Blocks of Items

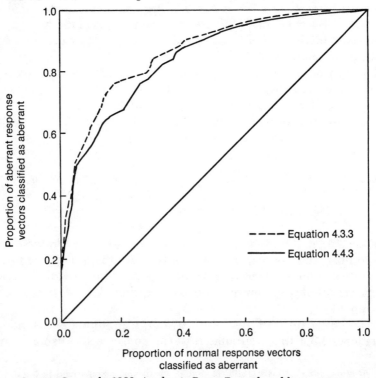

tude from only 15 to 18 items had a surprisingly small effect: appropriateness measurement was not substantially degraded. In fact, for detection rates up to 25 percent, there was virtually no difference between the two procedures. Furthermore, the false-alarm rates were quite low.

Parsons then studied Equation 4.4.3, using actual JDI data. He selected 100 actual JDI response vectors and applied the 33 percent spuriously low modification to the 51 items forming the Work, Supervision, and Co-workers scales. A normal group of 100 JDI response vectors was then selected so that the distribution of total JDI scores in this group matched the distribution in the spuriously low group. Separate attitudes for the Work, Supervisor, and Co-workers scales were then estimated for each response vector. Finally, ℓ_g was computed by Equation 4.4.3 for all response vectors.

Figure 4.4.7 presents the results of using Equation 4.4.3 with attitude estimates based on responses to 15 and 18 items for actual JDI data. This ROC curve is very interesting because it lies close to the

Figure 4.4.7
Appropriateness Index ℓ_g Based on Equation 4.4.3 for Actual JDI Data

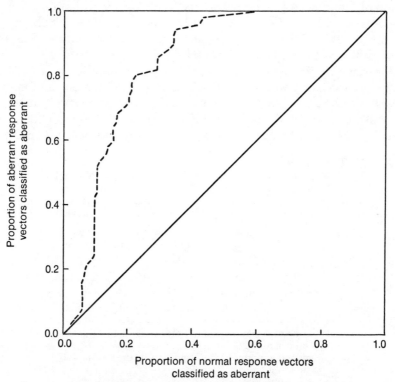

Source: Copyright 1983, Academic Press. Reproduced by permission.

diagonal for hit rates of less than 10 percent, but then rises sharply. An ROC curve of this shape would result if there were a sizable proportion (perhaps 15 percent) of the individuals in the normal group responding to the JDI in an aberrant fashion.

To investigate the possibility of truly aberrant responses to the JDI, Parsons computed appropriateness index scores for a sample of nominally normal JDI response vectors. Parsons used an index similar to Equation 4.4.3, except the standardized ℓ_z was computed for each JDI scale:

(4.4.4) $\bar{\ell}_z = \frac{1}{51}[18(\ell_z$ for Work)
                   $+ 18(\ell_z$ for Supervisor) $+ 15(\ell_z$ for Co-workers)].

On the basis of $\bar{\ell}_z$, Parsons separated response vectors into two groups. The 90 response vectors with the smallest $\bar{\ell}_z$ scores formed the "aberrant" sample and the remaining 947 response vectors formed the "normal" sample.

What predictions can be made about differences between normal response vectors and aberrant response vectors? Using classical test theory, it is possible to investigate some effects of *random* responding. For example, consider a population of individuals who respond randomly (choosing yes or no) to six items on an 18-item scale but respond normally to the remaining 12 items. Drasgow's (1982b) equations show that JDI scale means and validities will not be substantially different for the normal and partially random response vectors. If, for example, the mean, standard deviation, reliability, and validity of the Supervisor scale were 30, 12, .90, and .30 for the normal response vectors, then the mean and validity for the partially random response vectors would be 29 and .27 respectively. Nonetheless, the distributions of scale scores will be different in the two populations.

Table 4.4.4
Means and Variances of JDI Scale Scores for Normal and Aberrant Groups*

Scale	Group	Mean	SD	Variance
Work	Normal	25.70	14.55	211.69
	Aberrant	29.30	9.71	94.23†
Supervisor	Normal	40.79	13.10	171.48
	Aberrant	38.87	10.15	103.10†
Co-workers	Normal	24.62	9.03	81.60
	Aberrant	25.91	9.84	96.76

* The normal group contained 947 individuals; the aberrant group contained 90 individuals.
† Variance in normal group significantly greater ($\alpha = .01$) than in aberrant group.
Source: Copyright 1983, Academic Press. Reproduced by permission.

One important difference is that scores computed from partially random response vectors will have a *smaller variance* than scores in the normal group.

Table 4.4.4 contains summary statistics for the samples that were indicated to be normal and aberrant by ℓ_z. Note that on the Work and Supervisor scales there are clear and substantial differences between the response vectors that Parsons classified as normal and aberrant on the basis of Equation 4.4.4. This provides evidence in support of the hypothesis that there were a substantial number of aberrant response vectors contained in the nominally normal sample used to construct Figure 4.4.7.

4.5 SUMMARY AND DISCUSSION

The correlation of a scale with another variable may not be substantially affected if some scale scores are aberrant (e.g., Parsons's JDI data discussed above). Therefore, it appears that appropriateness measurement may not be especially useful to researchers who use correlations to investigate relations between variables for the purpose of theory building. However, if a test or scale is used to make decisions about individuals, or if specific values of test scores are used (e.g., minimum competency testing), then appropriateness measurement is very important. We reach this conclusion because the specific score obtained by an aberrant test taker does not have the same meaning as the identical score obtained by a normal test taker. As Parsons's JDI analyses illustrated, there can be substantial differences in the *distributions* of scores for normal and aberrant test takers. Thus a particular score should be interpreted only in the context of a population of examinees with a similar aberrance-inducing process. Since the underlying causes of aberrance are usually unknown, little meaning can be given to an individual's test score determined to be aberrant by an appropriateness index. Use of such test scores for college admissions and job hiring decisions is unwarranted.

The work of Levine and his colleagues has progressed to a point where practical applications of appropriateness measurement seem possible. The cost of computing an appropriateness index is quite small. The benefit can be enormous to those identified as measured poorly by a test.

In Chapter 9 we suggest that one of the primary causes of the controversy concerning the use of ability and aptitude tests in the United States is the asymmetry of the power relationship between an examinee and a testing organization. For example, a testing organization may unilaterally decide to discard test scores: The 12,000 Nursing Board examinees in New York who were reexamined (see Section 4.1) provide one example. When examinees believe their test scores to be inappropriate measures of ability, they may sometimes be allowed to retake the exam at their own expense, but they cannot have their original test scores removed from their records and transcripts. It is important to note that without appropriateness measurement *the testing organization does not have empirical evidence that a particular individual's test score is a truly valid measure of aptitude for that individual.* Appropriateness measurement provides theory-based methods for individuals to challenge the validity of their test scores as well as methods for testing organizations to ensure individualized quality control of their product.

REFERENCES

Brown, F. G., & Scott, D. A. The unpredictability of predictability. *Journal of Educational Measurement*, 1966, *3*, 297–301.

Donlon, T. F., & Angoff, W. H. The Scholastic Aptitude Test. In W. H. Angoff (Ed.), *The College Board Admissions testing program.* New York: College Entrance Examination Board, 1971.

Donlon, T. F., & Fischer, F. E. An index of an individual's agreement with group-determined item difficulties. *Educational and Psychological Measurement*, 1968, *28*, 105–113.

Drasgow, F. Statistical indices of the appropriateness of aptitude test scores (Doctoral dissertation, University of Illinois, 1978). *Dissertation Abstracts International*, 1979, *39*, 12B, p. 6095. (University Microfilms No. DEL79–13435)

Drasgow, F. Choice of test model for appropriateness measurement. *Applied Psychological Measurement*, 1982, *6*, 297–308. (a)

Drasgow, F. Biased test items and differential validity. *Psychological Bulletin*, 1982, *92*, 526–531. (b)

Drasgow, F., Levine, M. V., & Williams, E. Advances in appropriateness measurement. Manuscript in preparation, 1982.

Drasgow, F., & Parsons, C. K. Application of unidimensional item response theory models to multidimensional data. *Applied Psychological Measurement*, in press, 1983.

Fischer, F. E. Some properties of the personal biserial index. *Journal of Educational Measurement*, 1970, *7*, 275–277.

Ghiselli, E. E. The prediction of predictability. *Educational and Psychological Measurement*, 1960, *20*, 3–8.

Ghiselli, E. E. Moderating effects and differential reliability and validity. *Journal of Applied Psychology*, 1963, *47*, 81–86.

Ghiselli, E. E. *The validity of occupational aptitude tests.* New York: John Wiley & Sons, 1966.

Hoffman, B. *The tyranny of testing.* New York: Crowell-Collier Press, 1962.

Jacobs, P. I. *A study of large score changes on the Scholastic Aptitude Test* (Research Bulletin 63–20). Princeton, N.J.: Educational Testing Service, 1963.

Jensen, A. R. *Bias in mental testing.* New York: Free Press, 1980.

July licensing exam invalidated in New York. *American Journal of Nursing,* October 1979, pp. 1671; 1680; 1684.

Levine, M. V., & Drasgow, F. Appropriateness measurement: Review, critique, and validating studies. *British Journal of Mathematical and Statistical Psychology,* 1982, *35,* 42–56. (a)

Levine, M. V., & Drasgow, F. Appropriateness measurement: Validating studies and variable ability models. In D. J. Weiss (Ed.), *New horizons in testing: Latent trait test theory and computerized adaptive testing.* New York: Academic Press, 1982, in press. (b)

Levine, M. V., & Rubin, D. F. Measuring the appropriateness of multiple-choice test scores. *Journal of Educational Statistics,* 1979, *4,* 269–290.

Lord, F. M. An analysis of the Verbal Scholastic Aptitude Test using Birnbaum's three-parameter logistic model. *Educational and Psychological Measurement,* 1968, *28,* 989–1020.

Lord, F. M., & Novick, M. R. *Statistical theories of mental test scores.* Reading, Mass.: Addison-Wesley Publishing, 1968.

McNemar, Q. *Psychological statistics.* New York: John Wiley & Sons, 1969.

Parsons, C. K. The identification of people for whom JDI scores are inappropriate. *Organizational Behavior and Human Performance,* 1983, in press.

Sewall, G., Drake, S., & Lee, E. D. An epidemic of cheating. *Newsweek,* May 26, 1980, p. 63.

Smith, P. C., Kendall, L. M., & Hulin, C. L. *The measurement of satisfaction in work and retirement.* Skokie, Ill.: Rand McNally, 1969.

Wiggins, J. S. *Personality and prediction.* Reading, Mass.: Addison-Wesley Publishing, 1973.

Wright, B. D. Solving measurement problems with the Rasch model. *Journal of Educational Measurement,* 1977, *14,* 97–116.

Wright, B. D., & Stone, M. H. *Best test design.* Chicago: MESA Press, 1979.

Zedeck, S. Problems with the use of "moderator" variables. *Psychological Bulletin,* 1971, *76,* 295–310.

5

Item and Test Bias

5.0 OVERVIEW

We have shown in Chapter 4 that item responses can yield information about the appropriateness of a test score as a measure of θ for an individual. In this chapter the N by n data matrix displaying N individuals' responses to n items is considered from the complementary perspective. Our task is to examine the responses to a given item made by two or more identifiable groups rather than the responses made by one individual to all n items. Normally the groups are selected on the basis of theoretical interest or social and public policy concerns. For example, responses of groups protected by Titles VI or VII of the 1964 Civil Rights Act (United States Civil Rights Act, 1964) might be compared, for legal reasons, to responses of the majority group. In this chapter we shall present and discuss methods of examining differences in item responses between groups of individuals to detect item bias.

Item bias, defined more precisely below in Section 5.3, is said to occur when individuals with the same amount of an underlying trait from different subpopulations have different probabilities of responding to an item correctly (in ability measurement) or positively (in attitude measurement). The causes of item bias could be the use of highly idiosyncratic terms drawing on subcultural knowledge not widely shared in the population, items that refer to concepts not relevant to some subpopulation, or items that have been badly translated into a foreign language.

Item bias provides our second example of an application of IRT to a persistent measurement problem that is addressed only indirectly by classical measurement theory. By assessing item bias within an IRT framework, this very difficult measurement problem becomes tractable.

152

In Section 5.1 we provide an historical perspective by discussing *test* bias (not *item* bias) from the viewpoint of traditional measurement theory. The legal and social requirements for fairness in test usage have resulted in a heavy emphasis on examining test bias in relation to external criteria of performance. Section 5.2 contains a discussion of item bias defined and measured using heuristic procedures adapted from classical test theory. In Section 5.3 we define item bias in a way that is consistent with the theoretical perspective of item response theory, and we present methods of assessing item bias assuming one-, two-, and three-parameter logistic models.

The different definitions of item bias resulting from classical and item response theory are explicitly contrasted in Section 5.4; the strengths and weaknesses of each are emphasized. In Section 5.5 we note briefly the value of clinical insight and experience when administering tests to individuals from different subpopulations in the United States. These insights should be the source of hypotheses for rigorous analysis. The different approaches to item bias detection are summarized in Section 5.6.

Finally, we note that this chapter and the preceding chapter on appropriateness measurement have been stimulated, at least in part, by the social importance that tests have acquired. Many organizations and governmental agencies have decided to allocate opportunities and resources on the basis of measures of merit. Once this policy decision has been made, people who must make personnel decisions have chosen to rely on ability tests as assessments of merit. The social importance and necessity for unbiased and fair tests can be further stressed by noting the role of both general intelligence tests and narrow ability tests as selection devices in universities and as devices to place children into tracks in public schools. Outright denial of education on the basis of test scores is less of a problem than is the effect on the quality of education that is obtained.

One of the original purposes for developing ability tests should be kept in mind. The old school network, political patronage, family influence, and money were used historically as methods of resource and opportunity allocation. Ability tests were developed to assess merit and allocate opportunities in a more equitable fashion. That test scores are significantly related to many of the factors they were intended to supplant (socioeconomic status, family income, race) is at the heart of the current controversy. Attempts to replace an aristocracy with a meritocracy have been only marginally successful because the two systems appear to overlap substantially (White, 1982). These points are elaborated in Chapter 9. Thus, this chapter and Chapter 4 have social policy as well as practical measurement implications. Particularly in Chapter 5 we have strayed somewhat from an exposition of measurement theory to brief forays into the thickets of more controversial topics.

5.1   TEST BIAS, EXTERNAL CRITERIA

In this section we present three approaches to test bias that have been used, discussed, reviewed, and in some cases rejected by many practitioners. We do not discuss the *egalitarian hypothesis* of test fairness. This hypothesis implies that the existence of a significant difference in mean test scores among racial, sex, or ethnic groups is sufficient to conclude that test bias exists. Although this hypothesis seems to underlie some important federal court decisions (*Hobson* v. *Hansen*, 1967; *Larry P.* v. *Riles*, 1980), it involves an assumption of equal distributions of ability across groups. This assumption should be a question for empirical study, not part of a definition. We also do not discuss the constant ratio model (Thorndike, 1971), the conditional probability model (Cole, 1973), the equal probability model (Linn, 1973), or the equal risk model (Einhorn & Bass, 1971). The first three of these have been shown by Petersen and Novick (1976) to be internally inconsistent; the fourth has never achieved wide usage. Arvey (1979) provides a good nontechnical review and discussion of these models. They should perhaps be regarded as psychometric curios because of their internal inconsistencies and lack of adoption and use by practitioners. Although their use would achieve the goal of increasing the numbers of minority group members who are selected or hired, their theoretical shortcomings cannot be offset by their politically expedient (for some) results.

Single-group validity.   Single-group validity is defined as existing when a test is valid for predicting an external criterion for one group only. More precisely, the single-group validity hypothesis is stated as $0 = r_A < r_B$, where r_A and r_B are the test-criterion correlations in subpopulations A and B, respectively.

This definition of test fairness is nondirectional although it usually is assumed that tests are valid for whites, $r_W > 0$, but not for minorities, $r_M = 0$, and the use of such tests would be unfair to minorities. The unfairness results when test scores are used in selection decisions with a single cutting score because mean differences in test scores are commonly found between white and minority groups. Reliance on a test with single-group validity would result in a greater number of whites being selected (because $\overline{X}_W > \overline{X}_M$) even though the test was irrelevant for predicting performance of minority group members on the criterion (because $r_M = 0$).

Although the question of single-group validity has been controversial (Boehm, 1972; Humphreys, 1973; Schmidt, Berner, & Hunter,

1973; O'Connor, Wexley, & Alexander, 1975; Katzell & Dyer, 1977; Katzell & Dyer, 1978; Hunter, Schmidt, & Hunter, 1979), the issue appears to have been resolved. The available empirical evidence (Boehm, 1977; Katzell & Dyer, 1977; O'Connor et al., 1975; Schmidt et al., 1973) suggests rather conclusively that the frequency of obtaining single-group validities in *samples* does not exceed the frequency that would occur by chance given the assumption that the *population* validities are equal ($r_M = r_W$).

Differential validity hypothesis.   The differential validity hypothesis is less restrictive than the single-group validity hypothesis. It only states that the validity coefficients for the two subpopulations are unequal, that is $r_A \neq r_B$.

The differential validity hypothesis appears to be based upon the intuition that tests commonly measure information available to the majority group but not available to the minority group. Responses to items assessing such information may be useful for predicting criterion performance by majority group members, but will not be useful for the minority group. Thus, predictions of criterion performance should be more accurate for majority group members and, hence, yield a larger validity coefficient.

Evidence relating to the validity of the hypothesis is difficult to evaluate. With large enough sample sizes, any difference between population validity coefficients, no matter how trivial, will reach statistical significance. But, how large should a difference between groups be expected to be under the assumption that some measurement bias may exist? Keep in mind that individual studies normally will be based on relatively small samples. Their results are heavily influenced by sampling fluctuations, restrictions of range, criterion unreliability, and other sources of artifactual variance. Therefore, Hunter et al. (1979) argued that evidence must be cumulated across many studies where sampling fluctuations can be observed and other sources of variance estimated. Hunter et al. found 9 percent of 866 pairs of sample validity coefficients ($\hat{r}_M$ and $\hat{r}_W$) were significantly different from each other. Further, the cumulative test for the significance of the differences between the 866 *pairs* of coefficients was not significantly different from effects that would have been produced solely by restriction of range in test scores. They concluded that differential validity probably does not exist, and thus, validity is general rather than situation or group specific.

Drasgow (1982) has shown, however, that the difference between majority and minority group validity coefficients will typically be very small even when profound bias exists. He presented a hypothetical example where it was assumed that minority group members respond randomly to 25 "biased" items on a 100-item multiple-choice test.

Bias of this magnitude would adversely affect minority group members' chances of being hired or admitted. Drasgow found that this large proportion of profoundly biased items reduced the validity coefficient from .399 for the majority group to .385 in the minority group. Thus the difference in validity coefficients was only .014. The probabilities of obtaining statistically significant differences between majority and minority group validity coefficients under these biasing conditions are .0510, .0528, and .2731 when the minority and majority group sample sizes are (50, 100), (100, 1,000), and (10,000, 20,000), respectively, and where α is .05.

It is clear that the empirical finding of no significant difference between validity coefficients should *not* be taken as evidence of test fairness or lack of bias. This conclusion implies the many empirical differential validity studies that typically have not found a significant difference between majority and minority group validity coefficients *cannot* be used as evidence of test fairness. Even the Hunter et al. method of aggregating results across many studies has little power to detect bias. Other methods of analysis, which have statistical power to detect test bias, are required.

It is important to note that Drasgow did not conclude that test validity was either general or specific. He did conclude that evidence based on comparisons of majority sample validities and minority sample validities lacked power to address fairly the question of test bias.

Regression model. A third approach to test bias, referred to as the regression model or Cleary model, was articulated by Cleary (1968). This model for examining test bias states:

> A test is biased for members of a subgroup of the population if, in the prediction of a criterion for which the test was designed, consistent nonzero errors of prediction are made for members of the subgroup. In other words, the test is biased if the criterion score predicted from the common regression line is consistently too high or too low for members of the subgroup. With this definition of bias, there may be a connotation of "unfair," particularly if the use of the test produces a prediction that is too low. (p. 115)

For convenience, we shall refer to a test as fair in this subsection if a single regression line produces unbiased estimates of the criterion for all relevant subpopulations.

The regression model implies that separate regression lines for each relevant subpopulation should be determined. If the regression lines are identical within limits of sampling fluctuations, the test is considered fair. A single regression line can then be used to predict criterion performance; no advantage is given to any subpopulation.

If significantly different regression lines are determined to exist across subpopulations, test bias can be eliminated through the use of the separate regression lines estimated for each subpopulation. Separate equations would also be optimal in the statistical sense of minimizing squared errors of prediction. In this case, a rational test administrator would always use such separate regression lines to remove test bias. In practice, the use of separate regression lines for different subgroups simply means that selection decisions would *not* be based directly upon test score; an individual with a higher predicted criterion score would be preferred over one with a lower predicted criterion score. However, the prediction equations would be *different* across subpopulations in order to correct for bias in the test.

Regression lines for different subpopulations can differ in their standard errors of estimate (error variance), their slopes, or their intercepts. The significance of the differences in regression lines in different subpopulations can be evaluated by means of a test for the identity of regression equations in several populations (Neter & Wasserman, 1974). Examples of tests that are biased according to the regression model are shown in Figures 5.1.1 and 5.1.2.

Figure 5.1.1
Test Bias Caused by Intercept Differences

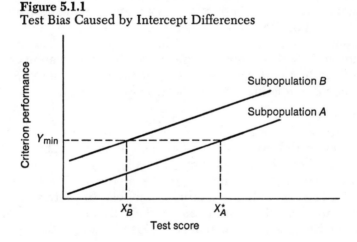

If Y_{min} is the minimum criterion performance that is acceptable, the different regression lines in Figures 5.1.1 and 5.1.2 imply different minimum predictor cutting or qualifying scores for the two subpopulations. In the figures, X_A^* and X_B^* denote the minimum test scores for subpopulations A and B that yield the minimally acceptable criterion performance, Y_{min}.

Figure 5.1.2
Test Bias Caused by Slope Differences

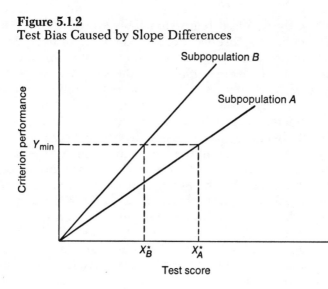

Because the fairness of a test according to the regression model depends in part on the equality of regression equations, it is important to examine the effects of errors of measurement on the determination of test bias. For the present discussion, assume that we have very large samples and consequently can ignore sampling fluctuations. It is easy to show that the slope b of the regression line relating criterion scores Y to test performance X is a function of the slope β of the regression line relating Y to true scores τ_X on the test:

$$(5.1.1) \qquad\qquad b = \rho_{xx'}\beta,$$

where $\rho_{xx'}$ is the classical measurement theory reliability of test scores. In other words, slopes of true score regression lines are reduced by errors of measurement in the predictor. The decrease in slope is a function of the reliability of the test. In contrast, it can be shown that errors of measurement *in the criterion* do not affect the regression line; the regression of τ_Y on X is identical to the regression of Y upon X.

The effects of errors of measurement in the predictor are illustrated in Figure 5.1.3. In this figure, the solid regression line is the regression of Y on τ_X, and the dashed lines are the regression lines of Y on X. The means of subpopulations A and B are indicated on the solid regression of Y on τ_X.

The effect of errors of measurement in the predictor leads to an interesting paradox. If the regression of Y on τ_X is the same for both groups *and* there are mean differences in predictor scores, then sepa-

Figure 5.1.3
Effects of Measurement Error in Predictor on Regressions of Y on X

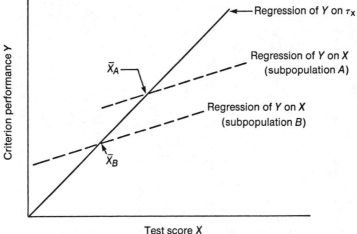

rate regressions of Y onto X will be required for unbiased prediction in the two groups. It can be shown that, if a single regression of Y onto X is used, criterion scores will be systematically overpredicted and underpredicted for the two different subpopulations. The paradox appears when we have an imperfect test X, with reliability of perhaps $\rho_{xx'} = .7$, that is fair by the regression model (i.e., a single regression line can be used for both samples). If we improve the test by doubling its length, its reliability will increase to $\rho_{xx'} = .82$ and test scores $\overset{\approx}{X}$ on the lengthened test (after dividing by two) will tend to be closer to true scores, τ_x. However, if X was a fair test, the more reliable test $\overset{\approx}{X}$ will not be fair. Thus, *improving* a test that is fair by the regression model produces an unfair test requiring the use of two separate regression lines. The effect of improving test reliability on regression lines can be seen in Figure 5.1.4.

The paradox discussed in conjunction with the regression model of test fairness has serious ramifications. The finding of equal regression lines for two subpopulations, with different means on the predictor test, is essentially happenstance. If the test under evaluation had been more reliable, the separate regression lines of Y onto X would have been steeper and the test would have been judged to be biased (see Figure 5.1.4). If the test had been less reliable, the within-sample regressions of Y onto X would have been flatter (as shown in Figure 5.1.3), and once again the test would have been judged to be biased. Conclusions about the equality of regressions of Y onto X require

Figure 5.1.4
Effects of Improving Test Reliability on Subpopulation Regression
Lines

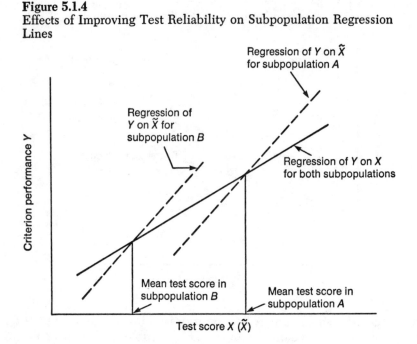

precise specifications of the measurement conditions (reliabilities and sample properties) as limitations on generalizations. This paradox suggests that claims of validity generalization are perhaps premature when based on inspection of subpopulation regressions. Tests that are apparently fair by the regression model can become unfair (and, hence, require two separate lines) if test reliability is increased or decreased.

Summary. All three definitions presented in this section examine bias in relation to an external criterion. Despite their problems, the differential validity hypothesis and the regression model have more than historical importance: Contemporary legal, public policy, and technical writings still stress these definitions and their implications.

5.2 TRADITIONAL HEURISTIC PROCEDURES FOR ASSESSING ITEM BIAS

In this section we present heuristic methods that define and assess item bias by reference to internal, measurement-related criteria. It is important to note that these definitions stress the importance of detecting bias at the point of measurement rather than fairness in decisions. The advantages and problems of different definitions will be discussed along with explications of their basic assumptions. The material in this section is presented to provide an additional perspective on item bias and to establish a point of departure for the discussion in Section 5.3 of methods of item bias detection derived from IRT.

Item discrimination statistics. Biserial or point biserial correlations between items and total test scores are frequently used measures of the extent to which responses to particular items are related to the trait assessed by the rest of the items on the test. (See Section 8.1 for a discussion of these correlations.) Comparisons of these correlations computed in different samples are often used to infer the presence or absence of item bias. For items to be unbiased according to this index, item-total correlations must be equivalent within the limits of sampling fluctuations across all subpopulations studied.

The logic of this approach is straightforward. Item-total correlations reflect the items' discriminatory power in the sense that individuals with high test scores are more likely to respond correctly to the item than individuals with lower test scores. If an item discriminates among ability levels for one group but not for another group, the conclusion is usually that the item contains material not generally available to the latter group; it is therefore biased. For example, if a verbal ability test contains a number of black slang items in addition to the usual items found on such tests, the slang items might discriminate reasonably well among blacks but probably would be nondiscriminating among whites. Such items would show larger item-total correlations for the black sample than they would for the white sample and would be considered biased. Similarly, if items require familiarity with material not generally available to members of different geographical subpopulations, they will not show similar correlations across these subpopulations. Items requiring a knowledge of sidewalk elevators will be biased against individuals from small towns just as items relying on agricultural terms would be biased against individuals from large cities.

Statistical tests of differences between item-total correlations can be performed. Unfortunately, correlations in general and item-total correlations in particular are very sensitive to restriction of range; differences across groups in total test score variance and item difficulty (and, hence, item variances) influence the sizes of item-total correlations. Differences in the distributions of ability among groups can therefore yield substantial differences in item-total correlations even when the items are assessing identical psychological traits with equal fidelity. Similarly, marked departures from normality of Y, the continuous variable assumed to underlie the dichotomously scored observed responses, influence biserial correlations. Bimodal distributions of the total test scores may produce biserial correlations greater than +1.00. These problems make the use of item-total biserial and point biserial correlations problematic.

Relative differences in item difficulties across samples. Item difficulties, defined as $(1 - \hat{p}_i)$ where $\hat{p}_i$ is the proportion of a sample responding correctly to the ith item, may be expected to differ across subpopulations because of differences in the distribution of θ across subpopulations. However, according to the relative item difficulty definition of item bias (Angoff & Ford, 1973), differences in θ distributions across subpopulations should have uniform effects on $1 - \hat{p}_i$. Thus, items should have uniformly larger values of $1 - \hat{p}_i$ in less able subpopulations. If the relative item difficulties or rank order of item difficulties differ markedly across two subpopulations, the items contributing to the differences in rank orders are said to be biased.

In use, this method requires that item difficulties, $\hat{p}_i$s, be calculated in each group. The $\hat{p}$s are then transformed into ETS Δs (Donlon & Angoff, 1971) by the process described in Section 4.2. Plotting the Δ values obtained in two samples against each other (each point represents the Δ values from two samples for the same item) graphically displays the relation between item difficulties evaluated in two different samples. Deviations of each item from the major axis of the bivariate Δ plot are direct indications of the extent to which items have different difficulties in the two samples. Large deviations indicate items that are relatively more difficult (in relation to the other items on the test) in one sample than the other. Consequently, a large deviation from the major axis is taken as evidence of bias for that item.

The relative difficulty approach can be illustrated by reference to Figure 5.2.1. In this bivariate distribution, transformed item difficulties Δ_{i_A} for the sample from subpopulation A are plotted along the abscissa, and transformed item difficulties Δ_{i_B} for the sample from subpopulation B are plotted along the ordinate. The equation for the major axis of the ellipse is given by $\Delta_{i_B} = T\Delta_{i_A} + V$. The slope T is calculated as

(5.2.1) $\quad T = \dfrac{(s_B^2 - s_A^2) \pm \sqrt{(s_B^2 - s_A^2) + 4[\hat{r}(\Delta_A, \Delta_B)]^2 s_A^2 s_B^2}}{2\hat{r}(\Delta_A, \Delta_B)s_A s_B}$

and the intercept is

(5.2.2) $\qquad\qquad\qquad V = \bar{\Delta}_B - T\bar{\Delta}_A$

(Angoff & Ford, 1973). In these equations, $\bar{\Delta}_A$ and $\bar{\Delta}_B$ represents the means of the transformed item difficulties in the two samples; s_A and s_B refer to the standard deviations of the Δ values in the two samples, and $\hat{r}(\Delta_A, \Delta_B)$ is the correlation between the Δ values from the two

Figure 5.2.1
Relation between Transformed Probabilities of Item Endorsement (Item
Difficulties) for 25 Selected Items Obtained from an English and Hebrew
Version of the JDI

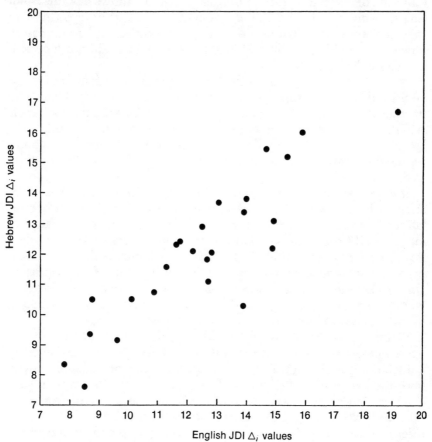

samples. Perpendicular distances, D_i, of each item from the major axis
are given by

(5.2.3)
$$D_i = \frac{T\Delta_{i_A} - \Delta_{i_B} + V}{\sqrt{T^2 + 1}}.$$

The limitations of the item difficulty definition and analysis of item
bias have been discussed by Hunter (1975). The most serious problem
is that the basic item statistics for the analysis, item difficulties, are
affected by the distributions of ability across groups. Lord's Paradox
(Lord, 1980; Section 2.5) is critical in this context because it shows

that the basic assumption of the relative difference hypothesis may be incorrect. In particular, the relative difference hypothesis supposes that differences in θ distributions across subpopulations "should have uniform effects on item difficulties." Figure 2.5.2 shows that this is not true if items vary in the IRT a_i parameter. Thus, if groups differ in their respective θ distributions and if items differ in discriminatory power, then using this method to detect item bias could produce artifactual evidence of item bias.

When the θ distributions of the two groups under consideration are very similar and the test contains items that do not vary substantially in item discriminatory power (or in the lower asymptotes of their ICCs), the relative item difficulty procedure will produce results similar to those determined by the IRT methods. Except for these conditions, investigators should be extremely cautious in using this method to detect item bias.

*Multivariate factor structures.** This approach requires that factor analyses be conducted on the item responses in all relevant subpopulations. If an item does not show similar loadings on appropriate factors across different subpopulations, it would be regarded as biased by this procedure. The problems, discussed in Chapter 8, that are caused by factoring binary data have limited the applications of this approach. Unless one is analyzing a) two-parameter logistic or normal ogive data where there is no guessing and b) where θ is normally distributed, factor analysis can give very misleading results.

When the assumptions of the two-parameter logistic and normal ogive models are reasonable, and θ is normally distributed, factoring tetrachoric correlations might be considered. Unfortunately, even here the sampling distribution of estimated factor loadings is very complex and requires computations that are too extensive for more than 20 to 25 items. As a heuristic device, multivariate factor structures across subpopulations provide insights into the meanings of the items across different samples. Recent advances in the factor analysis of binary data (Muthén and Christoffersson, 1981) may prove to be more useful than traditional factor analytic methods.

*Chi-squared indices of item bias.** Scheuneman (1979), Camilli (in Shepard, Camilli, & Averill, 1980), and Holland (see Scheuneman, 1980) have proposed methods of detecting item bias based on chi-squared statistics. These procedures make similar assumptions and involve similar calculations. Consequently, we will discuss only the most sophisticated methods. The interested reader is referred to Ironson (1980) for a comprehensive discussion and comparison of chi-squared bias indices.

In these methods, item bias is defined as existing when individuals from different subpopulations, but with the same total score on a test, have different probabilities of responding correctly to an item. The procedures provide a test for item bias by first dividing the total sample into relevant subpopulations (black/white, male/female, Catholic/other, etc.). Then the range of total scores on the test is divided into J discrete intervals. Usually five intervals are used although this can differ depending on the number of individuals in the samples, the item difficulty, and the skewness of the distributions of total test scores. The proportion of individuals in each test score interval who respond correctly (incorrectly) to an item is used as the estimate of the probability of individuals in that interval responding correctly (incorrectly). For an item to be unbiased, the probabilities of a correct response for individuals who fall within a particular test score interval must be identical across all relevant subpopulations. That is, Prob(u_i = 1|test score interval j) for subpopulation A should equal (within sampling fluctuations) Prob(u_i = 1|test score interval j) for subpopulation B.

The chi-squared approaches to the measurement of item bias are based on the assumption that the test is measuring a single latent trait. This assumption is also made by IRT approaches to item bias and is crucial for the definition of item bias. Basically, both the chi-squared approaches and the IRT approaches argue that if total test score or $\hat{\theta}$ is held constant, then differences in probabilities of correct responses to an item by members of different groups should not be observed because we are controlling the only trait being assessed by the items in question (since $X \doteq \tau_x$, and $\hat{\theta} \doteq \theta$). Different probabilities of correct responses indicate that we can distinguish among individuals by means of an item *after holding constant* the only attribute relevant to item responses. This contradiction implies that the item is functioning differently in the two groups (or, contrary to our assumption, the test is multidimensional). In either case, the item is biased in terms of its measurement of ability in the two groups. (Methods for examining the dimensionality of an item pool are discussed in Chapter 8.)

Camilli (Shepard et al., 1980) proposed a "full chi-squared" approach that uses expected frequencies of both correct and incorrect responses by the two groups in each score interval:

$$(5.2.4) \qquad \chi^2 = \sum_{j=1}^{J} \left[N_{jB} \frac{(\hat{p}_{jB} - \hat{p}_j)^2}{\hat{p}_j(1 - \hat{p}_j)} + N_{jA} \frac{(\hat{p}_{jA} - \hat{p}_j)^2}{\hat{p}_j(1 - \hat{p}_j)} \right],$$

with J degrees of freedom, where at each score interval j, j = 1, 2, $\cdots$, J,

> N_{jB} is the number of individuals sampled from subpopulation B in the jth total score interval,
> $\hat{p}_{jB}$ is the proportion of individuals in the jth total score interval

sampled from subpopulation B who correctly answered the item, and

$\hat{p}_j$ is the pooled proportion of individuals from both subpopulations who correctly answered the item.

N_{jA} and $\hat{p}_{jA}$ refer to the analogous quantities for subpopulation A. Note that Equation 5.2.4 is written as the sum of J independent χ^2 values, calculated at J total score intervals, using a 2 × 2 (right/wrong by subpopulation) table. The χ^2 value for each score interval j can be rewritten as

(5.2.5)
$$\chi_j^2 = \frac{N_j(ad - bc)^2}{(a + c)(b + d)(a + b)(c + d)},$$

where N_j is the total number of individuals in the jth interval, and a, b, c, and d are the cell frequencies in the 2 × 2 table:

		correct	incorrect
	A	a	b
Subpopulation	B	c	d

There are J such 2 × 2 tables for each item. This form of the chi-square test for item bias permits close examination of those score intervals that contribute most to a significant χ^2. Bias against a group in only some score ranges could be detected. This fine-grained analysis would possibly permit insightful hypotheses about the causes and nature of item bias if bias were consistently present in some score intervals but not others.

Equations 5.2.4 and 5.2.5 are very sensitive to sample sizes and expected cell frequencies. Frequencies of incorrect responses by majority samples in the highest total test score interval and correct responses by minority group members in the lowest score interval have been found to be very small (Ironson, 1980). These low frequencies may cause the statistic to deviate from a chi-squared distribution even when the item is unbiased. Ironson suggested changing the total score intervals that are used in the computation to overcome this problem. Note, however, that the ad hoc nature of these statistics is illustrated by their dependence on a number of arbitrary decisions. Ironson, for example, showed that small changes in the boundaries of the test score intervals changed the value of some chi-squared statistics from significant to nonsignificant and vice versa.

These and other criticisms of chi-squared statistics as indices of item bias are not meant to discourage their use by researchers. As long as the shortcomings and problems are known and usage of the statistics restricted to appropriate situations, this set of heuristic approaches has decided advantages over those deriving from IRT, both in terms of costs and conceptual simplicity.

5.3 IRT APPROACHES TO MEASUREMENT OF ITEM BIAS

In this section we shall present methods that have been developed to detect item bias for one-, two-, and three-parameter logistic models. These approaches all define item bias in terms of the similarity of ICCs for an item obtained in different groups or subpopulations. Specifically, *an item is biased if ICCs for the item estimated in samples from different subpopulations are not identical within the limits of sampling fluctuations.* Detecting item bias depends on procedures that compare ICCs from different groups and provide quantitative measures of their similarity. These measures can then be evaluated for statistical significance. The different operationalizations of this definition, however, do have different degrees of fidelity to the definition.

The procedures discussed in this section have several advantages over those based on conventional approaches. For example, the chi-squared procedures discussed in Section 5.2 require arbitrary but nonetheless critical decisions concerning the number of test score intervals and the cutting scores used to form these intervals. The chi-squared procedures also treat all examinees or respondents within a test score category as if they were of equal ability. Unless test score categories are infinitely narrow or unless the distributions of scores within each category from both samples are identical—neither situation is likely to be true in practice—then this assumption is wrong. When considered in light of the arbitrary nature of the score categories, it is apparent that ignoring information about individual examinees' abilities may lead to erroneous results.

The IRT procedures overcome many of these objections but they have substantial requirements. They require estimation of item and subject parameters in large samples and with relatively large numbers of items.

Item bias: One-parameter logistic model. As noted in Section 2.4, the one-parameter logistic model is a special case of the three-parameter logistic model in which it is assumed there is no guessing ($c_i = 0$ for all items) and items are all equal in discriminatory power ($a_i = 1.0$ for all items). Thus, according to the model, only one item parameter (difficulty) varies across items. Nonetheless, items can also differ in the extent to which they fit the one-parameter logistic model.

An item is biased within the framework of the one-parameter model if it displays a difficulty shift from one subpopulation to the other as shown in Figure 5.3.1, or if the item responses fit the model well in

Figure 5.3.1
Hypothetical One-Parameter Item Showing Greater Difficulty
in a Sample from Subpopulation A than in a Sample from Subpopulation B

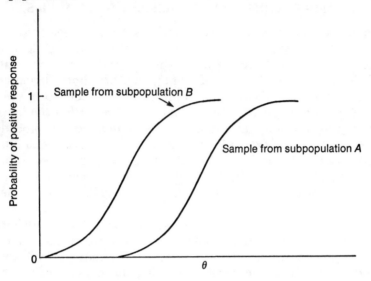

one sample but do not fit in the second sample as illustrated in Figure
5.3.2.

The difference in ICCs for the hypothetical item shown in Figure
5.3.1 could be a reflection of item content that was less familiar to one
subpopulation than the other, making it less likely for an equally able
member of one subpopulation to respond correctly. The hypothetical
item in Figure 5.3.2 could reflect different response selection strategies in subpopulation B than in subpopulation A. Alternatively, the
item may be less discriminating in subpopulation B because it reflects
item content that may be available but is not normally used by members of the subpopulation.

To detect item bias as displayed in Figure 5.3.1, estimates of item
difficulty must be obtained for the two subpopulations in question.
After equating θ-metrics by standardizing on $\hat{b}$, a test statistic proposed by Wright, Mead, and Draba (1976) is

$$(5.3.1) \qquad z_i = \frac{\hat{b}_{i_A} - \hat{b}_{i_B}}{[(\text{SE of } \hat{b}_{i_A})^2 + (\text{SE of } \hat{b}_{i_B})^2]^{1/2}},$$

where $\hat{b}_{i_A}$ and $\hat{b}_{i_B}$ are the estimated item difficulties for the ith item in
subpopulations A and B, and SE of $\hat{b}_{i_A}$ and SE of $\hat{b}_{i_B}$ are the corresponding standard errors of $\hat{b}$ in the two groups. (Section 2.7 contains

Figure 5.3.2
One Parameter Logistic ICC and Two Empirical ICCs* for a Hypothetical
Item Showing Better Fit to the Model in a Sample from Subpopulation A
than in a Sample from Subpopulation B

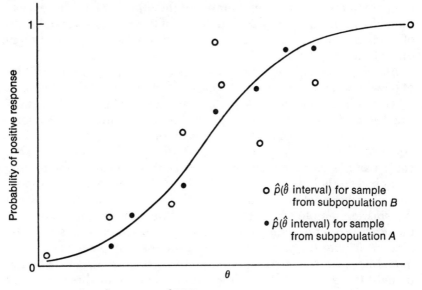

* Section 2.3 describes empirical ICCs.

formulae that can be used to compute the SE of b_i.) Under the null
hypothesis of no item bias, z_i should be asymptotically normally distributed with mean zero and unit variance. Obviously, a large value of
z_i indicates the item is relatively more difficult in one group than the
other.

When item bias is of the type indicated in Figure 5.3.2, items can
have equal item difficulties but a serious misfit in one subpopulation.
Consequently, item fit in both subpopulations should be examined.

Wright and Stone (1979) provide a statistic for the fit of the one-
parameter logistic model to item response data. This statistic, denoted
H_i for item i, is

$$(5.3.2) \qquad H_i = \sum_{j=1}^{N} \left\{ \frac{[u_{ij} - \hat{P}_i(\hat{\theta}_j)]^2}{\hat{P}_i(\hat{\theta}_j)\,\hat{Q}_i(\hat{\theta}_j)} \right\},$$

where u_{ij} is the dichotomously scored item response to item i by
examinee j, and $\hat{P}_i(\hat{\theta}_j)$ is computed by Equation 2.4.11 with $\hat{\theta}_j$ and
$\hat{b}_i$ substituted for θ and b_i. Wright and Stone (p. 79) state that this
statistic approximately follows a chi-squared distribution with $N - 1$
degrees of freedom.

Each test item could be examined for its fit to the one-parameter logistic model in both samples by means of Equation 5.3.2. Those items that fit the model in both samples could be tested for a shift in difficulty by Equation 5.3.1. Items would be eliminated for failure either to fit the model in one sample or the other, or for differences in difficulty in the two samples. The result of this process would be a set of items that fit the one-parameter model in both samples and do not differ in item difficulty.

Although the logic of the process is acceptable, the spectre of a lack of power to detect consistent deviations from the model in the minority or smaller sample must be recognized. A lack of power because of a small sample size suggests the possibility of retaining a collection of items that, although they all fit the one-parameter model and had equal difficulties *within the limits of statistical hypothesis testing,* could have serious cumulative effects. That is, if many of the retained items had slight but consistent difficulty shifts that favor one subpopulation but were not detected individually because of a lack of power in the smaller sample, the total test could be substantially biased. Although this is a problem with all item bias measures discussed in this section, it may be particularly acute for the one-parameter logistic model because this model is frequently applied to data sets that are thought to be too small to allow use of the two- or three-parameter models.

Once again, note that the mathematical simplicity of the one-parameter logistic model makes it a very attractive model for item analysis whenever the assumptions of the model can be met.

Item bias: Two-parameter logistic model. As previously noted, the two-parameter logistic model is a special case of the more general three-parameter logistic model in which all c_i parameters are equal to zero. Thus, it is more general than the one-parameter model in that item discrimination parameters are allowed to vary. This IRT model may be expected to be fit by data from attitude assessments, where there is no reason for examinees to attempt to maximize a score, or from free-response ability measures, where there may be differences in both item difficulty and item discrimination parameters but no guessing effects.

Hulin, Drasgow, and Komocar (1982) developed an indirect test of item bias for the two-parameter logistic model. The initial step in their procedure is to obtain, as described in Section 3.1, maximum likelihood estimates of item and subject parameters in the two samples, separately, standardizing on $\hat{b}_i$ rather than $\hat{\theta}$ to equate θ-metrics. Plotting $\hat{b}_i$s from the sample from subpopulation A against $\hat{b}_i$s from the sample from subpopulation B graphically displays the extent to which the two samples provide similar estimates of item difficulties. Lord

(1980), in a discussion of the closely related problem of item bias measurements in three-parameter models, suggests eliminating items with extreme values of $\hat{b}_i$ and low estimates of a_i; these items typically have extremely large standard errors of estimate for $\hat{b}_i$. They are excluded for the step involving computing the means and variances of $\hat{b}_i$ in the two samples, but may be replaced in the scale for purposes of assessing item bias. The reason for eliminating $\hat{b}_i$s that are poorly estimated when standardizing the $\hat{b}_i$s is to improve the equating of the θ-metric.

In the test proposed by Hulin et al., empirical ICCs are obtained by dividing the equated $\hat{\theta}$ continua in both samples into exhaustive and nonoverlapping intervals. Unlike the chi-squared methods described in Section 5.2, it is not necessary to use the same intervals in both samples. Proportions of positive responses to an item are determined within each $\hat{\theta}$ interval for each sample. These proportions are plotted against the midpoints of the $\hat{\theta}$ intervals to form an empirical ICC.

There is an obvious tradeoff that must be made in the division of the $\hat{\theta}$ continua into discrete intervals. More $\hat{\theta}$ intervals yield more points that define the empirical ICC. However, for a fixed sample size, increasing the number of $\hat{\theta}$ intervals decreases the number of examinees per interval and decreases the stability of the points that determine the empirical ICC.

To compare empirical ICCs, Hulin et al. transformed the proportions of positive responses, using a logit transformation. The reasoning that leads to this transformation can be seen by examining its effect on the ICC:

$$L\{P_i(\theta)\} = \log \left[\frac{P_i(\theta)}{1 - P_i(\theta)} \right]$$

$$\text{(5.3.3)} \qquad = \log \left[\frac{\{1 + \exp[-Da_i(\theta - b_i)]\}^{-1}}{1 - \{1 + \exp[-Da_i(\theta - b_i)]\}^{-1}} \right]$$

$$= Da_i(\theta - b_i)$$

and thus $L\{P_i(\theta)\}$ is a linear function of θ. The empirical proportions, $\hat{p}_i(\hat{\theta}$ interval) should also become linearly related to $\hat{\theta}$ after the logit transformation is applied. Following the logit transformation, the intercept of the linear regression line (i.e., the regression of the transformed empirical ICC onto $\hat{\theta}$) is a function of the item difficulty and discrimination parameters, and the slope of the regression line is a function of the item discrimination parameter.

The regressions of $L\{\hat{p}_i(\hat{\theta}$ interval)\}$ onto $\hat{\theta}$ are then computed within each sample. In the next step, one regression line is computed using all the empirical proportions. Let J_A and J_B denote the numbers of proportions obtained for the samples from subpopulations A and B. Then the single regression line, which is usually termed the *pooled regression line*, is estimated from the $(J_A + J_B)$ logit-transformed proportions. Finally, a statistical test of the equality of the regression lines estimated separately in the two subpopulations is performed (Neter & Wasserman, 1974). This test can be conducted by calculating the F-ratio

$$(5.3.4) \quad F = \frac{\text{SSE(pooled)} - [\text{SSE}(A) + \text{SSE}(B)]}{[\text{SSE}(A) + \text{SSE}(B)]} \cdot \frac{J_A + J_B - 4}{2},$$

where SSE(pooled) is the sum of squared errors for the pooled regression line, and SSE(A) and SSE(B) are the sums of squared errors in the samples from subpopulations A and B. This F-ratio has 2 and ($J_A + J_B - 4$) degrees of freedom.

An empirical ICC is shown in Figure 5.3.3 and the logit-transformed empirical ICC from the same data set is shown in Figure 5.3.4.

The F-test for item bias is basically a test of the hypothesis that the pooled regression line explains as much of the variance of logit-transformed proportions as two separate lines, one estimated in each sample. That is, if a common, pooled regression accounts for the transformed proportions as well as two separately estimated regression

Figure 5.3.3
Empirical ICC for Attitude Data with 18 $\hat{\theta}$ Intervals and Approximately 10 Examinees per $\hat{\theta}$ Interval

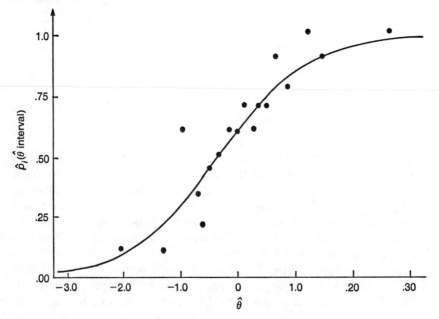

Figure 5.3.4
Logit-Transformed Empirical ICC Based on Proportions Shown in
Figure 5.3.3*

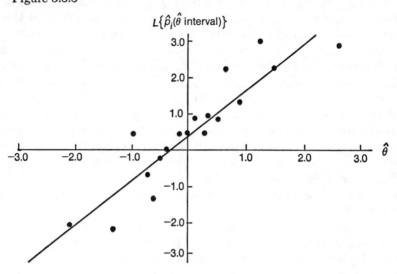

* See Section 6.4 for a discussion of transforming proportions of 0.0
and 1.0.

lines, then nothing is to be gained by considering the two samples
separately. This means the relations between item responses and $\hat{\theta}$ are
the same in both samples, and the item is functioning the same way as
a measure of θ in both samples. A statistically significant F-ratio from
Equation 5.3.4 means that the two separately estimated regression
lines account for more variance than the common, pooled regression
line; the two separate lines are *not* identical within the limits of sampling fluctuations. This means the item is functioning as a measure of
θ differently in the two samples. Hence, this is evidence that the item
is biased. This procedure is illustrated in more detail in Chapter 6
where it is applied to the analysis of translated attitude scales.

   Item bias: Three-parameter logistic model.[1]   The Hulin et al. test
for item bias in the two-parameter model is possible because there is a
simple transformation that renders the two-parameter logistic function
linear, and a statistical test of the equality of two linear regressions is
easily performed. When dealing with three-parameter logistic ICCs, a
nonzero c_i parameter precludes a convenient transformation to linear-

---

[1] This subsection utilizes matrix addition, multiplication, and inversion; these operations are described here.
   Matrix addition of two matrices, each with two rows and two columns, involves
computing

174

ity. Hence, with three-parameter ICCs and data, different approaches must be considered.

Lord (1980) outlined a procedure for detecting bias of items with three-parameter ICCs. It is based on a large sample version of Hotelling's T^2 statistic. In Lord's method, item parameters are initially estimated for both groups combined, standardizing on $\hat{b}$ rather than on $\hat{\theta}$. Each $\hat{c}_i$ is then fixed at the value obtained in the analysis of the combined sample for all remaining steps. Lord's decision not to reestimate cs when estimating parameters separately in the two samples was made because the values of many cs are poorly determined. After fixing each c_i at the value obtained in the combined sample, the item parameters are reestimated in each sample separately, again standardizing on $\hat{b}_i$ rather than $\hat{\theta}$. Items with extreme $\hat{b}_i$ and low $\hat{a}_i$ values are eliminated at the stage where the $\hat{b}$ parameters are standardized. This is similar to the initial stages of the test for bias of two-parameter logistic ICCs.

The $\hat{a}_i$ and $\hat{b}_i$ are now compared across relevant groups or subpopulations. The statistical test of the hypothesis that both $a_{i_A} = a_{i_B}$ and $b_{i_A} = b_{i_B}$ for the ith item is (in matrix notation)

(5.3.5) $$\chi^2 = v_i' \Gamma_i^{-1} v_i.$$

$$M + N = \begin{bmatrix} a & b \\ c & d \end{bmatrix} + \begin{bmatrix} e & f \\ g & h \end{bmatrix}$$
$$= \begin{bmatrix} (a + e) & (b + f) \\ (c + g) & (d + h) \end{bmatrix} = P,$$

where

$$M = \begin{bmatrix} a & b \\ c & d \end{bmatrix}$$

and

$$N = \begin{bmatrix} e & f \\ g & h \end{bmatrix}.$$

The matrices M, N, and P are referred to as "two-by-two" matrices because they have two rows and two columns. The *inverse* Q^{-1} of a two-by-two matrix $Q = \begin{bmatrix} a & b \\ b & c \end{bmatrix}$ is

$$Q^{-1} = \frac{1}{(ac - b^2)} \begin{bmatrix} c & -b \\ -b & a \end{bmatrix}.$$

Finally, the simultaneous *premultiplication* of Q by a row vector $v' = [d\ e]$ and *postmultiplication* by a column vector $v = \begin{bmatrix} d \\ e \end{bmatrix}$ yields

$$v'Qv = [d\ e] \begin{bmatrix} a & b \\ b & c \end{bmatrix} \begin{bmatrix} d \\ e \end{bmatrix}$$
$$= ad^2 + 2bde + ce^2.$$

Here,

$$\mathbf{v}'_i = (\hat{b}_{i_A} - \hat{b}_{i_B}, \hat{a}_{i_A} - \hat{a}_{i_B})$$

is the vector of differences of parameter estimates for item i obtained from samples from subpopulations A and B; $\boldsymbol{\Gamma}_i$ contains asymptotic sampling variances (squared standard errors) and covariances of $(\hat{b}_{i_A} - \hat{b}_{i_B})$ and $(\hat{a}_{i_A} - \hat{a}_{i_B})$ arranged in the two-by-two matrix

$\boldsymbol{\Gamma}_i =$

$$\begin{bmatrix} \text{sampling variance of } (\hat{b}_{i_A} - \hat{b}_{i_B}) & \begin{array}{c} \text{sampling covariance of} \\ (\hat{b}_{i_A} - \hat{b}_{i_B}) \text{ and } (\hat{a}_{i_A} - \hat{a}_{i_B}) \end{array} \\ \begin{array}{l} \text{sampling covariance of} \\ (\hat{b}_{i_A} - \hat{b}_{i_B}) \text{ and } (\hat{a}_{i_A} - \hat{a}_{i_B}) \end{array} & \text{sampling variance of } (\hat{a}_{i_A} - \hat{a}_{i_B}) \end{bmatrix} ;$$

and $\boldsymbol{\Gamma}_i^{-1}$ is the matrix inverse of $\boldsymbol{\Gamma}_i$. (Footnote 1 describes matrix inversion. "Sampling variances" and "sampling covariances" of item parameters were described in Section 2.7.) The test statistic follows a χ^2 distribution with 2 df.

　Lord's method for computing $\boldsymbol{\Gamma}_i^{-1}$ involves several steps. First, the information matrices for the $(\hat{b}, \hat{a})$ vectors must be computed separately for the two samples. Let $\mathbf{I}_{i_A}$ and $\mathbf{I}_{i_B}$ denote the information matrices for estimates of b_i and a_i in subpopulations A and B respectively. Then, substituting estimates of parameters into Lord's (p. 191) equations,

(5.3.6)　　　　　　　　$$\mathbf{I}_{i_A} = \begin{bmatrix} I_{b_i} & I_{a_i b_i} \\ I_{a_i b_i} & I_{a_i} \end{bmatrix},$$

where I_{b_i}, I_{a_i}, and $I_{a_i b_i}$ are defined in Equations 2.7.12, 2.7.13, and 2.7.14 respectively. I_{b_i}, I_{a_i}, and $I_{a_i b_i}$ are computed using parameters estimated for subpopulation A to obtain $\mathbf{I}_{i_A}$. $\mathbf{I}_{i_B}$ is obtained in a similar fashion for subpopulation B. Then $\boldsymbol{\Gamma}_{i_A}$ and $\boldsymbol{\Gamma}_{i_B}$, the asymptotic variance-covariance matrices of $(\hat{b}_i, \hat{a}_i)$ for subpopulations A and B respectively, are obtained by $\boldsymbol{\Gamma}_{i_A} = \mathbf{I}_{i_A}^{-1}$ and $\boldsymbol{\Gamma}_{i_B} = \mathbf{I}_{i_B}^{-1}$. Finally,

(5.3.7)　　　　　　　　$$\boldsymbol{\Gamma}_i = \boldsymbol{\Gamma}_{i_A} + \boldsymbol{\Gamma}_{i_B}$$

and $\boldsymbol{\Gamma}_i^{-1}$ is obtained by inverting $\boldsymbol{\Gamma}_i$.

　The null hypothesis that $a_{i_A} = a_{i_B}$ and $b_{i_A} = b_{i_B}$ is tested against the alternative hypothesis that either $a_{i_A} \neq a_{i_B}$ or $b_{i_A} \neq b_{i_B}$. Lord (Chapter 14) describes his test, presents some criticisms, and presents evidence in favor of his test. Readers should study Lord's Chapter 14 carefully before using his method.

　It is evident that Lord's procedure can be applied to two-parameter logistic ICCs also. In the case of three-parameter logistic ICCs, $\hat{c}_i$ is fixed at a constant across subpopulations for each item. With two-parameter ICCs, all the c_is are assumed, or demonstrated, to be zero. Because the test only depends on differences in a_i and b_i across groups and is mute regarding c_i, it is equally applicable to two-parameter logistic ICCs when parameters are estimated by the method of maximum likelihood.

A second procedure for examining possible bias of items with three-parameter logistic ICCs was developed by Linn, Levine, Hastings, and Wardrop (1981). This procedure is directly based on the difference between ICCs estimated in two different subpopulations. The cross-hatched regions in Figure 5.3.5 show several ways that items with three-parameter logistic ICCs can be biased. Panel A illustrates a hypothetical item with consistent bias against subpopulation B throughout the θ continuum; the item is uniformly more difficult for subpopulation B. Panel B illustrates an item with similar difficulty

Figure 5.3.5
Examples of Bias in Items with Three-Parameter Logistic ICCs

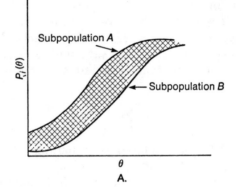

A.

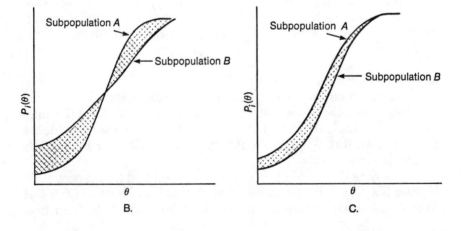

B.

C.

parameters for the two subpopulations but with less discriminatory power in subpopulation B. As a result, this item is biased against subpopulation B at the higher θ levels but biased against members of subpopulation A for lower θ values. Panel C depicts an item with similar difficulty and discrimination parameters but with a higher lower asymptote for subpopoulation A. Thus, the item is biased against members of subpopulation B at the lower θ values but is relatively unbiased at higher levels of θ. The bias illustrated in Panel C could perhaps be attributed to a test-taking strategy in subpopulation A that increases the likelihood of successful guessing.

Linn et al. discussed four different indices of bias.[2] The first three are directly related to the *area* between ICCs. The indices are defined in terms of a base and a comparison group. They are:

1. A *base-high area* that is the size of the region between $\theta = -3$ and $\theta = +3$ in which the base group ICC is above the comparison group ICC. Take subpopulations A and B as the comparison group and base group, respectively. Then the area of the cross-hatched region to the left of the point where the ICCs intersect in Panel B of Figure 5.3.5 is the base-high area.
2. A *base-low area* that is the size of the region between $\theta = -3$ and $\theta = +3$ in which the base group ICC is below the comparison group ICC. This is the area of the cross-hatched region to the right of the point of intersection of the ICCs in Panel B of Figure 5.3.5.
3. The *total area* between the two ICCs which is simply the sum of the first two indices.
4. The *root mean squared difference* between ICCs in the region $\theta = -3$ and $\theta = +3$. This index is obtained by computing

$$\text{RMSD} = \left\{ \frac{1}{600} \sum_{j=1} [\hat{P}_{i_A}(\theta_j) - \hat{P}_{i_B}(\theta_j)]^2 \right\}^{1/2}$$

for 600 θ values evenly spaced from -3 to $+3$.

Linn et al. approximated the area between two ICCs by dividing the θ continuum from -3 to $+3$ into 600 intervals. This assumes θ-metrics have been equated and almost all $\hat{\theta}$s are in the range of -3 to $+3$. The absolute values of the differences of the ICCs

$$|\hat{P}_{i_A}(\theta_j) - \hat{P}_{i_B}(\theta_j)|$$

at the midpoints of these 600 intervals were calculated and multiplied by the width of the interval (.01). Summing these 600 areas provides

---

[2] Linn et al. also discussed weighted versions of these indices of bias in which the differences between the curves were weighted by an estimate of the standard error of the difference between the ICCs. These weighted indices did not appear to be more useful than the simpler, unweighted indices.

an estimate of the total area between estimated ICCs. This area can be used to make inferences about the differences between ICCs in the two subpopulations.

Indices 1 and 2 provide estimates of the direction of bias (against the base group or against the comparison group), and indices 3 and 4 provide estimates of the total amount of bias in the item. Items with very similar ICCs in the two samples will have bias indices that are very close to zero. Items with seriously discrepant ICCs in the two samples would have bias indices (either index 3 or 4) that were substantially larger than zero.

Computing the indices discussed by Linn et al. is straightforward and the indices are intuitively appealing; they are based directly on differences between estimated ICCs. They also have an advantage over indices based upon comparisons of estimated item parameters: substantial differences in item parameters can exist without causing any practical differences in ICCs. Linn et al. presented a hypothetical example in which one item had $a = 1.8$, $b = 3.5$, and $c = .2$ and another item had $a = .5$, $b = 5.0$, and $c = .2$. These item difficulty and discrimination parameters are quite different, but the two ICCs differ by .05 or less in the interval $[-3.0, 3.0]$. Differences as small as .05 may well be tolerable for many practical measurement purposes.

There is a problem with using the Linn et al. indices in practice. The sampling distributions of the bias indices are unknown under the assumption of no difference between ICCs. Linn et al. described a method for evaluating their bias index values that involves additional calculations. Essentially, they suggested randomly dividing each sample into two halves, computing ICCs in each subsample, and then computing the bias index values for each item. This approach produces a distribution of bias index values for the situation where the null hypothesis is true. This distribution of a bias index is a bootstrapping approximation to the actual sampling distribution of the statistic under the null hypothesis of no bias.

Summary of IRT Indices of Item Bias

Statistic	Model	Hypothesis Being Tested
Lord's χ^2	3PL, 2PL	$a_{i_A} = a_{i_B}$ and $b_{i_A} = b_{i_B}$
Linn et al.	3PL, 2PL	Area or distance between ICCs in two subpopulations is zero
F-test	2PL	Regression of $\hat{p}_i(\hat{\theta}$ interval) on $\hat{\theta}$ is the same for both samples
Difficulty shift	Rasch	$b_{i_A} = b_{i_B}$
Fit of model to data	Rasch	One-parameter logistic model fits data in both subpopulations

Linn et al.'s bootstrapping approach would usually be undertaken in each study where their bias indices are used. Thus the effects of sample sizes, test lengths, distributions of θs, and distributions of item parameters on the sampling distribution of the bias index would be taken into account. Although it cannot be claimed that the value of the bias statistic that corresponds to the 90th or 95th percentile of the obtained sampling distribution truly produces an α-level of .10 or .05, it should be a good approximation.

5.4   CLINICAL EXPERIENCE AND INSIGHT

We note in passing that it is sometimes possible to detect item bias from clinical experience with a particular test, knowledge of different cultures within the United States, and familiarity with the content of the items. This method does not logically belong to classical test theory methods nor is it derived from IRT. Nevertheless, the quantitative methods discussed in this chapter should not preclude careful application of common sense. Some insights based on clinical experience are illustrated below.

Eisenman and McBride (1964) noted a problem with a particular item on the Wechsler Intelligence Scale for Children. In this test, males are asked, "What is the thing to do if you lose one of your friend's balls?" The correct answer is "buy him another" or "get him another." However, occasionally among rural samples some individuals respond, "get a doctor" and lose points. Apparently these children interpret the question as having anatomical significance. Given this interpretation, getting a doctor would be a correct response. Coyle (1965) similarly noted that occasionally an item on the information section of the same test will cause a related problem. This item asks, "What does C.O.D. mean?" This occasionally elicits an evasive answer from children from lower socioeconomic backgrounds in the South. *Cod*, of course, is a slang term for scrotum in that culture. When asked by an adult what C.O.D. means, some children apparently assume that the test administrator is being coy and spelling a vulgar term. Both items could be reworded slightly to retain their original content but remove bias against individuals from some subpopulations.

5.5   SUMMARY OF ITEM BIAS INDICES

The item bias indices discussed in this chapter should be regarded as different, rather than substitutable, solutions to the problem of detecting item bias. Because they make different assumptions, they are not necessarily competitive approaches. More importantly, slightly—

and at times substantially—different hypotheses are being tested. These differences in hypotheses illustrate both the necessity and futility of empirical studies that assess convergence among the different bias indices. It is important that such studies be done to learn how the statistics behave when applied to simulated data with varying amounts and types of bias. We need to learn the extent to which different indices yield similar conclusions about bias, and thus the extent and limits of substitutability of the indices.

Any set of empirical item responses may be poorly fit by an IRT model. Problems for bias indices caused by a lack of model fit must be examined because real empirical data usually (if not always) fail to correspond exactly to a tractable IRT model. Indices that are not robust to minor violations of the model may give erroneous results in real data. The effects of sample sizes and test lengths on item bias statistics are also largely unexplored. It is clear that sample size and test length are important to some extent because they jointly influence the stability of estimates of subject and item parameters (see Section 3.3). Sample sizes are also very important in determining the number of $\hat{\theta}$ or total test score intervals using the F-test and χ^2 approaches. In summary, both Monte Carlo and empirical comparisons are necessary; generalizations are as yet limited.

Careful examination of the hypothesis being tested by each index of item bias suggests limitations on their substitutability. One conventional approach discussed in Section 5.2, the transformed item difficulty analysis, assesses changes in relative item difficulties across samples. A second conventional approach, differences in item–total test score biserial correlations across subpopulations, is testing one type of relative discriminatory power across subpopulations. Regardless of the technical problems with these indices (discussed in Section 5.2), they do *not* represent tests of the same or even similar hypotheses.

The chi-squared item bias index described in Section 5.2 represents a test of a still different hypothesis. It examines discrepancies between proportions of correct and incorrect responses for groups of individuals with the same total test scores but who are from different subpopulations. Thus, the conventional chi-squared index is conditioning on a less informative measure of ability, total test score, than the F-test or Linn et al.'s test. The chi-squared methods seem more likely to be influenced by a single aberrant proportion in one total test score category than the F-test, Lord's method, or Linn et al.'s procedure.

IRT-based item bias indices test different hypotheses than those described above; further, the hypotheses tested within the IRT approaches are somewhat different from each other. Tests of item bias based on the one-parameter model assess item difficulty shifts and/or differential fits of the model to the data from two different samples. Because item difficulty parameters are sufficient to describe one-parameter ICCs, testing for item difficulty shifts across subpopulations is equivalent to testing for similarities of one-parameter logistic ICCs.

The F-test for item bias of two-parameter logistic ICCs is a direct application of a test for the similarity of linear regression lines estimated in two samples. The test examines differences in regression lines by comparing the variance of $L\{\hat{p}_i(\hat{\theta} \text{ interval})\}$ explained by the pooled regression line versus that explained by regression lines estimated in each sample separately. Thus, the fit of a line to a set of points is examined rather than point-to-point discrepancies.

Linn et al.'s area measure is perhaps the most appealing procedure because of its generality to either two- or three-parameter data and because of its fidelity to the theoretical definition of item bias in terms of similarity of ICCs. Its drawback is our lack of knowledge about the distribution of the indices under the null hypothesis of no differences in the ICCs. Monte Carlo estimates of the sampling distribution may provide a stopgap solution to the problem.

Lord's χ^2 test examines the significance of the difference of estimated item parameters across two samples. The test is mute regarding differences in the c parameter. It can be applied to either two- or three-parameter data with equal rigor. This procedure tests a hypothesis about differences between estimated parameters that define an ICC.

Applications of Lord's χ^2 test of item bias to two-parameter logistic ICCs will not necessarily yield the same results as F-tests for the similarity of the logit-transformed regression lines. Different hypotheses are being tested. The F-test is testing the similarity of empirical item characteristic curves. Lord's χ^2 test directly tests the equality of the theoretical item parameters a and b across groups. Even with a good fit of an IRT model to item response data, the F-test and χ^2 test may not yield identical results. If the data are not well fit by a model, all methods may encounter difficulties—Lord's because his formulae for standard errors of parameter estimates may be problematic, Hulin et al.'s because empirical proportions in $\hat{\theta}$ intervals may not become linearly related to $\hat{\theta}$ after the logit transformation, and Linn et al.'s because their parametric form for the ICC (e.g., the three-parameter logistic ICC) is inappropriate for the data.

In essence, we have attempted to present the strengths and weaknesses of the different procedures. We do not advocate the use of one specific item bias index. None appears to be universally or generally preferable. Researchers without access to LOGIST and high-speed, large-capacity computers are restricted to using the approaches discussed in Section 5.2 where some indices use only proportions of correct and incorrect responses within total score intervals, item-total correlations, and transformed item difficulties. The method based on Equation 5.3.1 is less demanding of computer time and money but is restricted to use with one-parameter logistic ICCs.

If a researcher has access to LOGIST (or a similar program) and a large-capacity computer, the choices are less restricted and any of the indices discussed in Section 5.3 are candidates for use. None, however, should be chosen for use without a careful consideration of the fidelity of the hypothesis being tested to the researcher's definition of item bias.

REFERENCES

Articles and Books

Angoff, W. H., & Ford, S. F. Item-race interaction on a test of scholastic ability. *Journal of Educational Measurement,* 1973, *10,* 95–106.

Arvey, R. D. *Fairness in selecting employees.* Reading, Mass.: Addison-Wesley Publishing, 1979.

Boehm, V. R. Negro-white differences in validity of selection procedures. *Journal of Applied Psychology,* 1972, 56, 33–39.

Boehm, V. R. Differential prediction: A methodological artifact? *Journal of Applied Psychology,* 1977, 62, 146–154.

Cleary, T. A. Test bias: Prediction of grades of Negro and white students in integrated colleges. *Journal of Educational Measurement,* 1968, 5, 115–124.

Cole, N. S. Bias in selection. *Journal of Educational Measurement,* 1973, *10,* 237–255.

Coyle, F. A., Jr. Another alternate wording on the WISC. *Psychological Reports,* 1965, *16,* 1276.

Donlon, T. F., & Angoff, W. H. The Scholastic Aptitude Test. In W. H. Angoff (Ed.), *The College Board Admissions testing program.* New York: College Entrance Examination Board, 1971.

Drasgow, F. Biased test items and differential validity. *Psychological Bulletin,* 1982, 92, 526–531.

Einhorn, H. J., & Bass, A. R. Methodological considerations relevant to discrimination in employment testing. *Psychological Bulletin,* 1971, 75, 261–269.

Eisenman, R., & McBride, J. W., Jr. "Balls" on the WISC. *Psychological Reports,* 1964, *14,* 266.

Hulin, C. L., Drasgow, F., & Komocar, J. Applications of item response theory to analysis of attitude scale translations. *Journal of Applied Psychology,* 1982, 67, 818–825.

Humphreys, L. G. Statistical definitions of test validity for minority groups. *Journal of Applied Psychology,* 1973, *58,* 1–4.

Hunter, J. E. *A critical analysis of the use of item means and item-test correlations to determine the presence or absence of content bias in achievement test items.* Paper presented at the National Institute of Education Conference on Test Bias, Bethesda, Maryland, December 1975.

Hunter, J. E., Schmidt, F. L., & Hunter, R. Differential validity of employment tests by race: A review and analysis. *Psychological Bulletin,* 1979, *86,* 721–735.

Ironson, G. H. Chi-square and latent trait approaches to the measurement of item bias. In *Test item bias methodology: The state of the art.* The Johns Hopkins University National Symposium on Educational Research, Washington, D.C., November 1980.

Katzell, R. A., & Dyer, F. J. Differential validity revived. *Journal of Applied Psychology,* 1977, *62,* 137–145.

Katzell, R. A., & Dyer, F. J. On differential validity and bias. *Journal of Applied Psychology,* 1978, *63,* 19–21.

Linn, R. L. Fair test use in selection. *Review of Educational Research,* 1973, *43,* 139–161.

Linn, R. L., Levine, M. V., Hastings, C. N., & Wardrop, J. L. Item bias in a test of reading comprehension. *Applied Psychological Measurement,* 1981, *5,* 159–173.

Lord, F. M. *Applications of item response theory to practical testing problems.* Hillsdale, N.J.: Erlbaum, 1980.

Muthén, B., & Christoffersson, A. Simultaneous factor analysis of dichotomous variables in several groups. *Psychometrika,* 1981, *46,* 407–419.

Neter, J., & Wasserman, W. *Applied linear statistical models.* Homewood, Ill.: Richard D. Irwin, 1974.

O'Connor, E. J., Wexley, K. N., & Alexander, R. A. Single-group validity: Fact or fallacy? *Journal of Applied Psychology,* 1975, *60,* 352–355.

Petersen, N. S., & Novick, M. R. An evaluation of some models for culture-fair selection. *Journal of Educational Measurement,* 1976, *13,* 3–29.

Scheuneman, J. A method of assessing bias in test items. *Journal of Educational Measurement,* 1979, *16,* 143–152.

Scheuneman, J. A posteriori analyses of biased items. In *Test item bias methodology: The state of the art.* The Johns Hopkins University National Symposium on Educational Research, Washington, D.C., November 1980.

Schmidt, F. L., Berner, J. G., & Hunter, J. E. Racial differences on validity of employment tests: Reality or illusion? *Journal of Applied Psychology,* 1973, *58,* 5–9.

Shepard, L., Camilli, G., & Averill, M. *Comparisons of six approaches for detecting test item bias using both internal and external ability criteria.* Paper presented at the Meeting of the National Council on Measurement in Education, Boston, April 1980.

Thorndike, R. L. Concepts of culture-fairness. *Journal of Educational Measurement,* 1971, *8,* 63–70.

White, K. R. The relation between socioeconomic status and academic achievement. *Psychological Bulletin,* 1982, *91,* 461–481.

Wright, B. D., & Stone, M. H. *Best test design.* Chicago: MESA Press, 1979.

Wright, B. D., Mead, R. J., & Draba, R. E. *Detecting and correcting test item bias with a logistic response model* (Research Memorandum No. 22). Chicago: University of Chicago, Department of Education, 1976.

Legal Cases

Hobson v. *Hansen,* 269 F. Supp. 401 (D.D.C. 1967), *affirmed sub nom. Smuck* v. *Hobson,* 408 F.2d 175 (D.C. Cir. 1969).

Larry P. v. *Riles,* 495 F. Supp. 926 (N.D. Cal. 1979) *appeal docketed,* No. 80-4027 (9th Cir., January 17, 1979).

United States Civil Rights Act, 1964, U.S.C. §§ 2000 et seq.

6

Applications of IRT to Language Translations

6.0 OVERVIEW

Many would probably not agree with Richards's statement that translating an instrument from a *source* (or original) language to a *target* language is "probably the most complex type of event yet produced in the evolution of the cosmos" (1953, p. 250). We can question the extremity of the statement but still agree that translation is a serious roadblock to progress in cross-cultural and international organizational research.

Although this chapter is concerned with translation, it is not intended as a review of language sciences. Others have done this (Brislin, 1976). We shall discuss some of the major problems raised by translations and their analyses, and show how applications of IRT to these problems provide solutions not available using other measurement theories. Clearly, IRT cannot provide solutions to all of the problems in this area. If it can solve some that other procedures cannot, significant progress has been made. We envision social science researchers and practitioners using methods described in this chapter in conjunction with construct validation studies to strengthen their claims of similarity of meanings across different language versions of scales and tests.

In Section 6.1 we briefly describe some problems in assessing the fidelity of a translation of material from a source language to a target language.[1] We focus on translations of major interest to social scien-

---

[1] Fidelity is used here in the sense of accurately reproducing, in the target language, the source version of an instrument. In engineering terms, the output of a high-fidelity system provides an accurate reproduction of the system's input. For scale or questionnaire translations, accurate reproduction of the input refers both to linguistic meaning (which is judged according to back translation procedures discussed in Section 6.3), and item measurement characteristics (which are evaluated according to methods discussed in Section 6.4). Thus, high-fidelity translations must reproduce both linguistic characteristics and measurement properties of items.

tists studying cross-cultural phenomena. Special attention is given to measurement scales developed for use in education, industrial/organizational psychology, and sociology.

Several types of translations are described in Section 6.2. Traditional methods of evaluating translations are reviewed in Section 6.3; their assumptions, strengths, and weaknesses are described. IRT methods of detecting item bias discussed in Chapter 5 are generalized to the problem of detecting mistranslated items from psychological scales in Section 6.4. These methods are illustrated in Section 6.4 using a set of attitude data gathered from a sample of bilingual Hispanics. IRT procedures are applied in Section 6.5 to another data set gathered from francophone and anglophone Canadians. The data set consists of responses to a verbal ability test originally written in English and its translation into Canadian French. This latter application involves three-parameter logistic ICCs, independent samples, and equating θ-metrics.

Discussed in Section 6.6 are restrictions on claims of equivalence of meanings in both cultures following IRT analysis of translations, problems raised by cross-cultural construct validation studies, and within and between cultural analyses.

6.1 TRANSLATIONS OF SCALES AND CROSS-CULTURAL RESEARCH

The ultimate goal of translating psychological scales into multiple languages is to permit research on psychological traits and constructs among members of different cultures. Very high-fidelity translations of psychological scales from one language to another are necessary to achieve this end. High-quality translations allow cross-cultural comparisons of the antecedents and correlates of psychological constructs. Further, scale development in the target language and culture may be shortened significantly. The problems of inferring, validating, and studying psychological constructs in one culture have been well documented (Campbell & Fiske, 1959; Cronbach & Meehl, 1955). Attempts to develop psychological scales that provide valid measurements in two cultures are more difficult. When one considers that the goals of cross-cultural research are to achieve this end *and* provide evidence that the meanings of the constructs assessed in the two cultures are the same *across* cultures, then the magnitude of the problems confronting research in this area become manifest.

Cross-cultural research on observable behaviors and responses (such as sexual practices or ceremonies), inferred from both verbal reports and public activities, suffers only to a limited extent from problems in the assessments of the variables being studied.

Childrearing practices or the exclusion of members of one sex from certain ceremonies can be ascertained by unobtrusive observations. Differences across cultures may be observed and the contextual meanings of these differences inferred. Similarly, ages at time of marriage and sexual contact with members of the same or opposite sex may be observed directly or unobtrusively. Once again, differences across cultures can be tabulated and studied.

Unfortunately, research—especially cross-cultural research—on antecedents and consequences of many psychological traits must proceed more circumspectly. It is more difficult to count events or provide observations that may be unambiguously interpreted as evidence of anxiety, intelligence, satisfaction, or even achievement. Within one culture the problems are difficult; solutions to problems of accurate measurement often seem to be rejected as soon as they are developed. Nonetheless, some progress has occurred in the measurement of abilities, satisfactions and attitudes, achievements, and even interests within cultures.

These considerations imply a distinction between what is directly observable and what is not—childrearing practices on the one hand and intelligence on the other. Both are subjects for study by scientists. Our commonsense usage of these terms as well as everyday observations suggest this is a valid distinction. However, a complete distinction is not crucial to our emphasis that research on constructs requiring introspections on the part of individuals and inferences about unobservables compounds the difficulties of cross-cultural research.

Glymour (1980) suggested that the distinction between observables and unobservables might be that observables are what a naive subject can be taught to recognize and discriminate *without reliance on a theory*. Maxwell (1962) provides an extensive discussion of the problems created by introducing unobservable terms and constructs into scientific discourse. Here we simply assert that concepts and constructs that evolve from language used to describe and report observable data are both necessary and logical. They allow necessary generalization and permit progress.

One procedure that could be used to evaluate a translation is to conduct construct validity studies (Cronbach & Meehl, 1955; Campbell & Fiske, 1959) on the original and translated measures in both cultures. There are problems with this approach. Operationally, construct validation studies tend to be never ending; there is always another construct as a candidate for inclusion in a study, and there is always another explanation for the observations. These problems are compounded when one attempts to determine the construct validity of a measure in two cultures *simultaneously*. The rules for specifying the meanings of constructs studied simultaneously in two cultures have not yet been fully explicated. Conclusions must therefore be tentative about the similarity or identity of meanings of a measure and its translations. When the rules for conducting such studies are poorly specified, the interpretations of the results are not precise, and judgments of the similarity or identity of the meanings of two measures of the same construct are a function of both the individual making the judgments and the obtained relations (Roberts, Hulin, & Rousseau, 1978).

Thus, this chapter does not provide a solution to the problems of establishing meanings of constructs in different cultures simultaneously. Theory-based methods are outlined which are designed to evaluate the equivalence of measurement across different language versions of items and psychological scales. With this evidence about the measurement equivalence of scales, the steps required for construct validation may proceed somewhat more easily.

6.2 TYPES OF TRANSLATIONS

Four types of translations can be identified by their goals. Casagrande (1954) presents a thorough discussion of these four types of translations, and Brislin (1976) summarizes the major differences. The first type of translation, termed *pragmatic translation,* refers to translation of a passage where the sole interest lies in communicating accurately in the target language what was contained in the source language. Here, the information conveyed is the criterion against which to evaluate the translation. Other linguistic aspects, such as style, are unimportant. Translations into English of Japanese instructions for assembling electronic components would be an example of pragmatic translations. Such a translation is successful to the extent that English-speaking individuals can understand and use the translated instructions, and so produce a functioning amplifier from the components.

Aesthetic-poetic translations have quite a different end. In this type of translation, the purpose is the evocation of moods, feelings, and affect in the target language that are identical to those evoked by the material in the source language. Although faithfulness to the original content is required, the translator is granted poetic license to achieve the desired ends.

In an *ethnographic translation,* the meaning and the cultural content of the source language materials must be maintained in the target language. Translators producing these translations must be familiar with both source and target cultures as well as source and target languages. They must know how words and phrases fit into cultures and use them appropriately in the translated version. Once again, some latitude must be granted because often there is no exact cultural equivalent in the target language and culture of the object in the source language. For example, England has no exact equivalent for a rural, southern United States accent and word usage. A translator would be required to select a region and accent in the target culture that conveyed the content as well as suggesting a regional accent and word usage which, while differing from English used by announcers from the British Broadcasting Company, did not convey other, unintended differences. Translating southern American English into Cockney would not suffice.

Linguistic translations are concerned with equivalence of meanings of both morphemes and grammatical forms of the two languages. Correspondence of structure becomes an important part of the analysis of the quality of a linguistic translation.

In this chapter we are concerned with evaluating translations of psychological instruments—ability tests; measures of attitudes, interests, values, satisfaction; personality inventories; projective techniques—that have been designed to assess individual differences with respect to any of a number of characteristics. These characteristics normally have been shown to have importance in the source culture and language for predicting and understanding human behavior—otherwise they would not have survived early validation attempts. They are hypothesized to have importance in the target culture—otherwise there would be little reason for producing the translation.

The translations considered in this area would likely be classified in Casagrande's scheme as ethnographic translations although the fit into this category is not perfect. The fidelity of a translation of a psychological instrument is judged, ultimately, by the fit of measures of constructs in the target culture and language into networks of relations. The fit of the target language construct into its network must be the same as the fit of the original language construct into its network. Thus, the goal of the translation is equivalence of meaning vis-à-vis a network of relations. The analysis of the degree of equivalence is ultimately determined by the extent of *convergence* of networks of relations. These statements imply an epistemological position that will be examined for dysfunctional consequences later in this chapter.

The position described above, prescribing how one infers meanings of psychological constructs, assumes that a communality exists between and among different cultures in the world. Of course, the assumption is highly speculative and is very likely to be false in the extreme. However, one can hypothesize about limited cultural communality among a restricted set of cultures with some degree of confidence. The psychic unity of man need not be invoked.

It needs to be stressed that we are not arguing that IRT-based analyses of translation quality are substitutes for rigorous construct validity research described in the preceding paragraphs. We see the goals of the two analyses as compatible, overlapping, and complementary. IRT analysis of translations is a theory-based attempt to determine the similarity of relations between item responses and an underlying trait θ in two languages. ICCs for the original item and its translation must be similar before one could conclude the original item and translated item had the same meaning in terms of the latent trait. Investigations of the meanings of latent traits in the two cultures are also necessary. Meanings are usually studied by the process of construct validation previously described.

6.3   ANALYSIS OF TRANSLATIONS BY TRADITIONAL METHODS

There are limited numbers of traditional procedures available for evaluating the quality of a translation. The most frequently used methods often include a comparison of the original scale to a translation of the target language version back into the source language. Comparisons of responses of *bilingual individuals* to both versions of an instrument are also used to assess a translation. Back translations and bilingual analysis are discussed in detail below.

Back translations.   This method involves three steps. The original version of the instrument is first translated into the target language. The target language instrument is then translated back into the source language by independent translators. Finally, the back translated instrument is compared to the original instrument by individuals who have not been involved in any of the previous steps. Discrepancies are noted, and frequently second and third iterations of troublesome items, questions, or instructions are required.

This procedure appears necessary but not sufficient to ensure comparability of meanings of psychological instruments. There are some shortcomings that should be noted. Highly skilled translators can sometimes produce acceptable back translations from badly garbled translations by a series of inferences and insightful guesses. A second problem is that reproduction of the original meaning by a back translation does not address directly the meaningfulness of the material in the *target* language. Thus, back translation seems a necessary first step in the analysis of any translation, but similarity of original material and the back translation does not guarantee equivalence. It is comforting to a cross-cultural researcher, however.

Bilingual responses.   Following a successful back translation, researchers may administer the two versions of the scales or tests to bilingual subjects, who complete both versions. The scales are scored following standard procedures, and the resulting sets of scores are correlated or otherwise analyzed to examine the extent to which the two versions of the scales yield highly similar information about the subjects. For example, if the subjects are equally skilled in both languages, one would expect a high degree of relation in the rank order of the subjects as well as similar means and variances of the items appearing in the two language versions of the scale. In a somewhat more sophisticated analysis, estimates might be obtained of the variance due to subjects, language differences, and subject-by-language interactions. The latter two sources of variance would indicate either constant error or random error introduced by the translation process. Strong linear relations between scores based on the two different versions of the scales would be interpreted as indicating that the translation had yielded equivalent scales in the two languages. Small amounts of variance due to language or to subject-by-language interactions would similarly indicate a high-fidelity translation.[2]

An unavoidable problem with this particular method of examining the quality of translations is caused by reliance on bilingual subjects. Because of their bilingualism, these individuals may interpret the meanings of words in ways that are different from monolinguals. That is, the relations (similarities and differences) among the words used by bilingual individuals may differ substantially from those used by monolingual individuals. Bilinguals' definitions of such objective terms as "yellow" can be different from either population of monolinguals with whom they share a common language (Landar, Ervin, & Horowitz, 1960). Bilinguals may see and report differences that are not shared by monolingual individuals; nonetheless it is monolingual individuals who are actually the focus of most cross-cultural research. Generalization of results for bilinguals to populations of monolinguals must be cautious and may prove misleading.

6.4   APPLICATIONS OF IRT TO ANALYSIS OF ATTITUDE SCALE TRANSLATIONS[3]

By way of introduction to this approach, consider again problems of item bias in psychological assessments in different ethnic samples in the United States (discussed in Chapter 5). Our questions about cross-cultural comparisons and meaningfulness of assessments are closely paralleled by the theoretical and practical problems of legal and statistical analysis of measurement bias within the heterogeneous population of the United States.

---

[2] See Katerberg, Hoy, and Smith (1977) for an example of this form of analysis based on Cronbach's generalizability theory (Cronbach, Gleser, Nanda, & Rajaratnam, 1972).

[3] Section 6.4 is a condensed and revised version of a paper by Hulin, Drasgow, and Komocar (1982). It is adapted here with permission of the American Psychological Association.

As we saw in Chapter 5, bias, from the perspective of IRT, is assessed by examining the relations between the conditional probabilities of responding correctly to an item (given θ) and θ, the unidimensional latent trait. Thus, ICCs for the two subpopulations are compared. Bias, or its lack, is judged relative to the underlying trait.

These IRT procedures can be directly applied to translation data to determine whether the relation between the underlying trait and the probability of endorsing an item is identical across cultures. Note that this provides *direct* evidence about the meanings of the items in terms of the underlying latent trait being measured by each version of the scale. ICCs for an item that differ across languages (after equating θ-metrics) pinpoint those items in need of revision (e.g., more or less difficult), indicate items with different discriminating power, and may even reveal problems with lower asymptotes (in terms of multiple-choice tests) resulting from ineffective or overly seductive distractors. In addition, similar ICCs of all items across both versions automatically result in equivalent tests and measurement scales. Thus, scale scores from either language version can be compared because they are in the same metric.[4] Different test norms may be required for two different cultures, however, and the same score may have a different relative standing (degree of extremity) in the different cultures.

In the remainder of Section 6.4 we shall present an analysis of a translation of the JDI, using the methods outlined above and in Chapter 5. The data set consists of responses to the JDI made by bilingual Hispanics employed by an international merchandising organization. This data set is used because it has previously been analyzed using traditional methods (Katerberg, Hoy, & Smith, 1977) and because it avoids the problem of equating θ-metrics and therefore provides a simpler application of the method.

The original sample analyzed by Katerberg et al. (1977) consisted of 203 bilingual employees. They were of Cuban or Puerto Rican extraction and employed in sales and sales support functions in company units in Miami or New York City. Respondents were asked to complete both English and Spanish versions of two attitude questionnaires on two different occasions, 30 days apart, in a counterbalanced order (Spanish-English and then English-Spanish). Only the responses to the JDI are analyzed here. Questionnaires were deleted that had greater than 10 percent missing data from either the English or Spanish versions of the scales of interest to the present study. This reduced the sample for the present study to 178 usable questionnaires. The scales examined here include the English and Spanish versions of the full 72-item, five-scale (measuring satisfaction with the

---

[4] This, of course, assumes near perfect statistical power and ability to detect small differences. Less than perfect detectability could result in small but consistent differences at the item level that accumulate to produce suspect scores.

Work Itself, Pay, Promotional Opportunities, Supervisor, and Co-workers) JDI. The two-parameter logistic model was selected as a statistical model for the JDI items because there is little reason to expect very dissatisfied employees to choose the positive response to any of the items. Thus the c parameter should be zero.

Our primary interest in this analysis is to compare the ICCs for the English version of JDI items to the corresponding ICCs for the Spanish version. The initial step involves separate maximum likelihood estimation of item and person parameters for the English and Spanish data sets by LOGIST (Wood, Wingersky, & Lord, 1976; Wood & Lord, 1976). Normally, the second step would involve equating θ-metrics since the parameters (and parameter estimates) of the two-parameter logistic model are not uniquely determined. However, a more direct procedure is possible for the present data because the bilingual subjects completed questionnaires in *both* English and Spanish. Thus, for each subject we can plot the estimate of job satisfaction from the Spanish version ($\hat{\theta}_S$) against the estimate of job satisfaction from the English version ($\hat{\theta}_E$). This plot is shown in Figure 6.4.1. The correlation between $\hat{\theta}_S$ and $\hat{\theta}_E$ is .92 and the regression of $\hat{\theta}_S$ on $\hat{\theta}_E$ is $\hat{\theta}'_S = -.01 + .96\hat{\theta}_E$. In light of the Monte Carlo research studying the standard error of estimate for $\hat{\theta}$ (Lord, 1975; Swaminathan & Gifford, 1979; Hulin, Lissak, & Drasgow, 1982), adjustment of the θ-metrics does not appear to be necessary. Figure 6.4.2 further confirms this conclusion. Here, estimated item difficulties for the English and Spanish versions of the JDI are plotted. The correlation between the two sets of estimated item difficulties is .93, and the regression of estimated item difficulty for Spanish items ($\hat{b}_{iS}$) on the estimated item difficulty of English items ($\hat{b}_{iE}$) is $\hat{b}'_{iS} = .01 + 1.02 \hat{b}_{iE}$.

Having determined that the $\hat{\theta}$ and $\hat{b}$ metrics are equivalent across the two versions of the JDI, we can now compare ICCs of the original and translated items. (A simple method for equating θ-metrics is described in Section 6.5.) Empirical ICCs are computed separately for each item in both languages by first dividing the $\hat{\theta}$ continuum into a number of mutually exclusive intervals. Then the proportions of positive responses from subjects within the intervals are determined. The plot of these proportions against the corresponding midpoints of each $\hat{\theta}$ interval constitutes an empirical ICC.

Figure 6.4.3 presents illustrative empirical ICCs for the Spanish and English versions of the item "challenging." (The ICCs estimated in the two separate samples are also shown.) These curves were obtained by dividing the $\hat{\theta}$ continuum into 18 intervals with approximately 10 respondents per interval; this appeared to be the most reasonable trade-off between (1) a large number of points in the empirical ICC and (2) accurately estimating each point of the empirical ICC.

Figure 6.4.1
Regression Line and Scatter Plot for Regression of $\hat{\theta}$ for Spanish Version of
JDI on $\hat{\theta}$ for English Version of JDI

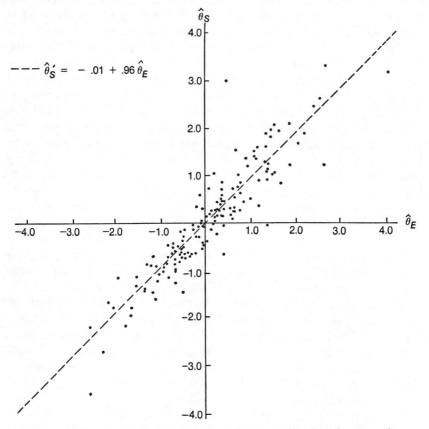

Source: Hulin, Charles L., Drasgow, F., & Komocar, John. "Applications of Item Response Theory to Analysis of Attitude Scale Translations," *JAP*, 1982, 67. 818–825. Copyright 1982 by the American Psychological Association. Reprinted/adapted by permission of the publisher and authors.

The empirical proportions $\hat{p}_i(\hat{\theta}$ interval) are then transformed by means of the logit transformation described in Section 5.3 (Equation 5.3.3) so that the transformed proportions are linearly related to θ. Following the logit transformation, the regression lines relating the transformed empirical proportions to $\hat{\theta}$ are estimated from each sample separately. The two regression lines should be identical within the limits of sampling fluctuations if the item provides equivalent measurement of θ in both languages.

A single regression line is fit to both sets of empirical proportions in the next step of the analysis. As described in Section 5.3, the data

Figure 6.4.2
Regression Line and Scatter Plot for Regression of $\hat{b}$ for Spanish Version of
JDI on $\hat{b}$ for English Version of JDI

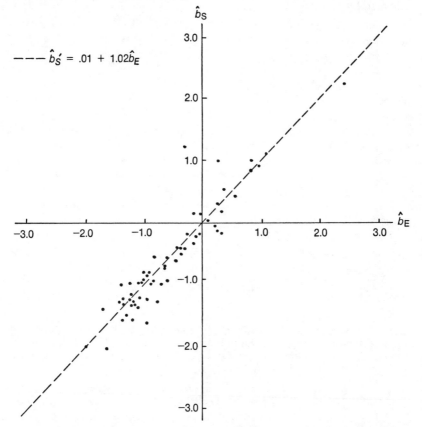

Source: Hulin, Charles L., Drasgow, F., & Komocar, John. "Applications of
Item Response Theory to Analysis of Attitude Scale Translations," *JAP*, 1982, 67.
818–825. Copyright 1982 by the American Psychological Association. Reprinted/
adapted by permission of the publisher and authors.

points for the pooled regression line consist of the transformed proportions from *both* the English and Spanish versions of the JDI. If J_S
and J_E empirical proportions are computed for the Spanish and English data sets respectively, then the pooled regression line is estimated from $(J_S + J_E)$ empirical proportions.

Finally, the test of the equality of two regression lines is accomplished by determining whether the two separate lines account for
significantly more variance in the dependent variable (i.e., in the
transformed proportions) than the pooled regression line. Equation
5.3.4 can be used to perform the test. A significant difference may be

Figure 6.4.3
Proportions of Positive Responses in 18 $\hat{\theta}$ intervals for English and Spanish Versions of the JDI Item "Challenging" and Corresponding ICCs Estimated by LOGIST

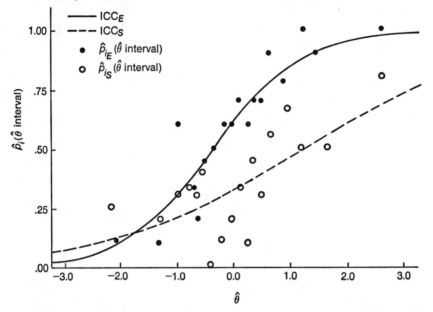

Source: Hulin, Charles L., Drasgow, F., & Komocar, John. "Applications of Item Response Theory to Analysis of Attitude Scale Translations," *JAP*, 1982, 67. 818–825. Copyright 1982 by the American Psychological Association. Reprinted/adapted by permission of the publisher and authors.

interpreted as indicating nonequivalence of ICCs across English and Spanish versions of the item. In addition, a significant effect can be examined more closely to determine whether the slopes of the regression lines differ (which would imply a difference in the two a parameters) or whether the intercepts differ (if the slopes do not differ, then significantly different intercepts imply a difference in the b parameters).

A completed example of the application of the Hulin, Drasgow, and Komocar procedure to the data set plotted in Figure 6.4.3 is provided below. The data for the example are listed in Table 6.4.1. In this table, midpoints of the $\hat{\theta}$ intervals for the English JDI are given in column 1; proportions of positive responses to the item in English and the logit transformation of these proportions are in columns 2 and 3. The midpoints of the $\hat{\theta}$ intervals for the Spanish data are listed in the fourth column and the corresponding proportions of positive responses and logit transformations of these proportions are in columns 5 and 6.

Note that two of the empirical proportions in Table 6.4.1 are 1.00

Table 6.4.1
Proportions of Positive Responses and Their Logit Transformations in $\hat{\theta}$ Intervals for English and Spanish JDI Data Sets

English $\hat{\theta}$ Interval Midpoints	$\hat{p}_E(\hat{\theta}\ Interval)$	$ln\left[\dfrac{\hat{p}_E(\hat{\theta}\ Interval)}{1-\hat{p}_E(\hat{\theta}\ Interval)}\right]$	Spanish $\hat{\theta}$ Interval Midpoints	$\hat{p}_S(\hat{\theta}\ Interval)$	$ln\left[\dfrac{\hat{p}_S(\hat{\theta}\ Interval)}{1-\hat{p}_S(\hat{\theta}\ Interval)}\right]$
-2.10	.11	-2.091	-2.17	.25	-1.099
-1.34	.10	-2.197	-1.33	.20	-1.386
-0.98	.60	0.406	-1.00	.30	-0.847
-0.73	.33	-0.708	-0.81	.33	-0.708
-0.64	.20	-1.386	-0.67	.30	-0.847
-0.54	.44	-0.241	-0.59	.40	-0.406
-0.37	.50	0.000	-0.42	.00*	-2.944
-0.17	.60	0.406	-0.24	.11	-2.091
-0.05	.60	0.406	-0.05	.20	-1.386
0.07	.70	0.847	0.10	.33	-0.708
0.25	.60	0.406	0.24	.10	-2.197
0.34	.70	0.847	0.32	.44	-0.241
0.46	.70	0.847	0.47	.30	-0.847
0.62	.90	2.197	0.65	.56	0.241
0.86	.78	1.266	0.90	.67	0.708
1.22	1.00*	2.944	1.20	.50	0.000
1.45	.90	2.197	1.64	.50	0.000
2.61	1.00*	2.944	2.62	.80	1.386

* See explanation in text.

and one is 0.00. Such extreme proportions occasionally occur when the sample size in a $\hat{\theta}$ interval is small. In the present example there were approximately 10 individuals in each of the 18 $\hat{\theta}$ intervals. Unfortunately, the logit transformation of a proportion of either 0.00 or 1.00 is undefined because it involves either a numerator or denominator of 0.00. To circumvent problems of undefined logit transformations, we use $(2N_j - 1)/2N_j$ as the "adjusted" proportion when the empirical proportion is 1.00, and $1/2N_j$ when the empirical proportion is 0.00, where N_j is the number of individuals in the jth $\hat{\theta}$ interval.

The adjustment of the empirical proportion is based on the following. Suppose that an additional sample of the same size were drawn from the same population. One would expect approximately the same observed proportions of positive responses in the new sample. However, with the general inconsistency of individuals, it seems unlikely that the extreme proportions of 1.00 or 0.00 would be obtained again. If only one individual in the second sample responded inconsistently, the proportion of positive or correct responses across the two samples combined would be $(2N_j - 1)/2N_j$ or $1/2N_j$. Thus, adjusting observed proportions of 1.00 or 0.00 reflects our intuitions about individuals' responses in additional samples. Note that adding or subtracting $1/2N_j$ has more of an effect on the observed proportions in small samples than large samples. If 10 individuals out of a possible 10 in the $\hat{\theta}$ interval responded positively, the adjusted proportion would be .95. If 20 out of 20 responded positively, the adjusted proportion would be .975. Smaller adjustments of observed proportions in larger samples reflect our increased confidence in the observed proportions.

The regression on $\hat{\theta}$ of the $J_E = 18$ logit-transformed proportions for the English sample is $.438 + 1.255\,\hat{\theta}$. The correlation between $\hat{\theta}$ and the logit-transformed proportions is .914. The sum of squares due to regression is 32.191, and the sum of squared errors (SSE) is 6.308. The regression of the $J_S = 18$ transformed Spanish proportions onto $\hat{\theta}$ is $-.770 + .564\,\hat{\theta}$. The correlation between $\hat{\theta}$ and the transformed Spanish proportions is .605. Here the sum of squares due to regression is 6.907, and the SSE is 11.938.

The regression of all 36 ($=J_E + J_S$) proportions onto $\hat{\theta}$ is $-.164 + .900\,\hat{\theta}$. The correlation between the transformed proportions and $\hat{\theta}$ is .692. The sum of squares due to regression is 34.174, and the SSE is 37.185. Thus the test for the equality of regression equations for the two samples is

$$F = \frac{37.185 - (6.308 + 11.938)}{(6.308 + 11.938)} \frac{(18 + 18 - 4)}{2} = 16.608,$$

which is significant ($\alpha = .01$). Based on these results, the conclusion would be that the item's measurement properties were different in the two languages. This means that the relation between probability of responding correctly to the item and the latent trait was different across the two language versions of the JDI.

Table 6.4.2 presents a summary of the significance tests for the 72-item JDI. Of the 72 F-ratios, ($df = 2,32$) 3 were significant at $\alpha = .05$.

Table 6.4.2
Summary of Significance Tests Comparing ICCs of
Corresponding English and Spanish Items

Nominal Alpha Level	Number Significant	Expected Number Significant
.01	1	.7
.05	3	3.6
.10	7	7.2
.25	12	18.0
.50	24	36.0

Taken alone, these results indicate that three Spanish JDI items have ICCs that differ from the ICCs of the corresponding English JDI items. However, these results could be Type I errors. Table 6.4.2 also presents the obtained and expected (under the null hypothesis assumption of no differences) numbers of significant F-ratios for selected α-levels from .01 to .50. There is little difference between the obtained and expected numbers of significant F-ratios at α-levels of .01, .05, and .10. Taken in total, Table 6.4.2 indicates that the translation of the JDI was quite good.

Figures 6.4.4 and 6.4.5 provide graphic examples of the regression method for comparing the equality of ICCs. In Figure 6.4.4, the transformed empirical ICCs of the English and Spanish versions of the item "challenging" are presented (the untransformed empirical ICC for this item was shown in Figure 6.4.3). An error may have occurred in the translation of this item. The item "challenging" was rendered as "retador" rather than "desafiante," which would be the preferred translation according to some language consultants. This apparent error perhaps introduced nonequivalent meaning into the Spanish item. It was detected as a biased item. However, we must stress that it is problematical whether a careful editorial review of the translation of the JDI items into Spanish would have brought this apparent mistranslation to light. A bilingual reviewer of the paper by Hulin, Drasgow, and Komocar argued that "retador" rather than "desafiante" was indeed the appropriate translation. The empirical analysis of the ICCs from the two language versions suggests that "retador" is inappropriate.

Figure 6.4.4
Regression Lines and Scatter Plots for Regressions of Logit-Transformed
Proportions of Positive Responses for 18 $\hat{\theta}$ Intervals on $\hat{\theta}$ for English and
Spanish Versions of the JDI Item "Challenging"

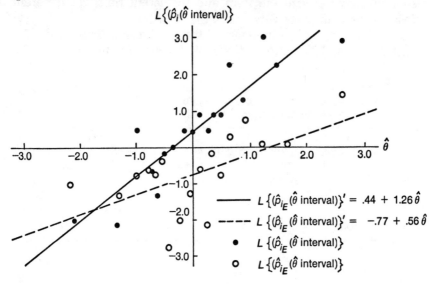

Figure 6.4.5
Regression Lines and Scatter Plots for Regressions of Logit-Transformed
Proportions of Positive Responses for 18 $\hat{\theta}$ Intervals on $\hat{\theta}$ for English and
Spanish Versions of the JDI Item "Influential"

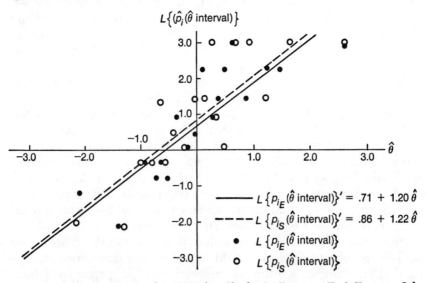

    Source for Figures 6.4.4 and 6.4.5: Hulin, Charles L., Drasgow, F., & Komocar, John.
"Applications of Item Response Theory to Analysis of Attitude Scale Translations,"
JAP, 1982, 67. 818–825. Copyright 1982 by the American Psychological Association.
Reprinted/adapted by permission of the publisher and authors.

Figure 6.4.5 shows a similar comparison for the item "influential." Conclusions based on visual inspections of the regression lines in Figures 6.4.4 and 6.4.5 agree with significance tests for the equality of the regression lines. The regression line for the item "challenging" in English differs from the regression line for the corresponding item in Spanish ($\alpha = .05$), and the regression line for the item "influential" in English does not differ significantly ($F = .13$, which is not significant for $\alpha = .05$). Visual inspection of the dispersions of the logit-transformed empirical proportions about the regression lines also reveals that more points, better estimated, would be desirable.

A problem deserving some discussion is the dimensionality of the JDI. One of the strong assumptions of IRT is that only a single latent trait underlies item responses. Chapter 8 contains a technical discussion of methods for examining the assumption of unidimensionality. The robustness of LOGIST to violations of a perfectly unidimensional latent trait was discussed in Section 3.3. The assumption of unidimensionality is clearly false for the JDI; factor analyses of the scales by the original developers (Smith, Kendall, & Hulin, 1969) and others (Smith, Smith, & Rollo, 1974) have repeatedly concluded that the 72 items assess five separate dimensions of satisfaction that are defined by the appropriate items.

Recent analyses (Parsons & Hulin, in press), using different procedures, suggest that treating the JDI as measuring a large, general affective component (i.e., general job satisfaction) may be warranted for some purposes. The subsets of items used to form the five satisfaction scales yield clusters of items with higher within-cluster correlations than expected on the basis of a single general affect dimension. Nonetheless, the general affect dimension of the JDI may be sufficiently prepotent for LOGIST to estimate individuals' standings on this dimension reasonably well. Thus, JDI item responses seem to be sufficiently unidimensional to allow use of IRT procedures: Violations of the unidimensionality assumption do not appear sufficiently severe to cause LOGIST to provide meaningless results.

Summary. Some limitations on claims for scale equivalence are apparent. We can conclude only that the translated JDI items are generally unbiased and are estimating equivalent traits within the two languages. The procedure is strictly an internal analysis; statements about equivalence must be made with this in mind. We have not examined relations between $\hat{\theta}$s derived from the translated scales and external variables, nor have we studied the translated JDI within networks of relations derived in Spanish language cultures. How the latent trait functions in the two cultures remains to be determined, but radically different meanings of the scales across the two cultures and languages would not be a fault of the translation.

6.5 APPLICATION OF IRT TO ANALYSIS OF ABILITY TEST TRANSLATION[5]

A second example of an IRT analysis of a translated scale is presented in this section. Here we describe the analysis of a translation, into Canadian French, of a verbal test originally developed and normed in English. The items forming the verbal scale were taken from the Otis-Lennon School Ability Test, Intermediate Level. The English version of this 60-item scale was administered to 727 English-speaking Ontario school children in grades 6, 7, and 8. The French language experimental version was administered to 1,373 French-speaking school children in grades 6, 7, and 8 in Quebec Province. Preliminary analyses indicated the two versions of the test were sufficiently unidimensional to apply the three-parameter logistic model (see Drasgow & Lissak, 1982, for details). In the initial analysis of the data by LOGIST, it was found that 10 of the original 60 items had extreme b parameters (i.e., greater than $+3$ or less than -3), and/or very low a parameters. These items were eliminated from all further analyses because their parameter estimates had very large standard errors.

The responses from the two groups of students were then reanalyzed separately by means of LOGIST to estimate both subject and item parameters. Both LOGIST analyses standardized on b rather than $\hat{\theta}$ in order to equate θ-metrics. That is, in the separate analyses of English- and French-speaking students' data, the item difficulties were scaled to have zero means and unit variances. This is accomplished by first computing the mean and standard deviation of the $\hat{b}$s obtained from the two data sets. Then the transformations

$$\text{Rescaled } \hat{b}_{iF} = \frac{\hat{b}_{iF} - \bar{\hat{b}}_F}{\text{SD of } \hat{b}_{iF}},$$

$$\text{Rescaled } \hat{\theta}_{kF} = \frac{\hat{\theta}_{kF} - \bar{\hat{b}}_F}{\text{SD of } \hat{b}_{iF}},$$

and

$$\text{Rescaled } \hat{a}_{iF} = \hat{a}_{iF}(\text{SD of } \hat{b}_{iF})$$

are applied to the item and person parameters for the French data set. Here $\bar{\hat{b}}_F$ and (SD of $\hat{b}_{iF}$) are the mean and standard deviation of item difficulties estimated from the French-speaking students' data, and $\hat{\theta}_{kF}$

---

[5] We would like to thank Charles E. McInnis, Georges Sarrazin, and Raymond Vaillancourt at the University of Ottawa for making these data available to us.

is the estimate of θ for the kth individual in the French sample. The mean and standard deviation of estimated item difficulties for the English version would also be computed and applied to parameter estimates ($\hat{b}_{iE}$, $\hat{\theta}_{kE}$, and $\hat{a}_{iE}$) from the English sample in a similar fashion. By standardizing the two distributions of $\hat{b}$ parameters to have equal means and variances, the effects of differences in ability distributions across samples were removed. ICCs from the two samples can then be directly compared.

The fourth bias index of Linn, Levine, Hastings, and Wardrop, (1981), which was described in Section 5.3, was computed for each item to indicate the discrepancies of the ICCs computed in the French- and English-speaking samples. (Index 4 is the root mean squared difference between ICCs for 600 θ values evenly spaced from -3 to $+3$). In order to obtain an approximate sampling distribution of the bias index for this collection of items, the French-speaking sample was divided randomly into two halves, ICCs were calculated separately for each half standardizing on $\hat{b}$ to equate θ metrics as described above, and the bias index was calculated for each item. This procedure is a bootstrapping technique that provides an approximation to the sampling distribution of the bias index under the null hypothesis of no differences between ICCs. Note that the null hypothesis is true here because the two French samples were randomly sampled from the same population.

This approximate distribution of the bias index was used to determine the values of the index that occur 10 percent of the time where there are no true differences. Thus, the 90th percentile of the observed distribution was established as the *critical value* that would be used to reject the null hypothesis and conclude that the ICCs from the two samples were indeed different. Note that we have attempted to set the α-level to be .10. Because the bootstrapping procedure only provides an *approximation* to the actual sampling distribution of the bias index under the null hypothesis, we cannot claim that our α-level is exactly .10.

Applying the decision rule to reject the null hypothesis when the bias index was larger than the critical value, 32 of the 50 items were found to be biased. Thus, it is apparent that many translated items of this verbal scale are not providing equivalent measurement in English and French. They should not be used to assess verbal ability of French-speaking students without further revision.

Figure 6.5.1 displays four items found to be nonequivalent by this procedure, and Figure 6.5.2 displays four items found to be equivalent. The item parameters estimated in both samples, as well as the values of the bias index, are presented in Tables 6.5.1 and 6.5.2.

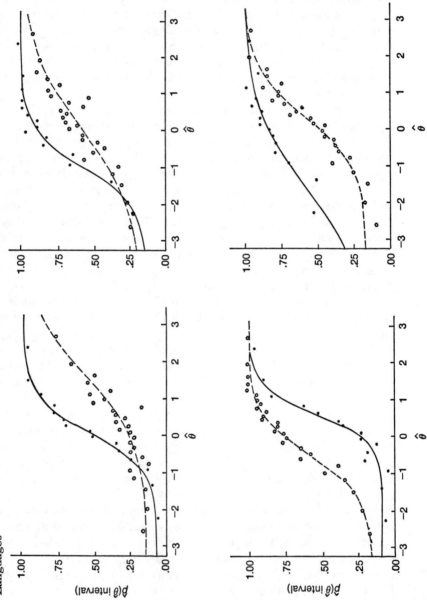

Figure 6.5.1
Four Items from the Otis-Lennon School Abilities Test Showing Nonequivalent Measurement across Languages

Figure 6.5.2
Four Items from the Otis-Lennon School Abilities Test Showing Equivalent Measurement across Languages

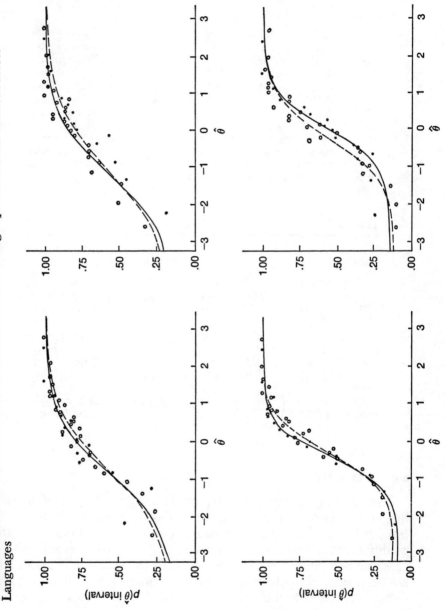

Table 6.5.1

Panel	$\hat{a}$	$\hat{b}$	$\hat{c}$	Linn et al. Bias Index 4	
A	.793	1.321	.160		Francophone
	1.288	.116	.145	.276	Anglophone
B	.615	.020	.160		Francophone
	1.119	−1.029	.145	.197	Anglophone
C	.522	− .478	.160		Francophone
	1.198	.846	.145	.331	Anglophone
D	1.032	.215	.160		Francophone
	.530	−1.714	.145	.479	Anglophone

Note: Item parameters estimated in anglophone and francophone samples and item bias index for four nonequivalent items from Canadian French translation of Otis-Lennon Test.

Table 6.5.2

Panel	$\hat{a}$	$\hat{b}$	$\hat{c}$	Linn et al. Bias Index 4	
A	.868	− .729	.160		Francophone
	.775	− .995	.145	.009	Anglophone
B	.799	−1.137	.160		Francophone
	.791	− .754	.145	.028	Anglophone
C	1.626	− .236	.160		Francophone
	1.534	− .417	.145	.009	Anglophone
D	1.361	− .156	.160		Francophone
	1.161	.016	.145	.011	Anglophone

Note: Item parameters estimated in anglophone and francophone samples and item bias index for four equivalent items from Canadian French translation of Otis-Lennon Test.

6.6 SUMMARY

It is not our purpose to comment on the quality of the translations of the Verbal Scale of the Otis-Lennon Test or the JDI. Instead, our interest lies in illustrating *procedures* one might use to evaluate the quality of translated scales. However, it should be stressed that the apparent nonequivalence in the translated Otis-Lennon items should not be attributed solely to the translation process. Both language and culture differentiate the two populations of students. Even good linguistic translations of items could appear to be biased due to cultural differences between the French- and English-speaking students. This point is highlighted by noting that when the Spanish version of the JDI was administered to *monolingual* Spanish-speaking Mexicans, the translation was found to have more biased than unbiased items. Thus, the two versions of the JDI appear to have different meanings in monolingual Spanish- and English-speaking samples, but not in the bilingual Hispanic sample from the United States. Cultural or language differences, or both, could contribute to this finding.

At this point, one could either attempt another iteration of the translation for the JDI and the Otis-Lennon into the target languages for use with monolingual individuals or conclude that, although the denotative meanings of the items were highly similar (as evidenced by the convergent back translations), the problems were inherent in cross-cultural research and not with the translation. If the latter conclusion was reached, an obvious next step would be to determine the different meanings of the scales in the target cultures on the basis of their relations with other relevant variables in nomological networks.

To argue that two scales have different meanings in two cultures on the basis of different behavioral correlates of the scales in the two cultures implies that we adopt a radical empirical epistemological position. This position attributes meaning to constructs, traits, and variables solely in terms of their relations with other variables, whose meanings also must be inferred from *their* relations with still other variables, etc., *ad infinitum*. Definitional and semantic legerdemain will not provide solutions to our problems except when the definitions are embedded within theories that suggest useful variables to include in the defining networks.

On the other hand, to conclude that the original and translated scales in two different languages are equivalent on the basis of similarity of ICCs implies that this form of internal consistency (evaluated by similarity of ICCs) is sufficient to allow claims of equivalence. This is a strong conclusion. Whatever epistemological position is adopted, applications of IRT to translation problems in psychology solve a number of research problems. IRT eliminates the necessity for bilingual samples, with their different perceptions of similarities and differences among the verbal terms denoting important concepts in their cultures and different interpretations of constructs—different from either group of monolingual individuals with whom they share one language. IRT procedures also eliminate the requirements that samples from the different populations be equivalent in terms of the distributions of their scores on the trait being measured by the scales.

Methodologically and conceptually, the applications of IRT seem to stand outside the continuum from strictly internal analyses derived from traditional item analyses and the laborious and time-consuming construct validation procedures outlined by Irvine and Carroll (1980). IRT procedures seem to provide more and better evidence about bias and measurement error than do traditional methods, but provide less information about the empirical meaning of the scales in the two cultures than would a process of construct validation. Although we disagree with many of the particulars outlined by Irvine and Carroll, we are in agreement with the necessity and purposes of some form of construct validation of the scales in the two cultures.

Establishing equivalence of scales in two languages and cultures is clearly difficult. At the extreme it may involve simultaneous development of extensive, fully articulated nomological networks in both cultures. This procedure, by itself, is difficult—perhaps even impossible in practical terms. Moreover, the crux of the problem is that the meanings of the variables most central to each network do not emerge unbidden from the background of quantitative and theoretical relations. The meanings depend as much on observers' fallible judgments, common sense, intuition, filtration of information, and many other unproved assumptions, as they do on objective descriptions of the relations obtained (Roberts et al., 1978). Different social scientists bring different intellectual backgrounds to bear on results of construct validation efforts. Different interpretations of the meanings of the variables will result. The application of IRT presented in this chapter circumvents some of the problems that must be solved before such nomological networks establishing construct validity can be developed, and may allow less slippage in networks of relations.

REFERENCES

Brislin, R. Translation research and its applications: An introduction. In R. Brislin (Ed.), *Translation: Applications and research*. New York: Wiley/ Halsted, 1976.

Campbell, D. T., & Fiske, D. W. Convergent and discriminant validation by the multitrait-multimethod matrix. *Psychological Bulletin*, 1959, 56, 81–105.

Casagrande, J. The ends of translation. *International Journal of American Linguistics*, 1954, 20, 335–340.

Cronbach, L. J., Gleser, G. C., Nanda, H., & Rajaratnam, N. *The dependability of behavioral measurements: Theory of generalizability for scores and profiles*. New York: John Wiley & Sons, 1972.

Cronbach, L. J., & Meehl, P. E. Construct validity in psychological tests. *Psychological Bulletin*, 1955, 52, 281–302.

Drasgow, F., & Lissak, R. I. Modified parallel analysis: A procedure for examining the latent dimensionality of dichotomously scored item responses. Manuscript under review, 1982.

Glymour, C. The good theories do. In *Construct validity in psychological measurement*. Princeton, N.J.: U.S. Office of Personnel Management and Educational Testing Service, 1980.

Hulin, C. L., Lissak, R. I., & Drasgow, F. Recovery of two- and three-parameter logistic item characteristic curves: A Monte Carlo study. *Applied Psychological Measurement,* 1982, 6, 249–260.

Hulin, C. L., Drasgow, F., & Komocar, J. Applications of item response theory to analysis of attitude scale translations. *Journal of Applied Psychology,* 1982, 67, 818–825.

Irvine, S. H., & Carroll, W. K. Testing and assessment across culture: Issues in methodology and theory. In H. C. Triandis & J. W. Berry (Eds.), *Handbook of cross-cultural psychology* (Vol. 2). Boston: Allyn & Bacon, 1980.

Katerberg, R., Hoy, S., & Smith, F. J. Language, time, and person effects in attitude scale translation. *Journal of Applied Psychology,* 1977, 62, 385–391.

Landar, H. J., Ervin, S. M., & Horowitz, A. E. Navaho color categories. *Language,* 1960, 36, 368–382.

Linn, R. L., Levine, M. V., Hastings, C. N., & Wardrop, J. L. Item bias in a test of reading comprehension. *Applied Psychological Measurement,* 1981, 5, 159–173.

Lord, F. M. *Evaluation with artificial data of a procedure for estimating ability and item characteristic curve parameters* (Research Bulletin 75–33). Princeton, N.J.: Educational Testing Service, 1975.

Maxwell, G. The ontological status of the theoretical entities. In *Minnesota studies in the philosophy of science* (Vol. III). H. H. Feigl & G. Maxwell (Eds.), Minneapolis, Minn.: University of Minnesota Press, 1962.

Parsons, C. K., & Hulin, C. L. An empirical comparison of latent trait theory and hierarchical factor analysis in applications to the measurement of job satisfaction. *Journal of Applied Psychology,* 1982, 67, 826–834.

Richards, I. Toward a theory of translation. Studies in Chinese thought. *American Anthropological Association,* 1953, 55, Memoir 75. Chicago: University of Chicago Press.

Roberts, K. H., Hulin, C. L., & Rousseau, D. M. *Developing an interdisciplinary science of organizations.* San Francisco: Jossey-Bass, 1978.

Smith, P. C., Kendall, L. M., & Hulin, C. L. *The measurement of satisfaction in work and retirement.* Skokie, Ill.: Rand McNally, 1969.

Smith, P. C., Smith, O. W., & Rollo, J. Factor structure for blacks and whites of the Job Descriptive Index and its discrimination of job satisfaction. *Journal of Applied Psychology,* 1974, 59, 99–100.

Swaminathan, H., & Gifford, J. A. *Estimation of parameters in the three-parameter latent trait models. (Report No. 90).* Amherst, Mass.: University of Massachusetts, School of Education, Laboratory of Psychometric and Evaluation Research, 1979.

Wood, R. L., & Lord, F. M. *A user's guide to LOGIST* (Research Memorandum 76–4). Princeton, N.J.: Educational Testing Service, 1976.

Wood, R. L., Wingersky, M. S., & Lord, F. M. *LOGIST—A computer program for estimating examinee ability and item characteristic curve parameters* (Research Memorandum 76–6). Princeton, N.J.: Educational Testing Service, 1976.

7

Adaptive Testing

7.0 OVERVIEW

Standardized ability tests, achievement tests, and attitude assessment instruments typically attempt to provide precise measurement across a wide range of some latent characteristic. This is accomplished through the use of items with difficulty parameters that range across a broad interval. An unintended consequence of variability in item difficulties is that any particular examinee will encounter many times, frequently as many as half of the items on the test, that are too easy or too hard to be informative about his or her ability. Nonetheless, the examinee must spend time and effort attempting to answer these items.

The goal of adaptive or *tailored* testing[1] is to present items of appropriate difficulty to each examinee. By "tailoring" the difficulty of items to the ability of an examinee, items that are too easy or too hard to provide information about the ability of the examinee are not administered. Instead, IRT methods are used to select items of the appropriate difficulty level for each examinee. These items provide substantial information about the examinee's ability.

There are a variety of benefits that result from an adaptive test. Obviously, the number of test items required to reach a specified level of measurement precision is substantially reduced. Thus, less time is required to complete the test, and the likelihood of fatigue or boredom is minimized. Motivational problems should also be reduced: Low-ability examinees will not be daunted by very difficult items and high-ability examinees are not likely to become careless after answering several consecutive easy items. Additional valuable consequences of a computerized adaptive test (CAT) are discussed in Section 7.6.

---

[1] We shall use the terms *tailored testing* and *adaptive testing* interchangeably.

Throughout this chapter we assume that item parameters are known from pretesting and do not distinguish between estimated and actual item parameters. Table 3.3.1 shows that the effects of item parameter estimation errors on the accuracy of ability estimates are relatively small. Thus it appears that any problems created by treating item parameters as known should be minor, provided that the test norming samples were reasonably large by the standards described in Section 3.3.

In Section 7.1 a number of noncomputerized testing procedures are discussed. We do not intend to present an exhaustive review of these methods nor do we intend to present detailed descriptions. Weiss and Betz (1973), Weiss (1974), Killcross (1976), and McBride (1976) provide extensive reviews. Our purposes are to describe several noncomputerized adaptive tests, to indicate the variety of approaches that have been taken, and to point out some shortcomings. A nontechnical description of computerized adaptive testing is given in Section 7.2. Several critical decisions that must be made prior to implementing a CAT are also noted. More detailed descriptions of the underlying issues and relevant research findings are presented in Section 7.3. A Monte Carlo simulation is presented in Section 7.4 to show the reduction in test length that is possible for an adaptive test. Unfortunately, the item selection procedures used in Section 7.4 may not be useful in practice if cheating can occur. An ad hoc procedure devised to minimize the effects of cheating is described in Section 7.5. Because this procedure abandons optimal item selection, it is not as efficient as the test described in Section 7.4. Another Monte Carlo study is presented in Section 7.5 to illustrate the degree of inefficiency caused by nonoptimal item selection.

7.1 NONCOMPUTERIZED ADAPTIVE TESTS

Binet. There are a variety of adaptive testing methods that do not require a computer. In fact, Weiss and Betz point out that Binet's ability tests were adaptive: The sequence of items presented to a child depended upon the child's previous responses. Here the examiner monitored a child's responses and selected items of appropriate difficulty for presentation.

There are two chief objections to individualized clinical administration of items to examinees. The first objection is that examinees would undoubtedly perform inconsistently across examiners, with some examinees doing better for one type of examiner and other examinees doing better for other types of examiners. Race, sex, and ethnicity of examinee and examiner are possible sources of these positive and negative interactions. This reduces the objectivity of the test:

All examinees do not respond to the same test, where the "test" is the *gestalt* created by the examiner and test items.[2] Nonetheless, Kreitzberg and Jones (1980, p. 3) point out that clinical administration of test items "has the potential to elicit considerable information about the examinee."

Cost is also a serious objection to clinical presentation of test items. It is inconceivable (to the present authors at least) that the College Entrance Examination Board could administer over a million SAT exams annually using Binet's method of item presentation at a reasonable cost to the examinees. The requirement of quickly and inexpensively testing large numbers of individuals was the primary motivation for the original development of paper-and-pencil multiple-choice tests during World War I (Weiss & Betz, 1973) and continues to be an important reason for their use.

Two-stage tests. An adaptive test that uses a paper-and-pencil multiple-choice format is the *two-stage test*. In a two-stage test each examinee first answers a short *routing test*. This test is scored immediately, and the results are used to direct each examinee to one of several longer *measurement tests*.

The basic idea underlying two-stage testing is that lower-ability examinees should perform relatively poorly on the routing test and can therefore be directed to an easier measurement test. High-ability examinees, in contrast, should score well on the routing test and can be directed to a more difficult measurement test.

The scoring of a two-stage test must take into account the systematic differences in difficulties of the measurement tests. For example, imagine that all measurement tests consist of 20 items, examinee A answered 10 items correctly on the most difficult measurement test, and examinee B answered 10 items correctly on the easiest measurement test. *The number right score of examinee A should not be compared to the number right score of examinee B,* because examinee A answered 10 *difficult* items correctly (and incorrectly answered 10 difficult items) and examinee B answered 10 *easy* items correctly (and incorrectly answered 10 easy items).

A number of scoring methods for two-stage tests have been devised. A simple method is the *average difficulty score* (Weiss, 1974). In this method of scoring, an examinee's total test score is taken as the average of the difficulties of all items he or she answered correctly.[3]

---

[2] Killcross provided a detailed argument that objectivity is the principal motivation for paper-and-pencil multiple-choice tests.

[3] This method of scoring a test is unlikely to be satisfactory if an examinee can guess the correct answer. Correctly guessing the answer to the most difficult item, but responding incorrectly to all other items, yields the highest score possible on a measurement test.

IRT methods would provide a convenient means to estimate ability in the context of two-stage tests. However, these methods have not been used extensively because most of the research in this area was conducted prior to widespread availability of the necessary IRT software and computer hardware.

Two-stage tests have been examined by Angoff and Huddleston (1958); Cleary, Linn, and Rock (1968); Linn, Rock, and Cleary (1969); and Lord (1971a, 1980). The results are generally favorable (Killcross, 1976); a reduction in test length is possible without degrading measurement accuracy. However, there are a number of problems with two-stage testing.

One practical question with two-stage tests concerns who should correct the routing test. Because large groups of examinees are usually tested simultaneously, the testing site is likely to become noisy and distracting unless examinees score their own routing test while remaining seated. We suspect that a nontrivial proportion of examinees will make errors in scoring their routing test and in selecting the appropriate measurement test.

A second problem encountered in two-stage testing is that the test is minimally adaptive: Item difficulty is adapted to the examinee only once during the test. Consequently, there is no recourse if the routing test directs an examinee to the wrong measurement test. The frequency of routing errors depends upon a number of factors (e.g., length of the routing test, the number of measurement tests); for some of the two-stage tests developed by the researchers listed above, approximately 20 percent of the examinees were not directed to the appropriate measurement test (Weiss & Betz, 1973).

If measurement tests consist of items with a narrow range of difficulties, there will be little information about the ability of examinees misclassified by the routing test. Measurement tests can be structured to have a broader range of item difficulties, but this is contrary to the purpose of adaptive testing. These problems can be circumvented through the use of more sophisticated methods of tailoring the measurement tests. Computerized adaptive testing is one possibility.

Flexilevel tests. Lord's (1971b, 1980) flexilevel test uses a cleverly constructed paper-and-pencil format to produce an adaptive test. Here a test with an odd number, say $n = 51$, of items has its items arranged in order of difficulty from easiest to hardest. Each examinee begins by answering the item with median difficulty (item 26). Examinees then score their own answers. If correct, they proceed forward in the test to the first item of greater difficulty that has not yet been attempted. If the current item is answered incorrectly, then the examinee proceeds backwards in the test to the first item of lesser difficulty not yet attempted. For our example of a 51-item test, an examinee would start with the median item, item 26, and a sequence of items and item responses might be:

Current Item	Update Rule	Examinee's Answer
26	If correct go to 27; if incorrect go to 25	Incorrect
25	If correct go to 27; if incorrect go to 24	Correct
27	If correct go to 28; if incorrect go to 24	Correct
28	If correct go to 29; if incorrect go to 24	Correct
29	If correct go to 30; if incorrect go to 24	Incorrect
24	Etc.	

Examinees continue until they answer half of the items, scoring their answers as they proceed through the test.

It is very easy to obtain test scores for a flexilevel test. Lord (1980, Chapter 8) showed that the number of correct answers is the appropriate test score for an examinee who correctly answers the last item attempted. Examinees who respond incorrectly to the last item they attempt should receive an additional one-half point: the number of correct answers plus one half is their appropriate test score.

Lord (1971b, 1980) demonstrated that a flexilevel test can be constructed to be nearly as effective as a peaked conventional test (which consists of all items with a common difficulty of b_o) in the ability range where the conventional test is most informative. The flexilevel provides superior measurement at other ability levels. In addition, Lord (1980) noted "unpeaked conventional tests cannot do as well in any part of the range [of θ] as a suitably designed flexilevel test" (p. 126).

Lord (1980) presented a list of questions that must be answered before flexilevel tests can be used. Two are noteworthy. First, Lord asked, "How can we score the examinee who does not follow directions?" The importance of this question is highlighted by Olivier's (1974) finding that approximately 15 percent of his sample of 635 examinees were unable to follow directions for a flexilevel test. A second question posed by Lord concerns the extent of the increase in testing time per item required by a flexilevel test. Clearly, the instructions for a flexilevel test are more complicated and require more time to present. The time needed to shuffle backwards and forwards through a test booklet may also be substantial. Both of Lord's questions can be circumvented by computerized presentation and scoring of test items.

Finally, note that the difficulty of items attempted by an examinee on a flexilevel test does not necessarily approach the examinee's ability as the exam progresses. For example, consider a hypothetical examinee of average ability who has made 10 correct and 10 incorrect responses to the 51-item flexilevel test previously described. The next item attempted would be item 16, which would be too easy for this examinee, or item 36, which would be too difficult. As the test continues, the examinee would be administered items that are even easier than item 16 and/or items that are even harder than item 36. No items of appropriate difficulty would be administered.

Branching tests.   In a *branching test* examinees start with an item of moderate difficulty. The general algorithm for selecting items in a branching test is to proceed to a more difficult item when a correct response is given and proceed to an easier item if an incorrect response is given. The branching pathways are established for all possible response patterns prior to any testing.

Figure 7.1.1 illustrates a branching network. An examinee who answered item 1 correctly would then attempt item 2, which would be an item somewhat more difficult than item 1. From item 2 the examinee would proceed to item 4 or item 5, depending upon whether the response to item 2 was correct or incorrect, respectively. Item 4 would of course be a more difficult item than item 5.

The branching test illustrated in Figure 7.1.1 allows examinees of moderate ability to attempt items of moderate difficulty throughout the test. For example, the moderately difficult item 13 in Figure 7.1.1 could be the last item attempted in the branching test.

Three variants of the branching test have received attention in the psychometric literature (see Lord, 1970, for a number of theoretical developments, and Killcross, 1976, and Weiss, 1974, for thorough reviews). In an *up-and-down* branching test, the item difficulty increases after a correct response and decreases after an incorrect response by a constant amount δ (delta). For example, if the ith item an examinee answers has difficulty b_i and if the examinee answers item i correctly, then the $(i + 1)$th item the examinee attempts will have difficulty $b_{i+1} = b_i + \delta$. If the examinee answers item i incorrectly, then $b_{i+1} = b_i - \delta$. In an up-and-down test, δ remains constant throughout the test. For the test in Figure 7.1.1, item 2 would be δ more difficult than item 1, δ less difficult than item 4, and exactly equal to the difficulty of item 8. Items 1, 5, and 13 would all be equally difficult as would items 3 and 9, 6 and 14, etc.

A second branching test studied by Lord (1970), termed the *H-L* test, is actually a generalization of the up-and-down test. Here H and L are positive integers, and the difficulty of the $(i + 1)$th item attempted by an examinee is related to the difficulty of the ith item by

$$b_{i+1} = \begin{cases} b_i + H\delta \text{ if item } i \text{ is answered correctly} \\ b_i - L\delta \text{ if item } i \text{ is answered incorrectly.} \end{cases}$$

Note that $H = 1$, $L = 1$ is the branching test previously described.

The *H-L* method allows steps of different size following correct and incorrect responses. For example, if $(H = 1, L = 2)$ and $\delta = .1$, then item difficulty will be increased by .1 following a correct re-

Figure 7.1.1
Pathways for an Up-and-Down Branching Test

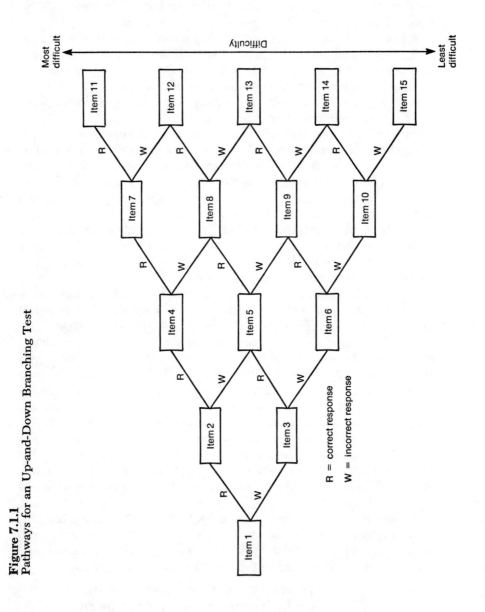

R = correct response

W = incorrect response

sponse but decreased by .2 following an incorrect response. Thus the decrease in item difficulty following an incorrect response is larger than the increase following a correct response. With multiple-choice items superior measurement should be obtained when L is larger than H. This is because it is possible to guess the answer to a multiple-choice item; consequently, a correct response is not unequivocal evidence that the examinee *knew* the answer. In contrast, an incorrect answer is relatively clear evidence that the examinee did not know the answer, and therefore should be given greater weight than a correct response.[4] Lord found the H-L combinations of $(H = 1, L = 3)$, $(H = 1, L = 2)$ and $(H = 2, L = 3)$ to be superior to up-and-down tests for simulated five-option multiple-choice tests (with $c_i = .2$ for all items).

Several methods of scoring up-and-down and H-L branching have been investigated. In one method, the average difficulty of all items attempted by an examinee is used as the test score. The difficulty of the last item administered to an examinee provides another method of scoring. This method can be improved slightly by defining the test score to be the difficulty of the next item that would have been administered had the test not ended. This method of scoring uses the information provided by the examinee's response to the last test item. Weiss and Betz (1973) and Lord (1970) provide further information on methods of scoring up-and-down and H-L branching tests.

A third general approach to branching tests described by Lord (1970, 1971c) is the Robbins-Monro procedure. In this method the step size between successive item difficulties is decreased during the test. Hence the Robbins-Monro procedure is called a *shrinking–step size* test.

When step size is decreased in accordance with the conditions stated by Robbins and Monro (1951) the difficulty of the final item presented to an examinee is a *consistent* estimate of the latent trait θ (Lord, 1970, p. 175). The proof of this result will not be discussed here. However, in this proof it is necessary to assume that the step size is reduced in a very precise manner. Thus an item bank of $2^n - 1$ items, with carefully prescribed item difficulties, is required for an n-item Robbins-Monro test (Lord, 1971c). It is unlikely that this type of test could be implemented for a test of more than 8 or 9 items; a 10-item Robbins-Monro test requires an item pool of 1,023 items.

In a Monte Carlo study, Lord (1971c) found a Robbins-Monro test to be superior to both up-and-down and H-L tests. However, he could not find a shrinking–step size test utilizing a realistically sized item

---

[4] Inattention, fatigue, and errors in entering an answer on the answer sheet can all lead to incorrect responses; nonetheless, these effects should be less important than the effects due to guessing.

pool that maintained the measurement effectiveness of the Robbins-Monro procedure. Lord found his best *H-L* tests to be superior to the approximate Robbins-Monro test.

There are a variety of theoretical and practical problems that have not yet been solved for branching tests. For example, Lord's work only considers the case where item discriminating power is constant for all items and item parameters are known. The effects of a_i that vary across items and the effects of using estimated item parameters are unknown.

7.2 COMPUTERIZED ADAPTIVE TESTING SCENARIO

Throughout the remainder of this chapter we shall discuss CAT with the following scenario in mind. The scenario begins as an examinee enters the testing site and checks in with the test monitor. The test site consists of a number of cathode ray tube (CRT) terminals. Each terminal is connected with its own mini- or microcomputer. The computers have disk drive attachments that allow convenient insertion and removal of disks. Stored on each disk is the item pool for one or more tests.

The test monitor then assigns a CRT to the examinee and inserts the appropriate disk. The computer provides instructions for signing on and can obtain various administative information such as the examinee's name, address, and social security number.

The test itself is preceded by test instructions. After verifying that the examinee understands the directions, the first test item is presented. This item is called the "initial item." The initial item can either be of moderate difficulty or selected for this examinee on the basis of some information such as the examinee's educational background. Choosing the initial item is the *starting point problem*.

If the examinee answers the initial item correctly, a more difficult item is presented next. A less difficult item is presented if the examinee answers incorrectly. At some point after 2, 3, or more items have been administered[5], an ability estimate is obtained and testing proceeds in the following iterative fashion:

a. Given the examinee's current ability estimate, the computer picks a new item that should be particularly useful for determining true ability. This is the *item selection problem*.

b. The item is presented and the examinee answers the item.

---

[5] In order to estimate ability by the method of maximum likelihood, the examinee must make at least one correct response and one incorrect response (otherwise the maximum likelihood ability estimate is $\pm\infty$). Thus two or more items must be administered prior to estimating ability. Other estimation techniques, such as Bayesian estimation, do not have this requirement.

c. The examinee's ability is reestimated, based on all the items that have been presented so far. This is the *ability estimation problem*.
d. Should another item be presented? This is the *termination criterion problem*.
e. If another item is to be presented, branch back to stage *a*. Otherwise, begin a new test or end the testing session.

As the testing session proceeds, administrative information about the examinee and his or her test scores are stored on the computer's disk. At the end of the testing session, the computer can check to see whether the transmission line to a central administrative computer is operative. If the line is operative, then the minicomputer transmits all relevant information about the examinee to the central computer. The central computer stores the information automatically in the appropriate data archive. Letters to the examinee and other appropriate parties summarizing test results can be printed automatically.

7.3 DISCUSSION OF CAT PROBLEMS

Starting point. As noted in the preceding section, two methods are frequently used for selecting the initial item. In a relatively homogeneous examinee population—for example, high school seniors—with further information about individual examinees unavailable, it is reasonable to administer an initial item of moderate difficulty. In Sections 7.4 and 7.5 we shall describe in detail two methods for picking an initial item when there is little prior information about examinees. In other situations, the examinee population may be very heterogeneous. For example, examinees' education levels may range from high school dropouts to college graduates. When information such as education level can be obtained prior to the beginning of the tailored test, an item of moderate difficulty for the appropriate educational level can be administered.

Lord (1977) found that the choice of starting item is relatively unimportant, at least for some types of adaptive tests. Lord simulated a 25-item, verbal ability adaptive test that used maximum likelihood estimation of ability (Section 2.6) and selected items that had maximum information (Section 2.7) at the current ability estimate. Initial items ranged in difficulty from moderate difficulty for fifth graders to very difficult for college-bound high school seniors. Surprisingly, the choice of the initial item had almost no effect on the accuracy of estimates of θ after 25 items were administered.

In sum, Lord's work clearly indicates that choice of an initial item can be unimportant provided that the adaptive test is reasonably long.

In attitude measurement, however, it is unlikely that as many as 25 items will be administered. Consequently, it is of interest to determine the number of items required for an adaptive test in order to circumvent the starting point problem. At present there is little information available concerning this topic.

Item selection and ability estimation. We shall discuss these two topics together because methods for selecting items are usually devised so that ability estimation is facilitated or optimized.

Two methods for estimating ability have been used frequently in adaptive testing: maximum likelihood estimation, discussed in Section 2.6, and Bayesian estimation, discussed below. Although either estimation method can be used in conjunction with any item selection technique, three item selection methods are conveniently used with maximum likelihood estimation, and a different item selection method is most conveniently used with Bayesian estimation. We shall first describe the item selection techniques used in conjunction with maximum likelihood estimation and then briefly discuss Bayesian estimation and its associated item selection technique.

Match b_i to $\hat{\theta}$ item selection. The simplest item selection rule used with maximum likelihood ability estimation involves examining all items not yet administered and selecting the item whose difficulty is closest to the current $\hat{\theta}$. We shall refer to this method as the "match b_i to $\hat{\theta}$" method. This method (or some variant of it) was used in early studies of tailored testing (Urry, 1970; Reckase, 1973, 1974; Weiss, 1974). The match b_i to $\hat{\theta}$ method is computationally simple, very inexpensive, and selects items of approximately appropriate difficulty.

Match m_i to $\hat{\theta}$ item selection. When there is guessing, the match b_i to $\hat{\theta}$ method will tend to select items that are too difficult. This is because the maximum of the item information function for item i occurs at the value of m_i along the θ continuum:

$$(7.3.1) \qquad m_i = b_i + \frac{1}{Da_i} \, ln\left[\frac{1 + \sqrt{1 + 8c_i}}{2}\right]$$

(Birnbaum, 1968), where $\ln(x)$ refers to natural logarithm of x. (In the derivation of Equation 7.3.1, Birnbaum assumed that items have three-parameter logistic ICCs.) The value of m_i for item i corresponds to the point along the θ continuum at which item i provides maximum information. Thus m_i corresponds to the ability level at which item i is most useful for maximum likelihood ability estimation.

Inspection of Equation 7.3.1 reveals that m_i is greater than b_i when $c_i > 0$. This means that an item with difficulty b_i is most useful for estimating ability when it is administered to an examinee whose ability is slightly higher than b_i. Consequently, the match b_i to $\hat{\theta}$ method can be improved if we match m_i to $\hat{\theta}$ by selecting, from the items not yet administered, the item whose m_i is closest to $\hat{\theta}$.

The match m_i to $\hat{\theta}$ method is almost as simple as the match b_i to $\hat{\theta}$ method. The only additional calculations involve computing m_i for each item. These values can be computed once and then stored or cataloged for each item in the same fashion as a_i, b_i, and c_i.

Table 7.3.1 presents estimated item parameters for three verbal ability items. If the next item to be presented were to be selected from

Table 7.3.1
Item Parameters for Three Items from
Verbal Ability Tests

Item	a_i	b_i	c_i	m_i	*Item Information at $\hat{\theta} = .40$*
140	.690	.217	.15	.402	.258
155	.690	.507	.13	.672	.260
174	1.104	.797	.12	.894	.643

these three items and if the current $\hat{\theta}$ were .40, then the match b_i to $\hat{\theta}$ method would select item 155. This is because $b_{155} = .507$ is closest to $\hat{\theta} = .40$. In contrast, the match m_i to $\hat{\theta}$ method would select item 140, since $m_{140} = .402$ is closest to $\hat{\theta}$.

Maximum information item selection. In Table 7.3.1, item 174 provides the most *information* about ability at $\hat{\theta} = .40$. The maximum information item selection method would select item 174. More generally, in the maximum information item selection method, item information $I(\hat{\theta}, u_i)$ is computed at the current value of $\hat{\theta}$ for all items not yet administered. (Section 2.7 provides the equations required to compute item information.) Then the unadministered item with maximum information at $\hat{\theta}$ is presented to the examinee.

In his recent work on adaptive testing, Lord has used the maximum information item selection method in conjunction with maximum likelihood ability estimation. An example of this research is Lord's (1977) Broad-Range Tailored Test (BRTT) of verbal ability. Lord compared the test information function of the 25-item BRTT to test information functions of three forms of the verbal section of the Preliminary Scholastic Aptitude Test (PSAT) adjusted to a length of 25 items.[6] The

---

[6] To adjust the test information function of a test with, say, 85 items to a length of 25 items, test information is multiplied by the ratio 25/85. Thus, the *shape* of the test information function remains the same, but the height of the function is reduced by a factor of 25/85 for all θ values.

BRTT was found to have roughly *twice* the information of the PSAT tests in the range of ability where the PSAT tests were *most* informative. Outside this range of ability, the BRTT was many times more informative.

*Bayesian estimation of ability.** The chief alternative to maximum likelihood estimation of ability in adaptive testing is Bayesian estimation. Although a technical description of Bayesian estimation is beyond the scope of this book (see Novick & Jackson, 1974, or Box & Tiao, 1973), it is relatively easy to obtain an intuitive understanding of this method. A Bayesian analysis in adaptive testing begins with the specification of a *prior distribution* for θ. The prior distribution summarizes what is known about a particular examinee's ability before testing begins. For the case of a homogeneous population with little or no further information available about particular examinees, we might assume that θ is normally distributed with a mean of zero and a variance of one.[7] Let us denote the prior distribution of θ by $f(\theta)$.

The prior distribution is then combined with the likelihood equation. Expanding the notation of Section 2.6, denote the likelihood of a vector $\mathbf{U}$ of item responses by an examinee with ability θ as $L(\mathbf{U}|\theta)$. Recall that in maximum likelihood estimation our estimate of θ is the value $\hat{\theta}$ that maximizes $L(\mathbf{U}|\theta)$. In Bayesian estimation, the likelihood equation is combined with the prior distribution via Bayes's theorem to yield

$$(7.3.2) \qquad f(\theta|\mathbf{U}) = kL(\mathbf{U}|\theta)f(\theta),$$

where $f(\theta|\mathbf{U})$ is the posterior distribution of ability and k is a constant needed for technical reasons.[8] The prior distribution $f(\theta)$ serves to rule out values of θ that are known a priori to be virtually impossible. For example, when only a few items have been administered, the likelihood $L(\mathbf{U}|\theta)$ often is maximized at a value of θ that is exceedingly large (perhaps $+10$) or small (perhaps -10). However, the height of the standardized normal curve $f(\theta)$ at extreme values of θ is very close to zero, and therefore the product of $L(\mathbf{U}|\theta)$ and $f(\theta)$ in Equation 7.3.2 is also near zero. Thus, only "reasonable" values of θ are considered when estimating ability. The Bayesian ability estimate can be taken as the mean of the posterior ability distribution. The variance of the posterior distribution then provides a measure of the uncertainty of the ability estimate.

Item selection for Bayesian ability estimation. The item selection method used most often with Bayesian estimation chooses the item

---

[7] This assumes, of course, that item parameters were estimated in a random or representative sample from this homogeneous population and that the θ-metric was scaled to have mean zero and variance one.

[8] The constant k is chosen such that the posterior distribution integrates to unity.

not yet administered that leads to the smallest expected posterior variance following the examinee's next response. This means that the next item to be administered should be the item that is expected to lead to the greatest reduction in uncertainty about the examinee's ability. The equations needed to determine which item minimizes the expected variance of the ability estimate following the examinee's next response are provided by Owen (1975) for the normal ogive model (see also Jensema, 1974b; 1977) and by Jensema (1974a) for the two- and three-parameter logistic models. Expressions are also provided in these papers for the posterior mean and variance of the ability distribution following correct and incorrect responses.

The *posterior* mean and variance calculated after the examinee's *i*th response are then taken as the mean and variance of the normal *prior* distribution of ability used to select item $i + 1$. They are also used in the prior distribution when computing the posterior mean and variance following the examinee's $(i + 1)$th response. This iterative process continues until the posterior variance becomes sufficiently small or until some fixed number of items is presented.

Termination criteria for adaptive tests. Two criteria for terminating adaptive tests merit attention. One criterion involves administering a fixed number of items, say $n = 25$, to all examinees. This criterion is quite useful in Monte Carlo simulations because it allows direct comparisons among test information curves for various n item adaptive and conventional tests. In actual practice, however, administering the same number of items to all examinees is not appropriate. For some examinees, fewer than n items are needed for satisfactory measurement; requiring these examinees to answer additional items wastes time and may cause fatigue and carelessness that degrade measurement quality. Other examinees' abilities, achievements, or attitudes may not be satisfactorily assessed with n items, and additional items are required. Thus, in practical applications of CAT, items should be administered until the standard error of $\hat{\theta}$ falls below the level required by the organization administering the test. For maximum likelihood ability estimation, $1/I(\hat{\theta})$ gives the squared standard error of $\hat{\theta}$. The standard error of $\hat{\theta}$ for a Bayesian ability estimate is the square root of the posterior variance of the ability distribution. Note that the accuracy of estimation of θ that is required by the testing organization could be different in different ranges of θ.

7.4 ADAPTIVE TESTING USING MAXIMUM INFORMATION ITEM SELECTION

In this section and in Section 7.5 we carefully examine implications of two adaptive testing procedures via Monte Carlo simulation. The

224

simulated test in Section 7.4 uses maximum information item selection and maximum likelihood ability estimation, and terminates after
25 items have been administered. These are the same methods used
by Lord (1977). We partially replicate Lord's work in order to illustrate the mechanics of adaptive testing, note some objections to this
type of adaptive testing, and establish a baseline against which we can
judge the adaptive test in Section 7.5. This latter adaptive test is designed to reduce cheating, a practical problem that may be particularly serious with maximum information item selection.

The item bank simulated in Sections 7.4 and 7.5 is based on item
parameter estimates obtained from actual verbal ability items administered to large samples of examinees. Thus, the item parameters used
in the simulations are realistic in that they correspond to item parameters actually estimated in large samples of real examinees. Item parameter estimates were taken from (1) Levine and Drasgow's (1982)
analysis of the 85 items on the April 1975 Scholastic Aptitude Test—
Verbal section (SAT-V); (2) Drasgow's (1979) analysis of the 95 items
on the April 1973 Graduate Record Examination—Verbal section
(GRE-V); and (3) Lord's (1968) analysis of the May 1964 SAT-V.[9] Estimates of parameters for 80 items from Lord's study were included in
the item bank.

The items on all three tests used a multiple-choice format. Because
the examinees were motivated to maximize their scores, it is likely
that some guessing occurred, and therefore the lower asymptotes of
ICCs would not be zero. Consequently, LOGIST was used to estimate
parameters of the three-parameter logistic model for each of the three
tests. These item parameter estimates were used as item parameters
throughout the simulations described in Sections 7.4 and 7.5.

Levine and Drasgow used a sample of 3,000 examinees to estimate
item parameters; the sample was created by taking every 10th examinee from a much larger sample. Drasgow estimated item parameters
from the responses of the first 3,000 examinees in a larger data set.
Although neither of these two samples was randomly selected, both
are representative of the populations of examinees taking the exams.
Due to the nature of their samples and the manner in which LOGIST
scales ability estimates (i.e., a mean of zero and a standard deviation of
one), such item parameters were scaled so that additional random
samples from each of the populations would be expected to have
ability estimates with a mean of zero and a standard deviation of one.

Lord's sample of 2,862 examinees was not a representative sample.
Instead, Lord selected examinees from a sample of 5,000 examinees
by choosing individuals with the lowest and highest scores on the

---

[9] The two forms of the SAT-V were composed of different items.

SAT-Math section. Selecting examinees with a wide range of abilities increases the accuracy of item parameter estimates. However, if Lord's θ-metric were used, the variance of $\hat{\theta}$ in a random or representative sample of examinees would be substantially less than one, because Lord deliberately selected high- and low-ability examinees and then scaled their ability estimates to have a standard deviation of one. Transforming Lord's item parameter estimates by the equations

$$\text{rescaled } \hat{b}_i = \frac{\text{Lord's } \hat{b}_i - .55}{.69}$$

and

$$\text{rescaled } \hat{a}_i = .69 \text{ (Lord's } \hat{a}_i)$$

rescales the item parameters so that a *random* sample of SAT-V examinees would be expected to have ability estimates with a mean of zero and a standard deviation of one.[10]

After rescaling Lord's item parameter estimates by the above transformations, all three tests would be expected to yield ability estimates with a mean of zero and a variance of one in random samples from their respective populations. For the Monte Carlo simulations described here, it is not necessary to equate θ-metrics for the different examinee populations in a fashion similar to Lord's (1977) equating. It is important, however, that the distributions of a_i, b_i, and c_i parameters realistically mimic distributions from actual tests. Furthermore, it is important that the *combinations* of a_i, b_i, and c_i for particular items are realistic. From the method by which it was constructed, we believe our hypothetical item bank has characteristics that realistically simulate a carefully developed item bank.

We did not want to generate an item bank according to a list of specifications for good items, where the specifications describe exceptional items with characteristics that are not observed in actual practice. Consequently, our item bank contained items with a_i values as low as .24, which is far less than the minimum usually suggested for adaptive tests. When carefully designed tests can contain items like this, we believe that it is unrealistic to exclude this type of item in an adaptive test simulation

---

[10] The constants used to rescale item parameter estimates were obtained using the normal distribution and Lord's (1968, p. 1011) Table 1. In particular, an examinee at the 50th percentile of SAT-V examinees obtained a score of approximately .55 on the $\hat{\theta}$ scale. Similarly, a $\hat{\theta}$ of -1 was at the 2d percentile and a $\hat{\theta}$ of 1.5 was at the 93.5th percentile. Fitting a normal distribution to these points indicates that a random sample of SAT-V examinees would have approximately a mean $\hat{\theta}$ ability estimate of .55 and a standard deviation of .69.

Simulation design. The simulated adaptive test described in this section begins by administering the item with maximum information at $\theta = 0$. If a simulated correct (incorrect) response is made, then the item with maximum information at $\theta = 1$ ($\theta = -1$) is presented. If another correct (incorrect) response is made, then the item with maximum information at $\theta = 2$ ($\theta = -2$) is administered. A third consecutive correct (incorrect) response is followed by presentation of the item with maximum information at $\theta = 3$ ($\theta = -3$). Further correct (incorrect) responses are followed by presentation of the item with maximum information at $\theta = 3$ ($\theta = -3$) that has not yet been administered.

The first maximum likelihood estimate $\hat{\theta}$ of ability is computed when the simulated examinee has made at least one correct and one incorrect response (see footnote 5). Thus two or more items must be administered before θ can be estimated. The item not yet administered with maximum information at $\hat{\theta}$ is presented next. This sequence of selecting the unused item with maximum information at the current value of $\hat{\theta}$, presenting the item and reestimating ability continues until a total of 25 items has been presented.

To reduce the computational burden of the adaptive test, item information for all 260 items was not recomputed for every new $\hat{\theta}$. Instead, a method sometimes termed *stratified maximum information item selection* was used. Item information was computed in a preliminary analysis for all 260 items at θ values of -3.00, -2.99, . . . , 2.99, 3.00. Then item information was rank ordered from highest to lowest at each θ value. A 25-row by 601-column matrix containing the top 25 items at each of the 601 values of θ was then generated. Row 1 contained the item number of the most informative item at each of the 601 values of θ, row 2 contained the item number of the second most informative item at each of the 601 θ values, etc. This matrix was stored as a disk file and then used during simulated adaptive testing. The column of this matrix corresponding to the θ value closest to $\hat{\theta}$ was examined to determine the item with maximum information not yet administered. Because the item pool contained little information outside the $[-3.0, 3.0]$ interval and examinees with ability outside this interval would be encountered only rarely in an actual testing situation, the first column of the information matrix was searched when $\hat{\theta}$ was less than -3.0 and the (601st) column was searched when $\hat{\theta}$ was greater than 3.

In sum, the item selection method used here approximates a true maximum information method because inside the $[-3.0, 3.0]$ interval, item information was determined at values of θ not more than .005 away from $\hat{\theta}$. From other analyses, the approximation was found to determine accurately the item with maximum information not yet administered inside $[-3.0, 3.0]$. Item selection was somewhat less accurate outside $[-3.0, 3.0]$ for obvious reasons. However, because there were few items that had information substantially greater than zero outside $[-3.0, 3.0]$ and because the item information curves were flat in this region, true maximum information item selection would have selected essentially the same set of items to administer as the approximation method.

The maximum likelihood ability estimation was accomplished by Newton-Raphson iterations. (See Lord, 1980, pp. 180–181, for a technical discussion of how to use the Newton-Raphson method for ability estimation.) This is a numerical method for determining the maximum of a nonlinear equation. The Newton-Raphson method converges to the maximum of the likelihood equation very quickly, provided that a good starting value of $\hat{\theta}$ is provided to the algorithm. The ability estimate based on $(i - 1)$ item responses usually provided a good starting point when estimating ability based on i item responses. A few iterations of the "method of golden sections" provided a good starting point for the Newton-Raphson algorithm when no previous ability estimate was available or when the previous ability estimate caused the Newton-Raphson method to diverge (i.e., go to $+\infty$ or $-\infty$). A good discussion of the method of golden sections is provided by Wagner (1969, Chapter 14).

Although comparisons of execution time for computer analyses across various computers must be performed with care, description of the computer time required for the adaptive test simulated here can provide a general understanding of the computational burden and expense. Using the methods described above, the computations included: (1) administering 25 items to each simulated examinee; (2) obtaining approximately 20 to 23 maximum likelihood estimates of θ; and (3) selecting the item with maximum information not yet administered following each estimation of θ. The FORTRAN program performing these calculations required approximately one half of a second of execution time *per simulated adaptive test* on an IBM 370/158 computer.

Finally, adaptive tests for examinees with true abilities of -2.75, $-2.50, \ldots, 2.75$ were simulated. Two hundred adaptive tests at each of these 23 θ levels were conducted, yielding a total of 4,600 simulated tests.

Results. The increase in measurement accuracy as the adaptive test proceeded is illustrated in Figure 7.4.1 for the 200 simulated examinees with $\theta = 0.0$. Note that the estimated information function increases approximately linearly as the number of test items increases.[11]

---

[11] Because maximum likelihood estimates of θ appeared to be nearly unbiased, the estimated information function was taken as the reciprocal of the estimated variance of $\hat{\theta}$ for examinees with a common θ.

228

Figure 7.4.1
Estimated Information and Standard Error of $\hat{\theta}$ for Maximum Information
Item Selection when $\theta = 0$

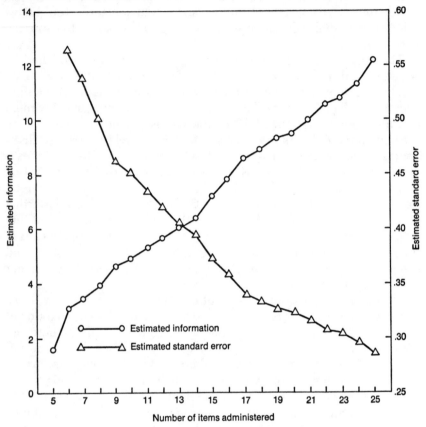

The decrease in the estimated standard error $1/\sqrt{I(\hat{\theta})}$ of $\hat{\theta}$ is quite
rapid in the beginning of the adaptive test but is relatively slow near
the end of the test.

The estimated test information function of the 25-item adaptive test
is shown in Figure 7.4.2. The test information functions for the GRE-V
and the two forms of the SAT-V, after adjusting to a common length of
25 items, are also shown in Figure 7.4.2. It is clear that the adaptive
test provides measurement that is superior to all three conventional
tests. Note that, for examinees with θ as low as -1.75 in the adaptive
test, θ is estimated more accurately than at *any* θ value for the conventional tests. Thus the adaptive test is more informative at a θ value
approximately three standard deviations away from its peak than are
the conventional tests at their peaks.

Figure 7.4.2
Approximate Test Information Functions for 25-Item
Adaptive Tests and Conventional Tests Adjusted to a
Length of 25 Items

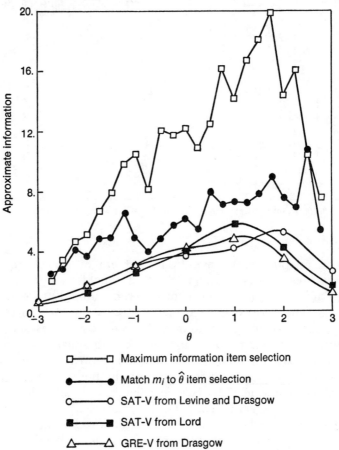

An examination of Table 7.4.1 makes apparent two interrelated problems with the maximum information item selection method and the use of Figure 7.4.2 to compare this adaptive test to conventional tests. This table presents the frequency distribution of the number of times each item was administered. Note that 141 items were *never* administered to any examinee when items were selected using the maximum information method. Thus, only 119 items in the item bank of 260 items were used. The improvement in measurement due to adaptive testing that is shown in Figure 7.4.2 may be overstated: The conventional tests contain 141 items with so little information that they were never used in the adaptive test. A fairer comparison be-

Table 7.4.1
Frequency of Item Presentation*

Number of Times Item Was Presented	Maximum Information Item Selection	"Match m_i to $\hat{\theta}$" Item Selection
0	141	0
1–200	16	36
201–400	9	98
401–600	13	74
601–800	8	28
801–1,000	14	8
1,001–1,200	21	14
1,201–1,400	15	2
1,401–1,600	12	0
1,601–1,800	6	0
1,801–2,000	2	0
2,001–3,000	2	0
3,001–4,600	1	0

* 200 examinees at each of 23 ability levels were simulated.

tween the adaptive and conventional tests might occur if the 141 unused items were deleted from the conventional tests prior to computing test information functions for the remaining 119 items. These functions, when adjusted to a length of 25 items, would cause the conventional tests to appear to provide more accurate estimation of θ.

A serious practical problem in many testing situations is cheating. Note that maximum information item selection facilitates cheating because (1) heavy use is made of a small number of items, so that the security of these questions is jeopardized; and (2) a cheater could memorize the answers to a small number of items and be assured of encountering several of the questions on the test. For the adaptive test described in this section, an examinee could memorize the answers to only 25 items and obtain a perfect score.

A different type of item selection can be used to reduce cheating. For example, the "match m_i to $\hat{\theta}$" item selection method should select a wider variety of items from the item pool than the maximum information item selection method. In Section 7.5 this item selection method is examined.

7.5 ADAPTIVE TESTING USING "MATCH m_i TO $\hat{\theta}$" ITEM SELECTION

The simulation described in this section is identical to the simulation in Section 7.4 except in item selection. The method of selecting an initial item and the method of selecting an item given a current ability estimate are designed to prevent heavy use of a few items. Consequently, these methods should reduce cheating.

In this simulation, the initial item presented to an examinee is randomly selected from the 30 hypothetical items in the item bank with m_i in the interval $[-.20, .21]$. If a correct (incorrect) response is made, the next item administered is randomly selected from the 30 items with m_i in the interval $[.86, 1.23]$ ($[-1.22, -.76]$). Further correct (incorrect) responses are followed by randomly selecting items not yet administered from the 30 items with the largest (smallest) m_i values.

When there is at least one correct response and one incorrect response, ability is estimated by the methods described in Section 7.4. The next item administered is selected by the "match m_i to $\hat{\theta}$" method. Item presentation, ability estimation, and item selection then continue until 25 items have been presented.

The test information function for the "match m_i to $\hat{\theta}$" method of adaptive testing is shown in Figure 7.4.2. As expected there is a substantial loss of information when that method of item selection is used in place of the maximum information method. There is, however, a substantial increase in information for the "match m_i to $\hat{\theta}$" method over the conventional tests. At ability levels of -1.25 and less, the adaptive test provides at least twice the information of the conventional tests. The adaptive test is usually about 50 percent more informative for ability levels above -1.25.

Table 7.4.1 presents the frequency of item selection for the "match m_i to $\hat{\theta}$" adaptive test. Note that all 260 items were used during testing. It is clear that this method of item selection uses more items than the maximum information method and avoids heavy use of a few items. The 16 items that were used more than 1,000 times were among the 22 items with the lowest m_i values in the item bank. These 22 items had m_i values that ranged from -3.54 to -1.53. Thus, the relatively heavy use of the easiest items resulted because there were very few easy items in the item bank.

Figure 7.4.2 and Table 7.4.1 clearly illustrate the tradeoff between avoiding heavy use of a few, very good items and maximizing the test information function. The maximum information method of item selection produces an excellent test information function through intensive use of a small number of highly discriminating items. The "match m_i to $\hat{\theta}$" method uses all items in the item bank but yields a substantially reduced test information function.

The implications of Section 7.4 and 7.5 for adaptive testing are clear. If cheating is not a problem—for example, in attitude measurement—then maximum information item selection should be used. If, however, the security of test items is questionable, then the "match m_i to $\hat{\theta}$" item selection is preferable.

7.6 SUMMARY

The simulations in Sections 7.4 and 7.5 document the increases in measurement accuracy that result from adaptive testing. Adaptive testing is substantially more efficient than conventional testing, especially for very high- and very low-ability examinees. Gains in information are less dramatic, however, if practical considerations preclude intensive use of a few items. Nonetheless, an adaptive test that uses the "match m_i to $\hat{\theta}$" item selection method provides more information about ability than typical conventional tests.

Increased measurement accuracy is not the only benefit of adaptive testing. Testing time, fatigue, and boredom should all be reduced in an adaptive test. Restrictions as to when a test is administered could also be reduced through the use of walk-in testing stations. The delays associated with scoring a paper-and-pencil test should be eliminated. Test scores would be available as soon as testing ends, and all concerned parties could be notified of the results immediately.

Urry (1977) predicted that:

> multiple-choice items will eventually become obsolete. The item writer will at last be liberated from the restraints imposed by the machine-scorable answer sheet, just as machine scoring alleviated the tedium of hand scoring a few decades ago (p. 193).

Thus, new item types may evolve that are superior to multiple-choice items. If such item types are devised, the advantage in measurement accuracy of adaptive testing over conventional tests may become even greater.

Appropriateness measurement methods could also be developed for adaptive tests. As noted in Chapter 9, this type of "quality inspection" of a test would help to reduce the asymmetry in the power relationship between examinees and the test user. Furthermore, appropriateness indices could be computed as the adaptive test progresses. If an anomaly were detected, remedial action could be taken immediately. For example, test directions could be presented to the examinee a second time, the examinee could be asked to reenter an apparently aberrant response, or the test length could be increased until an examinee reaches a reasonable level of consistency in his or her item responses.

In sum, we have presented a variety of benefits of adaptive testing. Since CAT is a relatively new field, it seems likely that many more innovations will be developed.

REFERENCES

Angoff, W. H., & Huddleston, E. M. *The multilevel experiment: A study of a two-level test system for the College Board Scholastic Aptitude Test* (Statistical Report 58-21). Princeton, N.J.: Educational Testing Service, 1958.

Birnbaum, A. Some latent trait models and their use in inferring an examinee's ability. In F. M. Lord & M. R. Novick, *Statistical theories of mental test scores*. Reading, Mass.: Addison-Wesley Publishing, 1968.

Box, G. E. P., & Tiao, G. C. *Bayesian inference in statistical analysis*. Reading, Mass.: Addison-Wesley Publishing, 1973.

Cleary, T. A., Linn, R. L., & Rock, D. A. An exploratory study of programmed tests. *Educational and Psychological Measurement*, 1968, *28*, 345–360.

Cronbach, L. J. Coefficient alpha and the internal structure of tests. *Psychometrika*, 1951, *16*, 297–334.

Drasgow, F. Statistical indices of the appropriateness of aptitude test scores (Doctoral dissertation, University of Illinois, 1978). *Dissertation Abstracts International*, 1979, *39*, 12B. (University Microfilms No. DEL79–13435, 6095)

Jensema, C. J. An application of latent trait mental test theory. *British Journal of Mathematical and Statistical Psychology*, 1974, *27*, 29–48. (a)

Jensema, C. J. The validity of Bayesian tailored testing. *Educational and Psychological Measurement*, 1974, *34*, 757–766. (b)

Jensema, C. J. Bayesian tailored testing and the influence of item bank characteristics. *Applied Psychological Measurement*, 1977, *1*, 111–120.

Killcross, M. C. *A review of research in tailored testing* (Report APRE No. 9/76). Franborough, Hants, England: Ministry of Defense, Army Personnel Research Establishment, 1976.

Kreitzberg, C. B., & Jones, D. H. *An empirical study of the broad range tailored test of verbal ability* (Research Report 80-5). Princeton, N.J.: Educational Testing Service, 1980.

Levine, M. V., & Drasgow, F. Appropriateness measurement: Review, critique, and validating studies. *British Journal of Mathematical and Statistical Psychology*, 1982, *35*, 42–56.

Linn, R. L., Rock, D. A., & Cleary, T. A. The development and evaluation of several programmed testing methods. *Educational and Psychological Measurement*, 1969, *29*, 129–146.

Lord, F. M. An analysis of the Verbal Scholastic Aptitude Test using Birnbaum's three-parameter logistic model. *Educational and Psychological Measurement*, 1968, *28*, 989–1020.

Lord, F. M. Some test theory for tailored testing. In W. H. Holtzman (Ed.), *Computer-assisted instruction, testing, and guidance*. New York: Harper & Row, 1970.

Lord, F. M. A theoretical study of two-stage testing. *Psychometrika*, 1971, *36*, 227–242. (a)

Lord, F. M. A theoretical study of the measurement effectiveness of flexilevel tests. *Educational and Psychological Measurement*, 1971, *31*, 805–813. (b)

Lord, F. M. Robbins-Monro procedures for tailored testing. *Educational and Psychological Measurement*, 1971, *31*, 3–31. (c)

Lord, F. M. A broad-range tailored test of verbal ability. *Applied Psychological Measurement*, 1977, *1*, 95–100.

Lord, F. M. *Applications of item response theory to practical testing problems.* Hillsdale, N.J.: Erlbaum, 1980.

McBride, J. R. *Research on adaptive testing, 1973–1976: A review of the literature.* Unpublished paper, University of Minnesota, 1976.

Novick, M. R., & Jackson, P. H. *Statistical methods for educational and psychological research.* New York: McGraw-Hill, 1974.

Olivier, P. An evaluation of the self-scoring flexilevel tailored test model. Unpublished doctoral dissertation, Florida State University, 1974.

Owen, R. J. A Bayesian sequential procedure for quantal response in the context of adaptive mental testing. *Journal of the American Statistical Association*, 1975, *70*, 351–356.

Reckase, M. D. *An interactive computer program for tailored testing based on the one-parameter logistic model.* Paper presented at the National Conference on the Use of On-Line Computers in Psychology, St. Louis, Mo.: 1973.

Reckase, M. D. *An application of the Rasch simple logistic model to tailored testing.* Paper presented at the Annual Meeting of the American Educational Research Association, 1974.

Robbins, H., & Monro, S. A stochastic approximation method. *Annals of Mathematical Statistics*, 1951, *22*, 400–407.

Wagner, H. M. *Principles of operations research.* Englewood Cliffs, N.J.: Prentice-Hall, 1969.

Urry, V. W. A Monte Carlo investigation of logistic test models. Unpublished doctoral dissertation, Purdue University, 1970.

Urry, V. W. Tailored testing: A successful application of latent trait theory. *Journal of Educational Measurement*, 1977, *14*, 181–196.

Weiss, D. J. *Strategies of adaptive ability measurement* (Research Report 74–5). Minneapolis: University of Minnesota, Department of Psychology, Psychometric Methods Program, 1974. (ED 104 930)

Weiss, D. J., & Betz, N. E. *Ability measurement: Conventional or adaptive?* (Research Report 73–1). Minneapolis: University of Minnesota, Department of Psychology, Psychometric Methods Program, 1973. (NTIS No. AD 757788)

8

Assessing the Dimensionality of an Item Pool

8.0 OVERVIEW

Determining the number of latent dimensions underlying item responses is important in attitude, ability, and achievement measurement. Assessing dimensionality is particularly important for IRT, because all the IRT models presented in Chapter 2 assume that a single latent trait underlies item responses. In Chapter 3 we examined the robustness of some IRT models and estimation methods to violations of unidimensionality, and found the models robust to small and moderate violations. In this chapter, methods are presented for assessing the latent structure underlying item responses. In conjunction with the material in Chapter 3, these methods can be used by researchers to determine whether their item response data are sufficiently unidimensional to employ IRT models.

The methods described in this chapter are based on the factor analytic model. Readers unfamiliar with factor analysis may wish to consult books by Kim and Mueller (1978a; 1978b) for elementary descriptions, and books by Thurstone (1947), Harman (1967), and Mulaik (1972) for more advanced discussions.

Two types of correlation coefficients (phi and tetrachoric) are used extensively in Chapter 8. These correlation coefficients are described in Section 8.1. The biserial and point biserial correlations, which are used throughout the book, are also discussed in this section. Because all of these correlation coefficients can be developed within a common theoretical framework, it is convenient to present this material in one section. Chapters 2 through 7 are *not* prerequisites for Section 8.1; this section can be read when required for understanding of points raised in any chapter.

The relations between one IRT model–the normal ogive model– and the factor analysis model are summarized in Section 8.2. This section is important because it provides a theoretical basis for using factor analysis to investigate the latent trait space of IRT. Without theoretical links between factor analysis and IRT there would be no reason for using factor analysis to assess empirically the unidimensionality assumption of IRT.

In Section 8.3 a simple method for assessing dimensionality, factoring phi coefficients, is presented. The "difficulty factors" that result from this procedure are also described in Section 8.3. For data sets where no guessing or response sets occur, factoring a matrix of tetrachoric correlations can be used to determine dimensionality. This method is illustrated in Section 8.4. Unfortunately, nonzero lower asymptotes of ICCs can cause artifactual "guessing factors" to emerge when tetrachoric correlations are factor analyzed. Section 8.5 describes the effects of nonzero lower asymptotes. Finally, a procedure is presented in Section 8.6 for examining the dimensionality of an item pool containing items that have either zero or nonzero lower asymptotes.

8.1 TYPES OF CORRELATION COEFFICIENTS

Table 8.1.1 presents the types of correlations that are important in Chapter 8. All three "observed" correlations are actually Pearson

Table 8.1.1
Types of Correlations as a Function of Measurement Level

Variable Types	Observed	Inferred
Continuous-Continuous	Product Moment (r)	—
Continuous-Dichotomous	Point Biserial (r_{pb})	Biserial (r_b)
Dichotomous-Dichotomous	Phi (r_p)	Tetrachoric (r_t)

product moment correlations and can be computed by the usual formula for a product moment correlation.[1] The term *inferred correlation* is used in this context to refer to a correlation that involves one or more *latent* variables. Specific distributional assumptions must be

[1] A useful mnemonic is that all three Pearson product moment correlations begin with the letter "P": product moment, point biserial, and phi.

made in order to estimate these correlations. An inferred correlation is estimated using the values of observed variables, but is interpreted in reference to one or two latent variables.

The *point biserial correlation* is the product moment correlation between a continuous variable Y and a dichotomous variable u. We are free to choose any scoring system for u because the absolute value of a product moment correlation is unaffected by a linear transformation of the form $u^* = mu + b$. Consequently, the $0 - 1$ scoring of item responses can be used to score any dichotomous variable when computing a point biserial correlation.

The $0 - 1$ scoring of u is convenient because it allows the formula for the product moment correlation to be simplified. For example, the sample point biserial correlation $\hat{r}_{pb}$ can be computed by the equation

$$(8.1.1) \qquad \hat{r}_{pb} = \frac{\bar{Y}^+ - \bar{Y}}{s_y} \sqrt{\frac{\hat{p}}{\hat{q}}},$$

where $\bar{Y}^+$ is the mean of Y among individuals with $u = 1$, $\bar{Y}$ is the mean of Y among all individuals, s_y is the standard deviation of Y, $\hat{p}$ is the proportion of individuals with $u = 1$ and $\hat{q} = 1 - \hat{p}$.

A *phi coefficient* is a product moment correlation coefficient between two dichotomously scored variables. For example, the Pearson product moment correlation between two test items that are scored $u_i = 1$ if correct and $u_i = 0$ if incorrect is referred to as a phi coefficient.

The formula for computing a product moment correlation can also be simplified when calculating a sample phi coefficient. In the following table, let A refer to the proportion of examinees who answered both items i and j correctly, B refer to the proportion who answered item i incorrectly and item j correctly, etc.:

	Item j		
	$u_j = 1$	$u_j = 0$	
Item i $u_i = 1$	A	C	$A + C$
$u_i = 0$	B	D	$B + D$
	$A + B$	$C + D$	

Then

$$(8.1.2) \qquad \hat{r}_p = \frac{A - (A + B)(A + C)}{\sqrt{(A + B)(C + D)(A + C)(B + D)}}.$$

The *biserial correlation* is the correlation between a hypothesized latent continuous variable that underlies a dichotomous variable, and another continuous variable. In particular, denote the hypothesized latent variable by Y (upsilon) and assume

1. Y is normally distributed, with mean zero and unit variance.
2. The observed dichotomous variable, u, results from categorizing Y by imposing a threshold γ (gamma):

$$u = \begin{cases} 1 \text{ if } Y \geq \gamma \\ 0 \text{ if } Y < \gamma. \end{cases}$$

Thus, if an individual's standing on Y is less than the threshold value γ, the individual's score on u is zero. If the individual's standing on Y exceeds the threshold value, the individual's score on u is one.

3. The regression of the observed continuous variable, Y, onto Y is linear.

Lord and Novick (1968, pp. 337–340) use these assumptions to show

(8.1.3) $$r_{pb} = tr_b,$$

where the *attenuation factor t* is

(8.1.4) $$t = \frac{h(\gamma)}{\{\Phi(\gamma)[1 - \Phi(\gamma)]\}^{1/2}}.$$

Here $h(\gamma)$ is the height of the standardized normal curve at γ, and $\Phi(\gamma)$ is the area under the standard normal curve to the left of γ. The maximum value of t occurs when $\Phi(\gamma)$ (which can be interpreted as the proportion of examinees with $u = 0$) is .50; then $t = .798$. As $\Phi(\gamma)$ increases to 1 or decreases to 0 (i.e., as the proportion of examinees with $u = 0$ approaches 1 or 0), t becomes smaller and thus the point biserial correlation becomes substantially smaller than the biserial correlation.

The point biserial correlation between u_i and θ is the product moment correlation between item responses on item i and θ. The biserial correlation between u_i and θ is the inferred correlation between the latent response strength variable Y (Bock & Lieberman, 1970) on item i and θ, *provided that the above assumptions are valid. Guessing* the correct response violates assumption 2 (above) and invalidates the relation in Equation 8.1.3.

The *tetrachoric correlation* is similar to the biserial correlation, except that *both* observed variables are dichotomous and a latent continuous variable is assumed to underlie each of the two observed dichotomous variables. The latent variables are assumed to follow a bivariate normal distribution, and each dichotomous variable is assumed to be generated by the process described in assumption 2 for the biserial correlation. Unfortunately, no simple relation, as in Equation 8.1.3, exists between phi and tetrachoric correlations. Instead, an infinite series derived by Pearson (1900) and cited by Lord and Novick (1968, p. 346) relates the phi and tetrachoric correlation. The IMSL (1975) subroutine BECTR can be used to calculate tetrachoric correlations.

8.2   RELATIONS BETWEEN THE NORMAL OGIVE MODEL AND THE FACTOR ANALYSIS MODEL[2]

In this section, relations between the two-parameter normal ogive model and the factor analysis model are described. Our purpose is to provide a conceptual understanding of the assumptions and the relations that can then be derived. We omit proofs; the interested reader is referred to Lord and Novick (1968, pp. 365–383).

We begin with the assumption that θ is normally distributed with mean zero and unit variance in the population under consideration. It is unlikely that θ will exactly follow a normal distribution in practice. However, the distribution of θ may approximate a normal distribution in many populations that have not been subjected to some type of range restriction.

We next assume that there is a set of n latent variables, Y_i, $i = 1, 2, \ldots, n$, that underlie responses to the n dichotomously scored test items. Each Y_i is assumed to have mean zero, unit variance, and be related to θ by

$$(8.2.1) \qquad Y_i = \alpha_i \theta + (1 - \alpha_i^2)^{1/2} S_i,$$

where α_i is the *factor loading* of Y_i on the *common factor* θ, and S_i is the *specific factor* for Y_i. S_i is assumed to be normally distributed with mean zero and unit variance, and to be uncorrelated with θ. Equation 8.2.1 has the form of the common-factor model with a single common factor, θ. A standard result from factor analytic theory is that the product moment correlation between Y_i and θ equals α_i.

Finally, assume that each of the n dichotomous response variables, u_i, is related to its corresponding Y_i by

$$(8.2.2) \qquad u_i = \begin{cases} 1 \text{ if } Y_i \geq \gamma_i \\ 0 \text{ if } Y_i < \gamma_i \end{cases}$$

where $u_i = 1$ indicates a correct response to item i, $u_i = 0$ indicates an incorrect response, and γ_i is the threshold for item i. The relation in Equation 8.2.2 states that examinees whose response strength on item

---

[2] This section explains *why* factor analysis is useful for assessing the dimensionality of the latent trait space. Section 8.2 is not essential for understanding how to use factor analysis to assess dimensionality.

i equals or exceeds the threshold on item i will respond correctly. In contrast, examinees with response strength Y_i below threshold will not respond correctly.

The biserial correlation between u_i and θ is the product moment correlation between the latent continuous variable that underlies u_i (i.e., Y_i) and θ. The product moment correlation between Y_i and θ is α_i; thus α_i is the biserial correlation between u_i and θ. From Equations 8.1.3 and 8.1.4, the point biserial between u_i and θ is

$$(8.2.3) \qquad r_{pb}(u_i, \theta) = \frac{h(\gamma_i)\alpha_i}{\{\Phi(\gamma_i)[1 - \Phi(\gamma_i)]\}^{1/2}}.$$

Using factor analytic theory, it can be shown that the product moment correlation between Y_i and Y_k is $\alpha_i\alpha_k$, which results because Y_i and Y_k share the single common factor θ. Since Y_i and Y_k are the latent variables that underlie u_i and u_k, the tetrachoric correlation between u_i and u_k is

$$(8.2.4) \qquad r_t(u_i, u_k) = r(Y_i, Y_k) = \alpha_i\alpha_k.$$

Using assumptions similar to the ones stated above, Lord and Novick (1968) proved that ICCs for all n items are normal ogives with the form

$$(8.2.5) \qquad P_i(\theta) = \frac{1}{\sqrt{(2\pi)}} \int_{-\infty}^{a_i(\theta-b_i)} \exp\left[\frac{-y^2}{2}\right]dy,$$

where

$$(8.2.6) \qquad a_i = \frac{\alpha_i}{\sqrt{(1 - \alpha_i^2)}}$$

and

$$(8.2.7) \qquad b_i = \frac{\gamma_i}{\alpha_i}.$$

A practical result of this is that knowledge of $\hat{a}_i$ from IRT analysis of two-parameter normal ogive or logistic item responses allows one to estimate the loading of an item on the common factor as

$$(8.2.8) \qquad \hat{\alpha}_i \doteq \frac{\hat{a}_i}{\sqrt{1 + \hat{a}_i^2}}.$$

8.3 FACTORING PHI COEFFICIENTS

Perhaps the simplest method for examining the dimensionality of an item pool involves factor analyzing the matrix of item-item product moment (i.e., phi) correlations. In the following paragraphs we describe this analysis and show its chief failing.

To illustrate the analysis in concrete terms, a truly unidimensional data set was generated by:

a. Selecting the one-parameter logistic model as the model for simulating item responses to 25 dichotomously scored items.
b. Setting the item difficulties to be uniformly spaced from -2.0 to 2.0. Thus, the item difficulties were $-2.0, -1.833, -1.667, \ldots ,$ 2.0.
c. Sampling a value for θ from a normal distribution with mean zero and unit variance.
d. Computing the probability of a correct response, $P_i(\theta)$, for each item i using the θ obtained in step (c) and the item difficulty from step (b). Equation 2.4.11 was used to compute $P_i(\theta)$.
e. Independently sampling a number between zero and one from a uniform distribution for each of the 25 items. If the ith number sampled was less than or equal to $P_i(\theta)$, then item i was scored as correct; otherwise the ith item was scored as incorrect.
f. Repeating steps (c) through (e) so that 500 simulated answer sheets were generated.

Thus, item responses were simulated by a process that precisely matches the one-parameter logistic model with abilities sampled from a normal distribution.

The phi correlations for the 25 items are presented in Table 8.3.1 with the items ordered according to difficulty. Clearly, there is structure to the pattern of correlations in this table. Note that correlations are largest near the diagonal, and tend to decrease further away from the diagonal. The lowest correlations are in the lower left corner of the matrix, which contains correlations of easy items with difficult items. In addition, items of moderate difficulty (b_i near zero) generally have the largest correlations.

A principal axes factor analysis was performed on the phi coefficients using squared multiple correlations as estimates of communalities. The largest 12 eigenvalues of the reduced correlation matrix (i.e., the matrix of phi coefficients with communality estimates in the diagonal) appear in Figure 8.3.1, and the loadings on the first two factors (before rotation) appear in Table 8.3.2. From the plot of eigenvalues, it appears that there is a strong first factor and a weaker second factor. This interpretation is supported by Table 8.3.2. The loadings on the second factor are related to item difficulty.

The second factor in Table 8.3.2 is an example of a *difficulty factor* that results when factoring product moment correlations obtained from dichotomous items of unequal difficulty. Because we know that

Table 8.3.1
Phi Coefficients for 25 Items Simulated according to the One-Parameter Logistic Model

Item	1	2	3	4	5	6	7	8	9	10	11	12	13	14	15	16	17	18	19	20	21	22	23	24	25	Item Difficulty
1	—																									−2.000
2	21	—																								−1.833
3	31	16	—																							−1.667
4	27	15	21	—																						−1.500
5	38	17	32	28	—																					−1.333
6	28	24	22	30	28	—																				−1.167
7	32	28	23	35	30	29	—																			−1.000
8	27	20	23	27	29	24	25	—																		−.833
9	27	24	27	34	30	27	37	31	—																	−.667
10	28	15	29	22	32	21	35	30	31	—																−.500
11	25	24	25	30	29	33	37	28	34	32	—															−.333
12	24	22	26	38	28	26	35	21	39	35	33	—														−.167
13	14	16	21	27	25	20	26	23	26	38	33	35	—													.000
14	20	16	23	23	29	24	32	23	35	31	33	33	31	—												.167
15	24	18	24	28	22	28	25	30	28	26	36	38	31	35	—											.333
16	20	20	21	24	21	18	29	28	35	34	33	29	27	37	30	—										.500
17	19	17	19	24	20	23	23	26	27	31	29	33	22	31	27	34	—									.667
18	16	18	19	22	19	25	20	21	28	28	30	29	27	31	36	32	27	—								.833
19	14	17	18	18	22	23	23	25	25	31	25	30	36	31	28	28	30	25	—							1.000
20	15	14	14	19	20	17	21	22	21	26	25	25	24	27	25	28	24	42	25	—						1.167
21	13	11	16	14	15	14	19	17	21	25	22	26	28	25	24	34	21	24	22	31	—					1.333
22	12	12	16	14	16	16	14	14	22	20	21	23	21	24	24	27	21	24	25	28	26	—				1.500
23	07	13	12	15	13	13	15	16	16	21	21	20	17	17	28	26	30	23	25	26	22	17	—			1.667
24	09	11	14	11	13	15	14	18	18	16	21	19	21	17	23	18	24	29	24	25	25	19	25	—		1.833
25	09	08	11	10	12	12	13	18	15	14	15	19	16	10	20	18	17	19	24	25	17	08	24	33	—	2.000

Note: To conserve space, decimal points are omitted and only the first two digits of the correlations are present. All calculations used at least four significant digits.

Figure 8.3.1
Eigenvalues Computed from Phi Coefficients in Table 8.3.1

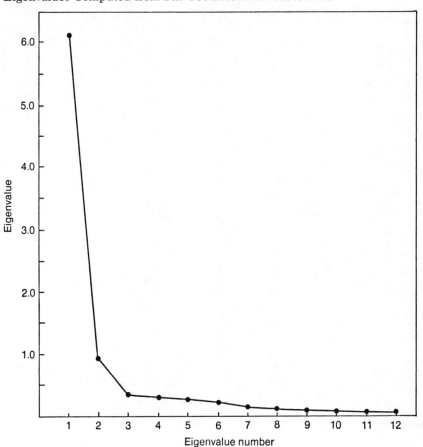

this data set was generated by a process involving only a single latent dimension, it is clear that the difficulty factor is an artifact of our analysis, and *cannot* be related to a second latent dimension.

A careful consideration of the dichotomous nature of item responses helps explain difficulty factors. The common factor model assumes that there is a linear relation between the latent variables (common and unique factors) and the observed variables. Because item responses are dichotomous, they cannot be linearly related to continuous latent variables. This is a serious violation of the factor model. The nonlinearity becomes even more of a problem when items have different difficulties. Here one can conceptualize the dichotomous item responses as resulting from *different* nonlinear transforma-

Table 8.3.2
Factor Loading Matrix
Obtained from Phi
Coefficients in Table 8.3.1

Item	Factor 1	Factor 2
1	.43	−.33
2	.35	−.13
3	.43	−.19
4	.48	−.22
5	.48	−.26
6	.46	−.19
7	.54	−.24
8	.48	−.12
9	.56	−.16
10	.56	−.07
11	.58	−.12
12	.60	−.06
13	.52	.03
14	.56	.02
15	.57	.07
16	.58	.13
17	.54	.16
18	.53	.19
19	.52	.22
20	.49	.22
21	.46	.27
22	.40	.12
23	.40	.24
24	.40	.31
25	.33	.23

tions (i.e., step functions with the step in different locations) of latent variables that *are*, in turn, linear combinations of common and unique factors. Carroll (1961) states that Ferguson (1941) was apparently the first researcher to recognize the problems associated with factoring phi coefficients.

8.4 FACTORING TETRACHORIC CORRELATIONS

If item responses result from dichotomization in the fashion described in Section 8.1, then tetrachoric correlations between pairs of items are unaffected by the respective item difficulties, meet the assumptions of factor analysis, and will *not* yield difficulty factors. The number of factors obtained by factoring a tetrachoric correlation matrix provides a valid estimate of the dimensionality of the latent trait space if sample size is sufficiently large.

Tetrachoric correlations were computed for the 25 simulated items described in the preceding subsection. These correlations, which were computed by the IMSL (1975) subroutine BECTR, appear in Table 8.4.1.

Because (1) logistic ICCs are virtually indistinguishable from corresponding normal ogive ICCs (see Equation 2.4.3 from Chapter 2) and (2) the normal ogive model is related to the common factor model by Equation 8.2.1, we can use Equation 8.2.6 to obtain the factor loading of each simulated item. Since a_i is unity for all one-parameter logistic items,

$$(8.4.1) \qquad\qquad 1.0 = \frac{\alpha_i}{\sqrt{1 - \alpha_i^2}},$$

where α_i is the factor loading of the ith item. This equation can be solved to yield $\alpha_i = \sqrt{.5}$. Finally, Equation 8.2.4 can be used to show that the tetrachoric correlations between all pairs of items simulated in Section 8.3 are .50. Thus, the population correlations estimated by the sample tetrachoric correlations in Table 8.4.1 are all .50, and the departures of sample tetrachoric correlations from .50 represent errors of estimation.

When the estimated tetrachoric correlations in Table 8.4.1 are compared to .50, it is clear that the population values are *not* well estimated. Using Guilford's (1956) Equation 83, the standard errors estimated by the IMSL subroutine BECTR for the sample tetrachoric coefficients range from .070 to .145, with most estimates near .10. Although the sampling distribution of the tetrachoric correlation is unknown (Kendall & Stuart, 1979, p. 329), it is interesting to note that roughly 75 percent of sample correlations were within one estimated standard error of .50, and 96 percent were within two estimated standard errors.

It is clear that the absolute magnitudes of the errors of estimate of the tetrachoric correlations are quite large (the standard error was roughly .10). Using Fisher's approximation (McNemar, 1969, p. 157), the standard error for sample Pearson product moment correlations is roughly .035 when samples of $N = 500$ are drawn from a population where the population correlation is .50. It is clear that researchers who wish to use and interpret tetrachoric correlations require very large samples.

Two related problems encountered with sample tetrachoric correlations are also illustrated in Table 8.4.1. First, note that there are missing values in Table 8.4.1. When each missing value is replaced with a .50, which is the population tetrachoric correlation, a second problem arises; the resulting matrix is non-Gramian. This means that the correlations in Table 8.4.1 could *not* result from any collection of

Table 8.4.1
Tetrachoric Correlations for 25 Items Simulated According to the One-Parameter Logistic Model

Item	1	2	3	4	5	6	7	8	9	10	11	12	13	14	15	16	17	18	19	20	21	22	23	24	25
1	—																								
2	43	—																							
3	56	33	—																						
4	51	30	39	—																					
5	65	33	56	42	—																				
6	53	45	40	52	49	—																			
7	58	50	42	58	52	48	—																		
8	52	37	42	48	50	39	41	—																	
9	51	45	48	58	52	44	59	48	—																
10	54	28	52	40	56	36	57	47	48	—															
11	51	45	47	53	52	53	60	44	53	49	—														
12	50	42	48	66	51	43	57	34	59	53	50	—													
13	29	31	40	49	47	34	45	36	42	58	53	53	—												
14	46	32	48	45	58	35	57	38	57	49	51	51	47	—											
15	64	39	54	62	47	44	47	51	48	43	57	60	48	53	—										
16	49	46	45	51	43	53	55	48	54	55	52	46	48	46	52	—									
17	52	41	44	56	45	35	46	46	48	52	48	54	43	57	47	59	—								
18	47	48	50	54	46	53	50	40	54	50	51	49	37	50	43	54	53	—							
19	42	49	51	45	60	51	44	50	51	59	36	54	46	51	58	52	56	45	—						
20	54	42	38	55	63	40	58	46	56	53	48	47	44	47	47	48	50	43	55	—					
21	43	30	50	37	42	32	53	36	46	52	40	48	52	45	43	57	41	67	43	53	—				
22	*	39	*	45	55	43	55	31	57	45	47	58	42	46	45	51	39	45	41	50	47	—			
23	*	*	47	*	50	37	42	42	41	53	50	55	38	51	54	51	57	45	48	50	43	36	—		
24	26	44	*	38	48	48	48	35	50	38	52	49	48	37	46	51	47	56	54	48	49	39	50	—	
25	*	35	*	41	*	39	50	*	47	40	40	52	47	25	45	40	38	41	50	51	38	20	50	63	—

Note: To conserve space, decimal points are omitted.
* The tetrachoric correlation could not be computed because no simulated examinee incorrectly answered the easier item while correctly answering the more difficult item.

500 persons' scores on 25 variables. Lord and Novick (1968) noted that "Difficulties may arise if certain common statistical techniques are incautiously applied to non-Gramian sample tetrachoric matrices" (p. 349). For example, squared multiple correlations were not used as communality estimates when Table 8.4.1 was factored, because some squared multiple correlations computed by SAS (1979) were greater than one.

Despite the problems noted above, a principal axes factor analysis was performed on the tetrachoric correlations in Table 8.4.1 with .5s entered for those correlations that could not be computed. The maximum correlation of an item with the remaining 24 items was used as the item's communality estimate. Eigenvalues of the reduced correlation matrix are presented in Figure 8.4.1 and the unrotated factor pattern matrix is shown in Table 8.4.2.

Figure 8.4.1
Eigenvalues Computed from Tetrachoric Correlations in Table 8.4.1

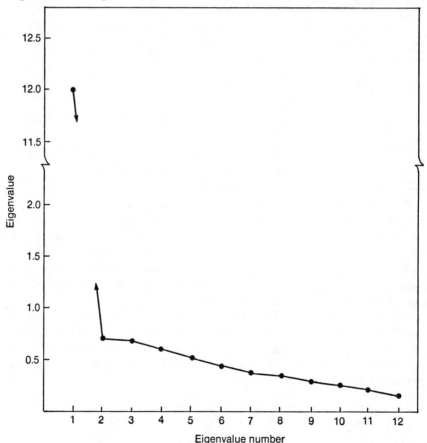

Table 8.4.2
Factor Loading Matrix
Obtained from Tetrachoric
Correlations in Table 8.4.1

Item	Factor 1	Factor 2
1	.72	−.15
2	.58	.11
3	.68	.06
4	.71	−.16
5	.74	−.02
6	.63	.04
7	.74	−.14
8	.63	.11
9	.74	−.10
10	.71	−.05
11	.72	−.08
12	.75	−.08
13	.64	.05
14	.68	−.25
15	.73	−.03
16	.73	−.01
17	.70	−.03
18	.71	.01
19	.72	.18
20	.72	.00
21	.66	−.01
22	.66	−.32
23	.69	.13
24	.68	.39
25	.64	.46

From the eigenvalue plot, it appears that the simulated 25-item instrument is unidimensional. Thus, factoring tetrachoric correlations yielded the *correct* conclusion about dimensionality. The factor pattern matrix in Table 8.4.2 further supports the decision to retain one factor: loadings on the second factor are generally small. Note that loadings on the first factor are all reasonably close to .71, which is the population value for all item loadings.

We have found a simple procedure that works well for replacing a small number of tetrachoric correlations that could not be computed when the one- or two-parameter logistic model is appropriate. This procedure begins with the estimation of IRT item parameters. Then $\hat{a}_i$ is substituted into Equation 8.2.8:

$$\alpha_i \doteq \hat{\alpha}_i = \frac{\hat{a}_i}{\sqrt{1 + \hat{a}_i^2}}.$$

For example, assume we find $a_1 = .6$ and $a_2 = 1.1$ for the first two items fit by a two-parameter logistic model. Then

$$\hat{\alpha}_1 = \frac{.6}{\sqrt{1 + .6^2}} = .51 \quad \text{and} \quad \hat{\alpha}_2 = \frac{1.1}{\sqrt{1 + 1.1^2}} = .74.$$

Using Equation 8.2.4, the tetrachoric correlation between u_1 and u_2 should be approximately $\hat{\alpha}_1 \hat{\alpha}_2 = (.51)(.74) = .38$. This value can then be used to replace the undefined tetrachoric correlation. Note, however, that this ad hoc procedure should be applied with caution, and then only if a small number of tetrachoric correlations cannot be computed. It should not be used when a substantial number of correlations are missing.

8.5 EFFECTS OF GUESSING

Unfortunately, guessing violates assumptions used to derive the tetrachoric correlation. In particular, each observed item response does not arise by dichotomizing a latent response variable (denoted by Y in Section 8.1). The procedure for assessing dimensionality described in Section 8.4 may consequently be misleading.

Carroll (1945) proposed a correction for the effects of guessing on the two-by-two tables used in computing tetrachoric correlations. Let the following table contain the expected proportions of responses to items i and j if *there were no guessing:*

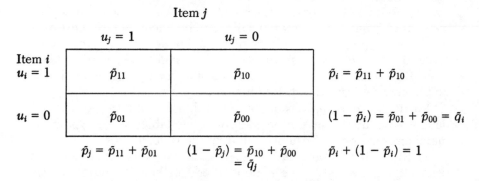

For example, $\tilde{p}_{10}$ is the proportion of examinees who know the answer to item i but did not know the answer to item j. Let c_i and c_j denote the probabilities of guessing the answers to items i and j, respectively. Using elementary probability, Carroll showed that the matrix of expected proportions of observed response patterns is:

250

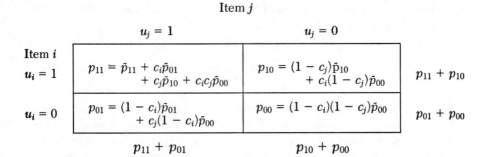

Item j

	$u_j = 1$	$u_j = 0$	
Item i $u_i = 1$	$p_{11} = \tilde{p}_{11} + c_i\tilde{p}_{01}$ $\quad + c_j\tilde{p}_{10} + c_ic_j\tilde{p}_{00}$	$p_{10} = (1 - c_j)\tilde{p}_{10}$ $\quad + c_i(1 - c_j)\tilde{p}_{00}$	$p_{11} + p_{10}$
$u_i = 0$	$p_{01} = (1 - c_i)\tilde{p}_{01}$ $\quad + c_j(1 - c_i)\tilde{p}_{00}$	$p_{00} = (1 - c_i)(1 - c_j)\tilde{p}_{00}$	$p_{01} + p_{00}$

$$p_{11} + p_{01} \qquad p_{10} + p_{00}$$

Therefore, the proportions without guessing can be obtained from the (observed) proportions *with* guessing by the set of equations

(8.5.1)
$$\tilde{p}_{00} = p_{00}/[(1 - c_i)(1 - c_j)]$$
$$\tilde{p}_{10} = [p_{10} - c_i(1 - c_j)\tilde{p}_{00}]/(1 - c_j)$$
$$\tilde{p}_{01} = [p_{01} - c_j(1 - c_i)\tilde{p}_{00}]/(1 - c_i)$$
$$\tilde{p}_{11} = 1 - (\tilde{p}_{10} + \tilde{p}_{01} + \tilde{p}_{00}).$$

Carroll suggested that the adjusted proportions should be used to compute the tetrachoric correlation between items i and j. For this procedure to function effectively, it is clear that the following conditions are needed: (1) sample size is large (so that the observed proportions are relatively unaffected by sampling fluctuations); (2) θ is normally distributed; (3) the three-parameter logistic model is appropriate,[3] (4) assumptions 2 and 3 of Section 8.1 are valid; and (5) c_i and c_j are known. In practice, estimation of c_i and c_j will usually be necessary. Some of the problems likely to be encountered in estimating lower asymptotes of ICCs are discussed in Section 2.6. Note, however, that the items most affected by guessing (i.e., very difficult items) are the items for which estimates of lower asymptotes are likely to be most accurate (Lord, 1968).

Finally, a factor analysis of the reduced matrix of tetrachoric correlations computed from corrected two-by-two tables should show the number of latent dimensions underlying item responses.

To illustrate this procedure, a second data set was generated. This data set was created by the same methods as the data set previously described, except that guessing was introduced. In particular, the

---

[3] Strictly speaking, the ICC should be a three-parameter normal ogive model, with Equation 2.4.1 replacing the logistic function in Equation 2.4.4. However, due to Equation 2.4.3, it is apparent that the differences between the three-parameter normal ogive and logistic ICCs are very small.

probability of a correct response to item i for a simulated examinee with ability θ was

$$(8.5.2) \qquad P_i(\theta) = c_i + (1 - c_i)\frac{1}{1 + \exp[-D(\theta - b_i)]} .$$

The item difficulties were again set equal to -2.000, -1.833, . . . , 2.000 for 25 items. Estimates of c_i obtained by Lord (1968) for the SAT-V were taken as the c_i for the items simulated here. They are listed in Table 8.5.2. A total sample of 1,000 examinees was generated by this procedure.

Table 8.5.1 presents the tetrachoric correlations from the unadjusted two-by-two tables of proportions. The nonzero c_i parameters had effects that ranged from small to profound on these tetrachoric correlations. Among the 10 easiest items, the average tetrachoric correlation is .43. This is slightly below the .50 that is expected when there is no guessing. In contrast, the average tetrachoric correlation among the five most difficult items is .11. The relation between item difficulty and magnitude of the observed tetrachoric correlation is apparent.

A principal axes factor analysis, with the maximum correlation of an item with the remaining 24 items as the communality estimate, was carried out on the tetrachoric correlations presented in Table 8.5.1. Table 8.5.2 shows the loadings on the first two factors and Figure 8.5.1 contains the eigenvalue plot. A spurious factor is again evident, *despite the fact that tetrachoric correlations* (and not phi coefficients) *were factored.* Gourlay (1951) was apparently the first researcher to demonstrate that factoring tetrachoric correlations could produce artifactual "guessing" factors.

Carroll's procedure for adjusting the two-by-two tables was then applied to the data set. For example, consider items 10 and 21. The observed two-by-two matrix of proportions is:

Item 10

		$u_{10} = 1$	$u_{10} = 0$	
	$u_{21} = 1$	$p_{11} = .255$	$p_{10} = .083$	.338
Item 21				
	$u_{21} = 0$	$p_{01} = .414$	$p_{00} = .248$	.662
		.669	.331	

Table 8.5.1
Tetrachoric Correlations for 25 Items with Nonzero Lower Asymptotes

Item	1	2	3	4	5	6	7	8	9	10	11	12	13	14	15	16	17	18	19	20	21	22	23	24	25
1	—																								
2	37	—																							
3	42	41	—																						
4	36	28	38	—																					
5	39	39	38	48	—																				
6	42	50	48	48	54	—																			
7	54	33	43	42	41	50	—																		
8	40	35	40	44	46	54	46	—																	
9	39	33	34	35	39	46	47	47	—																
10	50	40	41	39	48	50	48	45	46	—															
11	31	36	32	39	36	47	41	43	43	49	—														
12	37	32	33	28	44	36	39	38	38	43	33	—													
13	36	28	24	36	38	43	36	42	42	41	40	36	—												
14	22	32	32	38	44	40	45	39	46	41	44	27	39	—											
15	41	33	46	40	48	49	41	40	41	47	48	35	47	39	—										
16	32	29	34	34	33	41	25	36	42	35	40	29	44	37	46	—									
17	22	28	42	34	32	36	36	46	39	38	36	31	35	31	33	31	—								
18	32	40	32	29	36	48	35	36	36	38	36	30	28	37	34	40	31	—							
19	23	34	26	22	25	34	36	25	31	33	31	23	35	38	36	38	32	32	—						
20	40	16	22	41	42	38	27	30	41	34	35	34	29	33	30	37	34	35	25	—					
21	30	20	16	12	09	15	27	24	16	22	24	22	21	23	25	28	26	24	27	28	—				
22	18	10	12	23	22	11	20	18	25	24	24	22	15	17	22	25	28	17	21	26	13	—			
23	17	21	19	15	17	11	20	16	32	20	26	14	22	33	22	23	26	26	19	20	11	19	—		
24	19	06	12	08	04	11	09	07	23	16	12	00	18	13	17	08	13	07	20	04	12	13	12	—	
25	-02	08	-02	11	11	16	10	15	18	17	19	12	20	15	18	15	20	18	21	09	11	12	11	-02	—

Note: To conserve space, decimal points are omitted.

Figure 8.5.1
Eigenvalues Computed from Tetrachoric Correlations in Table 8.5.1

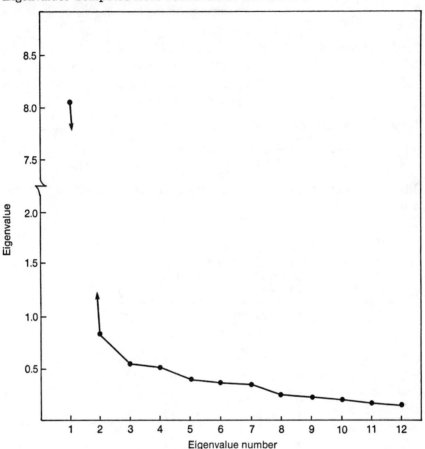

The tetrachoric correlation for this table is .22. From Equation 8.5.1,

$$\tilde{p}_{00} = .248/[(1 - .05)(1 - .20)] = .326$$
$$\tilde{p}_{10} = [.083 - .20(1 - .05).326]/(1 - .05) = .022$$
$$\tilde{p}_{01} = [.414 - .05(1 - .20).326]/(1 - .20) = .501$$
$$\tilde{p}_{11} = 1 - (.326 + .022 + .501) = .150,$$

since $c_{10} = .05$ and $c_{21} = .20$. The tetrachoric correlation for the adjusted two-by-two table is .44, which is a substantially improved measure of the association between items 10 and 21.

Unfortunately, the procedure for adjusting two-by-two tables sometimes encounters problems. For example, the observed two-by-two table for items 23 and 14 is

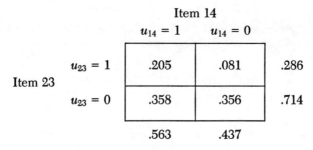

Item 14

		$u_{14} = 1$	$u_{14} = 0$	
Item 23	$u_{23} = 1$	.205	.081	.286
	$u_{23} = 0$	.358	.356	.714
		.563	.437	

Because $c_{14} = .20$ and $c_{23} = .20$, we see

$$\tilde{p}_{00} = .356/[(1 - .20)(1 - .20)] = .556$$
$$\tilde{p}_{10} = [.081 - .20(1 - .20).556]/(1 - .20) = -.010 \,.$$

Obviously, $\tilde{p}_{10}$ has been adjusted too much due to sampling fluctuations.

Table 8.5.2
Factor Loading Matrix Obtained
from Tetrachoric Correlations in
Table 8.5.1

Item	Factor 1	Factor 2	c_i
1	.61	−.28	.20
2	.56	−.18	.20
3	.57	−.35	.20
4	.60	−.09	.20
5	.66	−.18	.16
6	.72	−.20	.12
7	.67	−.17	.20
8	.67	−.09	.20
9	.67	.11	.06
10	.69	−.08	.05
11	.65	.11	.20
12	.56	−.10	.20
13	.61	.13	.16
14	.61	.14	.20
15	.67	−.01	.11
16	.60	.18	.12
17	.56	.27	.16
18	.58	.05	.13
19	.51	.22	.09
20	.54	.11	.09
21	.36	.16	.20
22	.34	.22	.20
23	.35	.26	.20
24	.20	.12	.20
25	.23	.29	.20

The problems encountered in computing tetrachoric correlations from adjusted two-by-two tables can be serious. About 6 percent of these correlations could not be computed due to negative or zero cell entries. An additional 9 percent of the correlations were more than three estimated standard errors from .50. Because so many adjusted tetrachoric correlations were missing or aberrant, no further analyses were undertaken involving Carroll's correction.

8.6 MODIFIED PARALLEL ANALYSIS

Drasgow and Lissak (1982) developed a method for assessing the dimensionality of an item pool which they termed *modified parallel analysis* (MPA). MPA consists of three major steps:

1. The eigenvalues of the matrix of item tetrachoric correlations are computed using an item's largest off-diagonal tetrachoric correlation as a communality estimate.[4]
2. LOGIST is used to estimate item parameters. Then a truly unidimensional item pool is generated by using estimated item parameters as the parameters of the simulated items. This *synthetic data set* should have the same number of simulated examinees and items as the real data set. If the distribution of $\hat{\theta}$ is approximately unimodal and symmetric with gradually decreasing tails, then the θ values used to create the synthetic data can be sampled from a normal distribution with mean zero and unit variance. Otherwise, $\hat{\theta}$ values from LOGIST can be used as the θ values when creating the synthetic data.
3. The eigenvalues of the matrix of tetrachoric correlations *obtained from the synthetic data* are computed using an item's largest off-diagonal tetrachoric correlation as a communality estimate.

The difference between *second* eigenvalues of the real and synthetic data sets can be examined to determine whether application of IRT to a real data set is justified. A useful criterion for evaluating the difference between second eigenvalues is derived from Drasgow and Parsons's (1983) research investigating the robustness of LOGIST to multidimensionality (see Section 3.3). In particular, Drasgow and Lissak performed MPA analyses for data sets generated to have the levels of multidimensionality studied by Drasgow and Parsons. Thus, it was possible to determine the magnitudes of differences between second eigenvalues for data sets that were sufficiently unidimensional for LOGIST and the magnitudes of differences for data sets that were too

---

[4] If a small number of tetrachoric correlations cannot be computed, the approximation method described at the end of Section 8.4 may be used.

multidimensional for LOGIST. Researchers can perform MPA analyses on their data sets and then compare their results to the results obtained by Drasgow and Lissak. If the differences between second eigenvalues in their MPA analyses are less than the differences found by Drasgow and Lissak for the third level of general factor prepotency (which Drasgow and Parsons found to be sufficiently prepotent to allow use of LOGIST), then applications of IRT appear justified.

MPA analyses were performed on the first 40 items of the hypothetical 50-item tests examined by Drasgow and Parsons. These 40 items were composed of four clusters of items with higher within-cluster correlations than expected on the basis of a single latent trait. Table 8.6.1 contains correlations (corrected for unreliability) between subscales formed from the four clusters of items. Note that the latent trait space was truly unidimensional for latent structure 1. In contrast, the general latent trait was very weak in latent structure 5. Drasgow and Parsons found that LOGIST performed satisfactorily for item responses simulated from latent structure 3. This was true both for item responses generated with guessing and for item responses generated with no guessing.

MPA was first examined in samples of $N = 750$ generated from each of the five latent structures in Table 8.6.1. In these data sets, the general latent trait was normally distributed and there was no guessing. Note that here the truly unidimensional data set created from latent structure 1 meets all the assumptions of the normal ogive model and that factoring tetrachorics as described in Section 8.4 is an appropriate method for assessing dimensionality.

The results of this first set of analyses are shown in Figure 8.6.1, where the five panels are arranged in the same order as the data sets in Table 8.6.1. Two points are noteworthy. First, in all five panels the synthetic data set appears to be multidimensional: The second and sometimes the third eigenvalues are noticeably larger than the rest of the eigenvalues. This effect is due to sampling error. In panel B the eigenvalues for a synthetic data set of $N = 5,000$ are shown. Here it is clear that the synthetic data set is unidimensional. As noted in Section 8.4, tetrachoric correlations have large sampling errors; samples of $N = 750$ apparently are not sufficient for the second and third eigenvalues to be well behaved.

The second point concerning Figure 8.6.1 is that MPA has substantial power for detecting multidimensionality. Drasgow and Parsons found that multidimensionality of the magnitude found in latent structure 4 could cause serious problems: LOGIST was no longer necessarily drawn to the general factor. In Figure 8.6.1, panel D, it is apparent that MPA detects this level of multidimensionality. In fact, the item responses generated from latent structure 3 are clearly identified as

Table 8.6.1
Correlations between Subscales Formed from Clusters of Items with High Within-Cluster Correlations

Latent Structure

Subscale	1			2			3			4			5		
Subscale	*1*	*2*	*3*	*1*	*2*	*3*	*1*	*2*	*3*	*1*	*2*	*3*	*1*	*2*	*3*
2	1.00			.86			.46			.36			.14		
3	1.00	1.00		.81	.77		.49	.46		.39	.33		.04	.04	
4	1.00	1.00	1.00	.76	.72	.68	.56	.52	.56	.29	.25	.27	.08	.07	.02

Note: Correlations were corrected for subscale unreliability. There were 15 items on subscale 1, 5 items on subscale 2, 10 items on subscale 3, and 10 items on subscale 4.

Figure 8.6.1
MPA for Item Responses Generated with No Guessing and a Normal Distribution of the General Latent Trait

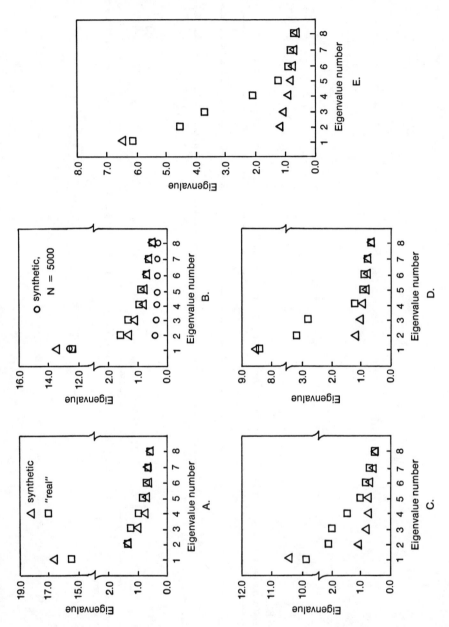

Figure 8.6.2
MPA for Item Responses Generated with Guessing and a Normal Distribution of the General Latent Trait

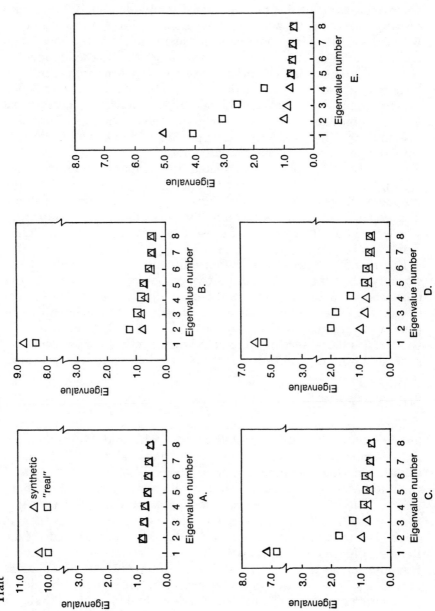

multidimensional, even though LOGIST was found to be robust to these violations of unidimensionality.

In other analyses, Drasgow and Lissak obtained similar results when scores on the latent traits were sampled from (1) a uniform distribution with mean zero and unit variance, and (2) a χ^2 distribution with one degree of freedom that was transformed to have a mean zero and unit variance. These findings are important for practitioners because the latent variables underlying item responses are assumed to be normally distributed in the derivation of the tetrachoric correlation (see Section 8.1). Drasgow and Lissak's results, however, indicate that MPA is robust to violations of the tetrachoric correlation normality assumptions. Thus, practitioners apparently do not need to be concerned with these distributional assumptions.

MPA was also applied to simulated item responses with guessing. Again, the five latent structures in Table 8.6.1 were used. For odd-numbered items, c_i was .20, and c_i was .15 for even-numbered items. The general latent trait was normally distributed, and sample size was $N = 1,000$. The results of these analyses are shown in Figure 8.6.2.

Figure 8.6.2 shows that it is more difficult to detect multidimensionality when there is guessing. Item responses generated from the third latent structure are not clearly indicated to be multidimensional in panel C. The evidence for multidimensionality is compelling in panel D of Figure 8.6.2. This appears to be satisfactory, because LOGIST encountered serious difficulties when applied to item responses generated from the fourth latent structure when there was guessing.

8.7 SUMMARY

MPA is an ad hoc procedure: It cannot be shown to be an optimal test for dimensionality. Christofferson (1975) and Muthén (1978) have developed theory-based tests of dimensionality of dichotomous variables, but their methods are not yet feasible for more than 20 to 25 variables. Moreover, it is not clear that an optimal test for dimensionality is desirable: virtually all real item pools are multidimensional to some extent. For the purposes of IRT, the essential questions seem to be: (1) Does a general latent variable underlie responses to most of the items in the pool (even though other latent variables may underlie responses to clusters of items to a lesser extent)? (2) Can the relations between item responses and the general latent variable be determined from sample data? The research described in Section 3.3 shows that the answer to the second question is positive provided that the general factor is sufficiently prepotent. MPA provides a way for researchers to determine whether in fact there is a latent variable that is strong enough to allow application of IRT in an item pool.

REFERENCES

Bock, R. D., & Lieberman, M. Fitting a response model for n dichotomously scored items. *Psychometrika,* 1970, *35*, 179–197.

Carroll, J. B. The effect of difficulty and chance success on correlations between items or between tests. *Psychometrika,* 1945, *10*, 1–19.

Carroll, J. B. The nature of the data, or how to choose a correlation coefficient. *Psychometrika,* 1961, *26*, 347–372.

Christoffersson, A. Factor analysis of dichotomized variables. *Psychometrika,* 1975, *40*, 5–32.

Drasgow, F., & Lissak, R. I. Modified parallel analysis: A procedure for examining the latent dimensionality of dichotomously scored item responses. Manuscript under review, 1982.

Drasgow, F., & Parsons, C. K. Application of unidimensional item response theory models to multidimensional data. *Applied Psychological Measurement,* in press, 1983.

Ferguson, G. A. The factorial interpretation of test difficulty. *Psychometrika,* 1941, *6*, 323–329.

Gourlay, N. Difficulty factors arising from the use of tetrachoric correlations in factor analysis. *British Journal of Psychology, Statistical Section,* 1951, *4*, 65–73.

Guilford, J. P. *Fundamental statistics in psychology and education* (4th ed.). New York: McGraw-Hill, 1956.

Harman, H. H. *Modern factor analysis* (2d ed.). Chicago: University of Chicago Press, 1967.

IMSL Library (5th ed.). Houston, Tex.: International Mathematical and Statistical Libraries, 1975.

Kendall, M., & Stuart, A. *The advanced theory of statistics* (Vol. 2, 4th ed.). New York: Macmillan, 1979.

Kim, J.-O., & Mueller, C. W. *Introduction to factor analysis.* Beverly Hills, Calif.: Sage Publications, 1978. (a)

Kim, J.-O., & Mueller, C. W. *Factor analysis.* Beverly Hills, Calif.: Sage Publications, 1978. (b)

Lord, F. M. An analysis of the Verbal Scholastic Aptitude Test using Birnbaum's three-parameter logistic model. *Educational and Psychological Measurement,* 1968, *28*, 989–1020.

Lord, F. M., & Novick, M. R. *Statistical theories of mental test scores.* Reading, Mass.: Addison-Wesley Publishing, 1968.

McNemar, Q. *Psychological statistics* (4th ed.). New York: John Wiley & Sons, 1969.

Mulaik, S. A. *The foundations of factor analysis.* New York: McGraw-Hill, 1972.

Muthén, B. Contributions to factor analysis of dichotomized variables. *Psychometrika,* 1978, *43,* 551–560.

Pearson, K. On the correlation of characters not quantitatively measurable. *Royal Society Philosophical Transactions* (Series A), 1900, *195,* 1–47.

SAS users guide (1979 ed.). Raleigh, N.C.: SAS Institute, 1979.

Thurstone, L. L. *Multiple factor analysis.* Chicago: University of Chicago Press, 1947.

9

Measurement and Public Policy

9.0 OVERVIEW

In this chapter we return to some of the issues that were introduced in Chapter 1. Specifically, we shall present a discussion of the areas in which psychological assessments and psychometrics influence social and public policies in the United States. Once again, our concerns about measurement and public policy go beyond the problems of race, sex, and ethnic group differences in cognitive ability test scores. Test-based decisions that may be in conflict with political and social goals are the basis of our concerns.

Many of the specific points in this chapter concern two major themes. The first theme is that the goals of politics and psychometrics have not been kept distinct. An example of this can be seen in the drafting and enforcement of the "Uniform Guidelines on Employee Selection Procedures" (Equal Employment Opportunity Commission et al., 1978). To a great extent, the "Uniform Guidelines" relied on the *Standards for Educational and Psychological Tests* (American Psychological Association et al., 1966, 1974) as a source of technical information. The federal courts have followed this practice also (Novick, 1981). However, when the *Standards* have interfered with achieving the goals of the Equal Employment Opportunity Commission (EEOC), the federal agency given enforcement responsibility for Title VII of the 1964 Civil Rights Act, attempts to maintain consistency between the "Uniform Guidelines" and the *Standards* gave way. Ad hoc procedures were substituted that were designed to accomplish the goals of the governmental agency—a workforce more representative of the racial and ethnic groups in the United States. This is not surprising given the political nature of the enforcement agency. However, it is to be regretted that the political nature of the decision to abandon consistency in favor of political goals was not made explicit. The ad hoc nature of the procedure should have been enunciated in the interests of making clear what rules were being enforced to achieve which goals. By maintaining a public posture that stressed the consistency between the "Uniform Guidelines" and the *Standards,* the EEOC has attempted to make psychometric procedures carry the burden of achieving both the political goal of a racially balanced work force and the psychometric goal of selection on the basis of merit. Failures to achieve simultaneously the political and psychometric goals are often attributed to biased tests—tests biased against minorities. A clearer distinction between political and psychometric decisions might have resulted in better realizations of the political ends, without making psychological tests the scapegoats in the failure to achieve this goal.

It is difficult, perhaps even impossible, to keep politics and psychological testing separate when testing is itself political in nature. Whatever the rhetoric, tests are designed for and used to accomplish a political goal. Thomas Jefferson, for example, wanted to substitute an aristocracy of talent, a meritocracy, for an aristocracy of wealth and family ties as a political goal. Indeed, the Virginia legislature passed a bill that had been introduced by Jefferson eliminating primo geniture (the exclusive right of inheritance belonging to the first born). This bill moved the Commonwealth of Virginia closer to the meritocratic ideal Jefferson envisaged.

Measures of ability and knowledge are tools used to achieve a meritocracy. However, the meritocracy of one generation tends to become the wealthy of the next generation, because the meritocracy's money can be used to obtain better educations for their children regardless of their children's ability (within broad limits) and, hence, better jobs. Thus, a mechanism designed to eliminate the influence of family backgrounds and wealth on admission and hiring decisions may become a mechanism for perpetuating the status quo and the influence of family ties.

This chain of events depends neither on the evil intent of those who rely on psychological tests for personnel decision making nor on bias against minority groups in standardized tests. It depends instead on what ability tests measure—an individual's current repertoire of skills and knowledge—and what they are useful for—to predict performance on related tasks. Education provides one mechanism for acquiring the skills and knowledge tapped by measures of cognitive ability.

The second major theme of the controversy concerning psychological tests is the marked difference in power between the test administrator and the examinee or job applicant. National testing organizations have occasionally required retesting large numbers of examinees when there was evidence of widespread cheating or violations of test security. It is easy to understand why this is done. However, the same testing organizations do not allow individual examinees an opportunity to dispute the validity of their test scores as measures of their ability (Novick, 1981). Examinees' arguments that a score from a specific test administration is aberrant and an invalid indication of their ability typically are not heeded. At the very best, the examinee might be allowed to retake the test at his or her expense and inconvenience. At worst, the suspect test score is used in decisions with profound long-term consequences for individuals.

Some personality tests used in personnel selection decisions, such as the Minnesota Multiphasic Personality Inventory (MMPI), have validity scales in addition to their clinical or content scales. These scales can be used to discard an entire test protocol because of excessive use of the "?" option or improbable claims to saintliness. Some individuals may introspect very little; they can truly be uncertain about many aspects of their relationships with others and the world around them. Use of the "?" option by these individuals to indicate uncertainty about many questions is justifiable. Similarly, some individuals may read all of the editorials, everyday, in every paper to which they subscribe. Others may truly appreciate medieval Welsh poetry. Endorsing such low-probability items will cause elevated scores on validity scales even though in some unusual individuals the statements may be true. Eliminating entire test protocols on the basis of these validity scales without allowing the individuals to provide an explanation of their responses is arbitrary. Such actions highlight the asymmetry of the power relationship between examinees and test administrators. The powerlessness of the examinee or applicant is especially serious when test scores are used by the powerful to make employment or educational decisions.

Social policies related to psychological tests and assessments are tied to legal challenges to the use of tests, and subsequent court decisions. The majority of public concerns about psychological testing is with apparent biases and discriminations against race, sex, and ethnic groups protected by the constitution and various federal statutes. In particular, the 1964 Civil Rights Act and the Rehabilitation Act of 1973 were designed to remove barriers to employment and *to increase the flow of ethnic minorities and women into positions of responsibility and authority in organizations.* Space does not allow a thorough exploration of all legal ramifications and specifications of all relevant court decisions. In Section 9.1 we shall review the major and most recent decisions in the area of employment discrimination and testing, and in Section 9.2 we consider educational discrimination and testing.

9.1 PSYCHOLOGICAL TESTS AND EMPLOYMENT DECISIONS

The major points covered in this section are concerned with legal decisions in employment discrimination cases involving psychological tests. Other important considerations—such as characteristics of relevant labor pools, proper criteria of performance, and even procedures for determining validity—are not addressed because they are only tangentially related to psychological measurement. We limit our discussion to psychometric issues in these cases in order to maintain the focus of this book.

The watershed decision in testing and discrimination in employment is *Griggs* v. *Duke Power Company* (1971). *Griggs* was the first case involving employment tests argued before the United States Supreme Court under the provisions of the 1964 Civil Rights Act. The facts of the case were never contested by the defendant, Duke Power. Willie B. Griggs, a black laborer employed by the Duke Power Company, applied for a job that would have resulted in a promotion. The requirements for the new job were possession of a high school diploma or a score at or above the 50th percentile on a general intelligence test. Griggs was denied the promotion because he did not meet either of the minimum qualifications. The Supreme Court, in a unanimous decision, ruled that Title VII of the 1964 Civil Rights Act *proscribed employment practices that are fair in form but have the result of discrimination in operation*. Further, the Supreme Court stated that once the plaintiff has established that adverse impact or discrimination practices exist, usually by statistical evidence showing disproportionate numbers of minority group members not hired or promoted, the burden of proof shifts to the defendant to show the job relatedness of the selection procedures being used.[1]

The decision, although leaving vague a number of important details, was a landmark in employment discrimination law. Because cognitive ability tests usually yield mean differences in test scores among race, ethnic, and sex groups, almost any test used for selection purposes will have adverse impact on minority groups. Nearly *any* challenge to the use of a test will require the employer to present acceptable evidence of job relatedness of the test. Common sense suggests that an employer would not use tests in selection programs without evidence of their validity, but empirical evidence establishing validity of tests comes in many varieties—when it exists at all.

---

[1] "Adverse impact" of a selection procedure for a minority group is usually defined to exist when the selection ratio (number hired divided by number of applicants) for the minority group is less than 80 percent of the selection ratio of the majority group.

Griggs, although introducing the concept of job relatedness into discrimination law, did not spell out how job relatedness could be established. Instead, the court decision noted that the existing EEOC *Guidelines* (1966) should be given "great deference" because they had been written by the agency charged with implementing the Civil Rights Act. The Supreme Court's deference to the *Guidelines* had a profound effect. EEOC regulations, without being subjected to adversarial comment, virtually became law in Title VII cases. It must be emphasized that the Supreme Court in a later decision modified their early position and stated that "To the extent that the EEOC *Guidelines* conflict with well-grounded expert opinion and accepted professional standards, they need not be controlling" (*National Education Association* v. *State of South Carolina*, 1978, p. 38).

A second important case in this area is *Washington* v. *Davis* (1976). Once again, the facts were undisputed. A written test designed to assess verbal ability excluded disproportionate numbers of black applicants for the position of policeman in Washington, D.C. The Supreme Court articulated that Title VII required test validation in any number of ways designed to determine if a test, in fact, selected those applicants who were most qualified for the job in question. However, the plaintiff had filed and argued the case under the equal protection clause of the 14th Amendment to the Constitution of the United States; the rigorous validity standards required by Title VII [actually required by the EEOC *Guidelines* and later by the "Uniform Guidelines" (EEOC et al., 1978)] were not appropriate for the constitutional question. The court interpreted the Constitution as requiring only that a defendent show a rational basis for the tests being used.

In *Albemarle Paper Co.* v. *Moody* (1975), the Supreme Court decided that a company's failure to analyze the particular skills needed in the jobs in question rendered the selection system, particularly the criterion used, defective. Once again, the Court referred to the EEOC *Guidelines* and legitimized their deference to this document by noting that the *Guidelines* relied on professional standards of test validation established by the American Psychological Association, the American Educational Research Association, and the National Council on Measurement in Education.

Of greater importance than the ultimate decision in *Albemarle* was the solidifying of earlier interpretations that there were three basic methods of establishing validity: criterion-related validity, content validity, and construct validity. Guion (1980) has commented that the courts, the EEOC *Guidelines*, and the "Uniform Guidelines" establish the illusion that there are three different roads to psychometric salvation. In fact, as noted below, there may be only one safe road, criterion-related validity, to the promised land where litigation about selection devices never occurs.

Two recent cases, *Guardians Association of New York City* v. *Civil Service Commission* (1980) and *Firefighters Institute (FIRE)* v. *St. Louis* (1980) (both of which the Supreme Court declined to review), seem to emphasize Guion's point: There may be three roads to psychometric salvation, but two of them (content and construct validity) are taken at the pilgrim's peril. In *FIRE*, for example, the court agreed that content validation procedures are appropriate for justifying the use of a selection test. However, the court rejected the particular tests in the case because the evidence offered to support their content validity was not judged to be adequate.

The court also held that content valid tests could only be used to set minimum standards and not to rank order job applicants for selection. Tests used to rank order candidates apparently require more stringent empirical validation efforts. The wording of the decision, however, is chilling for those who rest their cases for job relatedness of selection procedures on arguments about content. The court concluded that a pencil-and-paper test asking questions based on projected color slides of a simulated fire scene was measuring verbal skills far removed from a captain's actual work, and was not critical for that job.

Finally, the Supreme Court has agreed to hear during the 1981–82 session the case of *Teal* v. *Connecticut* (1981). In *Teal* the lower courts stated that if *any segment* of a sequential selection procedure has adverse impact against members of protected minority groups, then it must have demonstrated relevance to job-related criteria. A segment with adverse impact must be shown to be job related even when the selection procedure *as a whole* does not have adverse impact. This case, if upheld, would mean that a finding of no adverse impact of an entire selection procedure does not necessarily lead to a conclusion of no discrimination. Instead, every step in a sequential procedure would be considered as a selection device in and of itself. The implications of *Teal*, if upheld, cannot be anticipated at this time. That the Supreme Court has decided to hear the case suggests a questioning of the operation of a selection system as a whole as a basis for judging its legality. The lower court's decision in *Teal* seems to have been made in spite of the emphasis in the "Uniform Guidelines" on evaluating a selection system by the overall effect. Once again, ad hoc procedures have been used to achieve a political goal at the expense of consistency.

Public interest rights. There are three public policy considerations involved in employment testing and hiring. We should consider the rights and interests of the institution conducting the testing and hiring, the rights and interests of the test takers as applicants, and the public interest. It is unlikely that there exist any true solutions that satisfactorily address all aspects of the problems of psychological employment tests and minority group underrepresentation in the workforce. What follows are a number of suggestions, each of which addresses one issue in employment testing.[2]

The first suggestion emphasizes the joint political and psychometric nature of employment decisions. The decisions and the utility of any personnel system depend on relations both between test scores and job performance *within* subpopulations and relations *between* subpopulations in terms of their mean test scores and mean job performance (see, for example, Figure 5.1.3). This suggests we might explicitly recognize that decision making can be divided into two components: a political component determining the ratio of majority and minority employees desirable in a workforce, and a psychometric component determining how those individuals from subpopulations will be selected. (Whether such a division *should* be made is an entirely separate question.) For example, an organization might decide to avoid EEOC litigation and make a decision to hire minority employees at a rate equal to the hiring rate for the majority group. Following this political decision, individuals could be selected from the top down within these two (or more) groups on the basis of merit as assessed by psychological tests. Such a separation makes both the political and psychometric components explicit and open to debate.

Cronbach (1980) has shown that political decisions to increase substantially the numbers of minority group members hired may have relatively little impact on the quality of employees hired if the decisions within both groups are made on the basis of merit (applicants are hired from the top down on the basis of ability measures). This suggests that substantial deviations from psychometrically optimal decisions, deviations designed to achieve political goals, may have relatively small effects on the quality of applicants hired and, from an institution's point of view, may entail relatively small costs.

A warning is necessary. It may be an oversimplification to think that because a particular set of assumed test validities, hiring rates, and mean test score differences between groups produce small effects on the quality of applicants hired, then the true costs to organizations of suboptimal hiring are small. Translating quality of newly hired workers into utility (in terms of dollars or any other general measure of utility) is extremely difficult and involves many assumptions. Small differences in the quality of applicants hired may be translated into

---

[2] It is evident that employment testing discussed in Section 9.1 and educational testing discussed in Section 9.2 have many roots in common. Thus, proposed solutions are likely to be applicable to both problems, with different degrees of appropriateness.

either trivial or bankruptcy-producing results. The magnitude of the effect depends on many factors. Any particular organization may decide to evaluate the costs of such political decisions and be willing to incur them; others may not. The decision should be explicit.

A second suggestion that addresses an issue in employment testing arises from the realization that selection systems are designed or chosen to maximize or minimize some specified mathematical or statistical function. The choice of the function is up to the decision maker. For example, a selection system based strictly on within-group regressions is usually designed to minimize the sum of the squared deviations of obtained criterion scores, Y, about the predicted criterion scores $\tilde{Y}$. This simply requires that a prediction equation be developed to minimize $\Sigma_{i=1}^{N} (Y_i - \tilde{Y}_i)^2/N$, also referred to as a squared error loss function.[3] Different tests could be considered for use in the prediction equation. That test or weighted combination of tests would normally be chosen that minimized the squared error loss function over all individuals tested.

Choosing a selection device or system that minimizes a squared error loss function is objective in the sense that the loss function itself is quantitative, explicit, and value free. Note, however, that the *decision* to rely on this loss function is not objective; it involves a value judgment just as surely as if one decided to hire 20 percent (or any other percentage) minority employees. The squared error loss function treats squared errors of prediction, errors that result in the same value of $(Y_i - \tilde{Y}_i)^2$, as equivalent prediction errors for members of *all subpopulations* in the applicant pool. A decision to treat squared errors of prediction differently depending on the subpopulation in which the errors occurred would still yield a quantitative loss function that is objective in the sense defined above.

A different loss function may make this approach clearer. Rather than evaluating the squared error loss of different selection tests, one might decide to emphasize only those errors of prediction that lead to an error in a decision. That is, the focus is on the *decisions* that must be made. In this regard, it makes no difference if we predict that an individual will achieve a criterion standard score of +3.0 and the obtained score is only +2.0, provided that the individual is above the level on the criterion considered acceptable and would have been hired whether $\tilde{Y}_i = +2.0$ or +3.0. No error of decision making has occurred. In this instance, squared error is an inappropriate loss function. It has little meaning in terms of selection decisions (Cronbach & Gleser, 1965).

---

[3] It is called a loss function because decision makers are assumed to incur a loss whenever their predictions are in error. Squared error simply identifies the specific loss assumed to be incurred.

Focusing on a decision-making approach to employee selection normally means that a psychological test is evaluated in terms of the correct and incorrect decisions that are made using a test. These decisions typically can be framed in terms of a two-by-two, decision-by-outcome display as shown in Table 9.1.1.

Table 9.1.1
Two-By-Two Table Relating Decisions
Based on Test Score X to Outcomes with
Implicit $(+1, -1)$ Utilities

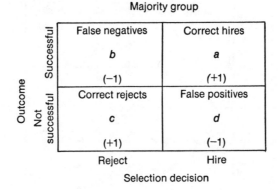

Evaluating specific tests or selection systems in terms of correct decisions involves summing the frequencies of correct decisions, cells a and c, and subtracting the frequencies of incorrect decisions in cells b and d. The test or selection system normally would be chosen that maximized the number of correct decisions. However, counting correct and incorrect decisions is equivalent to treating false negatives and false positives (cells b and d) as equally bad (a utility to the organization of -1) and both kinds of correct decisions (cells a and c) as equally good (a utility to the organization of $+1$). The different errors (false negatives and false positives) and the different correct decisions (correct hires and correct rejects) are treated as equivalent across all subpopulations.

In the context of this chapter, it is useful to consider personnel decisions as a sum of the decisions that are made within two or more subpopulations, e.g., a minority and a majority subpopulation. Thus, the frequencies in Table 9.1.1 can be separated into two tables as shown in Table 9.1.2. In this table, a total of N decisions are made: N_A decisions made about members of subpopulation A, and N_B decisions made about members of subpopulation B. One set of possible explicit *differential* utilities is indicated for the minority group in Table 9.1.2 $(k > 1)$. This is a set of weights that might result from an explicit goal

Table 9.1.2
Two-By-Two Tables from Two Subpopulations
Relating Decisions Based on Test X to
Outcomes, with Explicit Differential
Subpopulation Utilities

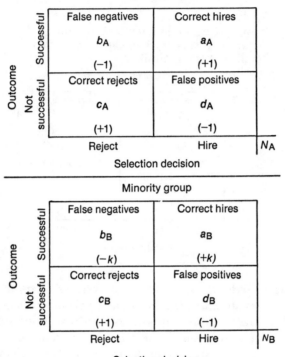

Majority group

		Reject	Hire	
Outcome	Successful	False negatives b_A (−1)	Correct hires a_A (+1)	
	Not successful	Correct rejects c_A (+1)	False positives d_A (−1)	N_A

Selection decision

Minority group

		Reject	Hire	
Outcome	Successful	False negatives b_B (−k)	Correct hires a_B (+k)	
	Not successful	Correct rejects c_B (+1)	False positives d_B (−1)	N_B

Selection decision

of an organization to increase the number of minority group members in the workforce. Such a decision would not necessarily be made because increasing the number of minority group members in the workforce is assumed to be better for the organization. It could be recognized explicitly that false negatives, those who would have been successful if hired, in a subpopulation that was already underrepresented in the workforce were much more serious social or public interest errors than false negatives in the majority population that is overrepresented in the workforce. Similar adjustments could be made in the utilities for cells c and d.

The important point to keep in mind is that the explicit utilities indicated in Table 9.1.2 are no more subjective than the implicit weights of +1 and −1 indicated in Table 9.1.1. One difference is that, in Table 9.1.2, the social values of the decision maker are made explicit. A second difference is that hiring decisions based on the utilities indicated in Table 9.1.2 would benefit minority group members; hiring decisions would not be made strictly on the basis of merit. Hiring on the basis of merit is usually considered to reflect our social values. The utilities in Table 9.1.2 reflect, on the other hand, an attempt to redress another part of the social system, discrimination against minority group members, that has existed for most of our history. We offer them as an example without evaluating their merit. The values of the utilities in Table 9.1.2 can be subjected to comment and debate. The weights in Table 9.1.1 are rarely subjected to such comment and debate because they are rarely made explicit. Not incidently, they also reflect most strongly the rights of the hiring organization.

Adopting utilities for the eight cells in Table 9.1.2 that differ between subpopulations implies that different cutting scores, X_A^* and X_B^*, will be chosen in the two subpopulations to maximize the sum of cell frequencies weighted by utilities. That is, cutting scores will be chosen to maximize the utility of the personnel decisions evaluated across both subpopulations. In this example, it would be expected that the minority group cutting score X_B^* would be less than the majority group cutting score X_A^* in order to increase the numbers of minority individuals in cell a_B and reduce the number of minority individuals in cell b_B. This would result from a decision by an organization to incur the costs of hiring a substantial number of false positives with utilities of -1 in order to avoid false negatives with utilities $-k$ $(k > 1)$.

The "solutions" suggested above (discussed in detail by Novick & Petersen, 1976) to problems of psychological testing and underrepresentation of minority group members in the workforce have the advantage of being explicit. They also recognize the political nature of the employment decision-making process and consider the public interest. Weights can be chosen to increase the flow of some minority groups into the work force. Note carefully that *political decisions to provide some specified groups an advantage in employment decisions must simultaneously erect barriers to other groups.* For this reason, political decisions may not always be made to provide minority groups with increased access to employment. In fact, historically, such political decisions have usually given majority group members an advantage. Blacks in the United States (except for the periods from 1860 to about 1875 and from 1970 to the present), and Jews in Nazi Germany and in the United States before World War II were systematically denied equal access to employment and educational opportunities. Legislation or court interpretations providing advantages to some groups today can easily be reinterpreted tomorrow to provide advantages to different groups with more political influence.

Thus, a decision could easily be made to *decrease* the flow of minority group members into the workforce by erecting barriers to employment for these groups. Depending on the shifting winds of politics to achieve "fairness" of hiring decisions is a high-risk venture.

Finally, and by no means least, it is not sufficient to consider the effects of hiring policy decisions on the percentage of minority group members employed or on the individual minority group members who are hired. It is also necessary to consider which majority group members are *not* hired or selected because of political decisions. It is not accurate, for example, to consider the majority subpopulation as an undifferentiated group. Selection decisions based on tests of cognitive ability rather than on an examination of education credentials benefit (relatively) blue-collar, working-class whites at the expense of blacks and middle-class whites. Decisions based on an examination of credentials followed by random selection helps (relatively) blacks and middle-class whites at the expense of working-class whites (Jencks, 1972). Applicants from different racial and socioeconomic groups are competing in a "zero-sum" game: decisions and outcomes benefiting one group are made at the expense of another group or groups. Which group (if any) is given an advantage must be an explicit political decision.

Individual applicant rights. As noted in Section 9.0, one reason for the focus of attention on testing and public policy is the asymmetry in the power relation between institutions and individual test takers. Institutions can arbitrarily discard the results of an entire test administration because of evidence of a breach of test security, and discard an individual's test results because of excessive use of a "?" option or an elevated score on a so-called validity scale. Individual test takers should be presented with evidence indicating why their vectors of responses are considered either valid or invalid assessments. An institution should automatically calculate theory-based appropriateness indices for every individual they test. If the use of the "?" option or excessive numbers of omitted responses results in an apparently aberrant response vector, the individual should be informed and the reasons for the lack of appropriateness detailed. If the use of large numbers of "?" options seems reasonable, given that the individual just never thinks about such things as how the top of his or her head feels (see similar items in the MMPI), then the clinical scores should be used as obtained. If excessive numbers of omitted responses on ability measures are the apparent cause of the lack of appropriateness, the individual should be told how to maximize his or her score on the test and then be retested.

Automatic calculation of appropriateness indices for all individuals does not completely equalize the power differential between the organization and the individual applicant. It does help, however. It provides a rational, theory-based procedure for assessing the relevance of every test score that is used to make important decisions about individuals. It also provides a mechanism by which applicants who use suboptimal response strategies can be detected and instructed how to maximize their scores. Individuals with inappropriate strategies or those who are unnecessarily creative in their interpretations of questions would be less likely to be penalized by inappropriately low estimates of their ability.

Institutional rights. A third set of rights and interests important in the use of tests is that of the employer. Here we note a strategy for dealing with psychological tests that focuses exclusively on these institutional rights. This strategy states that an organization should continue to rely on psychological tests as selection devices, to make psychometrically optimal decisions without regard to minority group status, to defend the use of their tests on the basis of the best available validity evidence, and to accept the long-term consequences of a workforce that is decidedly unbalanced in terms of race, ethnicity, and sex. The consequences of this strategy need careful consideration.

Assume, for example, that the federal courts decide that organizations are free to use tests in selection decisions and to base test usage on the belief that a test shown to be valid for a certain type of job in one organization is almost surely valid for similar jobs in other organizations; this is termed *validity generalization* (see Hunter, Schmidt, and Hunter, 1979). We might expect to see an increase in the use of tests as selection devices by employers because of decreased costs and decreased risks of litigation. Moreover, let us assume the findings that general ability tests assessing broad cognitive ability are more likely to be related to behavioral measures of job performance than are those that assess specific, narrow abilities (Hulin & Humphreys, 1979). Thus, in the future we would be likely to see organizations using general intelligence tests as selection devices. These tests would likely be similar to each other across organizations and jobs. If an individual were below a cutoff score for a desirable job in one organization, he or she would probably be below the cutoff for similar—or even dissimilar—jobs in other organizations. Consequently, subpopulations of permanently unemployed individuals and individuals whose employment opportunities are limited to less desirable jobs may be created in the United States. The long-term negative consequences and impact of this selection strategy on the public interest are serious.

The advantages to organizations following this selection strategy are quite clear. Assuming their tests are related to job performance, they will gain advantage over organizations not following a psychometrically optimal strategy for selecting applicants. How long this advantage will last depends on the size and mobility of the available labor pool and the adaptations in strategies followed by other organizations competing for the same workers. If organization Z is the only organization following such a policy, their relative advantage will continue indefinitely. If other competing organizations adopt the same policy, the best of the available workers would likely be shuffled around among the competing organizations. No long-term advantage would be likely to be gained by any one organization.

The labor market of an organization is also important. An organization may be only competing with other organizations in the United States for both its sales market and its labor pool. The finite, common labor pool available for hiring means that organization Z and its competitors can adopt strategies that effectively distribute both the highly and the less highly qualified workers across all organizations. If the competition is with organizations from other nations that neither compete for the same labor pool nor are faced with substantial numbers of minority groups that may be less qualified, a strategy that reflects anything other than their hiring on the basis of merit may in the long run be self-defeating to the organization and the individuals within that labor pool.

9.2 PSYCHOLOGICAL TESTS IN EDUCATION

Educational systems are the second major set of organizations that use psychological tests for decision-making purposes. Within school systems, tests are generally used to make both admission and placement decisions. These two uses are discussed separately below.

Placement. The specific issues involved in using psychological tests in educational settings for educational placement are germane to school systems and pupils rather than to employers and job applicants. However, the implications and consequences of using standardized tests are analogous. Minority group children are typically overrepresented in special education classes for children who are handicapped or have learning disabilities. They are underrepresented in educational programs and institutions for the gifted. Psychological tests of cognitive ability were once seen as a boon because they could classify students into homogeneous ability clusters enabling specialized educational programs to be structured for the specific needs of different ability groups. Tests are now seen by many as instruments of the white middle-class establishment used to continue racial segregation and deny minority children high-quality educations.[4] Educational

---

[4] Karier (1976), for example, has argued that psychological tests are an instrument of control used by the "corporate liberal state." Karier's interpretation of the current social forces and policies may be as misleading as his inferences about the intent of testing in

testing is indeed undesirable if it perpetuates segregation in the class-rooms with no concomitant increase in educational benefits to minority group students.

Although most of the relevant cases reviewed in this section are racial discrimination cases, they are properly viewed as descendants of a racial segregation case, *Brown* v. *Board of Education of Topeka* (1954). The now familiar ruling in *Brown*, striking down racially segregated, "separate but equal" schools in the United States, established the principle that black and ethnic minority children have a right to integrated and equal education guaranteed by the 5th and 14th amendments to the Constitution. Cognitive ability tests, because of their adverse impact on minorities and the poor are often viewed by the courts as subtle methods of perpetuating de facto segregation in place of illegal de jure segregation.

Since *Brown* the discrimination cases involving testing have been subtle and complex in their facts, implications, and legal opinions. For example, one of the early cases involving psychological tests and racial discrimination was *Hobson* v. *Hansen* (1967) (see also *Smuck* v. *Hobson*, 1969). *Hobson* was both a segregation and racial discrimination case. The discrimination aspects of the case involved the use of group-administered tests of ability that were used to place school children into different tracks in the District of Columbia school system. The court noted that, although the group tests were only one aspect of the decision to place children in the special education tracks, they played a dominant role. The court found these tests deficient and unconstitutional under the 5th and 14th amendments to the Constitution as a basis for educational groupings.

The heart of the court's decision was that placement of a disproportionate number of black and poor children in the "basic" as opposed to "honors" tracks was not offset by demonstrable educational gains to these children. Indeed, the court noted that the educational content of the basic track was so watered down as to amount to "warehousing" of the children. The tests were mechanically applied, and the court argued they were not based on good psychological and educational theory. Further, there were no requirements for periodic retesting of the children in the basic track to determine if they should be reassigned. If the special education programs have the desired effects on

education. The use of tests in education has been paralleled by an increase in the diversity of routes one can take to a degree (high school diploma or General Education Diploma; private four-year college, state university, or community college; any of a number of majors that will lead to admission to an advanced program; full-time student status or part-time pursuit of a degree while working). There has also been an increase in college, state, and federal financial support for students over which the "corporate liberal state" exercises very little control. These factors suggest that perceptions of the use of testing as a tool of the corporate liberal state are based upon the political ideologies of the critics more than on the system as it operates.

the students in these classes, the students *must* be reassessed periodically. Those students who have made sufficient gains in verbal ability and other skills so that they could benefit from regular classes must be identified. Thus, in *Hobson* as in other cases, the proscription against using psychological tests was aimed as much at an educational system that was seriously deficient in the education provided in the special classes and the *misuse* of test scores as it was at psychological tests per se. Indeed, the court was eminently correct in striking down the poorly conceived and rigidly applied procedures involving group assessments that were not validated for the purposes for which they were being used and a system that did not take into consideration students' growth and development.

Generalizations of *Hobson* can be seen in two recent cases involving two individually administered tests of cognitive ability. These tests, the Stanford-Binet and the Wechsler Intelligence Scale for Children—Revised (WISC-R), are generally regarded as being among the best available tests of ability today. The tests were used to place students into educable mentally retarded (EMR) and educable mentally handicapped (EMH) classes that were maintained separately from regular classes. These two cases are *Larry P.* v. *Riles* (1979), docketed for appeal, and *PASE* v. *Hannon*[5] (1980). The facts in both cases are remarkably similar. Children were placed into special education (EMR or EMH) classes following a procedure that reviewed teachers' recommendations and scores on the Stanford-Binet or the WISC-R. Black and ethnic minority children were represented in special classes in disproportionately greater numbers than their representation in the school system as a whole.

In *Larry P.* the court ruled in favor of the plaintiff, against the California State Department of Education, and permanently enjoined the San Francisco school system from using *any* standardized tests for identifying mentally handicapped black children or for placing these children into special classes without the prior permission of the court. The court explicitly rejected an explanation, based on true differences between groups in cognitive ability and skills assessed by the tests, for the disproportionate numbers of blacks and minorities in the special education classes. The court found that explanations of the differences in mean scores based on socioeconomic and cultural differences were not persuasive. It concluded that the best explanation for the difference in test performance was that the tests were inherently biased against racial and ethnic minorities. (This application of the egalitarian hypothesis (see Section 5.1) was also an important part of the decision in *Hobson*.) The court also explicitly noted that, if the special

---

[5] Parents in Action against Special Education.

education classes were working as intended and providing good educational experiences, the plaintiffs would not have appeared in the courtroom. Nonetheless, even though it appears to have been the quality of special education that triggered the litigation, the ruling in *Larry P.* proscribes the use of standardized tests for placement purposes in California schools.

Use of the term *ability* by the Court in *Larry P.* seems to reflect its common usage rather than its technical meaning. Ability, as used by the Court, refers to native capacity. Thus, mean differences on ability tests are viewed within this definition as reflecting *either* differences in native capacity *or* test bias. In *Larry P.*, the Court rejected the hypothesis of differences in native ability and thus concluded the test must be biased. Unfortunately, the premise that ability tests measure innate capacity is incorrect; *there are no tests of innate ability* any more than there are measures of innate height. Ability tests measure an individual's current repertoire of skills and knowledge obtained from past learning and experiences. Measures of ability and measures of height may be related in important ways to performance on other tasks; but such measures reflect current standing on the dimension, not innate capacity.

The distinction between tests as measures of innate capacity and tests as measures of learned skills and knowledge is important. Scores on tests of academic achievement (and hence scores on tests of cognitive ability and aptitude) are related to variables such as parents' education, availability of reading materials in the home, parents' aspirations for the child, and family's attitude toward education (White, 1982). The Court's belief that mean differences on ability tests reflect either differences in native capacity or test bias is conceptually erroneous and empirically impossible to test. Disadvantaged minority groups probably differ from the majority group on variables such as parents' education, availability of reading materials, etc., and these variables are related to test performance. Thus, mean differences on cognitive ability tests are expected.

In spite of the similarity of facts in *Larry P.* and *PASE* v. *Hannon* (1980), the court in *PASE* ruled against the plaintiff and for the City of Chicago school system. The court in this latter case stated that the plaintiff had not presented a persuasive case that the tests in question (Stanford-Binet and WISC-R) were inherently biased. The disproportionate representation of minority children in special education classes was not convincing to the Court. Specifically, the Court noted that the expert witnesses for the plaintiffs appeared to be testifying from rigid, doctrinaire positions and not from data. They were unresponsive to direct questions from the Court about the basis for their testimony and their conclusions about the bias in the tests. Lacking any statistical or other acceptable evidence about the bias in these tests, the Court based the ruling, which allowed the test to be used for tracking purposes in the Chicago school system, on a personal inspection of the wording and content of the items of the Stanford-Binet and the WISC-R.[6] This method of detecting item bias was rational once the Court had concluded that the expert witnesses were not addressing relevant issues of the case. In a very real sense, the Court had no alternative in the case in view of its conclusions about the expert witnesses. This form of item analysis as a basis for a decision has been characterized by Bersoff (1981a) as naive, unintelligent, and empty of empirical substance, as well as "embarrassingly unsophisticated and ingenuous" (1981b, p. 1049).

It needs emphasis that the basis for the decision in *Larry P.* was equally naive. Assumptions based on the egalitarian hypothesis that ability (as rigorously defined) is equally distributed across all subpopulations are no more defendable than is an inspection of item content to detect item bias. Decisions of this degree of importance should be based on the best theory-based empirical evidence available and not on armchair analysis.

Once again, note the plaintiffs in *PASE* were questioning the entire system of special education classes. The use of psychological tests per se as screening devices was not the central issue.

The decision in *Larry P.* has been appealed; the appeal has been docketed but not heard. The decision in *PASE* has not been appealed by the plaintiffs; the case became moot when the City of Chicago signed a consent decree on the matter of school integration. One provision of this decree effectively proscribed the use of the Stanford-Binet and WISC-R for placement purposes. The divergent rulings in *Larry P.* and *PASE* will likely be resolved by the federal judiciary system. Until such resolution takes place, administrators in school systems who use tests for purposes of placement into special education classes do so at risk of litigation.

Three recent cases also bear on the issue of standardized tests in educational systems. Two of these cases, *Lora* v. *Board of Education of the City of New York* (1979) and *Mattie T.* v. *Holladay* (1979) are similar to *Hobson* (1967) in that both questioned the use of standardized tests for special education screening purposes and the lack of effective "treatment" afforded the children in special classes. Another case, *Debra P.* v. *Turlington* (1979), however, involves a standardized test of functional literacy used as a prerequisite for obtaining a diploma from Florida Public Schools. In *Debra P.*, the court found that

---

[6] In his decision the judge published every item on the two tests and destroyed the carefully maintained security of test items. This potentially ruins the usefulness of the tests as diagnostic devices.

the Florida state student assessment test was a valid and reasonable measure for dividing students into "diploma" and "no diploma" classifications. They further found that the test had adequate content and construct validity and was not unconstitutionally racially or ethnically biased against black students. However, because of the past history of de jure racial segregation in Florida schools from 1885 to 1967 and de facto segregation from 1967 to 1971, the court enjoined the Florida school system for a period of four years from denying diplomas to black students for failing to pass the examination. Even though integration of the schools was accomplished by 1977, the court held that the use of a functional literacy test without adequate prior notice of implementation violated the equal protection clause of the federal statutes and the 14th amendment of the Constitution. Thus, in spite of the court's generally positive evaluation of the validity of the functional literacy examination, the operation of the overall system prevented its immediate implementation.

Educational admission. Basing college, law school, medical school, and graduate school admissions in part on scores earned on standardized paper-and-pencil ability tests has led to a substantial amount of rhetoric aimed at both tests and testing companies. Several truth-in-testing bills have been introduced in Congress, and 17 bills have appeared in state legislatures. Only two have been passed (New York and California).

The controversy and rhetoric about standardized educational admission tests seem to have developed independently of the psychometric evidence about the usefulness of admission tests in reducing errors of prediction. Cleary, Humphreys, Kendrick, and Wesman (1975), Rubin (1980), Linn, Harnisch, and Dunbar (1981) among others, have provided summaries of large numbers of studies relating college and professional school admission test scores to performance in postsecondary and postgraduate educational institutions. The evidence is clear and consistent. Well-constructed tests of cognitive ability are significantly and consistently related to performance in school. When appropriate corrections are made for restriction of range and other statistical artifacts, the validities of the tests are appreciably large. These tests do not appear to be consistently or generally biased against racial minority groups when the Cleary (Section 5.1) definition of test bias is used (Linn, 1982). This is the definition of test bias used by most courts and the "Uniform Guidelines" (EEOC et al., 1978).

Both of the constitutional cases in this area arose from challenges by white male applicants to "reverse discrimination" in professional schools that involved reserving a specific number of places in an entering class for minority group members. In *Defunis* v. *Odegaard* (1974), the Supreme Court ruled the case was moot because, by the time it had been appealed through the system to their court, Defunis had obtained a law degree from Washington University. Defunis had been granted an injunction by a lower court ordering the university to admit him pending the outcome of the appeal procedure.

In *Bakke* v. *Board of Regents of the University of California* (1978), the Supreme Court in a very narrow ruling decided that, without a finding of previous racial discrimination, reserving a number of specific slots (or a quota) for minority applicants in the admission class while turning away majority group applicants with better qualifications violated the constitutional rights of the majority group members denied admission.

Except for these two reverse discrimination cases in which institutions have attempted to achieve a political goal of a balanced admission class and to undo the adverse impact of standardized cognitive ability tests, there are few constitutional cases to be considered.

Once again, it is useful to focus both on the asymmetry of the power relationship between applicants and educational institutions and on the political goal of increasing the proportion of minority group members in higher education. It is clear that in this area, just as in the area of employment testing and educational placement testing, psychological tests have substantial adverse impact on minority groups. It is also known that scores on college admission tests are correlated with demographic variables such as socioeconomic status, family income, parents' education, and other variables that index class membership in the United States. Thus, there are pressures on colleges to deemphasize the use of aptitude tests and other selection criteria that result in racial and ethnic imbalances in higher education. There is no evidence that the substitutes proposed, for example, by Nairn (1980) will provide valid predictions of college performance, or that those substitutes (interviews, weighted biographical information blanks, demographic data) will prove *less* biased in the long run than psychological tests.[7]

Just as in the case of employment testing, it is instructive to consider both political decisions and psychometric admission decisions. One alternative would be to combine ability grouping with random

[7] It is likely that interviews would be very expensive, less valid, and more biased. Their only virtue for those who view the results of cognitive ability tests as biased is that, in some cases, the biases might cancel out over many interviews and have a net effect of zero. If colleges and universities turn to alumni for assistance in conducting interviews in order to decrease the expense involved, more bias *against* blacks and poor whites and bias *in favor of* children of alumni and friends of alumni is likely to result. Alumni of private colleges and large, prestigious state universities are frequently well-to-do financially, have friends in similar socioeconomic groups, and are generally white. It is a safe bet that interviews by alumni would increase the proportions of offsprings of alumni and their friends and decrease the proportions of less advantaged youths in our colleges and universities.

selection so that those with the highest grades in high school and the best SAT or ACT scores would be admitted to a college or university with a probability of 10 out of 10, those in the next lower grouping would be admitted with a probability of .9, the next grouping with a probability of .8, etc., down to the lowest grouping with a probability of .1. The odds would be substantially against admission to any specific college or university for those in the lower ability groupings, but no one would *necessarily* be precluded. With a sufficient number of schools participating in the system, the chances of gaining admission to at least one school would be appreciable for anybody. The spectre of admitting students into medical school who might become brain surgeons but yet have limited ability is more apparent than real. The lottery system would govern *admissions* only; graduation and certification should be on the basis of demonstrated competence.

This suggestion has significant costs. Introduction of an explicit random lottery into a selection system carries with it an element of capriciousness that may not be palatable to many taxpayers who support the educational system. (Randomness introduced through the mechanism of a screening interview with very low validity would probably be more acceptable.) Such a system would also influence educational institutions. Many graduate and professional schools as well as some universities and colleges admit students who are overwhelmingly likely to graduate. Teaching in many of these institutions has come to stress education to a great extent and evaluation to only a minor degree. An educational system into which students with low probabilities of success were admitted *as a matter of policy* would have to emphasize the role of evaluation so that unqualified students who were performing less than adequately could be identified and "deselected." This reemphasis of evaluation could easily have adverse effects on the educational process in many professional and advanced curricula.

Attempts to remove the power imbalance between test users and individual examinees have already begun. Public pressures and legislation requiring disclosure of items in nationally administered scholastic aptitude tests are a step in this direction. As a direct result, a small number of items on the SAT have been rescored because of errors; these errors would not have been rescored without item disclosure. That there are very few incorrectly scored items should not make us complacent. Rescoring only one or two items on a standardized ability test can make the difference for many students between being a National Merit Scholarship finalist and missing the cutoff. Similarly, rescoring one or two items on the GRE or LSAT can make the difference for some individuals between being admitted into the school of their choice or being denied admission (even though this is placing undue weight on test scores). Statistically, the effects are small and few. The results may nonetheless have profound impact on a small number of individuals.

Currently, appropriateness indices are not routinely computed for all examinees who take standardized examinations. As we have seen in Chapter 4 such indices, when based on sound psychometric theory, can frequently detect aberrant response vectors that produce invalid estimates of ability. By routinely computing these indices and taking action to retest or counsel those with aberrant response vectors, another step would be made in the direction of redressing power imbalances.

9.3 SUMMARY

In this chapter we have attempted to place the use of employment and educational testing in a broad social and political perspective. We have emphasized that relying on ability tests to make employment and educational decisions about individuals involves both political and psychometric goals. A recognition of the political component of decision making was stressed to help understand the current controversies. The marked power differences between individual test takers and testing organizations was also discussed. Voluntary and compulsory attempts on the part of test administrators to redress this imbalance were seen as first steps—necessary, but not yet sufficient to achieve the goal of equity in the relationship.

A consideration that appears repeatedly in this chapter is that tests per se are rarely challenged in courts. The *system*—educational or personnel—in which tests are used is usually the triggering mechanism for litigation or challenge. Similarly, *tests* do not stand or fall on the basis of court decisions; personnel or education *systems* survive or are changed. Thus, in most of the cases involving tests in educational systems, if the system had worked properly the case would never have been litigated. For example, if students placed into special education tracks had received obvious educational benefits that outweighed the social stigma resulting from being labeled as EMR or EMH students, there would have been little point in challenging the use of either the tests or the special education program. Greater attention to the complex, three-way consideration of individual rights, institutional rights, and the public interest could possibly have precluded much of the restrictive legislation aimed at national testing organizations that is under consideration or already passed.

Tests do not exist in a political or social vacuum. Their use to achieve political goals belies any claim to the contrary. Tests are integral parts of most placement and selection systems. Systems, not tests, sometimes operate to achieve political goals that at times are at cross-purposes with widely shared social goals and specific, narrow psychometric goals. A realization that we live and function in a political world does not mean we have to compromise our scientific standards as applied psychometricians. It must be recognized, however, that efforts in the area of applied psychometrics have direct consequences for social and public policies in the United States. If a society is unhappy with the long-term consequences of optimizing purely psychometric goals, we must be prepared to recognize and accommodate the multiple goals that operate in a political world; but we must do so while recognizing that political goals and psychometric optimality are in conflict. We must not pretend the psychometric evidence does not exist or that the goals are compatible. At present, the legislative and judicial branches of the United States government have not fully explicated these social and political goals. Psychometricians should welcome open debate concerning social and political goals, while insisting on a careful separation between social and psychometric issues.

It is worth emphasizing that this chapter has been written within the zeitgeist of a social policy that stresses *equal results* rather than *equal opportunity* for all. Lerner (1981) has noted that genuinely color-blind laws permitting no classes within American society were the laws of our land for two "hauntingly brief periods" in our history: the late 1860s and early 1870s, and more recently in the decade or so following *Brown* (1954). *Brown* and the 1964 Civil Rights Act were color-blind and were written in equal opportunity language. More recent interpretations, however, emphasize equal results. It is within that social framework that psychometric decisions must be made, while recognizing that the political component of test usage is highly volatile at this time.

Whether this current decade of egalitarianism is but a momentary aberration or a permanent social policy—as permanent as any social force can be—is important for our broader questions about social policy. Lerner (1979, 1980, 1981) has addressed these issues very cogently and thoroughly. However, for the purposes of this chapter, it is important to recognize that testing and social policy cannot be totally separated and that questions about the use of tests cannot be addressed without considering existing social forces, *whatever they are.* Different social policies tomorrow may dictate different emphases in selection decisions. They do not negate our emphasis that personnel decisions have both political and psychometric components that must be recognized and kept separate.

We must also recognize that federal judges are fallible in their decisions. Judges, no less than "expert" witnesses who testify from doctrinaire positions unsupported by data, allow their ideologies to influence interpretations of the empirical results that are available. At times, their decisions about tests are all too reminiscent of official policy concerning evolution in Russia endorsing Lysenko's theory stressing the inheritance of acquired traits. For example, in *Larry P. v. Riles,* the court permanently enjoined the California School System from using *any* standardized test of ability to place children in special education tracks within that system. The court reached this decision because it assumed, in the absence of evidence that would support such an assumption, the tests in question were inherently biased, and stated that tests could not be used unless the following results were obtained:

1. Tests would have to yield the same pattern of scores when administered to different groups of students.
2. Tests would have to yield approximately equal means when administered to different groups of students.
3. Tests would have to be correlated with relevant criterion measures, that is, IQ scores of black children would have to be correlated with classroom performance.

The third requirement is the sine qua non of the use of tests for educational placement. However, requirements 1 and 2 are unlikely to be met by any cognitive ability tests that meet normally accepted standards of construct validity. Further, the validity of the egalitarian hypothesis is *assumed* to be true, a result that should be subjected to rigorous empirical study and not a result that should be assumed a priori.

We cannot ignore the competing interests of individual examinees, job applicants, or the public interest in favor of organizational interests. That these interests have been ignored for too long may be the crux of our problem. However, as scientists we can insist that the best available data and psychometric theory should be used to examine possible bias in a particular test. We must, however, recognize the complex nature of the controversies facing us and the serious consequences of continued partial exclusion of minorities from the work force and higher education. The suggestions in this chapter recognize the often substantial differences in test scores among different subpopulations in the United States. A willingness to recognize the political nature of testing programs and a willingness to absorb some of the costs for achieving a more representative work force in no way perverts or ignores the data. It is simply based on a realization that continued maximization of a desirable psychometric or statistical goal may be seriously deficient and shortsighted. However, honesty and openness about what is being done, and *why* it is being done, is required.

REFERENCES

Articles and Books

American Psychological Association, American Educational Research Association, & National Council on Measurement in Education. *Standards for educational and psychological tests*. Washington, D.C.: American Psychological Association, 1966.

American Psychological Association, American Educational Research Association, & National Council on Measurement in Education. *Standards for educational and psychological tests*. Washington, D.C.: American Psychological Association, 1974.

Bersoff, D. N. Testing and the law. *American Psychologist*, 1981, *36*, 1047–1056. (a)

Bersoff, D. N. *Testing, the law, and pubic policy*. Paper presented at the Conference on Testing, Assessments, and Public Policy, American Psychological Association, Los Angeles, August 25, 1981. (b)

Cleary, T. A., Humphreys, L. G., Kendrick, S. A., & Wesman, A. Educational uses of tests with disadvantaged students. *American Psychologist*, 1975, *30*, 15–41.

Cronbach, L. J. Selection theory for a political world. *Public Personnel Management*, 1980, *9*, 37–51.

Cronbach, L. J., & Gleser, G. C. *Psychological tests and personnel decision* (2d ed.). Urbana: University of Illinois Press, 1965.

Equal Employment Opportunity Commission, Civil Service Commission, Department of Labor, & Department of Justice. Adoption by four agencies of uniform guidelines on employee selection procedures. *Federal Register*, 1978, *43*, 38290–38315.

Equal Employment Opportunity Commission. *Guidelines on employee selection procedures*. Washington, D.C.: August 24, 1966. (29 C.F.R. 1607).

Guion, R. On trinitarian doctrines of validity. *Professional Psychology*, 1980, *11*, 385–398.

Hulin, C. L., & Humphreys, L. G. Foundations of test theory. In E. B. Williams (Ed.) *Construct validity in psychological measurement*. Princeton, N.J.: Educational Testing Service, 1979.

Hunter, J. E., Schmidt, F. L., & Hunter, R. Differential validity of employment tests by race: A comprehensive review and analysis. *Psychological Bulletin*, 1979, *86*, 721–735.

Jencks, C. *Inequality: A reassessment of the effects of family and schooling in America*. New York: Harper & Row, 1972.

Karier, C. J. Testing for order and control in the corporate liberal state. In C. J. Karier, P. Violas, and J. Spring (Eds.), *Roots of crises: American education in the twentieth century*. Chicago: Rand-McNally, 1973.

Lerner, B. Employment discrimination: Adverse impact, validity, and equality. In P. B. Kurland and G. Gasper (Eds.), *1979 Supreme Court Review*. Chicago: University of Chicago Press, 1979.

Lerner, B. The war on testing: David, Goliath, and Gallup. *The Public Interest*, 1980, *60*, 119–147.

Lerner, B. Representative democracy, "men of zeal," and testing legislation. *American Psychologist*, 1981, *36*, 279–285.

Linn, R. L. Ability testing: Individual differences, prediction, and differential prediction. In A. K. Wigdor and W. R. Garner (Eds.), *Ability testing: Uses, consequences, and controversies, part II*. Washington, D.C.: National Academy Press, 1982.

Linn, R. L., Harnisch, D. L., & Dunbar, S. B. Corrections for range restriction: An empirical investigation of conditions resulting in conservative corrections. *Journal of Applied Psychology*, 1981, *66*, 655–663.

Nairn, A., & Associates. *The reign of ETS: The corporation that makes up minds*. Washington, D.C.: Nader, 1980.

Novick, M. R. Federal guidelines and professional standards. *American Psychologist*, 1981, *36*, 1035–1046.

Novick, M. R. & Petersen, N. S. Towards equalizing educational and employment opportunity. *Journal of Educational Measurement*, 1976, *13*, 77–88.

Rubin, D. R. Using empirical Bayes techniques in the law school validity studies. *Journal of the American Statistical Association*, 1980, *75*, 801–816.

White, K. R. The relation between socioeconomic status and academic achievement. *Psychological Bulletin*, 1982, *91*, 461–481.

Legal Cases

Albermarle Paper Co. v. *Moody*, 422 U.S. 405 (1975).

Bakke v. *Board of Regents of the University of California*, 432 U.S. 265 (1978).

Brown v. *Board of Education of Topeka*, 347 U.S. 483 (1954).

Debra P. v. *Turlington*, 474 F. Supp. 244 (M.D. Fla. 1979).

Defunis v. *Odegaard*, 416 U.S. 312 (1974).

Firefighters Institute v. *City of St. Louis*, 616 F.2d 350 (8th Cir. 1980), *cert denied sub nom., United States* v. *City of St. Louis*, 49 U.S.L.W. 3931, (June 15, 1981).

Griggs v. *Duke Power Co.*, 401 U.S. 424 (1971).

Guardians Association of New York City v. *Civil Service Commission*, 630 F.2d 79 (2d Cir. 1980), *cert denied*, 49 U.S.L.W. 3932 (June 15, 1981).

Hobson v. *Hansen*, 269 F. Supp. 401 (D.D.C. 1967). *affirmed sub nom. Smuck* v. *Hobson*, 408 F.2d 175 (D.C. Cir. 1969).

Larry P. v. *Riles*, 495 F. Supp. 926 (N.D. Cal. 1979) *appeal docketed*, No. 80–4027 (9th Cir. January 17, 1980).

Lora v. *Board of Education of the City of New York*, 456 F. Supp. 1211 (E.D. N.Y. 1979) *vacated and remanded* 623 F.2d 248 (2d Cir. 1980).

Mattie T. v. *Holladay,* D.A. No. DC–75–31–S (consent decree filed N.D. Miss., January 26, 1979).

National Education Association v. *State of South Carolina,* 434 U.S. 1026 (1978).

PASE v. *Hannon,* 506 F. Supp. 831 (N.D. Ill. 1980).

Teal v. *Connecticut,* 645 F.2d 133 (2d Cir., 1981).

Washington v. *Davis,* 426 U.S. 229 (1976).

Glossary

Frequently used symbols and abbreviations in the order of their appearance in the book are listed below. Numbers in parentheses refer to chapter and section where the symbol or abbreviation is first used or defined.

i	Lower case italic i, indicates the ith item on a test or scale. (1.3)
CTT	Classical test theory. (2.0)
SAT-V	Scholastic Aptitude Test-Verbal section. (2.1)
θ	Lower case Greek theta, denotes a value of the latent trait underlying observed item responses; also refers to the underlying latent continuum. (2.1)
ICC	Item characteristic curve. (2.2)
b	Lower case italic b, item characteristic curve difficulty parameter. (2.2)
c	Lower case italic c, item characteristic curve lower asymptote parameter. (2.2, 2.4)
$P_i(\theta)$	Capital italic P with subscript i, model-based probability of correct or positive response to item i among individuals with ability or attitude θ. (2.2, 2.4)
a	Lower case italic a, item characteristic curve discrimination parameter. (2.2, 2.4)
JDI	Job Descriptive Index. (2.3)
Empirical ICC	Empirical item characteristic curve. (2.3)
$\hat{\theta}$	Lower case Greek theta with a caret, maximum likelihood estimate of θ based on observed item responses, (2.3, 2.6).
π	Lower case Greek pi, mathematical constant 3.1415926. . . . (2.10)

e	Lower case italic e, mathematical constant 2.7183. . . . (2.10)
$\int$	Integral sign. (2.10)
$\exp(x)$	Raise e to the power x; $\exp(x) = e^x$. (2.4, 2.10)
m	Lower case italic m, number of options for a multiple-choice item. (2.4)
D	Capital italic D, constant usually set to 1.7 or 1.702. (2.4)
u	Lower case italic u, dichotomously scored item response; $u = 1$ for a correct or positive response, $u = 0$ for an incorrect or negative response. (2.5)
n	Lower case italic n, number of items on test or scale. (2.5)
Π	Capital Greek pi, product sign. (2.5)
E	Capital italic E, expected value. (2.5)
$\text{Prob}(u_i = 1\|\theta)$	Conditional probability of a positive response to item i among individuals with a standing of θ on the latent trait, $\text{Prob}(u_i = 1\|\theta) = P_i(\theta)$. (2.5)
$\text{Prob}(u_i = 0\|\theta)$	Conditional probability of a negative response to item i among individuals with a standing of θ on the latent trait, $\text{Prob}(u_i = 0\|\theta) = 1 - P_i(\theta)$. (2.5)
d	Lower case italic d, error of estimate of θ, $d = \theta - \hat{\theta}$. (2.5)
p_i	Lower case italic p, population proportion of correct responses to item i. (2.5)
MLE	Maximum likelihood estimation. (2.6)
L	Capital italic L, likelihood function, likelihood of data given parameter values. (2.6)
N	Capital italic N, number of examinees or subjects. (2.6)
$Q_i(\theta)$	Capital italic Q, probability of an incorrect response to item i among individuals with a standing of θ on the latent trait, $Q_i = 1 - P_i(\theta)$. (2.6)
$\ln$	Lower case ln, natural logarithm. (2.6)
l	Lower case italic l, natural logarithm of the likelihood function, $l = \ln(L)$. (2.6)
∂	Partial derivative sign. (2.10)
Σ	Capital Greek sigma, summation sign. (2.6)
$P_i(\theta)'$	Capital italic P with subscript i, θ in parentheses with a single quotation mark read as "prime," derivative of $P_i(\theta)$ with respect to θ. (2.6)
$\hat{a}_i$	Lower case italic a with a caret, maximum likelihood estimate of a_i. (2.6)
$\hat{b}_i$	Lower case italic b with a caret, maximum likelihood estimate of b_i. (2.6)
$\hat{c}_i$	Lower case italic c with a caret, maximum likelihood estimate of c_i. (2.6)

292

$\overline{X}$	Capital italic X with a bar, sample mean. (2.7)
σ_x	Lower case Greek sigma with subscript x, population standard deviation of X. (2.7)
$\sigma_{\overline{x}}$	Lower case Greek sigma with $\overline{x}$ as a subscript, standard error of the mean $\overline{X}$. (2.7)
$I_{\overline{x}}$	Capital italic I with $\overline{x}$ as a subscript, information about population mean, reciprocal of the squared standard error of $\overline{X}$. (2.7)
$I(\theta)$	Test information function, which equals the reciprocal of the asymptotic sampling variance of $\hat{\theta}$ for individuals with a standing on the latent trait of θ. (2.7)
$\sigma_{\hat{\theta}\|\theta}$	Lower case Greek sigma with subscript $\hat{\theta}\|\theta$, standard error of $\hat{\theta}$ for individuals with ability or attitude θ. (2.6)
$I(\theta,u_i)$	Item information function for ith item, information about θ provided by ith item. (2.7)
X	Capital italic X, observed test score. (2.7)
w_i	Lower case italic w, weight given to ith item when computing test score X. (2.7)
$I_x(\theta)$	Information about θ provided by the test scoring procedure that produces the test score X. (2.7)
I_a, I_b, I_{ab}	Terms in item parameter information matrix. (2.7)
SE of $\hat{b}$	Asymptotic standard error of maximum likelihood estimate $\hat{b}$ of item difficulty parameter b. (2.7)
SE of $\hat{a}$	Asymptotic standard error of maximum likelihood estimate $\hat{a}$ of item discrimination parameter a. (2.7)
$\mathrm{Cov}(\hat{a},\hat{b})$	Asymptotic sampling covariance of maximum likelihood estimates $\hat{a}$ and $\hat{b}$. (2.7)
τ	Lower case Greek tau, classical test theory true score. (2.9)
r_b	Lower case italic r with subscript b, population biserial correlation. (2.9, 8.1)
$\rho_{xx'}$	Lower case Greek rho with subscript xx', classical test theory reliability. (2.9)
σ_e^2	Lower case Greek sigma squared with a subscript lower case e, variance of classical test theory error scores. (2.9)
σ_τ^2	Lower case Greek sigma squared with subscript lower case Greek tau, variance of classical test theory true scores. (2.9)
$\sigma_{e\|\tau}$	Lower case Greek sigma with subscript lower case e, vertical bar, and lower case Greek tau, conditional standard deviation of classical test theory error scores for individuals with true score τ. (2.9)
$\sigma_{x\|\tau}^2$	Lower case Greek sigma squared with subscript lower case x, vertical bar, and lower case Greek tau, condi-

	tional variance of observed scores for individuals with classical test theory true score τ. (2.9)
$\sigma_{x\|\theta}^2$	Lower case Greek sigma squared with subscript lower case x, vertical bar, and lower case Greek theta, conditional variance of observed test scores for individuals with standing θ on the item response theory latent trait. (2.9)
coefficient α	Lower case Greek alpha, classical test theory measure of a test's internal consistency. (2.9, 3.1)
$\hat{r}_b$	Lower case italic r with a caret and the subscript b, biserial correlation (also referred to as the continuous biserial correlation) computed in a sample. (3.1, see also 8.1)
$\hat{r}_{pb}$	Lower case italic r with a caret and the subscript pb, point biserial correlation computed in a sample. (3.1, see also 8.1)
$\hat{p}_i$	Lower case italic p with a caret, proportion of correct or positive responses to item i in a sample. (3.1)
RMSE	Root mean squared error, square root of the average of the squared differences between sample estimates and the parameter(s) they estimate. (3.3)
$\mathcal{J}$	Capital script J, Jacobs' weighted average. (4.2)
Υ	Capital Greek upsilon, latent item propensity variable underlying the dichotomously scored item response u. (4.2, 8.1)
Δ	Capital Greek delta, measure of item difficulty scaled to have a mean of 13 and a standard deviation of 4. (4.2)
Φ^{-1}	Capital Greek phi, inverse normal transformation that transforms a probability value into a standardized normal deviate. (4.2)
r_{perbis}	Lower case italic r with subscript perbis; Donlon and Fischer's personal biserial correlation. (4.2)
$h(z)$	Lower case italic h and z, height of standardized normal curve (i.e., ordinate of $N(0,1)$ density function) at z. (4.2, 8.1)
$\Phi(z)$	Capital Greek phi and z, area under standardized normal curve to the left of z. (4.2, 8.1)
s	Lower case italic s, standard deviation of a set of numbers, sum of squared deviations about the mean divided by N, and not by $N-1$. (4.2)
ℓ_o	Lower case script l with lower case o as a subscript, class of appropriateness indices developed by Levine et al., appropriateness index studied by Levine and Rubin. (4.3)
U	Capital boldface U, vector of item responses. (4.3)

ℓ_g — Lower case script l with a lower case g as a subscript, Drasgow's geometric mean likelihood appropriateness index. (4.3)

P_{ik} — Capital italic P with ik as a subscript, shorthand notation for probability of response k on item i by an individual examinee with ability or attitude θ: $P_{ik} = \text{Prob}(u_i = k|\theta)$. (4.3)

$\hat{P}_{ik}$ — Capital italic P with a caret and ik as a subscript, shorthand notation for probability of response k to item i at the maximum likelihood estimate $\hat{\theta}$ of ability θ: $\hat{P} = \text{Prob}(u_i = k|\hat{\theta})$. (4.3)

ℓ_z — Lower case script l with subscript z, standardized ℓ_o appropriateness index. (4.3)

LR — Capital italic LR, Levine and Rubin's likelihood ratio appropriateness index. (4.3)

$\hat{\sigma}_g$ — Lower case greek sigma with a caret and subscript g, maximum likelihood estimate of the standard deviation of an examinee's ability or attitude across items in Levine and Rubin's Gaussian model. (4.3)

W — Capital italic W, Wright's squared standardized residual appropriateness index. (4.3)

ROC curve — Receiver operating characteristic curve. (4.4)

p_z — Lower case script p with z as a subscript, standardized ℓ_o class index for polychotomous test model. (4.4)

r_A — Lower case italic r with subscript A, correlation in subpopulation A, (r_B, r_M, r_W, are correlations in subpopulations B, M, and W, respectively). (5.1)

$\hat{r}_A$ — Lower case italic r with a caret and subscript A, correlation in sample from subpopulation A. (5.1)

α — Lower case Greek alpha, probability of a type I error in a hypothesis test. (5.1)

Y_{min} — Capital italic Y with subscript min, minimally acceptable criterion performance. (5.1)

X_A^* — Capital italic X with a star and subscript A, minimum test score in subpopulation A that yields a predicted criterion performance equaling or exceeding Y_{min}. (5.1)

T — Capital italic T, slope of major axis of ellipse. (5.2)

V — Capital italic V, intercept of major axis of ellipse. (5.2)

D_i — Capital italic D with subscript i, perpendicular distance of ith point to major axis of ellipse. (5.2)

J — Capital italic J, number of nonoverlapping and exhaustive test score (either X or θ) intervals. (5.2 and 5.3)

$\hat{p}_{jB}$ — Lower case italic p with a caret and subscript j_B, proportion of individuals with test scores in the jth test score

	interval who were sampled from subpopulation B and correctly answered the item. (5.2)
$\hat{p}_j$	Lower case italic p with a caret and subscript j, proportion of individuals in jth test score interval who responded correctly (individuals from all subpopulations are pooled to compute $\hat{p}_j$). (5.2)
N_{j_B}	Capital italic N with subscript j_B, number of individuals sampled from subpopulation B in the jth test score interval. (5.2)
$\hat{p}(\hat{\theta} \text{ interval})$	Lower case italic p with a caret, observed proportion of individuals with ability estimates in a particular $\hat{\theta}$ interval who responded correctly, i.e., a point on the empirical ICC corresponding to a particular $\hat{\theta}$ interval. (2.3, 5.3)
H_i	Capital italic H with subscript i, Wright and Stone's statistic for fit of one-parameter logistic model to ith item. (5.3)
$\hat{P}_i(\theta)$	Capital italic P with a caret and subscript i, model based probability of a correct or positive response to item i computed with item parameter estimates instead of item parameters. Probability is computed for individuals with ability or attitude θ. (5.3)
$L\{P_i(\theta)\}$	Capital italic L with $P_i(\theta)$ in braces, logit transformation of $P_i(\theta)$. (5.3)
SSE	Sum of squared errors for a least squares regression equation. (5.3)
Γ	Capital boldface Greek gamma, asymptotic variance-covariance matrix. (5.3)
$\mathbf{I}_i$	Capital boldface I with subscript i, item information matrix for a and b parameters of item i. (5.3)
$\mathbf{Q}^{-1}$	Capital boldface Q with -1 as superscript, inverse of matrix Q. (5.3, footnote 1)
SD of $\hat{b}_{i_A}$	Standard deviation of $\hat{b}$s for a particular item pool, where bs were estimated from responses made by individuals from subpopulation A. (6.5)
H–L	Capital italic H–L, up and down branching test. (7.1)
m_i	Lower case italic m with subscript i, value along θ continuum where information function for item i reaches its maximum. (7.3)
$f(\theta)$	Lower case italic f with lower case Greek theta in parentheses, ability distribution. (7.3)
$f(\theta|\mathbf{U})$	Lower case italic f with lower case Greek theta, vertical line, and capital boldface U in parentheses, posterior distribution of ability. (7.3)

$\hat{q}$ Lower case italic q with a caret, sample proportion incorrect; $\hat{q} = 1 - \hat{p}$. (8.1)

$\hat{r}_p$ Lower case italic r with a caret and a subscript p, phi coefficient computed in a sample. (8.1)

$r(X,Y)$ Lower case italic r, Pearson product moment correlation coefficient between X and Y, sometimes written r_{xy} or r. (8.1)

t Lower case italic t, categorization attenuation factor. (8.1)

r_{pb} Lower case italic r with subscript pb, population point biserial correlation. (8.1)

r_t Lower case italic r with subscript t, population tetrachoric correlation coefficient. (8.1)

α_i Lower case Greek alpha with subscript i, factor loading of item i on common factor. (8.2)

S_i Capital italic S with subscript i, specific factor underlying latent item propensity variable Y_i. (8.2)

Index

A

a, item discrimination parameter, 34–35
(a,b) sampling covariance, 62
Abelson, R. P., 5, 11
Aberrance detection, 134–45
  JDI, 144–49
Aberrant examinees, detection, 134–45
Aberrant test scores, 111
Ability, 15
Ability measures, definition, 279
Ability parameter estimation, 52
Ability scale development, 75–83
Adams, E. F., 40, 71
Adaptive testing, 9, 68, 210; *see also*
  Computerized adaptive testing
Adaptive tests, noncomputerized, 211
Adverse impact, 268
Ajzen, I., 5, 11
Alexander, R. A., 155, 183
Alignment error, 112
Anderson, N. H., 5, 11
Angoff, W. H., 119, 150, 162, 182, 213,
  233
Appropriateness indices, IRT methods,
  121–49
  Gaussian model, 127–28
  ℓ_g, 124
  ℓ_o, 122–27
  LR, 128
  ℓ_z, 126
Appropriateness index, Jacob's weighted
  average, 116–18
Appropriateness measurement, 7–8,
  110–12, 114, 121
Area under normal curve, equation, 71
Aronson, E., 11
Arvey, R. D., 154, 182
Attitude-behavior consistencies, 5
Attitude measurement, 4–7
Attitude scale development, classical
  approach, 80–83
  IRT approach, 83–87
Averill, M., 164–65, 183

B

b, item difficulty parameter, 32–33, 36–
  37
Back translations, 190
Bass, A. R., 154, 182
Berner, J. G., 154–55, 183
Berry, J. W., 209
Bersoff, D. N., 280, 287
Betz, N. E., 211–13, 217, 234
BICAL, 53
Binet, A., 211–12
Birnbaum, A., 28–29, 52, 55, 57, 59–60,
  71, 73, 77, 151, 220, 233
Birnbaum's paradox, 59, 77
Biserial correlation, 75, 77, 237
Black-white test differences, 8
Bock, R. D., 25–26, 53, 67, 72
Boehm, V. R., 154–55, 182
Box, G. E. P., 222, 233
Branching tests, 215
Brislin, R., 185, 188, 209
Broad-Range Tailored Test, 221
Brown, F. G., 116, 150

C

c, lower asymptote of ICC, 31–32, 36
Camilli, G., 164–65, 183
Campbell, D. T., 77, 109, 186–87, 208
Carroll, J. B., 245, 249–55, 261
Carroll, W. K., 207, 209
Carroll's correction for guessing, 249
Casagrande, J., 188–89, 208
Cheating, 113
Christoffersson, A., 164, 183, 260–61
Civil Rights Act of, 1964, 266
Classical test theory and IRT, relations,
  67–69
Cleary, T. A., 156, 182, 213, 233, 281,
  287
Cleary definition of test bias, 156, 281
Cliff, N., 17, 72
Cole, N. S., 154, 182

This book has been set VIP, in 10 and 9 point Caledonia, leaded 2 points. Chapter numbers are 24 point Zapf Book Demi and chapter titles are 18 point Zapf Book Demi. The size of the type page is 27 × 46 picas.

ANii